Developing Bioinformatics Computer Skills

Developing Bioinformatics
Computer Skills

Cynthia Gibas and Per Jambeck

O'REILLY®

Beijing · Cambridge · Farnham · Köln · Paris · Sebastopol · Taipei · Tokyo

Developing Bioinformatics Computer Skills
by Cynthia Gibas and Per Jambeck

Published by O'Reilly & Associates, Inc., 101 Morris Street, Sebastopol, CA 95472.

Editor: Lorrie LeJeune

Production Editor: Mary Anne Weeks Mayo

Cover Designer: Ellie Volckhausen

Printing History:

> April 2001:   First Edition.

ISBN: 1-56592-664-1   5/01
[C]

Table of Contents

Preface

Computers and the World Wide Web are rapidly and dramatically changing the face of biological research. These days, the term "paradigm shift" is used to describe everything from new business trends to new flavors of cola, but biological science is in the midst of a paradigm shift in the classical sense. Theoretical and computational biology have existed for decades on the "fringe" of biological science. But within just a few short years, the flood of new biological data produced by genomics efforts and, by necessity, the application of computers to the analysis of this genomic data, has begun to affect every aspect of the biological sciences. Research that used to start in the laboratory now starts at the computer, as scientists search databases for information that might suggest new hypotheses.

In the last two decades, both personal computers and supercomputers have become accessible to scientists across all disciplines. Personal computers have developed from expensive novelties with little real computing power into machines that are as powerful as the supercomputers of 10 years ago. Just as they've replaced the author's typewriter and the accountant's ledger, computers have taken their place in controlling and collecting data from lab equipment. They have the potential to completely replace laboratory notebooks and files as a means of storing data. The power of computer databases allows much easier access to stored data than nonelectronic forms of recording. Beyond their usefulness for the storage, analysis, and visualization of data, however, computers are powerful devices for understanding any system that can be described in a mathematical way, giving rise to the disciplines of computational biology and, more recently, bioinformatics.

Bioinformatics is the application of information technology to the management of biological data. It's a rapidly evolving scientific discipline. In the last two decades, storage of biological data in public databases has become increasingly common, and these databases have grown exponentially. The biological literature is growing exponentially as well. It's impossible for even the most zealous researcher to stay on top of necessary information in the field without the aid of computer-based tools, and the Web has made it possible for users at any location to interact with programs and databases at any other site—provided they know how to build the right tools.

Bioinformatics is first and foremost a biological science. It's often less about developing perfectly elegant algorithms than it is about answering practical questions. Bioinformaticians (or bioinformaticists, if you prefer) are the tool-builders, and it's critical that they understand biological problems as well as computational solutions in order to produce useful tools. Bioinformatics algorithms need to encompass complex scientific assumptions that can complicate programming and data modeling in unique ways.

Research in bioinformatics and computational biology can encompass anything from the abstraction of the properties of a biological system into a mathematical or physical model, to the implementation of new algorithms for data analysis, to the development of databases and web tools to access them. To engage in computational research, a biologist must be comfortable using software tools that run on a variety of operating systems. This book introduces and explains many of the most popular tools used in bioinformatics research. We've included lots of additional information and background material to help you understand how the tools are best used and why they are important. We hope that it will help you through the first steps of using computers productively in your research.

Audience for This Book

Most biological science students and researchers are starting to use computers as more than word-processing or data-collection and plotting devices. Many don't have backgrounds in computer science or computational theory, and to them, the fields of computational biology and bioinformatics may seem hopelessly large and complex. This book, motivated by our interactions with our students and colleagues, is by no means a comprehensive bible on all aspects of bioinformatics. It is, however, a thoughtful introduction to some of the most important topics in bioinformatics. We introduce standard computational techniques for finding information in biological sequence, genome, and molecular structure databases; we talk about how to identify genes and detect characteristic patterns that identify gene families; and we discuss the modeling of phylogenetic relationships, molecular structures, and biochemical properties. We also discuss ways you can use your computer as a tool to organize data, to think systematically about data-analysis processes, and to begin thinking about automation of data handling.

Bioinformatics is a fairly advanced topic, so even an introductory book like this one assumes certain levels of background knowledge. To get the most out of this book you should have some coursework or experience in molecular biology, chemistry, and mathematics. An undergraduate course or two in computer programming would also be helpful.

Structure of This Book

We've arranged the material in this book to allow you to read it from start to finish or to skip around, digesting later sections before previous ones. It's divided into four parts:

Part 1, *Introduction*

Chapter 1, *Biology in the Computer Age*, defines bioinformatics as a discipline, delves into a bit of history, and provides a brief tour of what the book covers and why.

Chapter 2, *Computational Approaches to Biological Questions*, introduces the core concepts of bioinformatics and molecular biology and the technologies and research initiatives that have made increasing amounts of biological data available. It also covers the ever-growing list of basic computer procedures every biologist should know.

Part II, *The Bioinformatics Workstation*

Chapter 3, *Setting Up Your Workstation*, introduces Unix, then moves on to the basics of installing Linux on a PC and getting software up and running.

Chapter 4, *Files and Directories in Unix*, covers the ins and outs of moving around a Unix filesystem, including file hierarchies, naming schemes, commonly used directory commands, and working in a multiuser environment.

Chapter 5, *Working on a Unix System*, explains many Unix commands users will encounter on a daily basis, including commands for viewing, editing, and extracting information from files; regular expressions; shell scripts; and communicating with other computers.

Part III, *Tools for Bioinformatics*

Chapter 6, *Biological Research on the Web*, is about the art of finding biological information on the Web. The chapter covers search engines and searching, where to find scientific articles and software, how to use the online information sources, and the public biological databases.

Chapter 7, *Sequence Analysis, Pairwise Alignment, and Database Searching*, begins with a review of molecular evolution and then moves on to cover the basics of pairwise sequence-analysis techniques such as predicting gene location, global and local alignment, and local alignment-based searching against databases using BLAST and FASTA. The chapter concludes with coverage of multifunctional tools for sequence analysis.

Chapter 8, *Multiple Sequence Alignments, Trees, and Profiles,* moves on to study groups of related genes or proteins. It covers strategies for multiple sequence alignment with tools such as ClustalW and Jalview, then discusses tools for phylogenetic analysis, and constructing profiles and motifs.

Chapter 9, *Visualizing Protein Structures and Computing Structural Properties,* covers 3D analysis of proteins and the tools used to compute their structural properties. The chapter begins with a review of protein chemistry and quickly moves to a discussion of web-based protein structure tools; structure classification, alignment, and analysis; solvent accessibility and solvent interactions; and computing physicochemical properties of proteins. The chapter concludes with structure optimization and a tour through protein resource databases.

Chapter 10, *Predicting Protein Structure and Function from Sequence,* covers the tools that determine the structures of proteins from their sequences. The chapter discusses feature detection in protein sequences, secondary structure prediction, predicting 3D structure. It concludes with an example project in protein modeling.

Chapter 11, *Tools for Genomics and Proteomics,* puts it all together. Up to now we've covered tools and techniques for analyzing single sequences or structures, and for comparing multiple sequences of single-gene length. This chapter discusses some of the datatypes and tools that are becoming available for studying the integrated function of all the genes in a genome, including sequencing an entire genome, accessing genome information on the Web, annotating and analyzing whole genome sequences, and emerging technologies and proteomics.

Part IV, *Databases and Visualization*

Chapter 12, *Automating Data Analysis with Perl,* shows you how a programming language such as Perl can help you sift through mountains of data to extract just the information you require. It won't teach you to program in Perl, but the chapter gives you a brief introduction to the language and includes examples to start you on your way toward learning to program.

Chapter 13, *Building Biological Databases,* is an introduction to database concepts. It covers the types of databases used in biological research, the database software that builds them, database languages (in particular, the SQL language), and developing web-based software that interacts with databases

Chapter 14, *Visualization and Data Mining,* covers the computational tools and techniques that allow you to make sense of your results. The first part of the chapter introduces programs that are used to visualize data arising from bioinformatics research. They range from general-purpose plotting and statistical packages for numerical data, such as Grace and *gnuplot*, to programs such as T$_E$Xshade that are dedicated to presenting sequence and structural information in an interpretable form. The second part of the chapter presents tools for data mining—the process of finding, interpreting, and evaluating patterns in large sets of data—in the context of applications in bioinformatics.

Our Approach to Bioinformatics

We confess, we're structural biologists (biophysicists, actually). We have a hard time thinking about genes without thinking about their protein products. DNA sequences, to us, aren't just sequences. To a structural biologist, genes (with a few exceptions) imply 3D structures, molecular shapes and conformational changes, active sites, chemical reactions, and detailed intermolecular interactions. Our focus in this book is on using sequence information as structural biologists and biochemists tend to use it—to understand the chemical basis of biological function. We've probably neglected some applications of sequence analysis that are dear to the hearts of molecular biologists and geneticists, so feel free send us your comments.

URLs Referenced in This Book

For more information on the URLs we reference in this book and for additional material about bioinformatics, see the web page for this book, which is listed in the "Comments and Questions" section.

Conventions Used in This Book

The following conventions are used in this book:

Italic
> Used for commands, filenames, directory names, variables, URLs, and for the first use of a term

`Constant width`
> Used in code examples and to show the output of commands

`Constant width italic`
> Used in "Usage" phrases to denote variables.

The owl icon designates a note, which is an important aside to the nearby text.

 The turkey icon designates a warning relating to the nearby text.

Comments and Questions

Please address comments and questions concerning this book to the publisher:

O'Reilly & Associates, Inc.
101 Morris Street
Sebastopol, CA 95472
(800) 998-9938 (in the United States or Canada)
(707) 829-0515 (international or local)
(707) 829-0104 (fax)

We have a web page for this book, where we list errata, examples, or any additional information. You can access this page at:

http://www.oreilly.com/catalog/devbioinfo/

To comment or ask technical questions about this book, send email to:

bookquestions@oreilly.com

For more information about our books, conferences, software, Resource Centers, and the O'Reilly Network, see our web site at:

http://www.oreilly.com

Acknowledgments

From Cynthia: I'd like to thank all of the people who have restrained themselves from laughing when they heard me say, for the thousandth time during the last year, "We're almost finished with the book." Thanks to my family and friends, for putting up with extremely infrequent phone calls and updates during the last few months; the students in my Fall 2000 Bioinformatics course, for acting as guinea pigs in my first bioinformatics teaching experiment and helping me identify topics that needed to be explained more thoroughly; my colleagues at Virginia Tech, for a year's worth of interesting discussions of what bioinformatics means and what bioinformatics students need to know; and our friend and colleague Jim Fenton for his contributions early in the development of the book; and my thesis advisor Shankar Subramaniam. I'd also like to thank our technical reviewers, Sean Eddy, Peter Leopold, Andrew Odewahn, Clay Shirky, and Jim Tisdall, for their helpful comments and excellent advice. And finally, thanks goes to the staff of O'Reilly, and our editor, Lorrie LeJeune, for infinite patience and moral support during the writing process.

From Per: First, I am deeply grateful to my advisor, Professor Shankar Subramaniam, who has been a continuous source of inspiration and a mainstay of our lab's congenial working environment at UCSD. My thanks also go to two of my mentors, Professor Charles Elkan of the University of California, San Diego, and Professor Michael R. Brent, now of Washington University, whose wise guidance has shaped my understanding of computational problems. Sanna Herrgard and Markus Herrgard read early versions of this book and provided valuable comments and moral support. The book has also benefited from feedback and helpful conversations with Ewan Birney, Phil Bourne, Jim Fenton, Mike Farnum, Brian Saunders, and Winny Tan. Thanks to Joe Johnston of O'Reilly for providing Perl advice and code in Chapter 12. Our technical reviewers made indispensable suggestions and contributions, and I owe special thanks to Sean Eddy, Peter Leopold, Andrew Odewahn, Clay Shirky, and Jim Tisdall for their careful attention to detail. It has been a pleasure to work with the staff at O'Reilly, and in particular with our editor Lorrie LeJeune, who patiently and cheerfully guided us through the project. Finally, my part of this book would not have been possible without the support and encouragement of my family.

I

Introduction

1

Biology in the Computer Age

From the interaction of species and populations, to the function of tissues and cells within an individual organism, biology is defined as the study of living things. In the course of that study, biologists collect and interpret data. Now, at the beginning of the 21st century, we use sophisticated laboratory technology that allows us to collect data faster than we can interpret it. We have vast volumes of DNA sequence data at our fingertips. But how do we figure out which parts of that DNA control the various chemical processes of life? We know the function and structure of some proteins, but how do we determine the function of new proteins? And how do we predict what a protein will look like, based on knowledge of its sequence? We understand the relatively simple code that translates DNA into protein. But how do we find meaningful new words in the code and add them to the DNA-protein dictionary?

Bioinformatics is the science of using information to understand biology; it's the tool we can use to help us answer these questions and many others like them. Unfortunately, with all the hype about mapping the human genome, bioinformatics has achieved buzzword status; the term is being used in a number of ways, depending on who is using it. Strictly speaking, bioinformatics is a subset of the larger field of *computational biology*, the application of quantitative analytical techniques in modeling biological systems. In this book, we stray from bioinformatics into computational biology and back again. The distinctions between the two aren't important for our purpose here, which is to cover a range of tools and techniques we believe are critical for molecular biologists who want to understand and apply the basic computational tools that are available today.

The field of bioinformatics relies heavily on work by experts in statistical methods and pattern recognition. Researchers come to bioinformatics from many fields, including mathematics, computer science, and linguistics. Unfortunately, biology is a science of the specific as well as the general. Bioinformatics is full of pitfalls for those who look for patterns and make predictions without a complete understanding of where biological data comes from and what it means. By providing algorithms, databases, user interfaces, and statistical tools, bioinformatics makes it possible to do exciting things such as compare DNA sequences and generate results that are potentially significant. "Potentially significant" is perhaps the most important phrase. These new tools also give you the opportunity to overinterpret data and assign meaning where none really exists. We can't overstate the importance of understanding the limitations of these tools. But once you gain that understanding and become an intelligent consumer of bioinformatics methods, the speed at which your research progresses can be truly amazing.

How Is Computing Changing Biology?

An organism's hereditary and functional information is stored as DNA, RNA, and proteins, all of which are linear chains composed of smaller molecules. These macromolecules are assembled from a fixed alphabet of well-understood chemicals: DNA is made up of four deoxyribonucleotides (adenine, thymine, cytosine, and guanine), RNA is made up from the four ribonucleotides (adenine, uracil, cytosine, and guanine), and proteins are made from the 20 amino acids. Because these macromolecules are linear chains of defined components, they can be represented as sequences of symbols. These sequences can then be compared to find similarities that suggest the molecules are related by form or function.

Sequence comparison is possibly the most useful computational tool to emerge for molecular biologists. The World Wide Web has made it possible for a single public database of genome sequence data to provide services through a uniform interface to a worldwide community of users. With a commonly used computer program called fsBLAST, a molecular biologist can compare an uncharacterized DNA sequence to the entire publicly held collection of DNA sequences. In the next section, we present an example of how sequence comparison using the BLAST program can help you gain insight into a real disease.

The Eye of the Fly

Fruit flies (*Drosophila melanogaster*) are a popular model system for the study of development of animals from embryo to adult. Fruit flies have a gene called *eyeless*, which, if it's "knocked out (i.e., eliminated from the genome using molecular biology methods), results in fruit flies with no eyes. It's obvious that the *eyeless* gene plays a role in eye development.

Researchers have identified a human gene responsible for a condition called *aniridia*. In humans who are missing this gene (or in whom the gene has mutated just enough for its protein product to stop functioning properly), the eyes develop without irises.

If the gene for *aniridia* is inserted into an eyeless drosophila "knock out," it causes the production of normal drosophila eyes. It's an interesting coincidence. Could there be some similarity in how *eyeless* and *aniridia* function, even though flies and humans are vastly different organisms? Possibly. To gain insight into how *eyeless* and *aniridia* work together, we can compare their sequences. Always bear in mind, however, that genes have complex effects on one another. Careful experimentation is required to get a more definitive answer.

As little as 15 years ago, looking for similarities between *eyeless* and *aniridia* DNA sequences would have been like looking for a needle in a haystack. Most scientists compared the respective gene sequences by hand-aligning them one under the other in a word processor and looking for matches character by character. This was time-consuming, not to mention hard on the eyes.

In the late 1980s, fast computer programs for comparing sequences changed molecular biology forever. Pairwise comparison of biological sequences is the foundation of most widely used bioinformatics techniques. Many tools that are widely available to the biology community—including everything from multiple alignment, phylogenetic analysis, motif identification, and homology-modeling software, to web-based database search services—rely on pairwise sequence-comparison algorithms as a core element of their function.

These days, a biologist can find dozens of sequence matches in seconds using sequence-alignment programs such as BLAST and FASTA. These programs are so commonly used that the first encounter you have with bioinformatics tools and biological databases will probably be through the National Center for Biotechnology Information's (NCBI) BLAST web interface. Figure 1-1 shows a standard form for submitting data to NCBI for a BLAST search.

Labels in Gene Sequences

Before you rush off to compare the sequences of *eyeless* and *aniridia* with BLAST, let us tell you a little bit about how sequence alignment works.

It's important to remember that biological sequence (DNA or protein) has a chemical function, but when it's reduced to a single-letter code, it also functions as a unique label, almost like a bar code. From the information technology point of view, sequence information is priceless. The sequence label can be applied to a gene, its product, its function, its role in cellular metabolism, and so on. The user searching for information related to a particular gene can then use rapid pairwise sequence comparison to access any information that's been linked to that sequence label.

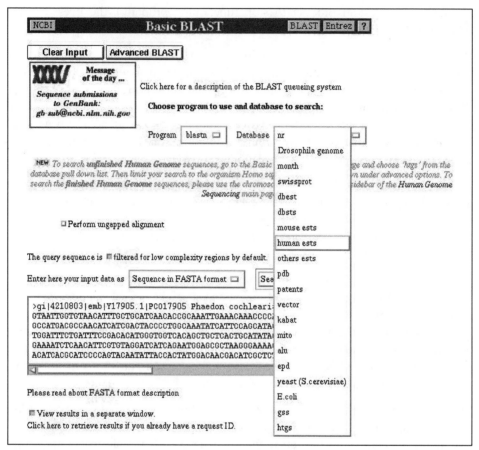

Figure 1-1. Form for submitting a BLAST search against nucleotide databases at NCBI

The most important thing about these sequence labels, though, is that they don't just uniquely identify a particular gene; they also contain biologically meaningful patterns that allow users to compare different labels, connect information, and make inferences. So not only can the labels connect all the information about one gene, they can help users connect information about genes that are slightly or even dramatically different in sequence.

If simple labels were all that was needed to make sense of biological data, you could just slap a unique number (e.g., a GenBank ID) onto every DNA sequence and be done with it. But biological sequences are related by evolution, so a partial pattern match between two sequence labels is a significant find. BLAST differs from simple keyword searching in its ability to detect partial matches along the entire length of a protein sequence.

Comparing eyeless and aniridia with BLAST

When the two sequences are compared using BLAST, you'll find that *eyeless* is a partial match for *aniridia*. The text that follows is the raw data that's returned from this BLAST search:

```
pir||A41644 homeotic protein aniridia - human
        Length = 447

   Score = 256 bits (647), Expect = 5e-67
   Identities = 128/146 (87%), Positives = 134/146 (91%), Gaps = 1/146 (0%)

Query: 24 IERLPSLEDMAHKGHSGVNQLGGVFVGGRPLPDSTRQKIVELAHSGARPCDISRILQVSN 83
          I R P+  M + HSGVNQLGGVFV GRPLPDSTRQKIVELAHSGARPCDISRILQVSN
Sbjct: 17 IPRPPARASMQNS-HSGVNQLGGVFVNGRPLPDSTRQKIVELAHSGARPCDISRILQVSN 75

Query: 84 GCVSKILGRYYETGSIRPRAIGGSKPRVATAEVVSKISQYKRECPSIFAWEIRDRLLQEN 143
          GCVSKILGRYYETGSIRPRAIGGSKPRVAT EVVSKI+QYKRECPSIFAWEIRDRLL E
Sbjct: 76 GCVSKILGRYYETGSIRPRAIGGSKPRVATPEVVSKIAQYKRECPSIFAWEIRDRLLSEG 135

Query: 144 VCTNDNIPSVSSINRVLRNLAAQKEQ 169
           VCTNDNIPSVSSINRVLRNLA++K+Q
Sbjct: 136 VCTNDNIPSVSSINRVLRNLASEKQQ 161


   Score = 142 bits (354), Expect = 1e-32
   Identities = 68/80 (85%), Positives = 74/80 (92%)

Query: 398 TEDDQARLILKRKLQRNRTSFTNDQIDSLEKEFERTHYPDVFARERLAGKIGLPEARIQV 457
           +++ Q RL LKRKLQRNRTSFT +QI++LEKEFERTHYPDVFARERLA KI LPEARIQV
Sbjct: 222 SDEAQMRLQLKRKLQRNRTSFTQEQIEALEKEFERTHYPDVFARERLAAKIDLPEARIQV 281

Query: 458 WFSNRRAKWRREEKLRNQRR 477
           WFSNRRAKWRREEKLRNQRR
Sbjct: 282 WFSNRRAKWRREEKLRNQRR 301
```

The output shows local alignments of two high-scoring matching regions in the protein sequences of the *eyeless* and *aniridia* genes. In each set of three lines, the query sequence (the *eyeless* sequence that was submitted to the BLAST server) is on the top line, and the *aniridia* sequence is on the bottom line. The middle line shows where the two sequences match. If there is a letter on the middle line, the sequences match exactly at that position. If there is a plus sign on the middle line, the two sequences are different at that position, but there is some chemical similarity between the amino acids (e.g., D and E, aspartic and glutamic acid). If there is nothing on the middle line, the two sequences don't match at that position.

In this example, you can see that, if you submit the whole *eyeless* gene sequence and look (as standard keyword searches do) for an exact match, you won't find anything. The local sequence regions make up only part of the complete proteins: the region from 24–169 in *eyeless* matches the region from 17–161 in the human *aniridia* gene, and the region from 398–477 in *eyeless* matches the region from 222–301 in *aniridia*. The rest of the sequence doesn't match! Even the two regions shown, which match closely, don't match 100%, as they would have to, in order to be found in a keyword search.

However, this partial match is significant. It tells us that the human *aniridia* gene, which we don't know much about, is substantially related in sequence to the fruit fly's *eyeless* gene. And we do know a lot about the *eyeless* gene, from its structure and function (it's a DNA binding protein that promotes the activity of other genes) to its effects on the phenotype—the form of the grown fruit fly.

BLAST finds local regions that match even in pairs of sequences that aren't exactly the same overall. It extends matches beyond a single-character difference in the sequence, and it keeps trying to extend them in all directions until the overall score of the sequence match gets too small. As a result, BLAST can detect patterns that are imperfectly replicated from sequence to sequence, and hence distant relationships that are inexact but still biologically meaningful.

Depending on the quality of the match between two labels, you can transfer the information attached to one label to the other. A high-quality sequence match between two full-length sequences may suggest the hypothesis that their functions are similar, although it's important to remember that the identification is only tentative until it's been experimentally verified. In the case of the *eyeless* and *aniridia* genes, scientists hope that studying the role of the *eyeless* gene in Drosophila eye development will help us understand how *aniridia* works in human eye development.

Isn't Bioinformatics Just About Building Databases?

Much of what we currently think of as part of bioinformatics—sequence comparison, sequence database searching, sequence analysis—is more complicated than just designing and populating databases. Bioinformaticians (or computational biologists) go beyond just capturing, managing, and presenting data, drawing inspiration from a wide variety of quantitative fields, including statistics, physics, computer science, and engineering. Figure 1-2 shows how quantitative science intersects with biology at every level, from analysis of sequence data and protein structure, to metabolic modeling, to quantitative analysis of populations and ecology.

Bioinformatics is first and foremost a component of the biological sciences. The main goal of bioinformatics isn't developing the most elegant algorithms or the most arcane analyses; the goal is finding out how living things work. Like the molecular biology methods that greatly expanded what biologists were capable of

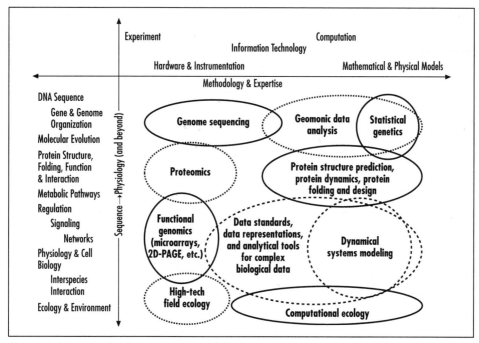

Figure 1-2. How technology intersects with biology

studying, bioinformatics is a tool and not an end in itself. Bioinformaticians are the tool-builders, and it's critical that they understand biological problems as well as computational solutions in order to produce useful tools.

Research in bioinformatics and computational biology can encompass anything from abstraction of the properties of a biological system into a mathematical or physical model, to implementation of new algorithms for data analysis, to the development of databases and web tools to access them.

The First Information Age in Biology

Biology as a science of the specific means that biologists need to remember a lot of details as well as general principles. Biologists have been dealing with problems of information management since the 17th century.

The roots of the concept of evolution lie in the work of early biologists who catalogued and compared species of living things. The cataloguing of species was the preoccupation of biologists for nearly three centuries, beginning with animals and plants and continuing with microscopic life upon the invention of the compound microscope. New forms of life and fossils of previously unknown, extinct life forms are still being discovered even today.

All this cataloguing of plants and animals resulted in what seemed a vast amount of information at the time. In the mid-16th century, Otto Brunfels published the first major modern work describing plant species, the *Herbarium vitae eicones*. As Europeans traveled more widely around the world, the number of catalogued species increased, and botanical gardens and herbaria were established. The number of catalogued plant types was 500 at the time of Theophrastus, a student of Aristotle. By 1623, Casper Bauhin had observed 6,000 types of plants. Not long after John Ray introduced the concept of distinct species of animals and plants, and developed guidelines based on anatomical features for distinguishing conclusively between species. In the 1730s, Carolus Linnaeus catalogued 18,000 plant species and over 4,000 species of animals, and established the basis for the modern taxonomic naming system of kingdoms, classes, genera, and species. By the end of the 18th century, Baron Cuvier had listed over 50,000 species of plants.

It was no coincidence that a concurrent preoccupation of biologists, at this time of exploration and cataloguing, was classification of species into an orderly taxonomy. A botany text might encompass several volumes of data, in the form of painstaking illustrations and descriptions of each species encountered. Biologists were faced with the problem of how to organize, access, and sensibly add to this information. It was apparent to the casual observer that some living things were more closely related than others. A rat and a mouse were clearly more similar to each other than a mouse and a dog. But how would a biologist know that a rat was like a mouse (but that rat was not just another name for mouse) without carrying around his several volumes of drawings? A nomenclature that uniquely identified each living thing and summed up its presumed relationship with other living things, all in a few words, needed to be invented.

The solution was relatively simple, but at the time, a great innovation. Species were to be named with a series of one-word names of increasing specificity. First a very general division was specified: animal or plant? This was the kingdom to which the organism belonged. Then, with increasing specificity, came the names for class, genera, and species. This schematic way of classifying species, as illustrated in Figure 1-3, is now known as the "Tree of Life."

A modern taxonomy of the earth's millions of species is too complicated for even the most zealous biologist to memorize, and fortunately computers now provide a way to maintain and access the taxonomy of species. The University of Arizona's Tree of Life project and NCBI's Taxonomy database are two examples of online taxonomy projects.

Taxonomy was the first informatics problem in biology. Now, biologists have reached a similar point of information overload by collecting and cataloguing information about individual genes. The problem of organizing this information and sharing knowledge with the scientific community at the gene level isn't being

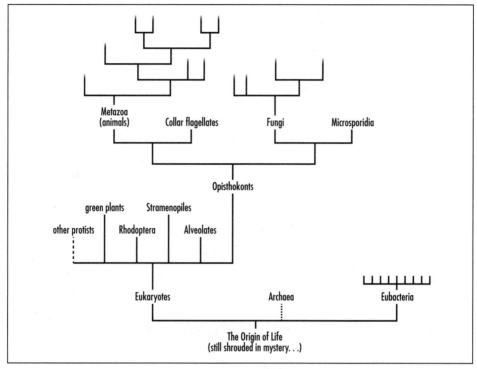

Figure 1-3. The "Tree of Life" represents the nomenclature system that classifies species

tackled by developing a nomenclature. It's being attacked directly with computers and databases from the start.

The evolution of computers over the last half-century has fortuitously paralleled the developments in the physical sciences that allow us to see biological systems in increasingly fine detail. Figure 1-4 illustrates the astonishing rate at which biological knowledge has expanded in the last 20 years.

Simply finding the right needles in the haystack of information that is now available can be a research problem in itself. Even in the late 1980s, finding a match in a sequence database was worth a five-page publication. Now this procedure is routine, but there are many other questions that follow on our ability to search sequence and structure databases. These questions are the impetus for the field of bioinformatics.

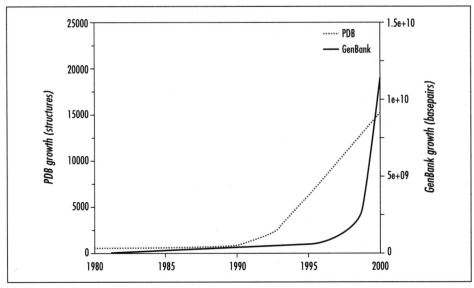

Figure 1-4. The growth of GenBank and the Protein Data Bank has been astronomical

What Does Informatics Mean to Biologists?

The science of informatics is concerned with the representation, organization, manipulation, distribution, maintenance, and use of information, particularly in digital form. There is more than one interpretation of what bioinformatics—the intersection of informatics and biology—actually means, and it's quite possible to go out and apply for a job doing bioinformatics and find that the expectations of the job are entirely different than you thought.

The functional aspect of bioinformatics is the representation, storage, and distribution of data. Intelligent design of data formats and databases, creation of tools to query those databases, and development of user interfaces that bring together different tools to allow the user to ask complex questions about the data are all aspects of the development of bioinformatics infrastructure.

Developing analytical tools to discover knowledge in data is the second, and more scientific, aspect of bioinformatics. There are many levels at which we use biological information, whether we are comparing sequences to develop a hypothesis about the function of a newly discovered gene, breaking down known 3D protein structures into bits to find patterns that can help predict how the protein folds, or modeling how proteins and metabolites in a cell work together to make the cell function. The ultimate goal of analytical bioinformaticians is to develop predictive methods that allow scientists to model the function and phenotype of an organism based only on its genome sequence. This is a grand goal, and one that will be approached only in small steps, by many scientists working together.

What Challenges Does Biology Offer Computer Scientists?

The goal of biology, in the era of the genome projects, is to develop a quantitative understanding of how living things are built from the genome that encodes them.

Cracking the genome code is complex. At the very simplest level, we still have difficulty identifying unknown genes by computer analysis of genomic sequence. We still have not managed to predict or model how a chain of amino acids folds into the specific structure of a functional protein.

Beyond the single-molecule level, the challenges are immense. The sheer amount of data in GenBank is now growing at an exponential rate, and as datatypes beyond DNA, RNA, and protein sequence begin to undergo the same kind of explosion, simply managing, accessing, and presenting this data to users in an intelligible form is a critical task. Human-computer interaction specialists need to work closely with academic and clinical researchers in the biological sciences to manage such staggering amounts of data.

Biological data is very complex and interlinked. A spot on a DNA array, for instance, is connected not only to immediate information about its intensity, but to layers of information about genomic location, DNA sequence, structure, function, and more. Creating information systems that allow biologists to seamlessly follow these links without getting lost in a sea of information is also a huge opportunity for computer scientists.

Finally, each gene in the genome isn't an independent entity. Multiple genes interact to form biochemical pathways, which in turn feed into other pathways. Biochemistry is influenced by the external environment, by interaction with pathogens, and by other stimuli. Putting genomic and biochemical data together into quantitative and predictive models of biochemistry and physiology will be the work of a generation of computational biologists. Computer scientists, mathematicians, and statisticians will be a vital part of this effort.

What Skills Should a Bioinformatician Have?

There's a wide range of topics that are useful if you're interested in pursuing bioinformatics, and it's not possible to learn them all. However, in our conversations with scientists working at companies such as Celera Genomics and Eli Lilly, we've picked up on the following "core requirements" for bioinformaticians:

- You should have a fairly deep background in some aspect of molecular biology. It can be biochemistry, molecular biology, molecular biophysics, or even molecular modeling, but without a core of knowledge of molecular biology you will, as one person told us, "run into brick walls too often."

- You must absolutely understand the central dogma of molecular biology. Understanding how and why DNA sequence is transcribed into RNA and translated into protein is vital. (In Chapter 2, *Computational Approaches to Biological Questions*, we define the central dogma, as well as review the processes of transcription and translation.)

- You should have substantial experience with at least one or two major molecular biology software packages, either for sequence analysis or molecular modeling. The experience of learning one of these packages makes it much easier to learn to use other software quickly.

- You should be comfortable working in a command-line computing environment. Working in Linux or Unix will provide this experience.

- You should have experience with programming in a computer language such as C/C++, as well as in a scripting language such as Perl or Python.

There are a variety of other advanced skill sets that can add value to this background: molecular evolution and systematics; physical chemistry—kinetics, thermodynamics and statistical mechanics; statistics and probabilistic methods; database design and implementation; algorithm development; molecular biology laboratory methods; and others.

Why Should Biologists Use Computers?

Computers are powerful devices for understanding any system that can be described in a mathematical way. As our understanding of biological processes has grown and deepened, it isn't surprising, then, that the disciplines of computational biology and, more recently, bioinformatics, have evolved from the intersection of classical biology, mathematics, and computer science.

A New Approach to Data Collection

Biochemistry is often an anecdotal science. If you notice a disease or trait of interest, the imperative to understand it may drive the progress of research in that direction. Based on their interest in a particular biochemical process, biochemists have determined the sequence or structure or analyzed the expression characteristics of a single gene product at a time. Often this leads to a detailed understanding of one biochemical pathway or even one protein. How a pathway or protein interacts with other biological components can easily remain a mystery, due to lack of hands to do the work, or even because the need to do a particular experiment isn't communicated to other scientists effectively.

The Internet has changed how scientists share data and made it possible for one central warehouse of information to serve an entire research community. But more importantly, experimental technologies are rapidly advancing to the point at which it's possible to imagine systematically collecting all the data of a particular type in a central "factory" and then distributing it to researchers to be interpreted.

In the 1990s, the biology community embarked on an unprecedented project: sequencing all the DNA in the human genome. Even though a first draft of the human genome sequence has been completed, automated sequencers are still running around the clock, determining the entire sequences of genomes from various life forms that are commonly used for biological research. And we're still fine-tuning the data we've gathered about the human genome over the last 10 years. Immense strings of data, in which the locations of only a relatively few important genes are known, have been and still are being generated. Using image-processing techniques, maps of entire genomes can now be generated much more quickly than they could with chemical mapping techniques, but even with this technology, complete and detailed mapping of the genomic data that is now being produced may take years.

Recently, the techniques of x-ray crystallography have been refined to a degree that allows a complete set of crystallographic reflections for a protein to be obtained in minutes instead of hours or days. Automated analysis software allows structure determination to be completed in days or weeks, rather than in months. It has suddenly become possible to conceive of the same type of high-throughput approach to structure determination that the Human Genome Project takes to sequence determination. While crystallization of proteins is still the limiting step, it's likely that the number of protein structures available for study will increase by an order of magnitude within the next 5 to 10 years.

Parallel computing is a concept that has been around for a long time. Break a problem down into computationally tractable components, and instead of solving them one at a time, employ multiple processors to solve each subproblem simultaneously. The parallel approach is now making its way into experimental molecular biology with technologies such as the DNA microarray. Microarray technology allows researchers to conduct thousands of gene expression experiments simultaneously on a tiny chip. Miniaturized parallel experiments absolutely require computer support for data collection and analysis. They also require the electronic publication of data, because information in large datasets that may be tangential to the purpose of the data collector can be extremely interesting to someone else.

Finding information by searching such databases can save scientists literally years of work at the lab bench.

The output of all these high-throughput experimental efforts can be shared only because of the development of the World Wide Web and the advances in communication and information transfer that the Web has made possible.

The increasing automation of experimental molecular biology and the application of information technology in the biological sciences have lead to a fundamental change in the way biological research is done. In addition to anecdotal research—locating and studying in detail a single gene at a time—we are now cataloguing all the data that is available, making complete maps to which we can later return and mark the points of interest. This is happening in the domains of sequence and structure, and has begun to be the approach to other types of data as well. The trend is toward storage of raw biological data of all types in public databases, with open access by the research community. Instead of doing preliminary research in the lab, scientists are going to the databases first to save time and resources.

How Can I Configure a PC to Do Bioinformatics Research?

Up to now you've probably gotten by using word-processing software and other canned programs that run under user-friendly operating systems such as Windows or MacOs. In order to make the most of bioinformatics, you need to learn Unix, the classic operating system of powerful computers known as servers and workstations. Most scientific software is developed on Unix machines, and serious researchers will want access to programs that can be run only under Unix. Unix comes in a number of flavors, the two most popular being BSD and SunOs. Recently, however, a third choice has entered the marketplace: Linux. Linux is an open source Unix operating system. In Chapters 3, 4, and 5, we discuss how to set up a workstation for bioinformatics running under Linux. We cover the operating system and how it works: how files are organized, how programs are run, how processes are managed, and most importantly, what to type at the command prompt to get the computer to do what you want.

Why Use Unix or Linux?

Setting up your computer with a Linux operating system allows you to take advantage of cutting-edge scientific-research tools developed for Unix systems. As it has grown popular in the mass market, Linux has retained the power of Unix systems for developing, compiling, and running programs, networking, and managing jobs started by multiple users, while also providing the standard trimmings of a desktop

PC, including word processors, graphics programs, and even visual programming tools. This book operates on the assumption that you're willing to learn how to work on a Unix system and that you'll be working on a machine that has Linux or another flavor of Unix installed. For many of the specific bioinformatics tools we discuss, Unix is the most practical choice.

On the other hand, Unix isn't necessarily the most practical choice for office productivity in a predominantly Mac or PC environment. The selection of available word processing and desktop publishing software and peripheral devices for Linux is improving as the popularity of the operating system increases. However, it can't (yet) go head-to-head with the consumer operating systems in these areas. Linux is no more difficult to maintain than a normal PC operating system, once you know how, but the skills needed and the problems you'll encounter will be new at first.

 As of this writing, my desktop computer has been reliably up and running Linux for nearly five months, with the exception of a few days time out for a hardware failure. No software crashes, no little bombs or unhappy faces, no missing *.dll* files or mysterious error messages. Installation of Linux took about two days and some help from tech support the first time I did it, and about one hour the second time (on a laptop, no less). Realistically, the main problem I have encountered being the only Linux user in a Mac/PC environment is opening email attachments from Mac users.—CJG

Fortunately, some of the companies selling packaged Linux distributions have substantially automated the installation procedure, and also offer 90 days of phone and web technical support for your installation. Companies such as Red Hat and SuSE and organizations such as Debian provide Linux distributions for PCs, while Yellow Dog (and others) provide Linux distributions for Macintosh computers.

There are a couple of ways to phase Linux in gradually. Of course, if you have more than one computer workstation, you can experiment with converting one of your machines to Linux while leaving your familiar operating system on the rest. The other choice is to do a *dual boot installation.* In a dual boot installation, you create two sections (called partitions) on your hard drive, and install Linux in one of them, with your old operating system in the other. Then, when you turn on your computer, you have a choice of whether to start up Linux or your other operating system. You can leave all your old files and programs where they are and start with new work in your Linux partition. Newer versions of Linux, such as Yellow Dog Linux for the PowerPC, allow users to emulate a MacOS environment within Linux and access software and files for both platforms simultaneously.

What Information and Software Are Available?

In Chapter 6, *Biological Research on the Web*, we cover information literacy. Only a few years ago, biologists had to know how to do literature searches using printed indexes that led them to references in the appropriate technical journals. Modern biologists search web-based databases for the same information and have access to dozens of other information types as well. Knowing how to navigate these resources is a vital skill for every biologist, computational or not.

We then introduce the basic tools you'll need to locate databases, computer programs, and other resources on the Web, to transfer these resources to your computer, and to make them work once you get them there. In Chapters 7 through 11 we turn to particular types of scientific questions and the tools you will need to answer them. In some cases, there are computer programs that are becoming the standard for solving a particular type of problem (e.g., BLAST and FASTA for amino acid and nucleic acid sequence alignment). In other areas, where the method for solving a problem is still an open research question, there may be a number of competing tools, or there may be no tool that completely solves the problem.

Why Do I Need to Install a Program from the Web?

Handling large volumes of complex data requires a systematic and automated approach. If you're searching a database for matches to one query, a web form will do the trick. But what if you want to search for matches to 10,000 queries, and then sort through the information you get back to find relationships in the results? You certainly don't want to type 10,000 queries into a web form, and you probably don't want your results to come back formatted to look nice on a web page. Shared public web servers are often slow, and using them to process large batches of data is impractical. Chapter 12, *Automating Data Analysis with Perl,* contains examples of how to use Perl as a driver to make your favorite program process large volumes of data using your own computer.

Can I Learn a Programming Language Without Classes?

Anyone who has experience with designing and carrying out an experiment to answer a question has the basic skills needed to program a computer. A laboratory experiment begins with a question, which evolves into a testable hypothesis, that is, a statement that can be tested for truth based on the results of an experiment or experiments. The processes developed to test the hypotheses are analogous to computer programs. The essence of an experiment is: if you take system X, and do something to it, what happens? The experiment that is done must be designed to have results that can be clearly interpreted. Computer programs must also be carefully designed so that the values that are passed from one part of a program to the next can be clearly interpreted. The human programmer must set up unambiguous instructions to the computer and must think through, in advance, what different types of results mean and what the computer should do with them. A large part of practical computer programming is the ability to think critically, to design a process to answer a question, and to understand what is required to answer the question unambiguously.

Even if you have these skills, learning a computer language isn't a trivial undertaking, but it has been made a lot easier in recent years by the development of the Perl language. Perl, referred to by its creator as "the duct tape of the Internet, and of everything else," began its evolution as a scripting language optimized for data processing. It continues to evolve into a full-featured programming language, and it's practical to use Perl to develop prototypes for virtually any kind of computer program. Perl is a very flexible language; you can learn just enough to write a simple script to solve a one-off problem, and after you've done that once or twice, you have a core of knowledge to build on. The key to learning Perl is to use it and to use it right away. Just as no amount of reading the textbook can make you speak Spanish fluently, no amount of reading O'Reilly's *Learning Perl* is going to be as helpful as getting out there and trying to "speak" it. In Chapter 12, we provide example Perl code for parsing common biological datatypes, driving and processing output from programs written in other languages, and even a couple of Perl implementations that solve common computational biology problems. We hope these examples inspire you to try a little programming of your own.

How Can I Use Web Information?

Chapter 6 also introduces the public databases where biological data is archived to be shared by researchers worldwide.

While you can quickly find a single protein structure file or DNA sequence file by filling in a web form and searching a public database, it's likely that eventually you will want to work with more than one piece of data. You may even be collecting and archiving your own data; you may want to make a new type of data available to a broader research community. To do these things efficiently, you need to store data on your own computer. If you want to process your stored data using a computer program, you need to structure your data. Understanding the difference between structured and unstructured data and designing a data format that suits your data storage and access needs is the key to making your data useful and accessible.

There are many ways to organize data. While most biological data is still stored in flat file databases, this type of database becomes inefficient when the quantity of data being stored becomes extremely large. Chapter 13, *Building Biological Databases*, covers the basic database concepts you need to talk to database experts and to build your own databases. We discuss the differences between flat file and relational databases, introduce the best public-domain tools for managing databases, and show you how to use them to store and access your data.

How Do I Understand Sequence Alignment Data?

It's hard to make sense of your data, or make a point, without visualization tools. The extraction of cross sections or subsets of complex multivariate data sets is often required to make sense of biological data. Storing your data in structured databases, which are discussed in Chapter 13, creates the infrastructure for analysis of complex data.

Once you've stored data in an accessible, flexible format, the next step is to extract what is important to you and visualize it. Whether you need to make a histogram of your data or display a molecular structure in three dimensions and watch it move in real time, there are visualization tools that can do what you want. Chapter 14, *Visualization and Data Mining*, covers data-analysis and data-visualization tools, from generic plotting packages to domain-specific programs for marking up biological sequence alignments, displaying molecular structures, creating phylogenetic trees, and a host of other purposes.

How Do I Write a Program to Align Two Biological Sequences?

An important component of any kind of computational science is knowing when you need to write a program yourself and when you can use code someone else has written. The efficient programmer is a lazy programmer; she never wastes effort writing a program if someone else has already made a perfectly good program available. If you are looking to do something fairly routine, such as aligning two protein sequences, you can be sure that someone else has already written the program you need and that by searching you can probably even find some source code to look at. Similarly, many mathematical and statistical problems can be solved using standard code that is freely available in code libraries. Perl programmers make code that simplifies standard operations available in modules; there are many freely available modules that manage web-related processes, and there are projects underway to create standard modules for handling biological-sequence data.

How Do I Predict Protein Structure from Sequence?

There are some questions we can't answer for you, and that's one of them; in fact, it's one of the biggest open research questions in computational biology. What we can and do give you are the tools to find information about such problems and others who are working on them, and even, with the proper inspiration, to develop approaches to answering them yourself. Bioinformatics, like any other science, doesn't always provide quick and easy answers to problems.

What Questions Can Bioinformatics Answer?

The questions that drive (and fund) bioinformatics research are the same questions humans have been working away at in applied biology for the last few hundred years. How can we cure disease? How can we prevent infection? How can we produce enough food to feed all of humanity? Companies in the business of developing drugs, agricultural chemicals, hybrid plants, plastics and other petroleum derivatives, and biological approaches to environmental remediation, among others, are developing bioinformatics divisions and looking to bioinformatics to provide new targets and to help replace scarce natural resources.

The existence of genome projects implies our intention to use the data they generate. The implicit goals of modern molecular biology are, simply stated, to read the entire genomes of living things, to identify every gene, to match each gene with the protein it encodes, and to determine the structure and function of each protein. Detailed knowledge of gene sequence, protein structure and function, and gene expression patterns is expected to give us the ability to understand how life works at the highest possible resolution. Implicit in this is the ability to manipulate living things with precision and accuracy.

2

Computational Approaches to Biological Questions

There is a standard range of techniques that are taught in bioinformatics courses. Currently, most of the important techniques are based on one key principle: that sequence and structural *homology* (or similarity) between molecules can be used to infer structural and functional similarity. In this chapter, we'll give you an overview of the standard computer techniques available to biologists; later in the book, we'll discuss how specific software packages implement these techniques and how you should use them.

Molecular Biology's Central Dogma

Before we go any further, it's essential that you understand some basics of cell and molecular biology. If you're already familiar with DNA and protein structure, genes, and the processes of transcription and translation, feel free to skip ahead to the next section.

The central dogma of molecular biology states that:

> DNA acts as a template to replicate itself, DNA is also transcribed into RNA, and RNA is translated into protein.

As you can see, the central dogma sums up the function of the genome in terms of information. Genetic information is conserved and passed on to progeny through the process of replication. Genetic information is also used by the individual organism through the processes of transcription and translation. There are many layers of function, at the structural, biochemical, and cellular levels, built on top of genomic information. But in the end, all of life's functions come back to the information content of the genome.

Put another way, genomic DNA contains the master plan for a living thing. Without DNA, organisms wouldn't be able to replicate themselves. The raw "one-dimensional" sequence of DNA, however, doesn't actually do anything biochemically; it's only information, a blueprint if you will, that's read by the cell's protein synthesizing machinery. DNA sequences are the punch cards; cells are the computers.

DNA is a linear polymer made up of individual chemical units called *nucleotides* or *bases*. The four nucleotides that make up the DNA sequences of living things (on Earth, at least) are adenine, guanine, cytosine, and thymine—designated A, G, C, and T, respectively. The order of the nucleotides in the linear DNA sequence contains the instructions that build an organism. Those instructions are read in processes called replication, transcription, and translation.

Replication of DNA

The unusual structure of DNA molecules gives DNA special properties. These properties allow the information stored in DNA to be preserved and passed from one cell to another, and thus from parents to their offspring. Two molecules of DNA form a double-helical structure, twining around each other in a regular pattern along their full length—which can be millions of nucleotides. The halves of the double helix are held together by bonds between the nucleotides on each strand. The nucleotides also bond in particular ways: A can pair only with T, and G can pair only with C. Each of these pairs is referred to as a *base pair*, and the length of a DNA sequence is often described in base pairs (or bp), kilobases (1,000 bp), megabases (1 million bp), etc.

Each strand in the DNA double helix is a chemical "mirror image" of the other. If there is an A on one strand, there will always be a T opposite it on the other. If there is a C on one strand, its partner will always be a G.

When a cell divides to form two new *daughter cells*, DNA is *replicated* by untwisting the two strands of the double helix and using each strand as a template to build its chemical mirror image, or *complementary strand*. This process is illustrated in Figure 2-1.

Genomes and Genes

The entire DNA sequence that codes for a living thing is called its *genome*. The genome doesn't function as one long sequence, however. It's divided into individual genes. A *gene* is a small, defined section of the entire genomic sequence, and each gene has a specific, unique purpose.

There are three classes of genes. *Protein-coding* genes are templates for generating molecules called proteins. Each *protein* encoded by the genome is a chemical

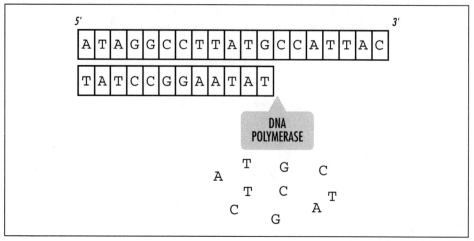

Figure 2-1. Schematic of a DNA molecule being replicated

machine with a distinct purpose in the organism. *RNA-specifying* genes are also templates for chemical machines, but the building blocks of RNA machines are different from those that make up proteins. Finally, *untranscribed genes* are regions of genomic DNA that have some functional purpose but don't achieve that purpose by being transcribed or translated to create another molecule.

Transcription of DNA

DNA can act not only as a template for making copies of itself but also as a blueprint for a molecule called ribonucleic acid (RNA). The process by which DNA is transcribed into RNA is called *transcription* and is illustrated in Figure 2-2. RNA is structurally similar to DNA. It's a polymeric molecule made up of individual chemical units, but the chemical backbone that holds these units together is slightly different from the backbone of DNA, allowing RNA to exist in a single-stranded form as well as in a double helix. These single-stranded molecules still form base pairs between different parts of the chain, causing RNA to fold into 3D structures. The individual chemical units of RNA are designated A, C, G, and U (uracil, which takes the place of thymine).

The genome provides a template for the synthesis of a variety of RNA molecules: the three main types of RNA are messenger RNA, transfer RNA, and ribosomal RNA. *Messenger* RNA (mRNA) molecules are RNA transcripts of genes. They carry information from the genome to the ribosome, the cell's protein synthesis apparatus. *Transfer* RNA (tRNA) molecules are untranslated RNA molecules that transport amino acids, the building blocks of proteins, to the ribosome. Finally, *ribosomal* RNA (rRNA) molecules are the untranslated RNA components of ribosomes, which are complexes of protein and RNA. rRNAs are involved in anchoring

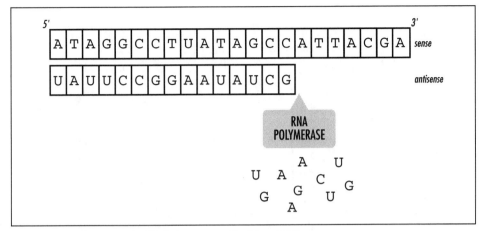

Figure 2-2. Schematic of DNA being transcribed into RNA

the mRNA molecule and catalyzing some steps in the translation process. Some viruses also use RNA instead of DNA as their genetic material.

Translation of mRNA

Translation of mRNA into protein is the final major step in putting the information in the genome to work in the cell.

Like DNA, proteins are linear polymers built from an alphabet of chemically variable units. The protein alphabet is a set of small molecules called *amino acids*.

Unlike DNA, the chemical sequence of a protein has physicochemical "content" as well as information content. Each of the 20 amino acids commonly found in proteins has a different chemical nature, determined by its side chain—a chemical group that varies from amino acid to amino acid. The chemical sequence of the protein is called its *primary structure*, but the way the sequence folds up to form a compact molecule is as important to the function of the protein as is its primary structure. The secondary and tertiary structure elements that make up the protein's final fold can bring distant parts of the chemical sequence of the protein together to form functional sites.

As shown in Figure 2-3, the *genetic code* is the code that translates DNA into protein. It takes three bases of DNA (called a *codon*) to code for each amino acid in a protein sequence. Simple combinatorics tells us that there are 64 ways to choose 3 nucleotides from a set of 4, so there are 64 possible codons and only 20 amino acids. Some codons are redundant; others have the special function of telling the cell's translation machinery to stop translating an mRNA molecule. Figure 2-4 shows how RNA is translated into protein.

$$4 \times 4 \times 4 = 64$$

	Second Position			
	U	**C**	**A**	**G**

First Position		U		C		A		G		Third Position
U	UUU	Phe	UCU	Ser	UAU	Tyr	UGU	Cys	U	
	UUC		UCC		UAC		UGC		C	
	UUA	Leu	UCA		UAA	Stop	UGA	Stop	A	
	UUG		UCG		UAG	Stop	UGG	Trp	G	
C	CUU	Leu	CCU	Pro	CAU	His	CGU	Arg	U	
	CUC		CCC		CAC		CGC		C	
	CUA		CCA		CAA	Gln	CGA		A	
	CUG		CCG		CAG		CGG		G	
A	AUU	Ile	ACU	Thr	AAU	Asn	AGU	Ser	U	
	AUC		ACC		AAC		AGC		C	
	AUA		ACA		AAA	Lys	AGA	Arg	A	
	AUG	Met (start)	ACG		AAG		AGG		G	
G	GUU	Val	GCU	Ala	GAU	Asp	GGU	Gly	U	
	GUC		GCC		GAC		GGC		C	
	GUA		GCA		GAA	Glu	GGA		A	
	GUG		GCG		GAG		GGG		G	

Figure 2-3. The genetic code

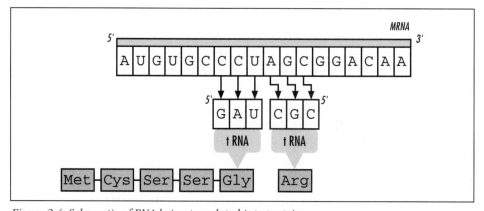

Figure 2-4. Schematic of RNA being translated into protein

Molecular Evolution

Errors in replication and transcription of DNA are relatively common. If these errors occur in the reproductive cells of an organism, they can be passed to its progeny. Alterations in the sequence of DNA are known as *mutations*. Mutations can have harmful results—results that make the progeny less likely to survive to adulthood. They can also have beneficial results, or they can be neutral. If a mutation doesn't kill the organism before it reproduces, the mutation can become fixed in the population over many generations. The slow accumulation of such changes is responsible for the process known as *evolution*. Access to DNA sequences gives us access to a more precise understanding of evolution. Our understanding of the molecular mechanism of evolution as a gradual process of accumulating DNA sequence mutations is the justification for developing hypotheses based on DNA and protein sequence comparison.

What Biologists Model

Now that we've completed our ultra-short course in cell biology, let's look at how to apply it to problems in molecular biology. One of the most important exercises in biology and bioinformatics is modeling. A *model* is an abstract way of describing a complicated system. Turning something as complex (and confusing) as a chromosome, or the cycle of cell division, into a simplified representation that captures all the features you are trying to study can be extremely difficult. A model helps us see the larger picture. One feature of a good model is that it makes systems that are otherwise difficult to study easier to analyze using quantitative approaches. Bioinformatics tools rely on our ability to extract relevant parameters from a biological system (be it a single molecule or something as complicated as a cell), describe them quantitatively, and then develop computational methods that use those parameters to compute the properties of a system or predict its behavior.

To help you understand what a model is and what kind of analysis a good model makes possible, let's look at three examples on which bioinformatics methods are based.

Accessing 3D Molecules Through a 1D Representation

In reality, DNA and proteins are complicated 3D molecules, composed of thousands or even millions of atoms bonded together. However, DNA and proteins are both *polymers*, chains of repeating chemical units (*monomers*) with a common backbone holding them together. Each chemical unit in the polymer has two subsets of atoms: a subset of atoms that doesn't vary from monomer to monomer and that makes up the backbone of the polymer, and a subset of atoms that does vary from monomer to monomer.

In DNA, four nucleic acid monomers (A, T, C, and G) are commonly used to build the polymer chain. In proteins, 20 amino acid monomers are used. In a DNA chain, the four nucleic acids can occur in any order, and the order they occur in determines what the DNA does. In a protein, amino acids can occur in any order, and their order determines the protein's fold and function.

Not too long after the chemical natures of DNA and proteins were understood, researchers recognized that it was convenient to represent them by strings of single letters. Instead of representing each nucleic acid in a DNA sequence as a detailed chemical entity, they could be represented simply as A, T, C, and G. Thus, a short piece of DNA that contains thousands of individual atoms can be represented by a sequence of few hundred letters. Figure 2-5 illustrates the simplified way to represent a polymer chain.

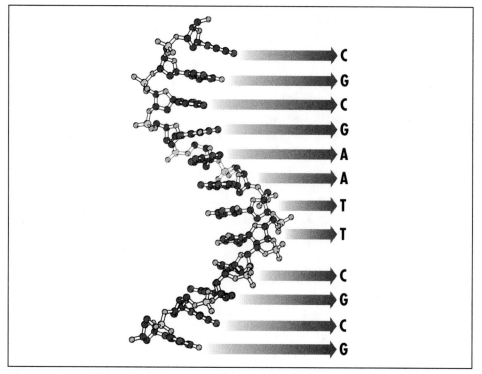

Figure 2-5. Simplifying the representation of a polymer chain

Not only does this abstraction save storage space and provide a convenient form for sharing sequence information, it represents the nature of a molecule uniquely and correctly and ignores levels of detail (such as atomic structure of DNA and many proteins) that are experimentally inaccessible. Many computational biology methods exploit this 1D abstraction of 3D biological macromolecules.

The abstraction of nucleic acid and protein sequences into 1D strings has been one of the most fruitful modeling strategies in computational molecular biology, and analysis of character strings is a long-standing area of research in computer science.* One of the elementary questions you can ask about strings is, "Do they match?" There are well-established algorithms in computer science for finding exact and inexact matches in pairs of strings. These algorithms are applied to find pairwise matches between biological sequences and to search sequence databases using a sequence query.

In addition to matching individual sequences, string-based methods from computer science have been successfully applied to a number of other problems in molecular biology. For example, algorithms for reconstructing a string from a set of shorter substrings can assemble DNA sequences from overlapping sequence fragments. Techniques for recognizing repeated patterns in single sequences or conserved patterns across multiple sequences allow researchers to identify signatures associated with biological structures or functions. Finally, multiple sequence-alignment techniques allow the simultaneous comparison of several molecules that can infer evolutionary relationships between sequences.

This simplifying abstraction of DNA and protein sequence seems to ignore a lot of biology. The cellular context in which biomolecules exist is completely ignored, as are their interactions with other molecules and their molecular structure. And yet it has been shown over and over that matches between biological sequences—for example, in the detection of similarity in eye-development genes in humans and flies, as we discussed in Chapter 1, *Biology in the Computer Age*—can be biologically meaningful.

Abstractions for Modeling Protein Structure

There is more to biology than sequences. Proteins and nucleic acids also have complex 3D structures that provide clues to their functions in the living organism. Molecular structures are usually represented as collections of atoms, each of which has a defined position in 3D space. Structure analysis can be performed on static structures, or movements and interactions in the molecules can be studied with molecular simulation methods.

Standard molecular simulation approaches model proteins as a collection of point masses (atoms) connected by bonds. The bond between two atoms has a standard length, derived from experimental chemistry, and an associated applied force that constrains the bond at that length. The angle between three adjacent atoms has a standard value and an applied force that constrains the bond angle around that value. The same is true of the dihedral angle described by four adjacent atoms. In a molecular dynamics simulation, energy is added to the molecular

---

* A *string* is simply an unbroken sequence of characters. A *character* is a single letter chosen from a set of defined letters, whether that be binary code (strings of zeros and ones) or the more complicated alphabetic and numerical alphabet that can be typed on a computer keyboard.

system by simulated "heating." Following standard Newtonian laws, the atoms in the molecule move. The energy added to the system provides an opposing force that moves atoms in the molecule out of their standard conformations. The actions and reactions of hundreds of atoms in a molecular system can be simulated using this abstraction.

However, the computational demands of molecular simulations are huge, and there is some uncertainty both in the *force field*—the collection of standard forces that model the molecule—and in the modeling of *nonbonded interactions*—interactions between nonadjacent atoms. So it has not proven possible to predict protein structure using the all-atom modeling approach.

Some researchers have recently had moderate success in predicting protein topology for simple proteins using an intermediate level of abstraction—more than linear sequence, but less than an all-atom model. In this case, the protein is treated as a series of beads (representing the individual amino acids) on a string (representing the backbone). Beads may have different characters to represent the differences in the amino acid sidechains. They may be positively or negatively charged, polar or nonpolar, small or large. There are rules governing which beads will attract each other. Like charges repel; unlike charges attract. Polar groups cluster with other polar groups, and nonpolar with nonpolar. There are also rules governing the string; mainly that it can't pass through itself in the course of the simulation. The folding simulation itself is conducted through sequential or simultaneous perturbation of the position of each bead.

Mathematical Modeling of Biochemical Systems

Using theoretical models in biology goes far beyond the single molecule level. For years, ecologists have been using mathematical models to help them understand the dynamics of changes in interdependent populations. What effect does a decrease in the population of a predator species have on the population of its prey? What effect do changes in the environment have on population? The answers to those questions are theoretically predictable, given an appropriate mathematical model and a knowledge of the sizes of populations and their standard rates of change due to various factors.

In molecular biology, a similar approach, called *metabolic control analysis*, is applied to biochemical reactions that involve many molecules and chemical species. While cells contain hundreds or thousands of interacting proteins, small molecules, and ions, it's possible to create a model that describes and predicts a small corner of that complicated metabolism. For instance, if you are interested in the biological processes that maintain different concentrations of hydrogen ions on either side of the mitochondrial inner membrane in eukaryotic cells, it's probably not necessary for your model to include the distant group of metabolic pathways that are closely involved in biosynthesis of the heme structure.

Metabolic models describe a biochemical process in terms of the concentrations of chemical species involved in a pathway, and the reactions and fluxes that affect those concentrations. Reactions and fluxes can be described by differential equations; they are essentially rates of change in concentration. What makes metabolic simulation interesting is the possibility of modeling dozens of reactions simultaneously to see what effect they have on the concentration of particular chemical species. Using a properly constructed metabolic model, you can test different assumptions about cellular conditions and fine-tune the model to simulate experimental observations. That, in turn, can suggest testable hypotheses to drive further research.

Why Biologists Model

We've mentioned more than once that theoretical modeling provides testable hypotheses, not definitive answers. It sometimes isn't so easy to maintain this distinction, especially with pairwise sequence comparison, which seems to provide such ready answers. Even identification of genes based on sequence similarity ultimately needs to be validated experimentally. It's not sufficient to say that an unknown DNA sequence is similar to the sequence of a gene that has been subject to detailed characterization, so therefore it must have an identical function. The two sequences could be distantly related but have evolved to have different functions. However, it's altogether reasonable to use sequence similarity as the starting point for verification; if sequence homology suggests that an unknown gene is similar to citrate synthases, your first experimental approach might be to test the unknown gene product for citrate synthase activity.

One of the main benefits of using computational tools in biology is that it becomes easier to preselect targets for experimentation in molecular biology and biochemistry. Using everything from sequence profiling methods to geometric and physicochemical analysis of protein structures, researchers can focus narrowly on the parts of a sequence or structure that appear to have some functional significance. Only a decade ago, this focusing might have been done using "shotgun" approaches to site-directed mutagenesis, in which random single-residue mutants of a protein were created and characterized in order to select possible targets. Functional genomics and metabolic reconstruction efforts are beginning to provide biochemists with a framework for narrowing their research focuses as well.

For the researcher focused on developing bioinformatics methods, the discovery of general rules and properties in data is by far the most interesting category of problems that can be addressed using a computer. It's also a diverse category and one we can't give you many rules for. Researchers have found interesting and useful properties in everything from sequence patterns to the separation of atoms in molecular structures and have applied these findings to produce such tools as genefinders, secondary structure prediction tools, profile methods, and homology modeling tools.

Bioinformatics researchers are still tackling problems that currently have reasonably successful solutions, from basecalling to sequence alignment to genome comparison to protein structure modeling, attempting to improve the accuracy and range of these procedures. Information-technology experts are currently developing database structures and query tools for everything from gene-expression data to intermolecular interactions. Like any other field of research, there are many niches of inquiry available, and the only way to find them is to delve into the current literature.

Computational Methods Covered in This Book

Molecular biology research is a fast-growing area. The amount and type of data that can be gathered is exploding, and the trend of storing this data in public databases is spilling over from genome sequence to all sorts of other biological datatypes. The information landscape for biologists is changing so rapidly that anything we say in this book is likely to be somewhat behind the times before it even hits the shelves.

Yet, since the inception of the Human Genome Project, a core set of computational approaches has emerged for dealing with the types of data that are currently shared in public databases—DNA, protein sequence, and protein structure. Although databases containing results from new high-throughput molecular biology methods have not yet grown to the extent the sequence databases have, standard methods for analyzing these data have begun to emerge.

While not exhaustive, the following list gives you an overview of the computational methods we address in this book:

Using public databases and data formats

> The first key skill for biologists is to learn to use online search tools to find information. Literature searching is no longer a matter of looking up references in a printed index. You can find links to most of the scientific publications you need online. There are central databases that collect reference information so you can search dozens of journals at once. You can even set up "agents" that notify you when new articles are published in an area of interest. Searching the public molecular-biology databases requires the same

skills as searching for literature references: you need to know how to construct a query statement that will pluck the particular needle you're looking for out of the database haystack. Tools for searching biochemical literature and sequence databases are introduced in Chapter 6, *Biological Research on the Web*.

Sequence alignment and sequence searching

As mentioned in Chapter 1, being able to compare pairs of DNA or protein sequences and extract partial matches has made it possible to use a biological sequence as a database query. Sequence-based searching is another key skill for biologists; a little exploration of the biological databases at the beginning of a project often saves a lot of valuable time in the lab. Identifying homologous sequences provides a basis for phylogenetic analysis and sequence-pattern recognition. Sequence-based searching can be done online through web forms, so it requires no special computing skills, but to judge the quality of your search results you need to understand how the underlying sequence-alignment method works and go beyond simple sequence alignment to other types of analysis. Tools for pairwise sequence alignment and sequence-based database searching are introduced in Chapter 7, *Sequence Analysis, Pairwise Alignment, and Database Searching*.

Gene prediction

Gene prediction is only one of a cluster of methods for attempting to detect meaningful signals in uncharacterized DNA sequences. Until recently, most sequences deposited in GenBank were already characterized at the time of deposition. That is, someone had already gone in and, using molecular biology, genetic, or biochemical methods, figured out what the gene did. However, now that the genome projects are in full swing, there's a lot of DNA sequence out there that isn't characterized.

Software for prediction of open reading frames, genes, exon splice sites, promoter binding sites, repeat sequences, and tRNA genes helps molecular biologists make sense out of this unmapped DNA. Tools for gene prediction are introduced in Chapter 7.

Multiple sequence alignment

Multiple sequence-alignment methods assemble pairwise sequence alignments for many related sequences into a picture of sequence homology among all members of a gene family. Multiple sequence alignments aid in visual identification of sites in a DNA or protein sequence that may be functionally important. Such sites are usually conserved; that is, the same amino acid is present at that site in each one of a group of related sequences. Multiple sequence alignments can also be quantitatively analyzed to extract information about a gene family. Multiple sequence alignments are an integral step in phylogenetic analysis of a family of related sequences, and they also provide the basis for identifying sequence patterns that characterize particular protein families. Tools for creating and editing multiple sequence alignments are introduced in Chapter 8, *Multiple Sequence Alignments, Trees, and Profiles.*

Phylogenetic analysis

Phylogenetic analysis attempts to describe the evolutionary relatedness of a group of sequences. A traditional phylogenetic tree or cladogram groups species into a diagram that represents their relative evolutionary divergence. Branchings of the tree that occur furthest from the root separate individual species; branchings that occur close to the root group species into kingdoms, phyla, classes, families, genera, and so on.

The information in a molecular sequence alignment can be used to compute a phylogenetic tree for a particular family of gene sequences. The branchings in phylogenetic trees represent evolutionary distance based on sequence similarity scores or on information-theoretic modeling of the number of mutational steps required to change one sequence into the other. Phylogenetic analyses of protein sequence families talks not about the evolution of the entire organism but about evolutionary change in specific coding regions, although our ability to create broader evolutionary models based on molecular information will expand as the genome projects provide more data to work with. Tools for phylogenetic analysis are introduced in Chapter 8.

Extraction of patterns and profiles from sequence data

A *motif* is a sequence of amino acids that defines a substructure in a protein that can be connected to function or to structural stability. In a group of evolutionarily related gene sequences, motifs appear as conserved sites. Sites in a gene sequence tend to be *conserved*—to remain the same in all or most representatives of a sequence family—when there is selection pressure against copies of the gene that have mutations at that site. Nonessential parts of the gene sequence will diverge from each other in the course of evolution, so the conserved motif regions show up as a signal in a sea of mutational noise. Sequence profiles are statistical descriptions of these motif signals; profiles can help identify distantly related proteins by picking out a motif signal even in a sequence that has diverged radically from other members of the same family. Tools for profile analysis and motif discovery are introduced in Chapter 8.

Protein sequence analysis

The amino-acid content of a protein sequence can be used as the basis for many analyses, from computing the isoelectric point and molecular weight of the protein and the characteristic peptide mass fingerprints that will form when it's digested with a particular protease, to predicting secondary structure features and post-translational modification sites. Tools for feature prediction are introduced in Chapter 9, *Visualizing Protein Structures and Computing Structural Properties*, and tools for proteomics analysis are introduced in Chapter 11, *Tools for Genomics and Proteomics.*

Protein structure prediction

It's a lot harder to determine the structure of a protein experimentally than it is to obtain DNA sequence data. One very active area of bioinformatics and computational biology research is the development of methods for predicting protein structure from protein sequence. Methods such as secondary structure prediction and threading can help determine how a protein might fold, classifying it with other proteins that have similar topology, but they don't provide a detailed structural model. The most effective and practical method for protein structure prediction is *homology modeling*—using a known structure as a template to model a structure with a similar sequence. In the absence of homology, there is no way to predict a complete 3D structure for a protein. Tools for protein structure prediction are introduced in Chapter 9.

Protein structure property analysis

Protein structures have many measurable properties that are of interest to crystallographers and structural biologists. Protein structure validation tools are used by crystallographers to measure how well a structure model conforms to structural rules extracted from existing structures or chemical model compounds. These tools may also analyze the "fitness" of every amino acid in a structure model for its environment, flagging such oddities as buried charges with no countercharge or large patches of hydrophobic amino acids found on a protein surface. These tools are useful for evaluating both experimental and theoretical structure models.

Another class of tools can calculate internal geometry and physicochemical properties of proteins. These tools usually are applied to help develop models of the protein's catalytic mechanism or other chemical features. Some of the most interesting properties of protein structures are the locations of deeply concave surface clefts and internal cavities, both of which may point to the location of a cofactor binding site or active site. Other tools compute hydrogen-bonding patterns or analyze intramolecular contacts. A particularly interesting set of properties are the electrostatic potential field surrounding the protein and other electrostatically controlled parameters such as individual amino acid pKas, protein solvation energies, and binding constants. Methods for protein property analysis are discussed in Chapter 10, *Predicting Protein Structure and Function from Sequence.*

Protein structure alignment and comparison

Even when two gene sequences aren't apparently homologous, the structures of the proteins they encode can be similar. New tools for computing structural similarity are making it possible to detect distant homologies by comparing structures, even in the absence of much sequence similarity. These tools also are useful for comparing constructed homology models to the known protein structures they are based on. protein structure alignment tools are introduced in Chapter 10.

Biochemical simulation

Biochemical simulation uses the tools of dynamical systems modeling to simulate the chemical reactions involved in metabolism. Simulations can extend from individual metabolic pathways to transmembrane transport processes and even properties of whole cells or tissues. Biochemical and cellular simulations traditionally have relied on the ability of the scientist to describe a system mathematically, developing a system of differential equations that represent the different reactions and fluxes occurring in the system. However, new software tools can build the mathematical framework of a simulation automatically from a description provided interactively by the user, making mathematical modeling accessible to any biologist who knows enough about a system to describe it according to the conventions of dynamical systems modeling. Dynamical systems modeling tools are discussed in Chapter 11.

Whole genome analysis

As more and more genomes are sequenced completely, the analysis of raw genome data has become a more important task. There are a number of perspectives from which one can look at genome data: for example, it can be treated as a long linear sequence, but it's often more useful to integrate DNA sequence information with existing genetic and physical map data. This allows you to navigate a very large genome and find what you want. The National Center for Biotechnology Information (NCBI) and other organizations are making a concerted effort to provide useful web interfaces to genome data, so that users can start from a high-level map and navigate to the location of a specific gene sequence.

Genome navigation is far from the only issue in genomic sequence analysis, however. Annotation frameworks, which integrate genome sequence with results of gene finding analysis and sequence homology information, are becoming more common, and the challenge of making and analyzing complete pairwise comparisons between genomes is beginning to be addressed. Genome analysis tools are discussed in Chapter 11.

Primer design

Many molecular biology protocols require the design of oligonucleotide primers. Proper primer design is critical for the success of polymerase chain reaction (PCR), oligo hybridization, DNA sequencing, and microarray experiments. Primers must hybridize with the target DNA to provide a clear answer to the question being asked, but, they must also have appropriate physicochemical properties; they must not self-hybridize or dimerize; and they should not have multiple targets within the sequence under investigation. There are several web-based services that allow users to submit a DNA sequence and automatically detect appropriate primers, or to compute the properties of a desired primer DNA sequence. Primer design tools are discussed in Chapter 11.

DNA microarray analysis

DNA microarray analysis is a relatively new molecular biology method that expands on classic probe hybridization methods to provide access to thousands of genes at once. Microarray experiments are amenable to computational analysis because of the uniform, standardized nature of their results—a grid of equally sized spots, each identifiable with a particular DNA sequence. Computational tools are required to analyze larger microarrays because the resulting images are so visually complex that comparison by hand is no longer feasible.

The main tasks in microarray analysis as it's currently done are an image analysis step, in which individual spots on the array image are identified and signal intensity is quantitated, and a clustering step, in which spots with similar signal intensities are identified. Computational support is also required for the chip-design phase of a microarray experiment to identify appropriate oligonucleotide probe sequences for a particular set of genes and to maintain a record of the identity of each spot in a grid that may contain thousands of individual experiments. Array analysis tools are discussed in Chapter 11.

Proteomics analysis

Before they're ever crystallized and biochemically characterized, proteins are often studied using a combination of gel electrophoresis, partial sequencing, and mass spectroscopy. 2D gel electrophoresis can separate a mixture of thousands of proteins into distinct components; the individual spots of material can be blotted or even cut from the gel and analyzed. Simple computational tools can provide some information to aid in the process of analyzing protein mixtures. It's trivial to compute molecular weight and pI from a protein sequence; by using these values in combination, sets of candidate identities can be found for each spot on a gel. It's also possible to compute, from a protein sequence, the *peptide fingerprint* that is created when that protein is broken down into fragments by enzymes with specific protein cleavage sites. Mass spec analyses of protein fragments can be compared to computed peptide fingerprints to further limit the search. Proteomics tools are covered in Chapter 11.

A Computational Biology Experiment

Computer-based research projects and computational analysis of experimental data must follow the same principles other scientific study do. Your results must clearly answer the question you set out to test, and they must be reproducible by someone else using the same input data and following the same process.

If you're already doing research in experimental biology, you probably have a pretty good understanding of the scientific method. Although your data, your method, and your results are all encoded in computer files rather than sitting on your laboratory bench, the process of designing a computational "experiment" is the same as you are used to.

Although it's easy in these days of automation to simply submit a query to a search engine and use the results without thinking too much about it, you need to understand your method and analyze your results thoroughly in the same way you would when applying a laboratory protocol. Sometimes that's easier said than done. So let's take a walk through the steps involved in defining an experiment in computational biology.

Identifying the Problem

A scientific experiment always begins with a question. A question can be as broad as "what is the catalytic mechanism of protein X?" It's not always possible to answer a complex question about how something works with one experiment. The question needs to be broken down into parts, each of which can be formulated as a hypothesis.

A *hypothesis* is a statement that is testable by experiment. In the course of solving a problem, you will probably formulate a number of testable statements, some of them trivial and some more complex. For instance, as a first approach to answering the question, "What is the catalytic mechanism of protein X?", you might come up with a preliminary hypothesis such as: "There are amino acids in protein X that are conserved in other proteins that do the same thing as protein X." You can test this hypothesis by using a computer program to align the sequences of as many protein X-type proteins as you can find, and look for amino acids that are identical among all or most of the sequences. Subsequently you'd move to another hypothesis such as: "Some of these conserved amino acids in the protein X family have something to do with the catalytic mechanism." This more complex hypothesis can then be broken down into a number of smaller ones, each of them testable (perhaps by a laboratory experiment, or perhaps by another computational procedure).

A research project can easily become interminable if the goals are ill-defined or the question can't feasibly be answered. On the other hand, if you aren't careful, it's easy to keep adding questions to a project on the basis of new information, allowing the goal to keep creeping out of reach every time its completion is close. It's easy to do this with computational projects, because the cost of materials and resources is low once the initial expense of buying computers and software is covered. It seems no big loss to just keep playing around on the computer.

We have found that this pathological condition can be avoided if, before embarking on a computational project, some time is spent on sketching out a specification of the project's goals and timeline. If you plan to write a project spec, it's easier to start from written answers to questions such as the following:

- What is the question this project is trying to answer?

- What is the final form you expect the results to take? Is the goal to produce a computer program, a data set that will be used in an ongoing project, a journal publication, etc.? What are the requirements for success or completion of the project?

- What is the approximate timeline of the project?

- What is the general outline of the project? Here, it would be appropriate to break the project down into constituent parts and describe what you think needs to be done to finish each part.

- How does your project fit in with the work of others? If you're a lone wolf, you don't have to worry about this, but research scientists tend to run in packs. It's good to have a clear understanding of where your work is dependent on others. If you are writing a project spec for a group of people to work on, indicate who is responsible for each part of the work.

- At what point will it be unprofitable to continue?

Thinking through questions like these not only gives you a clearer idea of what your projects are trying to achieve, but also gives you an outline by which you can organize your research.

Separating the Problem into Simpler Components

In Chapters 7 through 14, we cover many of the common protocols for using bioinformatics tools and databases in your research. Coming up with the series of steps in those protocols wasn't rocket science. The key to developing your own bioinformatics computer skills is this: know what tools are available and know how to use them. Then you can take a modular approach to the problems you want to solve, breaking them down into distinct modules such as sequence searching, sequence profile detection, homology modeling, model evaluation, etc., for each of which there are established computational methods.

Evaluating Your Needs

As you break down a problem into modular components, you should be evaluating what you have, in terms of available data and starting points for modeling, and what you need. Getting from point A to point B, and from point C to point D, won't help you if there's absolutely no way to get from point B to point C. For instance, if you can't find any homologous sequences for an unknown DNA sequence, it's unlikely you'll get beyond that point to do any further modeling. And even if you do find a group of sequences with a distinctive profile, you shouldn't base your research plans on developing a structural model if there are no homologous structures in the Protein Data Bank (PDB). It's just common sense, but be sure that there's a likely way to get to the result you want before putting time and effort into a project.

Selecting the Appropriate Data Set

In a laboratory setting, materials are the physical objects or substances you use to perform an experiment. It's necessary for you to record certain data about your materials: when they were made, who prepared them, possibly how they were prepared, etc.

The same sort of documentation is necessary in computational biology, but the difference is that you will be experimenting on data, not on a tangible object or substance. The source data you work with should be distinguished from the derived data that constitutes the results of your experiment. You will probably get your source data from one of the many biomolecular databases. In Chapter 13, *Building Biological Databases*, you will learn more about how information is stored in databases and how to extract it. You need to record where your source data came from and what criteria or method you use to extract your source data set from the source database.

For example, if you are building a homology model of a protein, you need to account for how you selected the template structures on which you based your model. Did you find them using the unknown sequence to search the PDB? Did that approach provide sufficient template structures, or did you, perhaps, use sequence profile-based methods to help identify other structures that are more distantly related to your unknown? Each step you take should be documented.

Criteria for selecting a source data set in computational biology can be quite complex and nontrivial. For instance, statistical studies of sequence information or of structural data from proteins are often based on a *nonredundant* subset of available protein data. This means that data for individual proteins is excluded from the set if the proteins are too similar in sequence to other proteins that are being included. Inclusion of two structure datafiles that describe the same protein crystallized under slightly different conditions, for example, can bias the results of a computational study. Each step of such a selection process needs to be documented, either within your own records, or by reference to a published source.

It's important to remember that all digital sequence and structure data is derived data. By the time it reaches you, it has been through at least one or two processing steps, each of which can introduce errors. DNA sequences have been processed by basecalling software and assembled into maps, analyzed for errors, and possibly annotated according to structure and function, all by tools developed by other scientists as human and error-prone as yourself. Protein structure coordinates are really just a very good guess at where atoms fit into observed electron density data, and electron density maps in turn have been extrapolated from patterns of x-ray reflections. This isn't to say that you should not use or trust biological data, but you should remember that there is some amount of uncertainty associated with each unambiguous-looking character in a sequence or atomic coordinate in a structure. Crystallographers provide parameters, such as R-factors and b-values, which quantify the uncertainty of coordinates in macromolecular structures to some extent, but in the case of sequences, no such estimates are routinely provided within the datafile.

Identifying the Criteria for Success

Critical evaluation of results is key to establishing the usefulness of computer modeling in biology. In the context of presenting various tools you can use, we've discussed methods for evaluating your results, from using BLAST E-values to pick the significant matches out of a long list of results to evaluating the geometry of a protein structural model. Before you start computing molecular properties or developing a computational model, take inventory of what you know, and look for further information. Then try to see the ways in which that information can validate your results. This is part of breaking down your problem into steps.

Computational methods almost always produce results. It's not like spectroscopy, where if there's nothing significant in the cuvette, you don't get a signal. If you do a BLAST search, you almost always get some hits back. You need to know how to distinguish meaningful results from garbage so you don't end up comparing apples to oranges (or superoxide dismutases to alcohol dehydrogenases). If you calculate physicochemical properties of a protein molecule or develop a biochemical pathway simulation, you get a file full of numbers. The best possible way to evaluate your results is to have some experimental results to compare them to.

Before you apply a computational method, decide how to evaluate your results and what criteria they need to meet for you to consider the approach successful.

Performing and Documenting a Computational Experiment

When managing results for a computational project, you should make a distinction between primary results and results of subsequent analyses. You should include a separate section in your results directory for any analysis steps you may perform on the data (for instance, the results of statistical tests or curve fitting). This section should include any observations you may have made about the data or the data collection. Keep separate the results, which are the data you get from executing the experiment, and the analysis, which is the insight you bring to the data you have collected.

One tendency that is common to users of computational biology software is to keep data and notes about positive results while neglecting to document negative results. Even if you've done a web-based BLAST search against a database and found nothing, that is information. And if you've written or downloaded a program that is supposed to do something, but it doesn't work, that information is valuable too—to the next guy who comes in to continue your project and wastes time trying to figure out what works and what doesn't.

Documentation issues in computational biology

Many researchers, even those who do all their work on the computer, maintain paper laboratory notebooks, which are still the standard recording device for scientific research. Laboratory notebooks provide a tangible physical record of research activities, and maintenance of lab records in this format is still a condition of many research grants.

However, laboratory notebooks can be an inconvenient source of information for you or for others who are trying to duplicate or reconstruct your work. Lab notebooks are organized linearly, with entries sorted only by date. They aren't indexed (unless you have a lot more free time than most researchers do). They can't be searched for information about particular subjects, except by the unsatisfactory strategy of sitting down and skimming the whole book beginning to end.

Computer filesystems provide an intuitive basis for clear and precise organization of research records. Information about each part of a project can be stored logically, within the file hierarchy, instead of sequentially. Instead of (or in addition to) a paper notebook on your bookshelf, you will have electronic record embedded within your data. If your files are named systematically and simple conventions are used in structuring your electronic record, Unix tools such as the *grep* command will allow you to search your documentation for occurrences of a particular word or date and to find the needed information much more quickly than you would reading through a paper notebook.

Electronic notebooks

While you can get by with homegrown strategies for building an electronic record of your work, you may want to try one of the commercial products that are available. Or, if you're looking for a freeware implementation of the electronic notebook concept, you can obtain a copy of the software being developed by the DOE2000 Electronic Notebook project. The eNote package lets you input text, upload images and datafiles, and create sketches and annotations. It's a Perl CGI program and will run on any platform with a web server and a Perl interpreter installed. When installed, it's accessible from a web URL on your machine, and you can update your notebook through a web form. The DOE project is designed to fulfill federal agency requirements for laboratory notebooks, as scientific research continues to move into the computer age.

The eNote package is extremely simple to install. It requires that you have a working web server installed on your machine. If you do, you can download the eNote archive and unpack it in its own directory, for example */usr/local/enote*. The three files *enote.pl, enotelib.pl,* and *sketchpad.pl* are the eNote programs. You need to move *enote.pl* to the */home/httpd/cgi-bin* directory (or wherever your executable CGI directory is; this one is the default on Red Hat Linux systems) and rename it *enote.cgi.* If you want to restrict access to the notebook, create a special subdirectory just for the eNote programs, and remember that the directory will show up in the URL path to access the CGI script. The *sketchpad.pl* file should also be moved to this directory, but it doesn't have to be renamed. Move the directories *gifs* and *new-gifs* to a web-accessible location. You can create a directory such as */home/httpd/enote* for this purpose. Leave the file *enotelib.pl* and the directory *sketchpad* where you unpacked them.

Finally, you need to edit the first line in both *enote.cgi* and *sketchpad.pl* to point to the location of the Perl executable on your machine. Edit the *enote.cgi* script to reflect the paths where you installed the eNote script and its support files. You also need to choose a directory in which you want eNote to write entries. For instance, you may want to create a */home/enote/notebook* directory and store eNote write files there. If so, be sure that directory is readable and writable by other users so the web server (which is usually identified as user *nobody*) can write there.

The eNote script also contains parameters that specify whether users of the notebook system can add, delete, and modify entries. If you plan to use eNote seriously, these are important parameters to consider. Would you allow users to tear unwanted pages out of a laboratory notebook or write over them so the original entry was unreadable? eNote allows you to maintain control over what users can do with their data.

The eNote interface is a straightforward web form, which also links to a Java sketchpad applet. If you want only specific users with logins on your machine to be able to access the eNote CGI script, you can set up a *.htaccess* file in the eNote subdirectory of your CGI directory. A *.htaccess* file is a file readable by your web server that contains commands to restrict access to a particular directory and/or where it can be accessed from. For more information on creating a *.htaccess* file, consult the documentation for the web server you are using—most likely Apache on most Linux systems.

If you do begin to use an electronic notebook for storing your laboratory notes, remember that you must save backups of your notebook frequently in case of system failures.

II

The Bioinformatics Workstation

3

Setting Up Your Workstation

In this chapter, we discuss how to set up a workstation running the Linux operating system. Linux is a free, open source version of Unix that makes it possible to turn an ordinary PC into a powerful workstation. By configuring your system with Linux and other open source software, you can have access to a lot of powerful computational biology and bioinformatics tools at a low cost.

In writing this chapter, we encountered a bit of a paradox—in order to get around in Unix you need to have your computer set up, but in order to set up your computer you need to know a few things about Unix. If you don't have much experience with Unix, we strongly suggest that you look through Chapters 4 and 5 before you set up a Linux workstation of your own. If you're already familiar with the ins and outs of Unix, feel free to skip ahead to Chapter 6, *Biological Research on the Web*.

Working on a Unix System

You are probably accustomed to working with personal computers; you may be familiar with windows interfaces, word processors, and even some data-analysis packages. But if you want to use computers as a serious component in your research, you need to work on computer systems that run under Unix or related multiuser operating systems.

What Does an Operating System Do?

Computer hardware without an operating system is like a dead animal. It isn't going to react, it isn't going to function; it's just going to sit there and look at you with glassy eyes until it rots (or rusts). The operating system breathes life into the inert body of your computer. It handles the low level processes that make hardware work together and provides an environment in which you can run and develop programs. The most important function of the operating system is that it allows you convenient access to your files and programs.

Why Use Unix?

So if the operating system is something you're not supposed to notice, why worry about which one you're using? Why use Unix?

Unix is a powerful operating system for multiuser computer systems. It has been in existence for over 25 years, and during that time has been used primarily in industry and academia, where networked systems and multiuser high-performance computer systems are required. Unix is optimized for tasks that are only fairly recent additions to personal-computer operating systems, or which are still not even available in some PC operating systems: networking with other computers, initiating multiple asynchronous tasks, retaining unique information about the work environments of multiple users, and protecting the information stored by individual users from other users of the system. Unix is the operating system of the World Wide Web; the software that powers the Web was invented in Unix, and many if not most web servers run on Unix servers.

Because Unix has been used extensively in universities, where much software for scientific data analysis is developed, you will find a lot of good-quality, interesting scientific software written for Unix systems. Computational biology and bioinformatics researchers are especially likely to have developed software for Unix, since until the mid-1990s, the only workstations able to visualize protein structure data in realtime were Silicon Graphics and Sun Unix workstations.

Unix is rich in commands and possibilities. Every distribution of Unix comes with a powerful set of built-in programs. Everything from networking software to word-processing software to electronic mail and news readers is already a part of Unix. Many other programs can be downloaded and installed on Unix systems for free.

It might seem that there's far too much to learn to make working on a Unix system practical. It's possible, however, to learn a subset of Unix and to become a productive Unix user without knowing or using every program and feature.

Different Flavors of Unix

Unix isn't a monolithic entity. Many different Unix operating systems are out there, some proprietary and some freely distributed. Most of the commands we present in this book work in the same way on any system you are likely to encounter.

Linux

Linux (LIH-nucks) is an open source version of Unix, named for its original developer, Linus Torvalds of the University of Helsinki in Finland. Originally undertaken as a one-man project to create a free Unix for personal computers, Linux has grown from a hobbyist project into a product that, for the first time, gives the average personal-computer user access to a Unix system.

In this book, we focus on Linux for three reasons. First, with the availability of Linux, Unix is cheap (or free, if you have the patience to download and install it). Second, under Linux, inexpensive PCs regarded as "obsolete" by Windows users become startlingly flexible and useful workstations. The Linux operating system can be configured to use a much smaller amount of system resources than the personal computer operating systems, which means computers that have been outgrown by the ever-expanding system requirements of PC programs and operating systems can be given a new lease on life by being reconfigured to run Linux. Third, Linux is an excellent platform for developing software, so there's a rich library of tools available for computational biology and for research in general.

You may think that if you install Linux on your computer, you'll be pretty much on your own. It's a freeware operating system, after all. Won't you have to understand just about everything about Linux to get it configured correctly on your system? While this might have been true a few years ago, it's not any more. Hardware companies are starting to ship personal computers with Linux preinstalled as an alternative to the Microsoft operating systems. There are a number of companies that sell distributions of Linux at reasonable prices. Probably the best known of these is the Red Hat distribution. We should mention that we (the authors) run Red Hat Linux. Most of our experience—and the examples in this book—are based on that distribution. If you purchase Linux from one of these companies, you get CDs that contain not only Linux but many other compatible free software tools. You'll also have access to technical support for your installation.

Will Linux run on your computere? Linux started out as a Unix-like operating system for PCs, but various Linux development projects now support nearly every available system architecture, including PCs of all types, Macintosh computers old and new, Silicon Graphics, Sun, Hewlett-Packard, and other high-end workstations and high-performance multiprocessor machines. So even if you're starting with a motley mix of old and new hardware, you can use Linux to create a multi-workstation network of compatible computers. See the section "Setting Up a Linux Workstation" for more information on installing and running Linux.

Other common flavors

There are many varieties (or "flavors") of Unix out there. The other common free implementation is the Berkeley Software Distribution (BSD) originally developed at the University of California-Berkeley. For the PC, there are a handful of commercial Unix implementations, such as The Santa Cruz Operation (SCO) Unix. Several workstation makers sell their own platform-specific Unix implementations with their computers, often with their own peculiarities and quirks. Most common among these are Solaris (Sun Microsystems), IRIX (Silicon Graphics), Digital Unix (Compaq Corporation), HP-UX (Hewlett Packard), and AIX (IBM). This list isn't exhaustive, but it's probably representative of what you will find in most laboratories and computing centers.

Graphical Interfaces for Unix

Although Unix is a text-based operating system, you no longer have to experience it as a black screen full of glowing green or amber letters. Most Unix systems use a variant of the X Window System. The X Window System formats the screen environment and allows you to have multiple windows and applications open simultaneously. X windows are customizable so that you can use menu bars and other widgets much like PC operating systems. Individual Unix shells on the host machine as well as on networked machines are opened as windows, allowing you to exploit Unix's multitasking capabilities and to have many shells active simultaneously. In addition to Unix shells and tools, there are many applications that take advantage of the X system and use X windows as part of their graphical user interfaces, allowing these applications to be run while still giving access to the Unix command line.

The GNOME and KDE desktop environments, which are included in most major Linux distributions, make your Linux system look even more like a personal computer. Toolbars, visual file managers, and a configurable desktop replicate the feeling of a Windows or Mac work environment, except that you can also open a shell window and run Unix programs.

Setting Up a Linux Workstation

If you are already using an existing Unix/Linux system, feel free to skip this section and go directly to the next.

If you are used to working with Macintosh or PC operating systems, the simplest way to set up a Linux workstation or server is to go out and buy a PC that comes with Linux preinstalled. VA Linux, for example, offers a variety of Intel Pentium-based workstations and servers preconfigured with your choice of several of the most popular Linux distributions.

If you're looking for a complete, self-contained bioinformatics system, Iobion Systems (*http://www.iobion.com*) is developing *Iobion*, a ground-breaking bioinformatics network server appliance developed using open source technologies. Iobion is an Intel-based hardware system that comes preinstalled with Linux, Apache web server, a PostgreSQL relational database, the R statistical language, and a comprehensive suite of bioinformatics tools and databases. The system serves these scientific applications to web clients on a local intranet or over the Internet. The applications include tools for microarray data analysis complete with a microarray database, sequence analysis and annotation tools, local copies of the public sequence databases, a peer-to-peer networking tool for sharing biological data, and advanced biological lab tools. Iobion promotes and adheres to open standards in bioinformatics.

If you already have a PC, your next choice is to buy a prepackaged version of Linux, such as those offered by Red Hat, Debian, or SuSE. These prepackaged distributions have several advantages: they have an easy-to-use graphical interface for installing Linux, all the software they include is packed into package manager (for Red Hat, it's the Red Hat Package Manager or RPM) archives or similar easily extracted formats, and they often contain a large number of "extras" that are easier to install from the distribution disk using a package manager than they are if you install them by hand.

That said, let's assume you've gone out and bought something like the current version of Red Hat. You'll be asked if you want to do a workstation installation, a server installation, or a custom installation. What do these choices mean?

Your Linux machine can easily be set up to do some things you may not be used to doing with a PC or Macintosh. You can set up a web server on your machine, and if you dig a little deeper into the manuals, you can find out how to give each user of your machine a place to create his own web page. You can set up an anonymous FTP server so that guests can FTP in to pick up copies of files you choose to make public. You can set up an NFS server to allow directories you choose to be mounted on other machines. These are just some options that set a server apart from a workstation.

If you are inexperienced in Unix administration, you probably want to set up your first Linux machine as a workstation. With a workstation setup, you can access the Internet, but your machine can't provide any services to outside users (and you aren't responsible for maintaining these services). If you're feeling more adventurous, you can do a custom installation. This allows you to pick and choose the system components you want, rather than taking everything the installer thinks you may want.

Installing Linux

We can't possibly tell you everything you need to know to install and run Linux. That's beyond the scope of this book. There are many excellent books on the market that cover all possible angles of installing and running Linux, and you can find a good selection in this book's *Bibliography*. In this section, we simply offer some advice on the more important aspects of installation.

System requirements

Linux runs on a range of PC hardware combinations, but not all possible combinations. There are certain minimum requirements. For optimum performance, your PC should have an 80486 processor or better. Most Linux users have systems that use Intel chips. If your system doesn't, you should be aware that while Linux does support a few non-Intel processors, there is less documentation to help you resolve potential problems on those systems.

For optimum performance your system should have at least 16 MB of RAM. If you're planning to run X, you should seriously consider installing more memory—perhaps 64 MB. X runs well on 16 MB, but it runs more quickly and allows you to open more windows if additional memory is available.

If you plan to use your Linux system as a workstation, you should have at least 600 MB of free disk space. If you want to use it as a server, you should allow 1.6 GB of free space. You can never have too much disk space, so if you are setting up a new system, we recommend buying the largest hard drive possible. You'll never regret it.

In most cases the installation utility that comes with your distribution can determine your system configuration automatically, but if it fails to do so, you must be prepared to supply the needed information. Table 3-1 lists the configuration information you need to start your installation.

Table 3-1. Configuration Information Needed to Install Linux

Device	Information Needed
Hard drive(s)	• The number, size, and type of each hard drive • Which hard drive is first, second, and so on • Which adapter type (IDE or SCSI) is used by each drive • For each IDE drive, if the BIOS is set in LBS mode
RAM	• The amount of installed RAM
CD-ROM drive(s)	• Which adapter type (IDE, SCSI, other) is used by each drive • For each drive using a non-IDE, non-SCSI adapter, the make and model of the drive
SCSI adapter (if any)	• The make and model of the card

Table 3-1. Configuration Information Needed to Install Linux (continued)

Device	Information Needed
Network adapter (if any)	• The make and model of the card
Mouse	• The type (serial, PS/2, or bus) • The protocol (Microsoft, Logitech, MouseMan, etc.) • The number of buttons • For a serial mouse, the serial port to which it's connected
Video adapter	• The make and model of the card • The amount of video RAM

To obtain information, you may need to examine your system's BIOS settings or open the case and look at the installed hardware. Consult your system documentation or your system administrator to learn how to do so.

Here are three of the more popular Linux distributions:

• Red Hat (*http://www.redhat.com/support/hardware/*)

• boot: Debian (*http://www.debian.org/doc/FAQ/ch-compat.html*)

• SuSE (*http://www.suse.com*)

All have well-organized web sites with information about the hardware their distributions support. Once you've collected the information in Table 3-1, take a few minutes to check the appropriate web site to see if your particular PC hardware configuration is supported.

Partitioning your disk

Linux runs most efficiently on a partitioned hard drive. *Partitioning* is the process of dividing your disk up into several independent sections. Each partition on a hard drive is a separate filesystem. Files in one filesystem are to some extent protected from what goes on in other filesystems. If you download a bunch of huge image files, you can fill up only the partition in which your home directories live; you can't make the machine unusable by filling up all the available space for essential system functions. And if one partition gets corrupted, you can sometimes fix the problem without reformatting the entire drive and losing data stored in the other partitions.

When you start a Red Hat Linux installation, you need the Linux boot disk in your floppy drive and the Linux CD-ROM in your CD drive. When you turn the computer on, you almost immediately encounter an installation screen that offers several installation mode options. At the bottom of the screen, there is a *boot:* prompt. Generally, you should just hit the Enter key; however, if you're using a new model of computer, especially a laptop, you may want to enter *text*, then press the Enter key for a text-mode installation, in case your video card isn't supported by the current Linux release.

Click through the next few screens, selecting the appropriate language and keyboard. You'll come to a point at which you're offered the option of selecting a GNOME workstation, a KDE workstation, a server, or a custom installation. At this point, you can just choose one of the single user workstation options, and you're essentially done. However, we suggest doing a custom installation to allow you greater control over what is installed on your computer and where it's installed.

If you have a single machine that's not going to be interacting with other machines on the network, you can probably get away with putting the entire Linux installation into one big filesystem, if that's what you want. But if you're setting up a machine that will, for instance, share software in its */usr/local* directory with all the other machines in your lab, you'll want to do some creative partitioning.

On any given hard disk, you can have four partitions. Partitions can be of two types: *primary* and *extended.* Within an extended partition, you can have as many subpartitions as you like. Red Hat and other commercial Linux distributions have simple graphical interfaces that allow you to format your hard disk. More advanced users can use the *fdisk* program to achieve precise partitioning. Refer to one of the "Learning Linux" books we recommend in the *Bibliography* for an in-depth discussion of partitioning and how to use the *fdisk* program.

Selecting major package groupings

After you've set up partitions on your disk, chosen mount points for your partitions, and completed a few other configuration steps, you need to pick the packages to install.

First, go through the Package Group Selection list. You'll definitely need printer support; the X Window System; either the GNOME or KDE desktop (we like KDE); mail, web, and news tools, graphics manipulation tools; multimedia support; utilities; and networked workstation support. If you'll be installing software (and you will), you need a number of items in the development package group (C, FORTRAN, and other compilers come in handy, as do some development libraries). You may also want to install the *Emacs* text editor and the authoring/publishing tools. Depending on where you use your system from, you may need dial-up workstation support.

The rest of the package groups add server functionality to your machine. If you want your machine to function as a web server, add the web server package group. If you want to make some of the directories on your machine available for NFS mounting, choose the NFS server group. If you plan to create your own databases, you may want to set up your machine as a PostgreSQL server. Generally, if you have no idea what it is or how you'd use it, you probably don't need to install it at this point.

If you're concerned about running out of space on your machine, you can now sift through the contents of each package grouping and get rid of software you won't be using. For example, the "Mail, Web and News" package grouping contains many different types of software for reading email and newsgroups. Don't install it all, just pick your favorite package, and get rid of the rest. (In case you're wondering what to choose, here's a hint: it's very easy to configure the Netscape browser to do all the mail and news reading you'll need.) If you're installing a Red Hat system, check under "Applications/Editors" and make sure you have the *vim* editor selected; in "Applications/Engineering," select *gnuplot*, and in "Applications/Publishing," select *enscript*. Don't worry if you don't install something at the beginning and find you need to install it later, it's pretty easy to do.

Other useful packages to add

Once you've done a basic Linux installation on your machine, you can add new packages easily using the *kpackage* command (if you're using the KDE desktop environment) or *gnorpm* (if you are using GNOME).

In order to compile some of the software we'll be discussing in the next few chapters, and to expand the functionality of your Linux workstation, you may want to install some of the following tools. The first set of tools are from the Red Hat Linux Power Tools CD:

R
A powerful system for statistical computation and graphics. It's based on S and consists of a high-level language and a runtime environment.

OpenGL/Mesa
A development kit for creating graphical user interfaces that enhances performance of some molecular visualization software.

LessTif
A widget set for application development. You might not use it directly, but it's used when you compile some of the software discussed later in this book. Install at least the main package and the client package.

Xbase
Another widget set.

MySQL
A database server for smaller data sets. It's useful if you're just starting to build your own databases.

octave
A MatLab-like high-level language for numerical computations.

xv   A multipurpose image-editing and conversion tool.

xemacs

A powerful X Windows-based editor with special extensions for editing source code.

plugger

A generic Netscape plug-in that supports many formats.

You can download from the Web and install the following tools:

JDK/JRE (http://java.sun.com)

A Java Development Kit and Java Runtime Environment are needed if you want to use Java-based tools such as the Jalview sequence editor we discuss in Chapter 4, *Files and Directories in Unix*. They are freely available for Linux from IBM, Sun, and Blackdown (*http://blackdown.org*). Blackdown also offers a Java plug-in for Netscape, which is required to run some of the applications we discuss.

NCBI Toolkit (ftp://ncbi.nlm.nih.gov/toolbox/ncbi_tools/README.htm)

A software library for developers of biology applications. It's required in order to compile some software originating at NCBI.

StarOffice (http://www.staroffice.com)

A comprehensive office productivity package freely available from Sun Micro-systems. It replaces most or all functionality of Microsoft Office and other familiar office-productivity packages.

How to Get Software Working

You've gone out and done the research and found a bioinformatics software package you want to install on your own computer. Now what do you do?

When you look for Unix software on the Web, you will find that it's distributed in a number of different formats. Each type of software distribution requires a different type of handling. Some are very simple to install, almost like installing software on a Mac or PC. On the other hand, some software is distributed in a rudimentary form that requires your active intervention to get it running. In order to get this software working, you may have to compile it by hand or even modify the directions that are sent to the compiler so that the program will work on your system. *Compiling* is the process of converting software from its human-readable form, *source code*, to a machine-readable *executable* form. A compiler is the program that performs this conversion.

Software that's difficult to install isn't necessarily bad software. It may be high-quality software from a research group that doesn't have the resources to produce an easy-to-use installation kit. While this is becoming less common, it's still common enough that you will need to know some things about compiling software.

Unix tar Archives

Software is often distributed as a *tar* archive, which is short for "tape archive." We discuss *tar* and other file-compression options in more detail in Chapter 5, *Working on a Unix System*. Not coincidentally, these archives are one of the most common ways to distribute Unix software on the Internet. *tar* allows you to download one file that contains the complete image of the developer's working software installation and unpack it right back into the correct subdirectories. If *tar* is used with the *p* option, file permissions can even be preserved. This ensures that, if the developer has done a competent job of packing all the required files in the *tar* archive, you can compile the software relatively easily.

tar archives are often compressed further using either the Unix *compress* command (indicated by a *.tar.Z* extension) or with *gzip* (indicated by a *.tar.gz* or *.tgz* extension).

Binary Distributions

Software can be distributed either as uncompiled source code or binaries. If you have a choice, and if you don't know any reason to do otherwise, choose the binary distribution. It will probably save you a lot of headaches.

Binary software distributions are precompiled and (at least in theory) ready to run on your machine. When you download software that is distributed in binary form, you will have a number of options to choose from. For example, the following listing is the contents of the public FTP site for the BLAST sequence alignment software. There are several archives available, each for a different operating system; if you're going to run the software on a Linux workstation, download the file *blast.linux.tar.Z*.

```
README.bls               52 Kb    Wed Jan 26 18:45:00 2000
blast.alphaOSF1.tar.Z  12756 Kb  Wed Jan 26 18:40:00 2000    Unix Tape Archive
blast.hpux11.tar.Z     11964 Kb  Wed Jan 26 18:43:00 2000    Unix Tape Archive
blast.linux.tar.Z       9334 Kb  Wed Jan 26 18:41:00 2000    Unix Tape Archive
blast.sgi.tar.Z        14746 Kb  Wed Jan 26 18:44:00 2000    Unix Tape Archive
blast.solaris.tar.Z    12724 Kb  Wed Jan 26 18:37:00 2000    Unix Tape Archive
blast.solarisintel.tar.Z 10679 Kb Wed Jan 26 18:43:00 2000   Unix Tape Archive
blastz.exe              3399 Kb   Wed Jan 26 18:44:00 2000    Binary Executable
```

Here are the basic binary installation steps:

1. Download the correct binaries. Be sure to use binary mode when you download. Download and read the instructions (usually a *README* or *INSTALL* file).

2. Follow the instructions.

3. Make a new directory and move the archive into it, if necessary.

4. *uncompress (*.Z)* or *gunzip (*.gz)* to uncompress the file.

5. Use *tar tf* to examine the contents of the archive and *tar xvf* to extract it.

6. Run configuration and installation scripts, if present.

7. Link binary into a directory in your default path using *ln −s,* if necessary.

RPM Archives

RPM archives are a new kind of Unix software distribution that has recently become popular. These archives can be unpacked using the command *rpm.* The Red Hat Package Manager program is included in Red Hat Linux distributions and is automatically installed on your machine when you install Linux. It can also be downloaded freely from *http://www.rpm.org* and used on any Linux or other Unix system. *rpm* creates a software database on your machine and simplifies installations and updates, and even allows you to create RPM archives. RPM archives come in either source or binary form, but aside from the question of selecting the right binary, the installation is equally simple either way.

(As we introduce commands, we'll show you the format of the command line for each command—for example, "Usage: `man` *name*"—and describe the effects of some options we find most useful.)

Usage: `rpm --[`*options*`] *.rpm`

Here are the important *rpm* options:

rebuild
Builds a package from a source RPM

install
Installs a new package from a binary RPM

upgrade
Upgrades existing software

uninstall (or *erase*)
Removes an installed package

query
Checks to see if a package is installed

verify
Checks information about installed files in a package

GnoRPM

Recent versions of Linux that include the GNOME user interface also include an interactive installation tool called GnoRPM. It can be accessed from the System folder in the main GNOME menu. To install software from a CD-ROM with GnoRPM, simply insert and mount the CD-ROM, click the Install button in GnoRPM, and GnoRPM provides a selectable list of every package on the CD-ROM you haven't already installed. You can also uninstall and update packages with GnoRPM, ensuring that the entire package is cleanly removed from your system. GnoRPM informs you if there are package dependencies that require you to download code libraries or other software before completing the installation.

Source Distributions

Sometimes the correct binary isn't available for your system, there's no RPM archive, and you have no choice but to install from source code.

Source distributions can be easy or hard to install. The easy ones come with a configuration script, an install script, and a *Makefile* for your operating system that holds the instructions to the compiler.

An example of an easy-to-install package is the LessTif source code distribution. LessTif is an open source version of the OSF/Motif window manager software. Motif was developed for high-end workstations and costs a few thousand dollars a year to license; LessTif supports many Motif applications (such as the multiple sequence alignment package ClustalX and the useful 2D plotting package Grace, for example) for free. When the LessTif distribution is unpacked, it looks like:

```
AUTHORS         KNOWN_BUGS     acconfig.h     configure      ltmain.sh
BUG-REPORTING   Makefile       acinclude.m4   configure.in   make.out
COPYING         Makefile.am    aclocal.m4     doc            missing
COPYING.LIB     Makefile.in    clients        etc            mkinstalldirs
CREDITS         NEWS           config.cache   include        scripts
CURRENT_NOTES   NOTES          config.guess   install-sh     test
CVSMake         README         config.log     lib            test_build
ChangeLog       RELEASE-POLICY config.status  libtool
INSTALL         TODO           config.sub     ltconfig
```

Configuration and installation of LessTif on a Linux workstation is a practically foolproof process. As the superuser, move the source *tar* archive to the */usr/local/ src* directory. Uncompress and extract the archive. Inside the directory that is created (*lesstif* or *lesstif.0-89*, for example), enter *./configure*. The configuration script will take a while to run; when it's done, enter *make*. Compilation will take several minutes; at the end, edit the file */etc/ld.so.conf*. Add the line */usr/lesstif/lib*, save the file, and then run *ldconfig −v* to make the shared LessTif libraries available on your machine.

Complex software such as LessTif is assembled from many different source code modules. The *Makefile* tells the compiler how to put them together into one large executable. Other programs are simple: they have only one source code file and no *Makefile*, and they are compiled with a one-line directive to the compiler. You should be able to tell which compiler to use by the extension on the program filename. C programs are often labeled *.c, FORTRAN programs *.f, etc. To compile a C program, enter *gcc program.c –o program*; for a FORTRAN program, the command is *g77 program.f –o program*. The manpages for the compilers, or the program's documentation (if there is any) should give you the form and possible arguments of the compiler command.

Compilers convert human-readable source code into machine-readable binaries. Each programming language has its own compilers and compiler instructions. Some compilers are free, others are commercial. The compilers you will encounter on Linux systems are *gcc*, the GNU Project C and C++ compiler, and *g77*, the GNU Project FORTRAN compiler.* In computational biology and bioinformatics, you are likely to encounter programs written in C, C++, FORTRAN, Perl, and Java. Use of other languages is relatively rare. Compilers or interpreters for all these languages are available in open source distributions.

Difficult-to-install programs come in many forms. One of the main problems you may encounter will be source code with dependencies on code libraries that aren't already installed on your machine. Be sure to check the documentation or the *README* file that comes with the software to determine whether additional code or libraries are required for the program to run properly.

An example of an undeniably useful program that is somewhat difficult to install is ClustalX, the X windows interface to the multiple sequence alignment program ClustalW. In order to install ClustalX successfully on a Linux workstation, you first need to install the NCBI Toolkit and its included Vibrant libraries. In order to create the Vibrant libraries, you need to install the LessTif libraries and to have XFree86 development libraries installed on your computer.

Here are the basic steps for installing any package from source code:

1. Download the source code distribution. Use binary mode; compressed text files are encoded.

2. Download and read the instructions (usually a *README* or *INSTALL* file; sometimes you have to find it after you extract the archive).

---

* The GNU project is a collaborative project of the Free Software Foundation to develop a completely open source Unix-like operating system. Linux systems are, formally, GNU/Linux systems as they can be distributed under the terms of the GNU Public License (GPL), the license developed by the GNU project.

3. Make a new directory and move the archive into it, if necessary.

4. *uncompress* (*.Z) or *gunzip* (*.gz) the file.

5. Extract the archive using *tar xvf* or as instructed.

6. Follow the instructions (did we say that already?).

7. Run the configuration script, if present.

8. Run *make* if a *Makefile* is present.

9. If a *Makefile* isn't present and all you see are *.f* or *.c* files, use *gcc* or *g77* to compile them, as discussed earlier.

10. Run the installation script, if present.

11. Link the newly created binary executable into one of the binary-containing directories in your path using *ln −s* (this is usually part of the previous step, but if there is no installation script, you may need to create the link by hand).

Perl Scripts

The Perl language is used to develop web applications and is frequently used by computational biologists. Perl programs (called *scripts*) have the extension *.pl* (or *.cgi* if they are web applications). Perl is an interpreted language; in other words, Perl programs don't have to be compiled in order to run. Instead, each command in a Perl script is sent to a program called the Perl interpreter, which executes the commands.*

To run Perl programs, you need to have the Perl interpreter installed on your machine. Most Linux distributions contain and automatically install Perl. The most recent version of Perl can always be obtained from *http://www.perl.com*, along with plenty of helpful information about how to use Perl in your own work. We discuss some of the basic elements of Perl in Chapter 12, *Automating Data Analysis with Perl.*

Putting It in Your Path

When you give a command, the *default path* or *lookup path* is where the system expects to find the program (which is also known as the executable). To make life easier, you can link the binary executable created when you compile a program to a directory like */usr/local/bin*, rather than typing the full pathname to the program every time you run it. If you're linking across filesystems, use the command *ln −s* (which we cover in Chapter 4) to link the command to a directory of executable

---

* There is now a Perl compiler, which can optionally be used to create binary executables from Perl scripts. This can speed up execution.

files. Sometimes this results in the error "too many levels of symbolic links" when you try to run the program. In that case, you have to access the executable directly or use *mv* or *cp* to move the actual executable file into the default path. If you do this, be sure to also move any support files the program needs, or create a link to them in the directory in which the program is being run.

Some software distributions automatically install their executables in an appropriate location. The command that usually does this is *make install*. Be sure to run this command after the program is compiled. For more information on symbolic linking, refer to one of the Unix references listed in the *Bibliography*, or consult your system administrator.

Sharing Software Among Multiple Users

Before you start installing software on a Unix system, one of the first things to do is to find out where shared software and data are stored on your machines. It's customary to install local applications in */usr/local*, with executable files in */usr/local/bin*. If */usr/local* is set up as a separate partition on the system, it then becomes possible to upgrade the operating system without overwriting local software installations.

Maintaining a set of shared software is a good idea for any research group. Installation of a single standard version of a program or software package by the system administrator ensures that every group member will be using software that works in exactly the same way. This makes troubleshooting much easier and keeps results consistent. If one user has a problem running a version of a program that is used by everyone in the group, the troubleshooting focus can fall entirely on the user's input, without muddying the issue by trying to figure out whether a local version of the program was compiled correctly.

For the most part, it's unnecessary for each user of a program to have her own copy of that program residing in a personal directory. The main exception to this is if a user is actually modifying a program for her own use. Such modifications should not be applied to the public, standard version of the program until they have been thoroughly tested, and therefore the user who is modifying the program needs her own version of the program source and executable.

What Software Is Needed?

New computational biology software is always popping up, but through a couple of decades of collective experience, a consensus set of tools and methods has emerged. Many scientists are familiar with standard commercial packages for sequence analysis, such as GCG, and for protein structure analysis, such as Quanta or Insight. For beginners, these packages provide an integrated interface to a variety of tools.

Commercial software packages for sequence analysis integrate a number of functions, including mapping and fragment assembly, database searching, gene discovery, pairwise and multiple sequence analysis, motif identification, and evolutionary analysis. One caveat is that these software packages can be prohibitively expensive. It can be difficult, especially for educational institutions and research groups on a limited budget, to purchase commercial software and pay the annual costs for license maintenance (which can be in the many thousands of dollars).

A related cost issue is that many commercial software packages, especially those for macromolecular structure analysis, don't yet run on consumer PCs. These packages were originally developed for high-end workstations when these workstations were the only computers with sufficient graphics capability to display protein structures. Although these days most home computers have high-powered graphics cards, the makers of commercial molecular modeling software have been slow to keep up.

While commercial computational biology software packages can be excellent and easy to use, they often seem to lag at least a couple of years behind cutting-edge method development. The company that produces a commercial software package usually commits to only one method for each type of tool, buys it at a particular phase in its development cycle, focuses on turning it into a commercially viable product, and may not incorporate developments in the method into their package in a timely fashion, or at all.

On the other hand, while academic software is usually on the cutting edge, it can be poorly written and hard to install. Documentation (beyond the published paper that describes the software) may be nonexistent. Graphical user interfaces in academic software packages are often rudimentary, which can be aggravating for the beginning user.

With this book, we've taken the "science on a shoestring" approach. In Chapters 6, 7, 9, 10, and 11 we've compiled quick-reference tables of fundamental techniques and free software applications you can use to analyze your data. Hopefully, these will help you to know what you need to do, how to seek out the tools that do it, and how to put them both together in the way that best suits your needs. This approach keeps you independent of the vagaries of the software industry and in touch with the most current methods.

Files and Directories in Unix

Now that you've set up your workstation, let's spend some time talking about how to get around in a Unix system. In this chapter, we introduce basic Unix concepts, including the structure of the filesystem, file ownership, and commands for moving around the filesystem and creating files.* Another important focus of this chapter, however, is the approach you should take to organizing your research data so that it can be accessed efficiently by you and by others.

Filesystem Basics

All computer filesystems, whether on Unix systems or desktop PCs, are basically the same. *Files* are named locations on the computer's storage device. Each filename is a pointer to a discrete object with a beginning and end, whether it's a program that can be executed or simply a set of data that can be read by a program. *Directories* or *folders* are containers in which files can be grouped. Computer filesystems are organized hierarchically, with a root directory that branches into subdirectories and subdirectories of subdirectories.

This hierarchical system can help organize and share information, if used properly. Like the taxonomy of species developed by the early biologists, your file hierarchy should organize information from the general level to the specific. Each time the filesystem splits into subdirectories, it should be because there are meaningful divisions to be created within a larger class of files.

---

* Throughout this chapter and Chapter 5, *Working on a Unix System*, we introduce many Unix commands. Our quick and dirty approach to outlining the functions of these commands and their options should help you get started working fast, but it's by no means exhaustive. The *Bibliography* provides several excellent Unix books that will help you fill in the details.

Why should you organize your computer files in a systematic, orderly way? It seems like an obvious question with an obvious answer. And yet, a common problem faced by researchers and research groups is failure to share information effectively. Problems with information management often become apparent when a research group member leaves, and others are required to take over his project.

Imagine you work with a colleague who keeps all his books and papers piled in random stacks all over his office. Now imagine that your colleague gets a new job and needs to depart in a hurry—leaving behind just about everything in his office. Your boss tells you that you can't throw away any of your colleague's papers without looking at them, because there might be something valuable in there. Your colleague has not organized or categorized any of his papers, so you have to pick up every item, look at it, determine if it's useful, and then decide where you want to file it. This might be a week's work, if you're lucky, and it's guaranteed to be a tough job.

This kind of problem is magnified when computer files are involved. First of all, many highly useful files, especially binaries of programs, aren't readable as text files by users. Therefore, it's difficult to determine what these files do if they're not documented. Other kinds of files, such as files of numerical data, may not contain useful header information. Even though they can be read as text, it may be next to impossible to figure out their purpose.

Second, space constraints on computer system usage are much more nebulous than the walls of an office. As disk space has become cheaper, it's become easier for users of a shared system simply never to clean up after themselves. Many programs produce multiple output files and, if there's no space constraint that forces you to clean up while running them, can produce a huge mess in a short time.

How can you avoid becoming this kind of problem for your colleagues? Awareness of the potential problems you can cause is the first step. You need to know what kinds of programs and files you should share with others and which you should keep in your own directories. You should establish conventions for naming datafiles and programs and stick to these conventions as you work. You should structure your filesystem in a sensible hierarchy. You should keep track of how much space you are using on your computer system and create usable archives of your data when you no longer need to access it frequently. You should create informative documentation for your work within the filesystem and within programs and datafiles.

The nature of the filesystem hierarchy means that you already have a powerful indexing system for your work at your fingertips. It's possible to do computer-based research and be just as disorganized as that coworker who piles all his books and papers in random stacks all over his office. But why would you want to do that? Without much more effort, you can use your computer's filesystem to keep your work organized.

Moving Around the Directory Hierarchy

Like all modern operating systems, the file hierarchy on a Unix system is structured as a tree. You may be used to this from PC operating systems. Open one folder, and there can be files and more folders inside it, layered as deep as you want to go. There is a root directory, designated as /. The root directory branches into a finite number of files and subdirectories. On a well-organized system, each of these subdirectories contains files and other subdirectories pertaining to a particular topic or system function.

Of course, there's nothing inside your computer that really looks like a tree. Files are stored on various media—most commonly the hard disk, which is a recordable device that lives in your computer. As its name implies, the hard disk is really a disk. And the tree structure that you perceive in Unix is simply a way of indexing what is on that disk or on other devices such as CDs, floppy disks, and Zip disks, or even on the disks of every machine in a group of networked computers. Unix has extensive networking capabilities that allow devices on networked computers to be mounted on other computers over the network. Using these capabilities, the filesystems of several networked computers can be indexed as if they were one larger, seamless filesystem.

Paths to Files and Directories

Each file on the filesystem can be uniquely identified by a combination of a filename and a path. You can reference any file on the system by giving its full name, which begins with a / indicating the root directory, continues through a list of subdirectories (the components of the path) and ends with the filename. The full name, or *absolute path,* of a file in someone's home directory might look like this:

```
/home/jambeck/mustelidae/weasels.txt
```

The absolute path describes the relationship of the file to the root directory, /. Each name in the path represents a subdirectory of the prior directory, and / characters separate the directory names.

Every file or directory on the system can be named by its absolute path, but it can also be named by a *relative path* that describes its relationship to the current working directory. Files in the directory you are in can be uniquely identified just by giving the filename they have in the current working directory. Files in subdirectories of your current directory can be named in relation to the subdirectory they are part of. From *jambeck*'s home directory, he can uniquely identify the file *weasels.txt* as *mustelidae/weasels.txt.* The absence of a preceding / means that the path is defined relative to the current directory rather than relative to the root directory.

If you want to name a directory that is on the same level or above the current working directory, there is a shorthand for doing so. Each directory on the system contains two links, ./ and ../, which refer to the current directory and its *parent* directory (the directory it's a subdirectory of), respectively. If user *jambeck* is working in the directory */home/jambeck/mustelidae/weasels*, he can refer to the directory */home/jambeck/mustelidae/otters* as ../otters. A subdirectory of a directory on the same level of the hierarchy as */home/jambeck/mustelidae* would be referred to as ../../didelphiidae/opossums.

Another shorthand naming convention, which is implemented in the popular *csh* and *tcsh* shell environments, is that the path of the home directory can be abbreviated as ~. The directory *home/jambeck/mustelidae* can then be referred to as ~/mustelidae.

Using a Process-Based File Hierarchy

Filesystems can be deep and narrow or broad and shallow. It's best to follow an intuitive scheme for organizing your files. Each level of hierarchy should be related to a step in the process you've used to carry out the project. A filesystem is probably too shallow if the output from numerous processing steps in one large project is all shoved together in one directory. However, a project directory that involves several analyses of just one data object might not need to be broken down into subdirectories. The filesystem is too deep if versions of output of a process are nested beneath each other or if analyses that require the same level of processing are nested in subdirectories. It's much easier to for you to remember and for others to understand the paths to your data if they clearly symbolize steps in the process you used to do the work.

As you'll see in the upcoming example, your home directory will probably contain a number of directories, each containing data and documentation for a particular project. Each of these project directories should be organized in a way that reflects the outline of the project. Each directory should contain documentation that relates to the data within it.

Establishing File-Naming Conventions for Your Work

Unix allows an almost unlimited variability in file naming. Filenames can contain any character other than the / or the null character (the character whose binary representation is all zeros). However, it's important to remember that some characters, such as a space, a backslash, or an ampersand, have special meaning on the command line and may cause problems when naming files. File-names can be up to 255 characters in length on most systems. However, it's wise to aim for uniformity rather than uniqueness in file naming. Most humans are much better at remembering frequently used patterns than they are at remembering unique 255-character strings, after all.

A common convention in file naming is to name the file with a unique name followed by a dot (.) and then an extension that uniquely indicates the file type.

As you begin working with computers in your research and structuring your data environment, you need to develop your own file-naming conventions, or preferably, find out what naming conventions already exist and use them consistently throughout your project. There's nothing so frustrating as looking through old data sets and finding that the same type of file has been named in several different ways. Have you found all the data or results that belong together? Can the file you are looking for be named something else entirely? In the absence of conventions, there's no way to know this except to open every unidentifiable file and check its format by eye. The next section provides a detailed example of how to set up a filesystem that won't have you tearing out your hair looking for a file you know you put there.

Here are some good rules of thumb to follow for file-naming conventions:

- Files of the same type should have the same extension.
- Files derived from the same source data should have a common element in their unique names.
- The unique name should contain as much information as possible about the experiment.
- Filenames should be as short as is possible without compromising uniqueness.

You'll probably encounter preestablished conventions for file naming in your work. For instance, if you begin working with protein sequence and structure datafiles, you will find that families of files with the same format have common extensions. You may find that others in your group have established local conventions for certain kinds of datafiles and results. You should attempt to follow any known conventions.

Structuring a Project: An Example

Let's take a look at an example of setting up a filesystem. These are real directory layouts we have used in our work; only the names have been changed to protect the innocent. In this case, we are using a single directory to hold the whole project.

It's useful to think of the filesystem as a family tree, clustering related aspects of a project into branches. The top level of your project directory should contain two text files that explain the contents of the directories and subdirectories. The first file should contain an outline of the project, with the date, the names of the people involved, the question being investigated, and references to publications related to this project. Tradition suggests that such informational files should be given a name along the lines of *README* or *00README*. For example, in the *shards* project, a minimal *README* file might contain the following:

```
98-05-22
Project: Shards
Personnel: Per Jambeck, Cynthia Gibas
Question: Are there recurrent structural words in the three-dimensional structure
of proteins?
Outline: Automatic construction of a dictionary of elements of local structure in
proteins using entropy maximization-based learning.
```

The second file should be an index file (named something readily recognizable like *INDEX*) that explains the overall layout of the subdirectories. If you haven't really collected much data yet, a simple sketch of the directories with explanations should do. For example, the following file hierarchy:

```
98-03-22 PJ
Layout of the Shards directory
(see README in subdirectories for further details)
/shards
/shards/data
/shards/data/sequences
/shards/data/structures
/shards/data/results
/shards/data/results/enolases
/shards/data/results/globins
/shards/data/test_cases
/shards/graphics
/shards/text
/shards/text/notebook
/shards/text/reports
/shards/programs
/shards/programs/source
/shards/programs/scripts
/shards/programs/bin
```

may also be represented in graphical form, as shown in Figure 4-1.

In this directory, we've made the first distinction between programs and data (*programs* contains the software we write, and *data* contains the information we get from databases, or files the programs generate). Within each subdirectory, we further distinguish between types of data (in this case, protein *structures* and protein *sequences*), and results (run on two sets of proteins, the *enolase* family and the *globin* superfamily) gleaned from running our programs on the data, and some

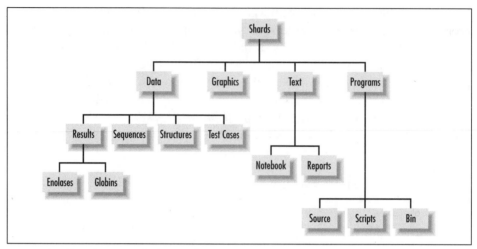

Figure 4-1. Tree diagram of a hierarchy

test cases. Programs are also subdivided according to types, namely whether they are the human-readable program listings (source code), scripts that aid in running the programs, or the binaries of the programs.

As we mentioned earlier, when you store data in files, you should try to use a terse and consistent system for naming files. Excessively long filenames that describe the exact contents of a file but change for different file types (like *all-GPCR-loops-in-SWISSPROT-on-99-7-14.text*) will cause problems once you start using the facilities Unix provides for automatically searching for and updating files. In the *shards* project, we began with protein structures taken from the Protein Data Bank (PDB). We then used a homegrown Perl program called *unique.pl* to generate a nonredundant database, in which no protein's sequence had greater than 25% similarity to any other protein in the set. Thus, we can represent this information economically using the filename *PDB-unique-25* for files related to this data set. For example, the list of the names of proteins in the set, and the file containing the proteins' sequences in FASTA format (a common text-file format for storing macromolecular sequence data), are stored, respectively, in:

```
PDB-unique-25.list
PDB-unique-25.fasta
```

Files containing derived data can be named consistently as well. For example, the file containing all seven-residue pieces of protein structure derived from the non-redundant set is called *PDB-unique-25-7.shard*. This way, if you need to do something with all files pertaining to this nonredundant database, you can use the wildcard *PDB-unique-25**, ignoring databases generated by different programs or those generated with *unique.pl* at different similarity thresholds.

File naming conventions can take you only so far in organizing a project; the simple naming schemes we've laid out here will become more and more confusing as a project grows. For larger projects, you should consider using a database management system (DBMS) to manage your data. We introduce database concepts in Chapter 13, *Building Biological Databases.*

Commands for Working with Directories and Files

Now that you have the basics of filesystems, let's dig into the specifics of working with files and directories in Unix. In the following sections, we cover the Unix commands for moving around the filesystem, finding files and directories, and manipulating files and directories.

As we introduce commands, we'll show you the format of the command line for each command (for example, "Usage: man *name*"), and describe the effects of some options we find most useful.

Moving Around the Filesystem

When you open a window on a Linux system, you see a command prompt:

```
$
```

Command prompts can look different depending on the configuration of your system and your shell. For example, the following user is using the *tcsh* shell environment and has configured the command prompt to show the username and current working directory:

```
[cgibas@gibas ~]$
```

Whatever the style of the command prompt, it means that your computer is waiting for you to tell it to do something. If you type an instruction at the prompt and press the Enter key, you have given your computer a command. Unix provides a set of simple navigation commands and commands for searching your filesystem for particular files and programs. We'll discuss the format of commands more thoroughly in Chapter 5. In this chapter, we'll introduce you to basic commands for getting around in Unix.

You are here: pwd

pwd stands for "print working directory," and that's exactly what it does. *pwd* sends the full pathname of the directory you are currently in, the current working directory, to standard output—it prints to the screen. You can think of being "in" a directory in this way: if the directory tree is a map of the filesystem, the current working directory is the "you are here" pointer on the map.

When you log in to the system, your "you are here" pointer is automatically placed in your *home directory*. Your home directory is a unique place. It contains the files you use almost every time you log into your system, as well as the directories that you create to store other files. What if you want to find out where your home directory is in relation to the rest of the system? Typing *pwd* at the command prompt in your home directory should give output something like:

    /home/jambeck

This means that *jambeck*'s home directory is a subdirectory of the home directory, which in turn is a subdirectory of the root (/) directory.

Changing directories with cd

Usage: cd *pathname**

The *cd* command changes the current working directory. The only argument commonly used with this command is the pathname of a directory. If *cd* is used without an argument, it changes the current working directory to the user's home directory.

In order for these "you are here" tools to be helpful, you need to have organized your filesystem in a sensible way in the first place, so that the name and location of the directory that you're in gives you information about what kind of material can be found there. Most of the filesystem of your machine will have been set up by default when you installed Linux, but the organization of your own directories, where you store programs and data that you use, is your responsibility.

Finding Files and Directories

Unix provides many ways to find files, from simply listing out the contents of a directory to search programs that look for specified filenames and the locations of executable programs.

Listing files with ls

Usage: ls [*-options*] *pathname*

---

* As you'll see when we cover the Unix shell and the command line in Chapter 5, Unix commands can be issued with or without arguments on the command line. The first word in a line is always a command. Subsequent words are arguments and can include options, which modify the command's behavior, and operands, which specify pathnames. Words in the command line are items separated by whitespace (spaces or tabs).

Now that you know where you are, how do you find out what's around you? Simply typing the Unix list command, *ls*, at the prompt gives you a listing of all the files and subdirectories in the current working directory. You can also give a directory name as an argument to *ls*. It then prints the names of all files in the named directory.

If you have a directory that contains a lot of files, you can use *ls* combined with the wildcard character * (asterisk) to produce a partial listing of files. There are several ways to use the *. If you have files in a series (such as *ch1* to *ch14*), or files with common characters (like those ending in *.txt*), you can use * to specify all of them at once. When given as the argument in a command, * takes the place of any number of characters in a filename. For example, let's say you're looking for files called *seq11*, *seq25*, and *seq34* in a directory of 400 files. Instead of scrolling through the list of files by eye, you could find them by typing:

```
% ls seq*
```

What if in that same directory you wanted to find all the text files? You know that text files usually end with *.txt*, so you can search for them by typing:

```
% ls *.txt
```

There are also a variety of command-line options to use with *ls*. The most useful of these are:

−a Lists all the files in a directory, even those preceded by a dot. Filenames beginning with a dot (.) aren't listed by *ls* by default and consequently are referred to as hidden files. Hidden files often contain configuration instructions for programs, and it's sometimes necessary to examine or modify them.

−R Lists subdirectories recursively. The content of the current directory is listed, and whenever a subdirectory is reached, its contents are also explicitly included in the listing. This command can create a catalog of files in your filesystem.

−1 Lists exactly one filename per line, a useful option. A single-column listing of all your source datafiles can quickly be turned into a shell script that executes an identical operation on each file, using just a few regular-expression tricks.

−F Includes a code indicating the file type. A / following the filename indicates that the file is a directory, * indicates that the file is executable, and @ following the filename indicates that the file is a symbolic link.

−s Lists the size of the file in blocks along with the filename.

−t Lists files in chronological order of when they were last modified.

−l Lists files in the long format.

−− color
   Uses color to distinguish different file types.

Interpreting ls output

ls gives its output in two formats, the short and the long format. The short format is the default. It includes only the name of each file along with information requested using the *–F* or *–s* options:

```
#corr.pl#         commands.txt      hi.c              psimg.c
#eva.pl#          corr.pl           nsmail            res.sty
#pitch.txt#       corr.pl~          paircount.pl      res.sty~
#wish-list.txt#   correlation.pl    paircount.pl~     resume.tex
Xrootenv.0        correlation.pl~   pj-resume.dvi     seq-scratch.txt
a.out             detailed-prac.txt pj-resume.log     sources.txt
```

The long format of the *ls* command output contains a variety of useful information about file ownership and permissions, file sizes, and the dates and times that files were last modified:

```
drwxrwxr-x   4   jambeck   weasel   2048   Mar5     18:23 ./
drwxr-xr-x   5   root      root     1024   Jan 20   12:13 ../
-rw-r--r--   1   jambeck   weasel   293    Jan 28   17:39 commands.txt
-rw-r--r--   1   jambeck   weasel   1749   Feb 21   12:43 corr.pl
-rw-r--r--   1   jambeck   weasel   559    Feb 23   14:52 correlation.pl
-rwxr-xr-x   1   jambeck   weasel   3042   Jan 21   17:05 eva.pl*
drwx------   2   jambeck   weasel   1024   Feb 16   14:44 nsmail/
```

This listing was generated with the command *ls –alF.* The first 10 characters in the line give information about file permissions. The first character describes the file type. You will commonly encounter three types of files: the ordinary file (represented by –), the directory (*d*), and the symbolic link (*l*).

The next nine characters are actually three sets of three bits containing file permission information. The first three characters following the file type are the file permissions for the user. The next set are for the user's group, and the final set are for users outside the group. The character string *rwxrwxrwx* indicates a file is readable (*r*), writable (*w*), and executable (*x*) by any user. We talk about how to change file permissions and file ownership in the section "Changing file ownership and permissions with chmod."

The next column in the long format file listing tells you how many links a file has; that is, how many directory listings for that file exist on the filesystem. The same file can be named in multiple directories. In the section "Manipulating Files and Directories," we talk about how to create links (directory listings) for new and existing files.

The next two columns show the ownership of the file. The owner of the files in the preceding example is *jambeck,* a member of the group *weasel.*

The next three columns show the size of the file in characters, and the date and time that the file was last modified. The final column shows the name of the file.

Finding files with find

Usage: `find pathname list -[test] criterion`

The *find* command is one of the most powerful, flexible, and complicated commands in the standard set of Unix programs. *find* searches a path or paths for files based on various tests. There are over 20 different tests that can be used with *find*; here are a few of the most useful:

–print

> This test is always **true** and sends the pathname of the current file to standard output. *–print* should be the last command specified in a line, because, as it's always **true**, it causes every file in the pathname being searched to be sent to the list if it comes before other tests in a sequence.

–name

> This is the test most commonly applied with *find* and the one that is the most immediately useful. *find –name weasel.txt –print* lists to standard output the full pathnames of all files on the filesystem named *weasel.txt*. The wildcard operator * can be used within the filename criterion to find files that match a given substring. *find –name weas* –print* finds not only *weasel.txt*, but *weasel.c* and *weasel*.

–user uname

> This test finds all files owned by the specified user.

–group gname

> This test finds all files owned by the specified group.

–ctime n

> This test is **true** if the current file has been changed *n* days ago. Changing a file refers to any change, including a change in permissions, whereas modification refers only to changes to the internal text of the file. *–atime* and *–mtime* tests, which check the access and modification times of the files, are also available.

Performing two *find* tests one after another amounts to applying a logical "and" between the tests. A *–o* between tests indicates a logical "or." A slash (*/*) negates a command, which means it finds only those files that fail the test.

find can be combined with other commands to selectively archive or remove particular files from a filesystem. Let's say you want a list of every file you have modified in your home directory and all subdirectories in the last week:

```
% find ~ -type f -mtime -7 -print
```

Changing the type to *d* shows only new directories; changing the –7 to +7 shows all files modified more than a week ago. Now let's go back to the original problem and find executable files. One way to do this with *find* is to use the following command:

```
% find / -name progname -type f -exec ls -alF '{' ';'
```

This example finds every match for *progname* and executes *ls –alF FullPathName* for every match. Any Unix command can be used as the object of *–exec*. Cleanup of the */tmp* directory, which is usually done automatically by the operating system, can be done with this command:

```
find /tmp -type f -mtime +1 -exec rm -rf '{' ';'
```

This deletes everything that hasn't been modified within the last day. As always, you need to refer to your manual pages, or manpages, for more details (for more on manpages, see Chapter 5).

Finding an executable file with which

Usage: `which` `progname`

The *which* command searches your current path and reports the full path of the program that executes if you enter *progname* at the command prompt. This is useful if you want to know where a program is located, if, for instance, you want to be sure you're using the right version of the program. *which* can't find a program in a directory that isn't in your path.

Finding an executable file with whereis

Usage: `whereis` `–[options]` `progname`

The *whereis* command searches a standard set of directories for executables, manpages, and source files. Unlike *which*, *whereis* isn't dependent on your path, but it looks for programs only in a limited set of directories, so it doesn't give a definitive answer about the existence of a program.

Manipulating Files and Directories

Of course, just as with the stacks of papers on your desk, you periodically need to do some housekeeping on your files and directories to keep everything neat and tidy. Unix provides commands for moving, copying, and deleting files, as well as creating and removing directories.

Copying files and directories with cp

Usage: `cp` `-[options]` `source destination`

The *cp* command makes a copy of a source file at a destination. If the destination is a directory, the source can be multiple files, copies of which are placed in the destination directory. Frequently used options are –*R* and –*r*. Both copy recursively; that is, they copy the source directory and all its subdirectories to the destination. The –*R* option prevents *cp* from following symbolic links; only the link itself is copied. The –*r* option allows *cp* to follow symbolic links and copy all files it finds. This can cause problems if the symbolic links happen to form a circular path through the filesystem.

Normally, new files created by *cp* get their file ownership and permissions from your shell settings. However, the POSIX version of *cp* provides an –*a* option that attempts to maintain the original file attributes.

Moving and renaming files and directories with mv

Usage: mv *source destination*

The *mv* command simply moves or renames *source* to *destination*. Files and directories can both be either *source* or *destination*. If both *source* and *destination* are files or both are directories, the result of *mv* is essentially that the file or directory is renamed. If the *destination* is a directory, and the intention is to move already existing files or directories under that directory in the hierarchy, the directory must exist before the *mv* command is given. Otherwise the *destination* is created as a regular file, or the operation is treated as a renaming of a directory. One problem that can occur if *mv* isn't used carefully is when *source* represents a file list, and *destination* is a preexisting single file. When this happens, each member of *source* is renamed to *destination* and then promptly overwritten, leaving only the last file of the list intact. At this point, it's time to look for your system administrator and hope there is a recent backup.

Creating new links to files and directories with ln

Usage: ln -[*options*] *source destination*

The *ln* command establishes a link between files or directories at different locations in the directory tree. While creating a link creates the appearance of a new file in the destination location, no data is actually copied. Instead, what's created is a new pointer in the filesystem index that allows the *source* file to be found at more than one location "on the map."

The most commonly used option, –*s*, creates a symbolic link (or *symlink*) to a file or directory, as in the following example:

```
% ln -s perl5.005_03 perl
```

This allows you to type in just the word *perl* rather than remembering the entire version nomenclature for the current version of Perl.

Another common use of the *ln* command is to create a link to a newly compiled binary executable file in a directory in the system path, e.g., */usr/local/bin.* Doing this allows you to run the program without addressing it by its full pathname.

Creating and removing directories with mkdir and rmdir

> Usage: `mkdir -[options] dirname`
> Usage: `rmdir -[options] dirname`

New directories can be created with the *mkdir* command, which has only two command-line options.

mkdir –p creates a directory and any intermediate components of the path that are missing. For instance, if user *jambeck* decides to create a directory *mustelidae/ weasels* in his home directory, but the intermediate directory *mustelidae* doesn't exist, *mkdir –p* creates the intermediate directory and its subdirectory *weasels.*

mkdir –m mode creates a directory with the specified file-permission mode.

rmdir removes a directory if it's empty. With the *–p* option, *rmdir* removes all the empty directories in a given path. If user *jambeck* decides to remove the directory *mustelidae/weasels,* and directory *mustelidae* is empty except for directory *weasels, rmdir –p ~/mustelidae/weasels* removes both *weasels* and its parent directory *mustelidae.*

Removing files with rm

> Usage: `rm -[options] files`

The *rm* command removes files and directories. Here are its common options:

–f Forces the removal of files without prompting. You still can't remove files you don't own, but the write permissions on files you do own are ignored. For example, *rm –f a** deletes all files starting with the letter a, but doesn't delete any subdirectories.

–i Prompts you with *rm: remove filename?* Files are removed only if you begin your answer with a *y* or *Y.*

–r (recursive option) Removes all directories and subdirectories in the list of files. Symbolic links aren't traversed; only the symlink itself is removed.

–v (verbose option) Echoes the names of all files/directories that are removed.

While *rm* is a fairly simple command, there are a few instances in which it can cause serious problems for the careless user.

The command *rm ** removes all files in a directory. Unless you have the files set as read-only or have the interactive flag set, you will delete everything in the directory. Of course this isn't as bad as using the command *rm –r ** or *rm –rf **, the last of which overrides any read-only file modes, traverses down through your directories and deletes everything in your current directory or below.

Occasionally you will find that you create odd files in your directories. For instance, you might have a file named *-myfile* where the *-* is part of the filename. Try deleting it, and you will get an error message concerning the fact that *rm* doesn't have a *-m* option. Your shell program interprets the *-m* as a command flag, not part of the filename. The solution to this problem is trivial but not always instantly apparent: simply provide a more complete path to the file, such as *rm ./-myfile* or *rm /home/jambeck/-myfile*. Similar solutions are needed if you accidently create a file with a space in the name.

Working in a Multiuser Environment

Unix systems are designed to allow multiple users to share system resources and software, yet at the same time to allow users to selectively protect their work from each other. To work with others in a multiuser environment, there are a number of general Unix concepts you need to understand.

Users and Groups

If you use a Unix system, you must be registered. You are identified by a login name and can log in only by entering the password uniquely associated with your login name. You have control over an area of the filesystem, which may be as large or small as system resources allow. You belong to one or more groups and can share files with other members of a group without needing to make the files accessible to other users. At any given time, only one of a your groups is active, and new files you create are automatically associated with the active, or primary, group. If you use group permissions to share files with other users, and you need to change to a particular group ID, the command *newgrp* allows you to change your primary group ID. The *id* command tells you what your user and primary group IDs are.

Information about your account is stored the */etc/passwd* file, a file that provides the system with information needed when you log in. Your username and user ID mapping are found here, along with your default groups, full name, home directory and default shell program. The shell program is described in Chapter 5. The encrypted version of your password used to be stored here, but on most systems, for security reasons, the actual password has been removed from the *passwd* file. Additional group information is found in the */etc/group* file. You can view the contents of these files with an editor, even though they are system files you normally can't overwrite.

User Directories

When your system administrator creates a new user account, the process includes creating an entry in the */etc/passwd* file, possibly adding you to a number of groups in */etc/group*, creating a home directory for you somewhere on the system, and then changing the ownership of that directory so that you own it and any files that are put into it at the time of creation. Your entry in */etc/passwd* needs to match the path to your home directory, and the user and group that own your home directory. There should also be a set of files in your home directory that set up your work environment when you log in and are specific to the Unix shell listed in your *passwd* entry. These files are discussed in more detail in Chapter 5.

File Permissions and Statistics

As we discussed in the section on the *ls* command, each file and directory has an owner and a group with which it's associated. Each file is created with *permissions* that allow or prevent you access to the file dependent on your user ID and group. In this section we discuss how to view and change file permissions and ownership.

Viewing file attributes with stat

> Usage: `stat -[options] filename`

stat lets you view the complete set of attributes of a file or directory, including permissions, modification times, and ownership. It may be more information than you need, but it's there if you want it. For example, the command *stat image1.rgb* returns:

```
image1.rgb:
inode 11750927; dev 77; links 1; size 922112
regular; mode is rw-------; uid 12430 (jambeck); gid 280 (weasel)
projid 0  st_fstype: xfs
change time - Sun Mar 14 14:21:50 1999 <921442910>
access time - Sat Mar 13 18:11:21 1999 <921370281>
modify time - Sat Mar 13 10:28:39 1999 <921342519>
```

Changing file ownership and permissions with chmod

On most Unix systems, you wouldn't want every file to be readable, writable, and executable by every user. The *chmod* command allows you to set the file permissions, or *mode*, on a list of files and directories. The recursive option, −*R*, causes *chmod* to descend recursively through a directory tree and change the mode of the files and directories.

For example, a long directory listing for a directory, a symlink, and a file looks like this:

```
drwxr-xr-x  7  jambeck  weasel  2048    Feb 10 19:08  image/
lrwxr-xr-x  1  jambeck  weasel  10      Mar 14 13:12  image.rgb-> image1.rgb
-rw-r--r--  1  jambeck  weasel  922112  Mar 13 10:28  image1.rgb
```

The first character in each line indicates whether the entry is a file, directory, symlink, or one of a number of other special file types found on Unix systems. The three listed here are by far the most common. The remaining nine characters describe the mode of the file. The mode is divided into three sets of three characters. The sets correspond—in the following order—to the user, the group, and other. The user is the account that owns the directory entry, the group can be any group on the system, and other is any user that doesn't belong to the set that includes the user and the group. Within each set, the characters correspond to read (*r*), write (*w*), and execute (*x*) permissions for that person or group.

In the previous example, to change the mode of the file *image1.rgb* so that it's readable only by the user and modified (writable) by no one, you can issue one of the following commands:

```
chmod  u-w,g-r,o-r image1.rgb
chmod  u=r,g=-,o=- image1.rgb
chmod  u=r,go=-    image1.rgb
```

Any one of these commands results in *image1.rgb*'s permissions looking like:

```
-r-------- 1 jambeck weasel 922112 Mar 13 10:28 image1.rgb
```

The first two commands should be fairly obvious. You can add or subtract user's, group's or other's read, write or execute permissions by this mechanism. The mode parameters are:

[u,g,o]

    User, group, other

[+,–,=]

    Add, subtract, set

[r,w,x]

    Read, write, execute

u, g, and *o* can be grouped or used singly. The same is true for *r, w,* and *x.* The operators +, –, and = describe the action that is to be performed.

Changing file and directory ownership with chown and chgrp

    Usage: chown –[*options*] *filenames item*
    Usage: chgrp –[*options*] *filenames*

The *chown* command lets you change the owner (or, in file-permission parlance, the user) of a file or directory. The operation of the *chown* command is dependent on the version of Unix you are running. For example, IRIX allows you to "give" the ownership to someone else, while this is impossible to do in Linux. We will cite only examples of the *chgrp* command, since in Linux, you can be a member of two groups and get this command to work for you.

chgrp lets you change the group of a file or directory. You must be a member of the group the file is being changed to, so you have to be a member of more than one group and understand how to use the *newgrp* command (which is described later in this chapter). Assume for a moment that you created *image/*, a directory containing files, while you were in your default group. Later, you realize that you want to share these files with members of another group on the system. So, at first, the permissions look like this:

```
drwxr-xr-x 7 jambeck weasel 2048 Feb 10 19:08 image/
```

Change to the other group using the command *newgrp wombat*, then type:

```
chgrp -R wombat image
```

to make all files in the directory accessible to the *wombat* group. Finally, you should change the permissions to make the files writable by the *wombat* group as well. This is done with the command:

```
chmod -R g+w image
```

Your entry should now appear as follows:

```
drwxrwxr-x 7 jambeck wombat 2048 Feb 10 19:08 image/
```

System Administration

Most files that control the configuration of the Unix system on your computer are writable only by the system administrator. Adding and deleting users, backing up and restoring files, installing new software in shared directories, configuring the Unix kernel, and controlling access to various parts of the filesystem are tasks normally handled by one specially designated user, with the username *root*. When you're doing day-to-day tasks, you shouldn't be logged in as root, because *root* has privileges ordinary users don't, and you can inadvertently mess up your computer system if you have those privileges. Use the *su* command from your command line to assume system-administration privileges temporarily, do only those tasks that need to be done by the system administrator, and then exit back to your normal user status.

If you set up a Unix system for yourself, you need to become the system administrator or superuser and learn to do the various system-administration tasks necessary to maintain your computer in a secure and useful condition. Fortunately, there are several informative reference books on Unix system administration available (several by O'Reilly), and an increasing number of easy-to-use graphical system-administration tools are included in every Linux distribution.

Conventions for Organizing Files

Unix uses a simple set of designations for the various types of files found on the system. Normally you can find what you need with *info, find,* or *which,* but sometimes it's necessary to search manually, and you don't want to look in */bin* for a library. These designations are used at the operating-system level, but they are also often used in project subdirectories or software distributions to separate files:

bin Executable files, or binaries

lib Libraries, both runtime or shared, and those needed when compiling

spool
　　Directories used by the system when communicating with external devices and machines

tmp
　　Temporary storage

src Source code for programs

etc Configuration information

man
　　Manual pages, documentation

doc Documentation

X X or X11R6 refers to X programs, libraries, *src,* etc.; directories typically have a fairly complete set of subdirectories

Once you have a basic understanding of how to organize and manage your files and directories, you're well on your way to understanding how to work in a Unix environment. In Chapter 5 we complete our lightning Unix tutorial with a discussion of many of the most commonly used Unix commands. In order to really master the art of Unix, we strongly recommend consulting one or more of the books in the *Bibliography.*

Locating Files in System Directories

While all your own files should be created in your home directory or in other areas specifically designated for users to share, you need to be aware of the locations of files in other parts of the system. One benefit of a system environment designed for multiple users is that many users can share common resources while controlling access to their own files.

To say there is a standard Unix filesystem is somewhat of an overstatement, but, like Plato's vision of the perfect chair, we will attempt to imagine one out in the ether. Since Linux is being developed by thousands of programmers on different continents and has the benefit of the development of both Berkeley and AT&T's SysV Unix, along with the POSIX standards, we will use the Linux filesystem as a template and point out major discrepancies when necessary. The current standard for the Linux filesystem is described at *http://www.pathname.com/fhs/*. Here, we present a brief skeleton of the complete filesystem and point out a few salient features. Most directories described in this section are configurable only by the system administrator; however, as a user, you may sometimes need to know where system files and programs can be found. Figure 4-2 illustrates the major subdirectories, which are further described in the following list.

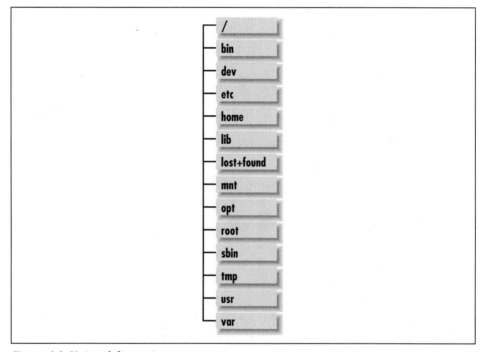

Figure 4-2. Unix subdirectories

/dev
    Contains all the device drivers needed to connect peripherals to the system. Drivers for SCSI, audio, IDE drives, PPP, mice, and most other devices are found here. In general there are no user-configurable options here.

/etc
    Houses all the configuration files local to your machine. This includes items such as the system name, Internet address, password file (unless your machine is part of some larger cluster), filesystem information, and Unix initialization information.

/home

A common, but not standard, part of Unix. */home* is usually a fairly large, separate partition that houses all user home directories. Having */home* on a separate partition has the advantage of allowing it to be shared in a cluster environment, and it also makes it difficult for users to completely fill an important system partition and cause it to lock up.

/lost+found

A system directory that is a repository for files and directories that have somehow been misplaced by the system. Typically, users can't *cd* into this directory. Files usually end up in the *lost+found* because of a system crash or a disk problem. At times it's possible that your system administrator can recover files that appear to be lost simply by moving them from *lost+found* and renaming them. There's a separate *lost+found* for each partition on the system.

/mnt

While not found on all systems, this is the typical place to mount any partitions not described by the standard Unix filesystem description. Under Linux, this is where you will find a mounted CD-ROM or floppy drive.

/nfs

Often used as the top-level directory for any mount points for partitions that are mounted from remote machines.

/opt

A relatively new addition to the Unix filesystem. This is where optional, usually commercial, packages are installed. On many systems you will find higher-end, optimizing compilers installed here.

/root

The home directory for root, i.e., for the system administrator when she is logged in as root.

/sbin, /bin, and */lib*

Since the machine may need to start the boot process without the */usr* partition present, any programs that are using it prior to mounting the */usr* partition must reside on the main or root partition. The contents of the */sbin* directory, for instance, are a subset of the */usr/sbin* directory. Labeling directories *sbin* indicates that only system-level commands are present and that normal users probably won't need them, and therefore don't need to include these directories in their path. The */lib* directory is a small subset of system libraries that are needed by programs in */bin* and */sbin*. Current Unix programs use *shared* libraries, which means that many programs can use functions from the same library, and so the library needs to be loaded into memory only once. What this means for practical purposes is that programs

don't take as much memory as they would if each program included all the
library routines, and the programs don't actually run if the correct library has
been deleted or hasn't been mounted yet.

/tmp and /var/tmp

Typically configured to be readable/writable/executable by all users. Many
standard programs, such as *vi*, write temporary files to one of these directories while they are running. Normally the system cleans out these directories
automatically on a regular basis or when the machine is rebooted. This is a
good place to write temporary files, but you can't assume that the system will
wait for you to erase them.

/usr

The repository for the majority of programs, compilers, libraries, and documentation for the Unix filesystem. The current recommendation for most Unix
systems is that the system should be able to mount */usr* as a separate, read-
only partition. In a workstation-cluster environment, this means that a server
can export a */usr* partition, and all the workstations in that cluster will share
the programs. This makes the system administrator's job easier and provides
users with a uniform set of machines.

/usr/local

The typical directory in which to install programs and documentation so that
they aren't overwritten by the operating system. You will often find programs
such as Perl and various others that have been downloaded from the Internet
installed in this location.

/var

The directory used by all system programs that write output to the disk. All
system logs, spools, and temporary data are written here. This includes log-
ging information such as that written during the boot process, by the mailer,
by the login program, and by all other system processes. Incoming and outgo-
ing mail is stored in the */var/spool* directory, as are files being sent to printers.
Information needed for *cron*, *batch*, and *at* jobs is also found here.

5

Working on a Unix System

Unix has a wealth of functions, and you'll want to be aware of a particular subset of them before you start running programs and collecting data. In Chapter 4, *Files and Directories in Unix*, we talked about how to organize and manage your files in Unix, as well as how to move around the filesystem. In this chapter we take you on a whirlwind tour through the common Unix commands you'll need to know to work efficiently. We discuss the Unix shell itself, issuing commands in Unix, viewing, editing, and extracting information from your files, shell scripts, and working in a multiuser environment.

Once you've learned to use some of these Unix commands, you'll find that they are astonishingly powerful and flexible, allowing you to modify files in ways that are impossible, or at least not easy, with a conventional word-processing program. For example, with a single command you can find all the instances of a pattern in every file under your home directory. A few simple tricks can create a script that will process every file in your source data directory identically. Another simple script can update a customized local copy of a database every night while you're sleeping.

The Unix Shell

When you log into a Unix system or open a new window in your system's window manager interface, the system automatically starts a program called a *shell* for you. The shell program interprets the commands you enter and provides you with a working environment and an interface to the operating system. It's possible to work in Unix without the shell using graphical file manager tools, but you'll find that many shell commands are useful for data processing and analysis. Entire books devoted to the various shells are available, and the manpages for some of the common shells exceed 100 pages when printed. We provide you only with a brief introduction to the commonly used shells, to get you started with as few hurdles as possible.

What Flavors of Shell Are There?

The shell program you use affects the feel of your command-line interface. Some of the features that can be built into the shell program include a simple arithmetic interpreter that lets you use the command line as a calculator; command aliasing, which lets you refer to standard Unix commands with other more convenient words; filename completion, which lets you type only the number of characters necessary to distinguish a file from other files in the directory, rather than typing the full filename; command editing and command history, which let you scroll back through the commands you've recently issued and edit them on the command line; spelling correction; and help functions for the shell program.

There are a number of common shell programs on Unix systems. You are automatically assigned a shell when your system administrator sets up your account. On Linux systems, the default shell program is the *bash* (Bourne Again) shell. However, you may prefer to use a shell other than *bash*. The two main classes of shell programs are shells derived from the Bourne shell, *sh*, and shells derived from the C shell *csh*. Bourne-type shells include *sh*, *bash*, *ksh* (the Korn shell), and *zsh* (the Z shell). C-type shells include *csh* and *tcsh*.

We tend to prefer C shells, for historical reasons. When we started working in Unix, the C shell was the best thing going, and the *tcsh* program has expanded the original *csh* into a powerful shell. *tcsh* implements most of the desirable shell features, including history, command aliasing, filename completion, command-line editing, arithmetic and functions, job control, and spelling correction. *tcsh* is also one of the most user-configurable shells. Therefore, we'll discuss the behavior of Unix commands from a C-shell perspective, as if you were using the *tcsh* program, which we use on our machines.

Your default shell will be listed as the last item in your entry in the */etc/passwd* file. If you aren't certain which shell you are currently using, you can find out by typing:

```
% finger your-user-name
```

For user *jambeck*, this command shows the following information:

```
Login name: jambeck        In real life: Per Jambeck
Directory: /home/jambeck    Shell: /bin/tcsh
```

This tells us that he is using *tcsh* as his default shell. For practical reasons, we will limit our discussions and most references to *csh* and *tcsh*. It must also be noted that many system processes (e.g., *batch*, *at*, and *cron*) use the Bourne shell by default, which makes it necessary to learn at least a minimal subset of its command language. On most systems there are commands to change your default shell as set in the *passwd* file. The *chsh* (change shell) command allows you to change your default login shell, if you're working on a Linux system.

Issuing Commands on a Unix System

There's a standard format for sending an instruction to Unix. In this book, we'll refer to commands and to the command line. Each of Unix's many native commands has a tangible existence as an executable program, and to issue the command is to tell Unix to execute that program. In this section and those that follow, we move fairly quickly through concepts and commands. While we can give you a brief overview of the Unix features we find most useful, this book isn't designed to replace a comprehensive Unix reference book. If you're new to Unix, we strongly recommend that you review the basics of Unix with the help of books such as *Learning the Unix Operating System, Running Linux,* or *Unix for the Impatient.* We've provided a list of recommended reading in the *Bibliography.*

The Command-Line Format

The command line consists of the command itself, optional arguments that modify how the command works, and operands such as files upon which the command operates. For example, the *chsh* (change shell) command, which we just discussed briefly, has several possible options. The first is the *–s* option, which must be followed by the name of a shell program as its argument. The second is the *–l* option, which needs no argument, and which lists the shells that are available on your system. The operand for the *chsh* command is the username of the user whose shell is being changed. So, to change your default shell program, you might first type:

```
% chsh -l
```

which gives you a list of the shell programs available on the system:

```
/bin/bash
/bin/sh
/bin/ash
/bin/bsh
/bin/bash2
/bin/tcsh
/bin/csh
/bin/ksh
/bin/zsh
```

Then, to actually change your shell to *tcsh*, you can type:

```
% chsh -s /bin/tcsh yourusername
```

Options can simply be single-letter codes, or they can have their own arguments. Options that take no arguments can be given as a group, while each option that takes an argument must be specified separately. Each option group and separate option must be preceded by a hyphen (–). The last option in a group, or separate options, can be followed by the option argument. The operands follow the final option in the list.

Many Unix commands have options that, frankly, you'll never use. And we're not going to talk about them. But there are ways of finding out more.

Unix Information Commands

Unix has its own built-in reference manual, which is quite comprehensive and informative, and which will give you the correct information about the commands and options available on the particular system you're using.

The *man* command is one of the most useful Unix commands; it allows you to view Unix manual pages. While some Unix systems have implemented a web browser-like interface to the Unix manpages, you can't always count on this option being available. The *man* command is available on all types of Unix systems.

> Usage: `man name`

where *name* can be a Unix command, such as *grep*, or a system file, such as the password file */etc/passwd*.

If you're not sure of the command you're looking for, you can sometimes find the right information using *man*'s slightly smarter cousin, *apropos*. The *apropos* command locates commands by keyword lookup.

> Usage: `apropos name`

For instance, if you're concerned about disk usage on your system, you can enter *apropos usage*. The output of this command on our PC running Red Hat Linux is:

```
du (1)- summarize disk usage
getrlimit, getrusage, setrlimit (2)- get/set resource limits and usage
quota (1)- display disk usage and limits
quotacheck (8)- scan a file system for disk usages
```

apropos doesn't always produce such brief and informative output. Entering a smart combination of keywords is (as always with such searches) the key to getting the output you want. If you want a predictable listing of Unix commands, it's probably best to pick up a comprehensive Unix book.

What should you do if you find the following text in a manpage?

```
This documentation is no longer being maintained and may be inaccurate or
incomplete. The Texinfo documentation is now the authoritative source.
```

The GNU* set of Unix tools are adopting a documentation system, called *texinfo*, that is different from the traditional *man* system. If you come across this message, you should be able to read the up-to-date documentation on the program by typing in the command *info progname*. For instance, *info info* gives you a complete set of documentation on the use of *info* and even provides instructions for creating your own *info* documentation when you start writing your own programs.

Standard Input and Output

By default, many Unix commands read from standard input and send their output to standard output. Standard input and output are file descriptors associated with your terminal. A program reading from standard input will simply hang out and wait for you to type something on your keyboard and press the Enter key. A program writing to standard output spews its output to your terminal, sometimes far faster than you can read it.

Some Unix commands read a hyphen (–) surrounded by whitespace on either side as "data from standard input." This construct can then be used in place of a filename in the command line. Absence of an output filename is sufficient to cause the program to write to standard output.

Redirection of Command Input and Output

The standard input and output descriptors are useful because you can redirect both standard input and output, associating them with filenames, with no effects on the functioning of the program. Here are the most common redirection constructs used by the C shell:

<   This redirector preceding a filename associates that filename with standard input, i.e., the contents of the file are presented to the program as if they are standard input.

>   This redirector associates a filename with standard output, so that the filename is created on execution of the command, or whatever is in an existing file of that name is overwritten by the output of the command.

>> This redirector associates a filename with standard output. It differs from > in that the output of the command is appended to the end of the existing file.

---

* GNU tools are distributed and maintained by the GNU Project at the Free Software Foundation. GNU stands for "GNU's Not Unix" and refers to a complete, Unix-like operating system that's built and maintained by the GNU Project (*http://www.Gnu.org*).

The *cat* command reads the contents of a file and writes them to standard output. If you want to use the *cat* command to combine the contents of three files into one new file, you can use a redirector like this:

```
% cat file1 file2 file3 > file4
```

This construct with *cat* would be useful if, for example, you'd just downloaded a bunch of individual sequence files from the NCBI web site and want to collect them into one large file that can be read by another program. (This is an example of something that seems like it should be simple, but is actually time-consuming and annoying to do with a standard PC word-processing program. Unix provides a neat solution that doesn't even require you to open any files).

You can also use redirectors to direct the contents of a file into a program at run-time, as standard input (useful if you are running a program that prompts you for input from the keyboard) or to capture output from a program that is normally written to standard output:

```
program < inputfile
program > outputfile
```

For example, let's say you've just finished an extensive BLAST search, and you want to send the results to your colleague. You can use the redirector < ("less than"), to scoop the file *huge_blast_report* out of your directory and mail it directly to your colleague:

```
% mail colleague@university.edu < huge_blast_report
```

If you want to increase the chances of your colleague opening the message, you can add a subject header to the mail message using the mail option *–s*. The command reads:

```
% mail -s "surprise!" colleague@university.edu < huge_blast_report
```

The reverse operation, sending the results of standard output (or text that's displayed on your screen) to a file, can be accomplished using > ("greater than"). Perhaps your colleague wants to write a quick reminder to herself to reply to your mail. She could do it using the *cat* command to take input from the keyboard and redirect it to a file, like this:

```
% cat > reminder_to_self
Ha! Send fifteen BLAST reports to colleague on Monday.
^D
%
```

Ctrl-D (^D) signals that you have finished entering text. Your colleague now has a file called *reminder_to_self* in her current working directory.

Operators

Operators are similar to redirectors in that they are ways of directing standard input and output. However, they direct input and output to and from other commands rather than to filenames.

The most commonly used operator is the pipe (|). The pipe directs standard output of one command into standard input for the next command. This allows you to chain together several different filtering commands or programs without creating input or output files each time.

You can use the *cat* command to direct the contents of a file into a program that reads information from standard input:

```
% cat inputfile | program
```

This command construct does the same thing as the example we showed earlier (*program < inputfile*). Both cause the output of the *cat* command to act as input for *program*. If you want to do a lot of runs of the same program using slightly different input, you can create multiple input files and then write a script that *cats* each of those input files in turn and pipes their contents to *program*.

Pipes can carry out a complete set of file-processing options without writing to disk. For instance, imagine that you have a datafile consisting of multiple tables concatenated together. The first table in the file takes up the first 67 lines, the second table takes up the next 100 lines, and the rest of the file is taken up by a third table.* You want the information that's contained in the second column of the middle table, which stretches from characters 30–39 in the row. Using filters and pipes, you can construct the following command to crop out the data you need:

```
% head -167 protein1.pka | tail -100 | cut -c30-39 > protein1.pka.data
```

In this example, *head* sends the top 167 lines of a specified file or files (in this case *protein1.pka*) to standard output; *tail* takes the last 100 lines of the output of *head*; and *cut* takes the correct column of characters out of the results of *head* and *tail* and then stores it in *protein1.pka.data*.

Wildcard Characters

A useful construct Unix shells recognize is the presence of wildcard characters in filenames. The shell locates matches for any wildcards before passing filenames on to the program. The two most commonly used wildcards are the asterisk (*) and the question mark (?). * means "any sequence of zero or more characters, except

---

* This isn't an imaginary format at all. It's pretty close to the format of the output file from a calculation that we do frequently: computing the pKa values of individual amino acids in a protein.

for the / character." ? means "any single character." Thus, "every file in this directory" can be denoted by a lone *, which is a useful shortcut.

The shell recognizes other wildcards as well. The construct [*cset*] refers to any
characters in the specified set. If you want to move all files beginning with letters
a through *m* to a new directory, you can structure the command as *mv [a–m]* ./
newdir*. If you want to move all files beginning with a number to a new directory,
enter *mv [0–9]* ./newdir*.

Running X Commands

On Unix systems running the X Window System, there are many commands available that initiate programs with functions that aren't command line-based. Once
these programs, which can include anything from graphics viewers to complicated scientific applications, are called from the command line, they use the X
Window System to open their own windows, which generally contain a complete,
independent graphical user interface.

Viewing and Editing Files

You're probably accustomed to the idea of using a program to open a file. If your
first introduction to computers has been sometime in the last 15 years, you're
probably used to simply clicking on a file icon, which is automatically recognized
by the right piece of software, which opens the file.

In Unix, commands are designed to operate on files that are sensibly readable and
printable as text whenever possible. Thus text files can be opened by a wide variety of commands that allow a great deal of flexibility in file manipulation. The file
reading and processing commands have such functions as sorting data based on
the value of a particular substring in each line of the file, cutting a particular column out of a file, pasting columns of data together side by side, checking to see
what the differences between two files are, and searching for instances of a pattern in a file or group of files. Often, these simple commands are all you need to
extract a desired subset of the data in a file and prepare it for analysis.

Unix has many ways to view and edit the contents of files. There are viewers for
text and programs that allow you to examine the contents of binary files, as well
as full-featured editors for modifying plain-text files.

Viewing and Combining Files with cat

Usage: `cat -[options] files`

cat dumps the contents of a file onto the screen. If your file is short, or if you've successfully completed a speed-reading course, this utility works well. If you need to see what's on each page of a file, though, *cat* is less useful, since the contents of the file scroll by without pausing.

Instead of viewing text, *cat* is most useful for combining (or con*cat*enating) files. For instance, if you have a series of files of program output named *meercat1.txt*, *meercat2.txt*, and *meercat3.txt*, and you want to combine them into a single file, you can type:

```
% cat meercat1.txt meercat2.txt meercat3.txt > big-meercat.txt
```

This command appends the contents of *meercat3.txt* to the end of *meercat2.txt*, the contents of *meercat2.txt* to the end of *meercat1.txt*, and so on, combining them into one big file named *big-meercat.txt*. If you've thought to number the outputs sequentially (as we have with the meercats), and want them in that order in the file, you can just type:

```
% cat meercat*.txt > big-meercat.txt
```

and it will have the same effect. Wildcard characters such as * use a strict alphabetical order: if they exist, files *meercat10.txt* and *meercat11.txt* come before *meercat2.txt*.

cat can also append files to the end of an existing file. For example, if your program generates another output file you need to attach to the end of the collection, the command:

```
% cat meercat10.txt >> big-meercat.txt
```

does just that. If you use > instead of >> in this situation, instead of being added at the end of the file, the new file *meercat.txt* overwrites the entire contents of *big-meercat.txt*.

Incidentally, if you want a command that's the reverse of *cat* to print the lines of a file in backward order, you're in luck: the command is called *tac*. Sadly, the command *acta*, for printing a file inside out, hasn't yet been implemented.

more: A Step in the Right Direction

Usage: `more -[options] [+linenumber] [+/pattern] filename`

more is a pager, which in Unix means a program that lets you view a file one page at a time. Suppose you have a file containing BLAST output named *blast-first.txt*. Typing:

```
% more blast-first.txt
```

shows you the first page of the file *blast-first.txt,* and steps forward one page every time you press the space bar. To leave *more,* hit the *q* key; to view other *more* commands while within *more,* enter *h.*

more is smart about moving around files. If you know where you want to go in the file, you can specify the line number (using the *+linenumber* option). If, on the other hand, you want to start at the first occurrence of a certain word or pattern, use the *+/pattern* option. When viewing a file in *more,* if you press the / key and then type a pattern to search for, *more* jumps to the next occurrence of that pattern in the file and repeats searches for each subsequent occurrence of that pattern every time you press / followed by the Enter key.

Here are some other useful options for *more:*

−r   Shows normally unprintable control characters as well as normal text

−s   Squeezes multiple empty lines into a single one

You can redirect the output of a program that generates more than a screen's worth of text to *more,* allowing you to page through the output one screen at a time. Let's say you want to know who is logged into your Unix system. If enough users are logged in, the output scrolls off the screen. By piping *who* to *more:*

```
% who | more
```

you can scroll through the output line-by-line using the Return key or screen-by-screen using the space bar.

more's most significant shortcoming is that some versions can't move backward through a file. *less* is a utility that remedies this simple problem.

less: The Gold Standard

There is a superior pager command, *less.* Most importantly, *less* rectifies *more*'s biggest flaw: it lets you page backward as well as forward in a file. *less* also doesn't load a file into memory all at once, which makes it less likely that your computer will grind to a halt if you view a huge file with it. Finally, it also handles binary files more gracefully, displaying readable text as characters and representing unreadable control characters in the form ^X. *less* uses the same options as *more,* but it also takes additional options. Be sure to check *info less* to see which ones your local version takes. And finally, while it hardly bears mentioning, why is it called *less*? Because *less* is *more.* Sigh.

Editing Files with vi and vim

Usage: `vim` *filename*

Because it's a text-based operating system that has historically been used for software development and computation, Unix did not traditionally provide the kind of full-featured, "what you see is what you get" text editing that exists on personal computers, although now such editors are available. In fact, WYSIWYG text editors are of limited utility for programmers because they often introduce invisible markup characters into documents.

It's worth learning to use the plain-text editors that are provided for Unix. They have a fairly steep learning curve, but they are the right tools for the job if you're writing programs or looking at plain-text data. If you download sequence data from a web server and open and work with it in a plain-text editor, the file you write out should be readable by a sequence-analysis program. If you opened the same file and worked with it in a WYSIWYG editor, then wrote it out in the file format used by that editor, it would be unreadable by other programs.

The *vi* editor is a standard feature of most Unix systems. It's a full-screen editor; it allows you to see as many lines of the file that you are editing as will fit into the terminal screen or window in which you run it. The cursor can be moved through the file using keyed instructions, but it can't be moved with the mouse. The bottom line on the screen is called the *status line*. Error messages from *vi* appear in the status line.

In the later section "The Language of Regular Expressions," we discuss the use of regular expressions for searching and replacement as a feature of the plain-text editor *vi*. The ability to use *vi* with the regular-expression language makes *vi* a powerful tool for file manipulation.

A few nice features have been added to *vi* in *vim* (*vi* improved). It's worth asking your system administrator to install *vim* if it's not already on your system, if only for the multiple undo feature that it introduces. We can't cover all the features of *vim* here, but we will present a few commands that will get you up and running.*

vim has three modes; in each, input from the keyboard is interpreted differently:

Command
> This is the main mode; you are automatically in command mode when you start working. Keystrokes are interpreted as *vim*'s short commands, most of which consist of one or two letters. You can always return to the command mode by hitting the Escape key once (or sometimes twice).

Input
> This mode is reached by issuing any command that requires input.

---

* See the *Bibliography* for pointers to complete references on *vi*.

Status line

This mode is for issuing longer, more complex commands. To reach status line mode, simply type a semicolon (;) in command mode. A semicolon appears at the left side of the status line, and anything you type appears in the status line. When you finish typing your command and hit the Enter key, the command is executed, and you return to command mode.

Here are some of the most useful *vim* command-mode commands:

h, j, k, l

Moves the cursor around in your file character-by-character or line-by-line. It's sort of like a pre-joystick video game: "h" moves you to the left, "l" to the right, "j" moves you down a line, and "k" up a line. On most systems, the arrow keys on your keyboard will also work to move you around within *vim*.

w, b

Moves the cursor forward ("w") or back ("b") by one word in the text. Words are delimited by whitespace.

), (

Moves the cursor forward ")" or back "(" by one sentence in the text. Sentences are recognized as sequences of words terminated by an end-of-sentence character (. ? !).

a, A, i, I, o, O

Initiates the insertion of text. "a" and "A" insert text after the cursor and at the end of the current line, respectively. "i" and "I" insert text before the cursor and at the beginning of the current line. "o" and "O" open a blank line below or above the current line, respectively, and begin inserting text on the new line.

x, X

Deletes the text under the cursor or before the cursor, respectively. Preceded by an integer number, they delete that number of characters after or preceding the cursor.

s, S

Substitutes for the character under the cursor or for the current line, respectively, by deleting the character either under the cursor or the line and initiating insertion of text in place of the deleted character. Preceded by an integer number, "s" replaces that number of characters with the new text, and "S" replaces the specified number of lines.

Here are some of the most useful *vim* status line mode commands:

:wq
> Saves changes to the file and quits the editing session. ":w" can be used by itself or with the name of the file to write to. ":q!" exits the session without saving changes.

r]   Followed by a filename, inserts the entire text of the named file.

:g/pattern/s//replacement/g
> Searches for and replaces *pattern* with *replacement* throughout the buffer. If the trailing "g" is left off, only the first occurrence of the pattern in any line is replaced.

:number
> Moves the cursor to the specified line number.

The GNU Emacs Editor

vim is a fairly flexible editor, and you can certainly learn to make it do any text-editing task that you need to do. However, there are other options for text editing on Unix systems. The best of these is probably the Emacs editor. Emacs is an editing program made available by the Free Software Foundation. It contains not only a text-editing facility with special modes for T_EX and LaT_EX documents, programs in various programming languages, and outlines, but also a file manager, mail and news readers, and access to the online documentation browser *info*. Whole books have been written on Emacs (see the *Bibliography*) so we won't go into it here except to recommend that, if you're working on a Unix system, learning to use Emacs is one of the better uses of your learning-curve time.

Viewing Binary Files with strings

Usage: `strings -[options] filenames`

In addition to the text files we've discussed up to now, there are also binary files that can't be read as text. They are almost always the output of a program or the executable form of a program itself (as opposed to the source code). Binary files and program executables aren't human-readable because they are in machine language. Because of this language gap, we'll unflinchingly make the prediction that, 9 times out of 10, it isn't worth the effort needed to read binaries. You'll have more luck taking another route, like talking to the person whose program created the file in the first place. Unfortunately, many programs today, such as commercial hidden Markov model software or data mining programs that directly write their internal representation of data structures to disk, use binary files to store proprietary data structures. For that tenth time, then, we present some tips on how to extract information from binaries without going crazy.

Your first step should be to use either the *less* command described earlier or the *strings* command. If any portions of the file are in plain text, they will be readable in *less*. The *strings* command cuts out any readable text characters in the file and prints them to the screen. For example, if you have an undocumented binary file named *badger* and want to see if it contains any clues as to what it does, try typing:

```
% strings -n 3 badger | less
```

(The *−n* option tells *strings* how many readable text characters in a row constitute a string. The default setting for *−n* is four). Piping the output to *less* will let you page through it if it's longer than one screen. If the output looks like:

```
ATCGTACTGATCGTCGATCGTCGATCATGCA
CGTAGCAGTCGATCATCATCGTACTAGCTAG
ATGCCTGAGCTATACACACTAGTCACGATGC
```

you might guess that *badger* contains some kind of binary encoding of data including a nucleotide sequence or a (not good) multiple sequence alignment.

od and Binary Data

Usage: `od -[`*options*`]` *filenames*

Sometimes, it may be necessary to do more than just identify a binary file. In these cases, the *od* program may provide a first step in understanding the file's contents. Before looking at *od* itself, let's take a quick detour through the ways in which binary information is represented in a moderately more human-friendly form.

Rather than using conventional decimal (base-10) notation, binary data is usually represented using a base that is a power of two: either octal (base-8) or hexidecimal (base-16) digits. Octal numbers are usually preceded by a 0. For example, the decimal number 25 corresponds to octal 031.* Hexidecimal digits, on the other hand, are usually preceded by a 0x and use the letters A through F to represent the decimal numbers 10 through 15. The decimal number 25 is 0x19 in hexidecimal.

If you want to delve into the heart of the binary file and see what's going on, you can use the *od* command to perform an *octal dump* (or hex dump) and see if your binary file is readily interpretable. Typing:

```
% od -c badger | less
```

---

* Giving rise to the old joke, "Why do programmers confuse Christmas and Halloween? Because OCT 31 is DEC 25."

creates an octal dump of *badger* you can step through a page at a time. It should look something like this:

```
0000000  \0  \0  \0 001      \0  \0  \0 006   R   T   D   C   Y   G  \0
0000020  \0  \0 006   R   T   D   C   Y   G  \0  \0  \0  \a  \0  \0  \0
0000040 001   1  \0  \0  \0 003   A   R   G  \0  \0  \0 001  \0  \0  \0
0000060 002   C   A  \0  \0  \0 002   B   Z 270   R   ? 200  \0  \0   @
```

od's primary options are:

−*c* Prints out text characters corresponding to bytes

−*x* Produces a hex dump of the file

−*o* Produces an octal dump (the default setting)

−*d* Produces a dump of unsigned decimal numbers

Unless you're a serious programmer, you're not likely to have to read binaries. However, on the off chance that you do, we hope these standard tools will help you start to get your questions answered.

Transformations and Filters

Filters are programs that take input data and transform it to produce output. They can accomplish tasks—such as extracting parts of files—that word processing and spreadsheet applications can't. A transformation involves a simple manipulation of the data format, or selection of specified lines or fields from the data. In this section, we discuss some of the more commonly used filters that are part of Unix. These filters can read from standard input and writing to standard output, allowing you to combine them and produce fairly complex transformations.*

Extracting the Beginning of a File with head

Usage: **head** − *number files*

Say you have a program that spits out a lengthy datafile that has several different tables of information concatenated together. Leaving aside the question of why anyone would write a program that creates such difficult output, there are commands that allow you to work with such data, and you need to know them. *head* is one such command.

---

* If you need to transform data in a way that isn't allowed by the standard Unix filters, see Chapter 12, *Automating Data Analysis with Perl*, in which we discuss the Perl scripting language. Perl is a very complete and sophisticated language that allows you to produce an infinite variety of specialized filters.

By default, *head* sends the top 10 lines of the specified file or files to standard output. Checking the head of a file this way is an easy way to see if there's something in the file without opening it using an editor or doing a full *cat* of the file.

With the *–number* flag, *head* becomes a tool for selecting a specified number of records from the top of a file. Combinations of *head* and *tail* commands can extract any set of lines from a file provided that you know their location in the file.

Extracting the End of a File with tail

Usage: `tail [-f] ` *`-number files`*

The *tail* command outputs the last 10 lines of a file by default, or the last *num* lines of the file if specified. With the *–f* option, *tail* gives constantly updated output of the last few lines in the file. This provides a way to monitor what is being added to a text output file as it's written by another program.

Splitting Files with split and csplit

Usage: `split -[` *`options`* `] ` *`filename`*
Usage: `csplit -[` *`options`* `] ` *`file criteria`*

The *split* command allows you to break up an existing file into smaller files of a specified size. Each file produced is uniquely named with a suffix (*aa, ab...az, ba,* etc.). The options to *split* are:

–l lines

  Splits the file into subfiles of length *lines*

–a length

  Uses *length* letters to form suffixes

If you have a file called *big-meercat.txt* and you want to split it into subfiles of length 100 lines using single-letter suffixes and writing the files out to subfiles named *meercat.**, the command form of the *split* command is:

```
% split -l 100 -a 1 big-meercat.txt meercat.
```

csplit also splits files into subfiles, but is somewhat more flexible than *split*, because it allows the use of criteria other than number of lines or bytes for splitting. Here are *csplit*'s options:

–f prefix

  Uses the specified file prefix to form subfile names

–n length

  Uses suffixes of a specified length to form subfile names; subfile suffixes are made up of numbers rather than letters

Split criteria are formed in two ways: either a regular expression is supplied as the criterion, possibly modified by an offset, or a number of lines can be specified.

A biological sequence database in FASTA format may contain many records of the form:

```
>identifying header information
PROTEINORNUCLEICACIDSEQUENCEDATA
```

The *csplit* command can split such a database into individual sequence files using the command:

```
% csplit -f dbrecord. -n 6 fastadbfile /^>/
```

The file is split into numbered subfiles, each containing a single sequence.

Separating File Components with cut

Usage: cut -c *list filenames*
or cut -f *list* -d *delim* -s *file*

The *cut* command outputs selected parts of each line of an input file. A line in a file is simply any stretch of characters that ends with a specific delimiter; a delimiter is a special nontext character an operating system or program recognizes. Lines in files are terminated with an *EOL* (end-of-line) character; files themselves are terminated with an *EOF* (end-of-file) character. These characters are usually invisible to you when you're working with the file, but they are important in how a file is treated by programs that read it.

For example, say you have a file called *sequence_data* that contains the following:

```
ATC   TAC
ATG   CCC
GAT   TCC
```

Here's how to use *cut* to output the first character of each line in the file:

```
% cut -c 1 sequence_data
A
A
G
```

And here's how to output the first line of fields 1 and 2:

```
% cut -f 1-2 sequence_data
AAT   TAC
```

Portions of each defined line can be selected by character number in the line with the *-c* option, or by field with the *-f* option. Fields are stretches of characters within a line that are defined by delimiters. The most obvious delimiter for use within the text of a file is simply the space character, but other characters can be used as well. Fields are different from columns, which are strictly defined by numbering each character in the input line.

The *list* argument specifies the range of each line, whether in characters or in fields, to be selected.

The list is in the form of single numbers or of two numbers separated by a – character. Multiple single columns or ranges can be selected by separating them with commas. Either the first or the last number can be omitted, indicating that the cut starts at the beginning of the line or that it ends at the end of the line. Characters and fields in each line are numbered starting at 1.

When the *–f* option is used, indicating that *cut* is to count fields rather than characters, a delimiter other than the default tab character can be specified with the *–d* option. The *–s* option causes *cut* to ignore lines that don't contain the specified delimiter. This option can be useful, for example, for ignoring header lines in a table.

Combining Files with paste

Usage: `paste -[options] files`

The *paste* command allows you to combine fields from several files into one larger file. Unlike the *join* command, which does a database-style merging of two files, *paste* is a purely mechanical combination of files. Lines are combined based solely on their line number in each file: i.e., the first line of *file1* is pasted next to the first line of *file2*, regardless of the content of the lines. Pasted data is separated by a tab character unless another delimiter is specified with the *–d* option. With the *–s* option and only one input filename, *paste* joins all the lines in the input file into one long line.

paste can prepare datafiles to be read by data-analysis applications. If you have a group of files in the same format and you have used other filter commands to remove corresponding information from each of them, you can prepare one input file that allows you to plot the corresponding information from each of the files without reading them independently. In a previous example, we used piped commands to extract a column from a table in a complicated output file:

```
% head -167 protein1.pka | tail -100 | cut -c30-39 > protein1.pka.data
```

If you have eight similar output files for proteins 1–8, you can process them all in the same way and then paste the results that you're interested in comparing into one big datafile:

```
% paste protein*.pka.data > allproteins.pka.data
```

Each individual file in this example might look something like this:

```
3.8
12.0
10.8
4.4
4.0
6.3
7.9
```

Each number represents the computed pKa value of one amino acid in a protein. If you have several sets of results that can be meaningfully combined into a table, *paste* creates a simple tab-delimited table that looks like this:

```
3.8 3.2 3.6
12.0 12.9 12.5
10.8 10.9 11.0
4.4 4.2 4.5
4.0 3.9 4.2
6.3 6.5 6.2
7.9 7.5 8.0
```

It's up to you, however, to understand how your data can be meaningfully combined into a table and to use the *paste* command correctly to get the result you want.

Merging Datafiles with join

Usage: `join -[options] file1, file2`

join merges two files based on the contents of a specified join field, where lines from the two files having the same value in the join field are assumed to correspond. Files are assumed to have a tabular format consisting of fields and a consistent field separator, and are assumed to be sorted in increasing order of their join fields.

Command-line options for *join* include:

−1 fieldnum

Uses the specified field number as the join field in *file 1*

−2 fieldnum

Uses the specified field as the join field in *file 2*

−t character

Uses the specified character as the delimiter throughout the join operation

−e string

Replaces empty output fields with the specified string

—a filenum

> Produces output for each unpairable line in the specified file; can be specified for both input files; fields belonging to the other output file are empty

—v filenum

> Produces output only for unpairable lines in the specified file

—o list

> Constructs the output lines from the list of specified fields, where the format of the field list is *filenum.fieldnum*; multiple items in the list can be separated by commas or whitespace

join is quite useful for constructing data tables from multiple files, and a sequence of *join* operations can construct a complicated file. In a simple example, there are three files:

```
mustelidae.color:
badger black
ermine white
long-tailed tan
otter brown
stoat tan

mustelidae.prey:
ermine mouse
badger mole
stoat vole
otter fish
long-tailed mouse

mustelidae.habitat:
river otter
snowfield ermine
prairie long-tailed
forest badger
plains stoat
```

First, combine *mustelidae.color* and *mustelidae.prey*. The field both have in common is the name of the animal, which is the first field in each file. *mustelidae.prey* isn't yet sorted. The form of the *join* command needed is:

```
% sort mustelidae.prey | join mustelidae.color - > outfile
```

which produces the following output:

```
badger black mole
ermine white mouse
long-tailed tan mouse
otter brown fish
stoat tan vole
```

Now combine the resulting file with *mustelidae.habitat*. If you want the resulting output to be in the form *habitat animal prey color*, use the command construct:

```
% sort -k2 mustelidae.habitat | join -1 2 -2 1 -o 1.1,2.1,2.3,2.2 - outfile
```

This operates on the standard input and the output file from the previous step to produce the output:

```
forest badger mole black
snowfield ermine mouse white
prairie long-tailed mouse tan
river otter fish brown
plains stoat vole tan
```

Sorting Files with sort

Usage: `sort -[general options] -o[outfile] -[key interpretation options] -t[char] -k[keydef]...[filenames]`

The *sort* command can sort a single file, sort a group of files and simultaneously merge them into a single file, or check a file for sortedness. This function has many applications in data processing. Each line in the file is treated as a single field by default, but keys can also be defined by the user on the command line.

The main options for *sort* are:

−c Tests a file for sortedness based on the user-selected options

−m Merges several input files

−u Displays only one instance of lines that compare as equal

−o outfile
   Sends the output to a file instead of sending it to standard output

−t char
   Uses the specified character to delimit fields

Options that determine how keys are interpreted can be used as global options, but they can also be used as flags on a particular key. The key interpretation options for *sort* are:

−b Ignores leading or trailing whitespace in a sort key.

−r Reverses the sort order for a particular key.

−d Uses "dictionary order" in making comparisons; i.e., characters other than letters, digits, and whitespace are ignored.

−f Reclassifies lowercase letters as uppercase for the purpose of making comparisons. Normally, L and l would be separated from each other due to being in

uppercase and lowercase character sets; with the *–f* flag, all L's end up together, whether capitalized or not.

Specifying sort keys

Key definitions are arguments of the *–k* option. The form of a key definition is *position1,position2*. Each is a numerical value that specifies where within the line the key starts and ends. Positions can have the form *field.character*, where *field* specifies the field position in the input line, and *character* specifies the position of the starting character of the key within its individual field. If the key is flagged with one of the key interpretation options, the form of the key is *field.character[flags]*. If the key interpretation option isn't applied to the whole sort, but merely to one key, then it's appended to the key definition without a preceding hyphen.

File Statistics and Comparisons

It's frequently useful to find out if two separate files are the same and, if not, where they have differences. For instance, if you have compiled a program on your local machine, and test cases are provided, you should run your copy of the program on the test cases and compare the output to the canonical output provided by the makers of the program. If you want to check that the backup copy of a file and the current version of the file are the same, file-comparison tools are very useful. Unix provides tools that allow you to do this without laboriously searching through the files by hand.

Comparing Files with cmp and diff

> Usage: `cmp -[options] file1 file2`
> Usage: `diff -[options] file1 file2`

Let's say you have two lists and, while they look similar, you can't tell by eye if they are exactly the same list. This can happen if you get a list of gene names back from database searches performed using two subtly different queries and want to know if they are equivalent. In order to compare them rigorously (and save your eyes in the process), you can try the semicomplementary commands *cmp* and *diff*. In short, *cmp* tells you whether two files are identical, and *diff* prints any lines that are different.

cmp is fairly simple-minded. Typing:

```
% cmp enolase1.list enolase2.list
```

produces no output if the two files are identical. Otherwise, *cmp* returns a message that the files differ and includes the character and line at which the first difference occurs.

diff is most useful for comparing different versions of a file to find exactly where the files differ. Before looking at *diff*'s rather obtuse output, it's worth a moment to see how to decrypt it. Without options, *diff* responds with a list of differences in the form of the changes required to make *file2* from *file1*:

x,y d i

> Lines *x* through *y* in *file1* are missing in *file2* after line *i* (i.e., they've been deleted from *file2*).

i a x,y

> Lines *x* through *y* in *file2* are missing in *file1* after line *i* (i.e., they've been added to *file2*).

i,j c x,y

> Lines *i* through *j* in *file1* have been changed to lines *x* through *y* in *file2*.

In practice, the output looks like this (where *enolase1.txt* and *enolase2.txt* are lists of names of putative enolases produced by two database searches performed at different times):

```
% diff enolase1.list enolase2.list
1a2
> ENO_MESCR
5a7
> ENOA_MOUSE
```

Here are two of the more immediately useful options *diff* uses:

−b Ignores differences in whitespace between lines

−B Ignores inserted or deleted blank lines between files

The *info* pages on *diff* and its variants are especially helpful. If you use this utility extensively, we strongly recommend you give them a look.

Counting Words with wc

Usage: `wc -[options] filename(s)`

wc is a simple and useful utility for counting things in text files. Given a text file, *wc* counts the number of lines, words, and bytes (characters) that it contains. The default setting for *wc* is to count all three entities, so that typing it at the command prompt returns a line that looks like:

```
% wc meercat1.txt
    27   98    559 meercat1.txt
```

This output tells you that there are 27 lines, 98 words, and 559 bytes in *meercat1. txt*. If you pass multiple files to *wc*, it returns counts both for individual files and for all of them combined. For example, if you run *wc* on the three meercat files:

```
% wc meercat1.txt meercat2.txt meercat3.txt
```

(or, to save time, *wc meercat*.txt*, being appropriately careful using the wildcard), the output looks like:

```
 41   130   905 meercat1.txt
 50   124   869 meercat2.txt
 10    19   156 meercat3.txt
101   273  1930 total
```

These are the options for *wc*:

–c Counts only bytes (characters)

–w Counts only words

–l Counts only lines

--help
> Prints a usage message

--version
> Prints the version of *wc* being used

Unix tools can often be used in combination to collect information you need. For instance, say you have a list of 1,000 files that need to be processed, and the output files are all saved together in the same directory. Instead of trying to list the contents of that directory using *ls*, you can use *ls –1 dirname* | *wc* to find how many output files have been created so far.

The Language of Regular Expressions

The pattern-matching language known as *regular expressions* allows you to search for and extract matches and to replace patterns of characters in files (given the right program). Regular expressions are used in the *vi* and Emacs text-editing programs. Since much of the data that biologists work with contains patterns, one of the first skills you need to learn is how to match patterns and extract them from files.

Regular expressions also are understood by the Perl language interpreter. Knowing how to use regular expressions along with the basic commands of Perl gives you a powerful set of data-processing tools. We'll cover the basics of regular expressions here, and return to them again in Chapter 12.

If you've ever used a wildcard character in a search, you've used a regular expression. Regular expressions are patterns of text to be matched. There are also special characters that can be used in regular expressions to stand for variable patterns, which means you can search for partial or inexact matches. Regular expressions can consist of any combination of explicit text and special characters.

The special characters recognized in basic regular expressions are:

\   The backslash acts as an escape character for a special character that follows it. If part of the pattern you are searching for is a dot, you give the regular expression *chars\.txt* to find the pattern *chars.txt*.

.   The dot matches any single character.

*   The behavior of the asterisk in regular expressions is different from its behavior as a shell wildcard. If preceded by a character, it matches zero or more occurrences of that character. If preceded by a character class description, it matches zero or more characters from that set. If preceded by a dot, it matches zero or more arbitrary characters, which is equivalent to its behavior in the shell.

^   The caret at the beginning of a regular expression matches the beginning of a line. Otherwise, it matches itself.

$ The dollar sign at the end of a regular expression matches the end of a line. Otherwise, it matches itself.

[charset]

A group of characters enclosed in square brackets matches any single character within the brackets. [badger] matches any of (a, b, d, e, g, r). Within the set, only –, caret,], and [are special. All other characters, including the general special characters, match themselves. A range of characters in the form [*c1–c2*] can also be given; e.g., [0–9] or [A–Z].

Searching for Patterns with grep

Usage: `grep –[options] 'pattern' filenames`

grep allows you to search for patterns (in the form of regular expressions) in a file or a group of files. GNU *grep* (the standard on Linux) searches for one of three kinds of patterns, depending on which of the following functions is selected:

–*G* Standard *grep*: searches for a regular expression (this is the default)

–*E* Extended *grep*: searches for an extended regular expression

–*F* Fast *grep*: rapidly searches for a fixed string (a pattern made of normal characters, as opposed to regular expressions)

Note that the –*E* and –*F* options can be explicitly selected by calling *egrep* or *fgrep* on some systems. If no files are specified to be searched, *grep* searches the standard input for the pattern, allowing the output of another program to be redirected to *grep* if you are looking for a pattern in the output.

As a simple example, consider the following commands:

```
% grep -c '>' SP-caspases-A.fasta SP-caspases-B.fasta
% grep '>' SP-caspases-A.fasta SP-caspases-B.fasta
```

These both search through a file of FASTA-formatted sequences (whose header lines, you will remember, begin with the > symbol). The first command returns the number of sequences in each file, while the second returns a list of the sequence headers. Be sure to enclose the > in quotes, though. Otherwise, as one of us once found out the hard way, the command is interpreted as a request for *grep* to search the standard input for no pattern and then redirect the resulting empty string to the files listed, overwriting whatever was already there.

grep takes dozens of options. Here are some of the more useful ones:

−*c*   Prints only a count of matching lines, rather than printing the matching lines themselves

−*i*   Ignores uppercase/lowercase distinctions in both file and pattern

−*n*   Prints lines and line numbers for each occurrence of a pattern match

−*l*   Prints filenames containing matches to *pattern*, but not matching lines

−*h*   Prints matching lines but not filenames (the opposite of −*l*)

−*v*   Prints only those lines that don't contain a match with *pattern*

−*q*   (quiet mode) Stops listing matches after the first occurrence

In protein structure files, protein sequence information is stored as a sequence of three-letter codes, rather than in the more compact single-letter code format. It's sometimes necessary to extract sequence information from protein structure files. In real life, you can do this with a simple Perl program and then go on to translate the sequence into single-letter code. But you can also extract the sequence with two simple Unix filter commands.

The first step is to find the SEQRES records in the PDB file. This is done using the *grep* command:

```
% grep SEQRES pdbfile > seqres
```

This gives you a file called *seqres* containing records that look like this:

```
SEQRES 1 357 GLU VAL LEU ILE THR GLY LEU ARG THR ARG ALA VAL ASN 2MNR 106
SEQRES 2 357 VAL PRO LEU ALA TYR PRO VAL HIS THR ALA VAL GLY THR 2MNR 107
SEQRES 3 357 VAL GLY THR ALA PRO LEU VAL LEU ILE ASP LEU ALA THR 2MNR 108
```

Not all the characters in each record belong to the amino-acid sequence. Next, you need to extract the sequences from the records. This can be done using the *cut* command:

```
% cut -c20-70 seqres > seqs
```

The output of this command, in the file *seqs*, looks like this:

```
GLU VAL LEU ILE THR GLY LEU ARG THR ARG ALA VAL ASN
VAL PRO LEU ALA TYR PRO VAL HIS THR ALA VAL GLY THR
VAL GLY THR ALA PRO LEU VAL LEU ILE ASP LEU ALA THR
```

If you don't want to create the intermediate file, you can pipe the commands together into one command line:

```
% grep SEQRES pdbfile | cut -c20-70 | paste -s > seqs.
```

Addition of the *paste –s* command joins the individual lines in the file into one long line.

Unix Shell Scripts

The various Unix shells also provide a mechanism for writing multistep scripts that let you automate your work. *Scripts* are labeled as such because they contain, verbatim, the sequence of commands you want to "say" to the shell, just as the script for a play contains the sequence of lines the author wants the actors to say.

Shell scripts—even the simplest ones—are still applications, and they behave accordingly. Let's say you want to start a series of calculations that will take a while, and then go home to eat dinner. By default, the shell will wait until one command is finished to execute the next command, so if the second command acts upon the output of the first, it won't start prematurely. The important thing is that you don't have to be there to type the second command.

Here's a relatively simple example. Assume you have just downloaded the entire set of GenBank DNA sequence files. You want the information in the files, but you need it to be in a different format so that a program you've downloaded can process it. You're going to use the program *gb2fasta* to convert the files from Gen-Bank to FASTA format. (This script assumes you've downloaded the GenBank files to your current working directory.) Then you want to process each file using the BLAST *formatdb* program. To make the script more flexible, you can write it so that it takes an optional file list on the command line to specify which files to process. The script might look like this:

```
#!/usr/bin/csh
foreach file ($*)
echo $file
gb2fasta $file > $file.na
formatdb -t "$file" -i $file.na -p F
end
```

After creating the file, you need to make it executable using the *chmod* command. For instance, if the filename of the script is *blastprep*, give the command:

```
% chmod a+x blastprep
```

The first line of the script tells the operating system which shell program to use, the shell is invoked, and the job is run. You can invoke your command immediately in the following way:

```
./blastprep gbest*.seq
```

In order to run the new script without giving its full path, you need to run the *rehash* command before typing this command. *rehash* is a C-shell command that updates the list of all executable files in your path.

In the previous example, all the GenBank EST files are automatically parsed and prepared for use with BLAST. The programs *gb2fasta* and *formatdb* run just as they do on the command line, but you don't have to wait for each command to complete. The script takes your command-line argument—in this case *gbest*.seq*, which is a list of filenames—and sequentially fills the variable *$file* with each value. It then loops through the lines between the "foreach" and "end" lines. The *echo* command simply sends the value of *$file* to standard output, so you can see in your terminal window how the job is progressing. The *gb2fasta* program normally prints to standard output, so you need to redirect the output to a specific filename. On the other hand, *formatdb* processes the input files and generates new files using an internal naming convention, so no output file is needed in the script.

Communicating with Other Computers

As we'll see in Chapter 6, *Biological Research on the Web*, the ability to plug into other computers and networks across the world allows you to read and download an amazing amount of information, as well as share data with your colleagues. In fact, your work as a bioinformatician depends on having access to public databases and other repositories of biological data. In this section, we look at how your computer communicates with other machines and the tools it uses to do so.

The Web

The easiest way to communicate with other computers is via the Web. Most distributions of Linux include web browser software—usually Netscape—which, if you select it from the list of installation options, is automatically installed for you. Setting up a web browser on a Linux system is the same as setting up a browser on other computers; you need to set the browser's preferences and tell it where the correct utilities are located to open different kinds of file attachments.

You may want to maintain a web page on your machine, and in order to do that, you need to install web server software. Again, most Linux distributions allow you to install the Apache web server software as one of your installation options. If you choose to install the Apache web server, you can publish a simple web site by placing the appropriate HTML files in the */home/httpd/html* directory.

IP Addresses and Hostnames

In the world of the Internet, computers recognize each other by their Internet Protocol (IP) addresses. Computers that are constantly connected to the Internet have permanently allocated IP addresses and hostnames, while computers that only connect to the Internet occasionally may have dynamically allocated IP addresses, or no IP address at all, depending on the protocol they use to connect.

IP addresses consist of four numbers separated by dots (e.g., 128.174.55.33). These are interpreted as directions to the *host* (a computer that communicates with other computers) by network software. Computers also have *hostnames*, such as *gibas. biotech.vt.edu*. *Name servers* are dedicated machines that maintain information about the relationships among IP addresses and hostnames.

telnet

    Usage: `telnet full.hostname`

The *telnet* command opens a shell on a remote Unix machine; the workstation on which the command is issued becomes a terminal for that machine. To *telnet* to another Unix machine, you must have a login on that machine. Once you're logged in to the remote host, the shell works just as if you were working directly on the remote machine.*

A "login:" prompt should appear, followed by a "password:" prompt after your ID is entered.

ftp

    Usage: `ftp full.host.name.edu`

The File Transfer Protocol (*ftp*) is a method for transferring files from one computer to another. You may be familiar with Fetch, Interarchy, or other PC-based FTP clients; Unix *ftp* is conceptually similar to these programs (and many of them have analogs that run under Linux, if you like their graphical user interfaces). When you use *ftp* to connect to another host, you will find yourself in an operating environment that is unique to *ftp*. Unix commands don't always work in the *ftp* environment, although the commands *ls* and *cd* have similar functions.

---

* If you are logged in as *root*, there are certain tasks you can't do from a remote terminal.

Again, a "login:" prompt appears, followed by a "password:" prompt. If you are accessing an anonymous FTP server (a common way to distribute software), the standard username is *anonymous*, and your email address is the password. Once in the FTP environment, the most important commands to know are:

help
> Prints out the list of *ftp* commands. *help command* prints out information on a specific command.

ls Lists the contents of the directory on the remote host.

cd Changes the working directory on the remote host.

lcd
> Changes the working directory on the local host.

get, mget
> *get* copies a single file from the remote host to the local host. *mget* copies multiple files.

put, mput
> *put* copies a single file from the local host to the remote host. *mput* copies multiple files.

binary, ascii
> Changes the file-transfer mode to binary or ASCII. You should choose binary when you are downloading binary executables, images, and other encoded file formats.

prompt
> Toggles the interactive mode that asks you to confirm every transfer when you transfer multiple files.

Displaying from a Remote Terminal

Sometimes you need to run an X program on another computer and have it display on your terminal. This is relatively simple to do. First, you need to set your own terminal to allow remote displays from other hosts. This is done using the *xhost* command:

```
% xhost +
```

A confirmation that access is allowed from other hosts is then printed to standard output.

Next, you need to change the display environment on the remote machine. This is done with the *setenv* command:

```
% setenv DISPLAY yourmachine.yoursubnet.wherever.edu:0
```

Not all X applications running on a remote server can use your terminal for display, generally because the remote machine and your machine don't have the same graphics capabilities. For instance, programs running on a remote Silicon Graphics machine can't display on your local Linux workstation, because Silicon Graphics uses proprietary graphics libraries that aren't currently available to Linux users. However, even if both machines are compatible, bandwidth limitations can make running large X programs over the network extremely slow.

Communication and File Sharing

One of the biggest inconveniences for Linux users in a primarily Mac/PC environment is the sharing of files generated by PC productivity software with other users. While it's not our purpose to teach you to use these packages here, we can mention a few options that will help you handle communication with non-Unix users.

Fortunately, there are relatively low-cost software products available for Linux that make it possible to work with common file types, such as Microsoft Word and rich-text format (RTF) documents, PowerPoint presentations, and Excel spreadsheets. Sun's StarOffice (*http://www.staroffice.com*) and Applix's Applixware (*http://www. vistasource.com*) are two possibilities; at the time of this writing, StarOffice seemed to do the cleanest job of converting files generated by Microsoft Word and other commonly used programs. Adding one of these packages to your Linux system will add most of the basic PC functions (word processing, electronic presentations, etc.) that may be vital to your work.

Most kinds of graphics files are easily handled and converted on Linux systems. One powerful tool for manipulating graphics files is called the GIMP (Gnu Image Manipulation Program, *http://www.gimp.org*). The GIMP is commonly included in Linux distributions, so be sure to select it as part of your installation if you will be doing anything with graphics files. The GIMP is analogous to Adobe Photoshop program and shares most of the same functionality.

Media Compatibility

Linux users can read and write files on Microsoft-formatted floppy disks and Zip disks. A floppy or Zip disk is treated as an additional filesystem on your computer. The most basic way to access this filesystem is to mount it using the *mount* command. To do this, you need to know the device ID of the disk you are trying to mount and establish a mount point for the new filesystem.

Determining the device IDs of the various drives is usually straightforward. One way is to open the file */var/log/dmesg*. This file contains the system information that is printed to standard output when the machine is booted. Scan through the file and find the drive information, which should look like this:

```
hdc: SAMSUNG SC-140B, ATAPI CDROM drive
hdd: IOMEGA ZIP 250 ATAPI, ATAPI FLOPPY drive
hdc: ATAPI 40X CD-ROM drive, 128KB Cache
Floppy drive(s): fd0 is 1.44M
```

This section of the file contains information about IDE devices. On this particular machine, the IDE devices include a CD-ROM drive, a Zip drive, and a floppy drive. The three-letter codes *hdc*, *hdd*, and *fd0* are the device IDs.

The next section of the file contains information about SCSI devices. On this particular machine, the main hard disk is a SCSI drive, and its ID is *sda*. *sda1*, *sda2*, etc., are the individual IDs of the partitions on the hard drive:

```
Detected scsi disk sda at scsi0, channel 0, id 0, lun 0 SCSI device
sda: hdwr sector= 512 bytes. Sectors= 35566499 [17366 MB] [17.4 GB]
sda: sda1 sda2 sda3 sda4 < sda5 sda6 sda7 sda8 sda9 >
```

Accessing Devices as Unix Filesystems

Once you know the device IDs, mounting these new filesystems is simple. If you're the root user of your own machine, the command is:

```
mount -t [filesystem type] devicefile mount point
```

For example, to mount a PC-formatted floppy disk at */mnt/floppy,* the command is:

```
% mount -t msdos /dev/fd0 /mnt/floppy
```

You can find a listing of allowed file types in the manpages for *mount.*

As a shortcut, you can modify your */etc/fstab* file to contain the following lines:

```
/dev/fd0          /mnt/floppy         vfat  noauto,owner  0 0
/dev/hdd4         /mnt/zip            vfat  noauto,owner  0 0
```

On this system, the Zip drive is located at */dev/hdd.* All PC-formatted Zip disks use partition number 4, and the device file for that partition is */dev/hdd4.* The *noauto* flag means that these disks aren't mounted automatically at boot time. Once these lines are added to */etc/fstab,* the devices can be mounted with the shortened command *mount devicefilename.*

Once the Zip or floppy is mounted as a partition, the files on that disk can be treated like any other file on the system.

Getting some of these devices working isn't as straightforward as we'd like it to be. For further help, you can search the Web for the Linux how-to pages for the particular device you're using.

Accessing Devices as DOS Disks

If you install the utility package *mtools* and its graphical frontend *mfm*, you can run *mfm* and move files to Zip or floppy disks, using a graphical interface similar to that on a PC. However, if you use this method to access devices, you can't run Unix commands on the files stored on your media until you move them onto the local hard disk.

By default, processes to access media may be run only by the root user. It's possible to configure your system so that other users can write to floppy and Zip drives. However, this creates a security hole in your system. You have to decide for yourself whether the benefits of easy disk access outweigh any potential risks.

Playing Nicely with Others in a Shared Environment

Unix environments traditionally have been multiuser environments. While the availability of new flavors of Unix for personal computers might change this on your computer at home, at work you will probably use a shared, networked Unix system at least some of the time. And even on a personal Unix system, you need to be aware of problems that can arise when you create an excessive load on your system, and of how background processes can interfere with your ability to run interactive processes.

Because the Unix operating system can interact with more than one user at a time, from terminals attached directly to the system or over a network, there can be many processes executing on your system. Some processes will be yours, and others will belong to users who may be working across the room from you or hundreds of miles away. To be a good citizen in a Unix environment, you need to share the system's resources. While administrators of large public systems make it nearly impossible for you to be a bad citizen by implementing quotas for space usage and queueing systems for process management, it isn't likely that all systems you use will be so tightly managed. On shared systems in which good faith is all that's keeping users from stepping on each other's toes, it's wise to manage your own processes responsibly. Otherwise someone's going to come gunning for you, and it won't be pretty.

Processes and Process Management

A Unix system carries out many different operations at the same time. Each of these operations, or processes, has a unique process ID that allows the user or the administrator to interact with that process directly.

There are a minimum number of processes that run on a system regardless of whether you actively initiate them. Each shell program, whether idle or active, has a process ID attached to it. Several system (or root) processes, sometimes known as *daemons*, are constantly active on the system. These processes often lie in wait for you to initiate some activity they handle: for instance, printing files, sending email, or initiating a *telnet* session.

Above and beyond this minimal system activity level are any processes you initiate by typing a command or running a program. The Unix kernel manages these processes, allocating whatever resources are available to the processes according to their needs.

Each process uses a percentage of the processing capacity of the system's CPU or CPUs. It also uses a percentage of the system's memory. When the processes running on a machine require more than 100% of the CPU's capacity to execute, each individual process will execute more slowly. While Unix does an extremely good job of juggling hundreds of processes that run at the same time without having the machine roll over and die, eventually you will see a situation where the load on the machine increases to the point that the machine becomes useless. The operating system uses many techniques to prevent this, such as limiting the absolute number of processes that can be started and swapping idle jobs out of memory. Even on a single processor system, it's possible to have multiple processes running concurrently as long as there is enough space for both jobs to remain in memory. At the point at which the CPU has to constantly wait for data to get loaded from the swap space on the hard drive, you will see a great drop in efficiency. This can be monitored using the *top* command, which is described in the "top" section. Many machines are more limited by lack of memory than they are by a slow CPU, and it's often now more cost-effective to put money into additional RAM than to buy the latest, greatest, and fastest CPU.

Checking the load average

Usage: **w**

The *w* command is available on most Unix systems. This command can show you which other users are logged into the system and what they are doing. It also shows the current load average on the system.

The standard output of the *w* command looks like this:

```
2:55pm up 37 days, 4:50, 4 users, load average: 1.00, 1.02, 2.00
USER     TTY    FROM      LOGIN@   IDLE    JCPU    PCPU WHAT
jambeck  tty1             22Jan99  37days  3:55m  0.06s startx
jambeck  ttyp0  :0.0      Wed 5pm  1:34m   0.22s  0.22s -csh
jambeck  ttyp3  :0.0      21Feb99  3:47    9.05s  8.51s telnet weasel
god      ttyp2  around    2:52pm   0.00s   0.55s  0.09s create world
```

The first line of the output is the header. It shows the time of day, how long the machine has been up, how many users are logged in, and what the load average on the system has been for the last 1 minute, 5 minutes, and 15 minutes. The load average represents the fractional processor use on the system. If you have a single processor system and a load average of 1, the system is being used at optimal capacity. A four-processor system with a load average of 2 is being used at only half of its capacity. If you log in to a system and it's already being used at or beyond its capacity, it's not polite to add other processes that will start running right away. The *batch* or *at* commands can set up a process to start when resources become available.

The information displayed for each user is the username, the tty name, the remote host from which the user is logged in, the login time, the idle time, the JCPU and PCPU times, and what the user is doing.

Listing processes with ps

Usage: `ps [options]`

ps produces a snapshot of what the processor is doing at the moment you issue the command. Depending on what your computer is doing at the time, typing *ps* at the prompt should give output along the lines of:

```
  PID TTY     TIME CMD
36758 ttyq10 0:02 tcsh
43472 ttyq10 0:00 ps
42948 ttyq10 4:24 xemacs-20
42967 ttyq10 1:21 fermats-last-theorem-solver
```

Most of *ps*'s options modify the types of processes on which *ps* reports and the way in which it reports them. Here are some of the more useful options:

a   Lists every command running on the computer, including those of other users

l   Produces a long listing of processes (process memory size, user ID, etc.)

f   Lists processes in a "tree" form, showing related processes

Notice that you don't need to preceed the option with a dash. There are actually a couple of dozen options for *ps*; check *info ps* to see which options are supported by your local installation.

top

Usage: `top -[options]`

The *top* command provides real-time monitoring of processor activity. It lists processes on the system, sorted by CPU usage, memory usage, or runtime. The *top*
screen looks like this:

```
4:34pm up 37 days, 6:29, 4 users, load average: 0.25, 0.07, 0.02
42 processes: 39 sleeping, 3 running, 0 zombie, 0 stopped
CPU states: 42.9% user, 6.4% system, 0.0% nice, 51.0% idle
Mem:  39092K av, 38332K used,   760K free, 13568K shrd,  212K buff
Swap: 33228K av, 20236K used, 12992K free              8008K cached

  PID USER    PRI NI  SIZE  RSS SHARE STAT LIB %CPU %MEM   TIME COMMAND
  516 jambeck  15  0  4820 3884  1544 R      0 30.4  9.9   4:23 emacs-fgyell
  415 root      9  0 10256 9340   888 R      0 15.5 23.8 161:41 /usr/X11R6/b
10756 cgibas    5  0   716  716   556 R      0  2.3  1.8   0:01 top-ci
```

The header is similar to the output of *w* but more detailed. It gives a breakdown
of CPU and memory usage in addition to uptime and load averages. The display
can be changed to show a variety of fields. The default configuration of *top* is set
in the user's *.toprc* file or in a systemwide */etc/toprc* file.

Here are the *top* options:

−*d* Updates with a frequency of *delay*

−*q* Refreshes without any delay, running at the highest possible priority

−*s* Runs in secure mode, with its most potentially dangerous commands disabled

−*c* Prints the full command line instead of just the command you're running

−*i* Ignores all processes except those currently running

While *top* is running, certain interactive commands can be entered, unless they are
disabled from the command line. The command *i* toggles the display between
showing all processes and showing just the processes currently running. *k* kills a
process. It prompts you for the process ID of the process to kill and the signal to
send to it. Signal 15 is a normal kill; signal 9 is a swift and deadly kill that can't be
ignored by the process. *r* changes the running priority of a process, implementing
the *renice* command discussed in the later section "Setting process priorities with
nice and renice." It prompts you for the process ID and the new priority value for
the job.

Signaling processes with kill

> Usage: kill [-s *signal* | -p] [-a] *PID*

The *kill* command lets you terminate a process abnormally from the command
line. While *kill* can actually send various types of signals to a process, in practice
it's most often used in the form *kill PID* or, if that fails to kill the process, *kill −9
PID*.

On most systems, *kill* −*l* lists the available types of signals that can be sent to a process. It's sometimes useful to know that jobs can be stopped and restarted with *kill* −s *STOP* and *kill* −s *CONT.*[*]

A PID is usually just the numerical process ID, which you can find with the *ps* or *top* commands. It can also be a process name, in which case a group of similarly named processes can be addressed. Another useful form of PID is −*n process group ID*, which allows the *kill* command to address all the processes in a group simultaneously.

Setting process priorities with nice and renice

    Usage: nice -n [val command arg]
    Usage: renice -n [incr] [-g|-p|-u] id

Processes initiated on a Unix system run at the maximum allowed priority unless you tell them to do otherwise. The *nice* and *renice* commands allow the owner of a process, or the superuser, to lower the priority of a job.

If limited computing resources are shared among many users and computers are used simultaneously for computation and interactive work, it's polite to run background jobs (jobs that run on the machine without any interactive interface) with a low priority. Otherwise, interactive jobs such as text editing or graphical-display programs run extremely slowly while background jobs hog the available resources. Jobs running at a low priority are slowed only if higher-priority processes are running. When the load on the system is low, background jobs with low priority expand to use all the available resources.

You can initiate a command at a low priority using *nice*. *n* is the priority value. On most systems, this is set to 10 by default and can range from 1–19, or 0–20. The larger the number, the lower the priority of the job, of course.

The *renice* command allows you to reset the priority of a process that's already running. *incr* is a value to be added to the current priority. Thus, if you have a background process running at normal priority (priority 1) and you want to lower its priority (by increasing the priority number), you can enter *renice −n 18* to increase the priority value to 19. You can also input a negative number to put the job at high priority, but unless you are root, you are limited to raising its priority to 1. The *renice* options, −*p*, −*g*, and −*u*, cause *renice* to interpret *id* as a process ID, a process group ID, or a user number, respectively.

---

[*] Discussion of the other signals can be found in any of the comprehensive Unix references listed in the *Bibliography*.

Scheduling Recurring Activities with cron

The *cron* daemon, *crond*, is a standard Unix process that performs recurring jobs for the system and individual users. System activities such as cleanup of the */tmp* directory and system backups are typically functions controlled by the *cron* daemon. Normal users can also submit their own jobs to *cron*, assuming they have permission to run *cron* jobs. Details about *cron* permissions are found in the *crontab* manpage. Since the *at* and *batch* commands, which are discussed later, are also controlled by *cron*, most systems are configured to allow users to use *cron* by default.

Submitting jobs to cron using crontab

Usage: `crontab -[options] file`

Submission of jobs to *cron* is done using the *crontab* command. *crontab –l > file* places the current contents of your *crontab* into a file so you can edit the list. *crontab file* sends the newly edited file back and initializes it for use by *cron*. *crontab –r* deletes your current *crontab*.

cron processes the contents of all *crontab*'s and then initiates jobs as scheduled. A *crontab* entry as produced by *crontab –l* looks like:

```
# Format of lines:
#min  hour  daymo  month  daywk  cmd
   50    2     *      *      *    /home/jambeck/runme
```

This entry runs the program *runme* at 2:50 A.M. every day. An asterisk in any field means "perform this function every time." In this entry, all output to either STDOUT or STDERR is mailed to user *jambeck*'s email account on the machine where the *cron* job ran.

Using cron to schedule a recurrent database search

What if your group performs DNA sequencing on a daily basis, and you want to use the sequence-alignment program BLAST to compare your sequences automatically against a nonredundant protein database? Consider this *crontab* entry:

```
01 4 * * * find /data/seq/ -name "*.seq" -type f -mtime -1 -exec
/usr/bin/csh /usr/local/bin/blastall -p blastx -d nr -i '{' ";'
```

This automatically runs at 4:01 A.M. and checks for all sequences that have been modified or added to the database in the last 24 hours. It then runs the BLASTX program to search your copy of the nonredundant protein sequence database for matches to your new sequences and mails you the results. This example assumes you have all the necessary environment variables set up correctly so that BLAST can find the necessary scoring matrixes and databases. It also uses a default parameter set, which may need to be modified to get useful results. Once you get it configured correctly, all you have to do is browse through your email while you drink your morning coffee.

Scheduling processes with batch and at

> Usage: at -[*options*] *time*
> Usage: batch -[*options*]

The *batch* and *at* commands are standard Unix functions and are commonly available on most systems. Jobs are submitted to queues, and the queues are processed by the *cron* daemon; jobs are governed by the same restrictions as *crontab* submissions. The *batch* command assigns priorities to jobs running on the system. Using *batch* allows a system administrator to sort jobs by priority—high to low—thereby allowing more important jobs to run first. Unless the system has a mechanism to kill interactive jobs that exceed a specified time limit, this use of the *batch* queue relies on users to work in a cooperative manner. On larger systems the function of *batch* is usually replaced by more complicated queuing systems. You need to get information from your system administrator about which *batch* and *at* queues are available.

at allows you to submit a job to run at some specified time. *batch* sequentially runs jobs whenever the machine load drops below a specified level and the number of concurrent *batch* jobs has not been exceeded. Once you initiate *at* or *batch*, all command-line entries are considered part of the job until you terminate the submission with a Ctrl-D keystroke. Like *cron*, any STDOUT and STDERR generated by the job are mailed to you, so you at least get notified of error conditions. Here are the common options:

−q queuename
> Specifies the queue. By default, *at* uses the "a" queue; *batch* uses the "b" queue.

−l   Causes *at* to list the jobs current in the specified queue.

−d jobid
> Tells *at* to delete a specified job.

−f filename
> Instructs *at* to run the job from a file rather than standard input.

−m Instructs *batch* and *at* to send mail upon completion, even when no output is generated.

time
> Time can be now, teatime, 7:00 P.M., 7:00 P.M. tomorrow, etc. Check the manpage for more details.

As an example, let's say that you want your boss to think you were slaving away at 3:00 A.M. Simply send her mail at 3:07 A.M. Even if you don't plan on being awake, it's no problem. At the *at* command prompt, just type:

```
> at 3:07am
Mail -s "big breakthrough" boss@wherever < /home/jambeck/news
<Ctrl-d>
```

Monitoring Space Usage and File Sizes

As fast as available disk space on a system expands, users seem to be able to expand their files to fill it. Software takes up more space; output files become larger and more complex; more layers of analysis can be created. Since the infinitely large data-storage medium has yet to be invented, you can still run up against disk-space limitations. So, you need to be able to monitor how much space you are using and, as we'll discuss in the section "Creating Archives of Your Data," how to make data archives and store them on appropriate media.

Checking disk usage with du

Usage: du -[*options*] *filenames*

du reports the number of disk blocks used by the specified file or files. Without a filename, it reports disk usage for all files in the current working directory. The *−s* flag causes *du* to report values only for the named file, rather than for the file and its subdirectories.

Checking for free disk space with df

Usage: df

df reports free diskspace for local and networked filesystems on your computer. *df* is a useful way to find out which filesystems are mounted on your computer. If a connection to a filesystem you would expect to find is down, that filesystem doesn't appear in the *df* output. The *df* output looks like this:

```
Filesystem              Type    blocks       use      avail %use Mounted on
/dev/root               xfs   17506496  14113592   3392904  81  /
/dev/xlv/xlv_raid_home  xfs   62783488  39506328  23277160  63  /scratch-res1
/dev/dsk/dks0d5s0       xfs   17259688  15000528   2259160  87  /mnt/root-6.4
/dev/dsk/dks12d1s7      xfs   17711872  11773568   5938304  67  /ip410
/mnt/local/jmd/balder:  NFS   server balder not responding
zeus:/hamr              nfs    2205816    703280   1502536  32  /nfs/zeus/hamr
zeus:/hamrscr           nfs    4058200   2153480   1904720  54  /nfs/zeus/hamrscr
zeus:/lcascr1           nfs  142241472 103956480  38284992  74  /nfs/zeus/lcascr1
```

The first column is the actual location of the filesystem. In this case, locations preceded with / are local, and those preceded with a name (e.g., */zeus:...*) are physically part of another machine. The second column shows which protocol can *mount* the remote filesystem—that is, connect it to your computer. The next three columns show how many blocks are available on the filesystem, how many of those are in use, and how many are available, followed by the percent use of each device. The final column shows the local path to the filesystem.

It's useful to know these things if you are working on a system that is made up of multiple networked machines. From time to time connections are lost, like that to *balder* in the previous example. You may log in to a machine that can't find your home directory because an NFS connection is down. At these times, it's useful to be able to figure out what the problem is so you can send a concise and helpful email to the system administrator rather than just saying "help! My home directory is missing."

Checking your compliance with system quotas with quota

On some Unix systems, especially those that provide services to many users, system administrators implement disk space quotas for each user. The consequences of exceeding a disk space quota may be obvious. You might find that you're unable to write files or that you are automatically prompted to delete files each time you log in. Or, the consequences may be silent, but very annoying. For instance, if you exceed a quota, you may be able to run a text editor, only to find that it has overwritten the file you were editing with a file of length zero. Or your older files may simply start to be deleted as space is needed by other users.

If you're paying for computer time on a shared system, it's in your interest to find out what the user quota for the system is, for how long you can exceed it, what will happen if you exceed it, and where and how you can archive your files.

The *quota* command gives basic information about space usage and quota limits on systems with quotas. On most Unix systems, issuing the command *quota –v* gives space use information even when user disk quotas haven't been exceeded.

Creating Archives of Your Data

So, after months of your time, hundreds of megabytes of files, and several layers of subdirectories, the otter project is finally complete. Time to move on to the next project with a clean slate. But as refreshing as it may sound, you can't just type:

```
% rm -rf otter/
```

Other people may need to look back at your findings or use them as a starting point for their own research. At the other extreme, you can't leave your files lying around or laboriously copy them a few at a time to another location. Not every file needs to be accessible at all times; some files are replaced, while others are more conveniently stored elsewhere. This section covers the tools provided by Unix for archiving your data so you don't have to worry about it on a day-to-day basis but can find things later when you need them.

tar: Hold the feathers

   Usage: `tar functions [options] [arguments] filenames`

After going through all the effort of setting up your filesystem rationally, it seems like a waste to lose that structure in the process of storing it away, like hastily packed dishes in an unexpected cross-country move. Fortunately, there is a Unix command that lets you work with whole directories of files while retaining the directory structure. *tar* compacts a directory and all its component files and (if you ask for it) subdirectories into a single file with the name of the compacted directory and a *.tar* extension. The options for *tar* break down into two types: functions (of which you must choose one) and options. *tar* is short for "tape archive," since the utility was originally designed to read and write archives stored on magnetic tape. Another common use of *tar* is to package software in a form that can be easily transferred over the Internet.

To run *tar*, you must choose one of the following functions:

c   Creates a new tape archive

r   Appends the files to an existing archive

u   Adds files to the archive if they aren't present or are modified

x   Extracts files from an existing archive

t   Prints a table of contents of the archive

The options for *tar* are as follows:

f archive
   Performs the specified operation on *archive*, which can either be a device (such as a tape drive or a removable disk) or a *tar* file

v   (verbose mode) Prints the name of each file archived or extracted with a character to indicate the function (*a* for archived; *x* for extracted)

w   (whiny mode) Asks for confirmation at every step

Note that neither functions nor options require the hyphen that usually precedes Unix command options.

If you type:

```
% tar cvf otter/
```

the *otter/* directory and all its subdirectories are rolled into a single file called *otter. tar*. It's good practice to use the *v* option, so you can see if something is going horribly wrong while the archive is being processed.

If, on the other hand, you want to make an archive of the *otter/* directory on the tape drive *nftape*, you can type:

```
% tar cvf /dev/nftape otter/
```

A couple of warnings about *tar* are in order. First, before you use *tar* on your system, you should use *which* to find out whether the GNU or the standard version is installed. Several of the options mean different things to each version; the ones listed earlier are the same in each version.

Second, the *tar* file you create will be as large as all the contents of the directory and subdirectories beneath it. This condition has dire implications if your archived directory is large and you have limited disk space, or you need to transfer large amounts of *tar*'d data. In these cases, you should break down the directory into subdirectories of a more manageable size, and *tar* those instead.

If you don't have the space on your current filesystem or partition for your files and the archive you are creating to exist simultaneously, or you wish to download a whole archive file and unpack it just to retrieve a few files, you can transfer your archive over the network or even just to another partition using a combination of *ftp* and *tar* commands. Sending an archive this way and then extracting it at the destination can be less time-consuming than a *cp −r* if a large number of files are involved. The *ftp* program recognizes a form in which a command replaces the input filenames. The command is executed in a subshell on the local machine and operates on files on the local filesystem. The construct is:

```
ftp command "| command" filename
```

Inside the *ftp* program, here's how to send the output of the *tar* command, enclosed in quotes, into the filename specified as the target on the remote machine:

```
put "|tar cvBf - *" filename
```

Here's how to direct the downloaded archive through the *tar* command, resulting in extraction of only the files in the specified directory within the archive:

```
get filename.tar "|tar xvf - dirname"
```

Finally, here's how to list the contents of the remote archive:

```
get filename.tar "|tar t - *"
```

compress

Usage: `compress -[options] filenames`

Ultimately, you don't want to be left with large—if more manageable—*tar* files cluttering up your filesystem. In this situation, data-compression utilities are important, since they allow you to cheat and reduce the amount of space that files take up on your hard disk. *compress* is the standard Unix file-compression command.

It's the opposite of *uncompress*, the command used in Chapter 3, *Setting Up Your Workstation*, to open compressed papers and software. *compress* adds a *.Z* to the end of the filename.

Here are the most useful options for *compress*:

–f Forces compression; even if there is already a compressed version of the file, the main effect is to not overwrite an existing compressed file

–v (verbose mode) Prints percentage compression achieved by the file

–r (recursive mode) If *compress* is applied to a directory that contains subdirectories, compresses their contents as well as those of the original directory

If you have a text file named *stoat.txt* and the *tar* file of the *otter/* directory from the last section, and you want to compress both and look at the resulting compression ratio achieved, type:

```
% compress -v stoat.txt otter.tar
```

This command produces two files *stoat.txt.Z* and *otter.tar.Z*. The files can be uncompressed using the *uncompress* command or *gzip –d* (described next). In case you were wondering, natural languages (the kind humans use) end up with a compression ratio around 60%, and programming languages get around 40%. Try compressing the sequences of some of your favorite proteins to see what sort of ratio you get: the values can be wildly variable, depending on whether there are repeats in the sequence.

gzip

Usage: `gzip -[options] filenames`

As usual, in addition to the standard Unix *compress*, there's a faster and more efficient GNU utility: *gzip*. *gzip* behaves in much the same way as *compress*, except that it gets better compression on average, since it uses a superior algorithm. *gzip* adds the suffix *.gz* to a file that it compresses. It emulates the *compress* options described earlier and adds a few of its own:

–N (default setting) Preserves the original name and timestamp from the file being compressed

–q (quiet mode) Suppresses warnings when running

–d Returns a file that has been compressed by *gzip* to its uncompressed state; *gzip* can also recognize and uncompress files produced by *compress*

III

Tools for Bioinformatics

## Chapter 6

Biological Research
on the Web

The Internet has completely changed the way scientists search for and exchange information. Data that once had to be communicated on paper is now digitized and distributed from centralized databases. Journals are now published online. And nearly every research group has a web page offering everything from reprints to software downloads to data to automated data-processing services.

A simple web search for the word *bioinformatics* yields tens of thousands of results. The information you want may be number 345 in the list or it may not be found at all. Where can you go to find only the useful software and data, and scientific articles? You won't always get there by a simple web search. How can you judge which information is useful? Publication on the Web gives information an appearance of authority it may not merit. How can you judge if software will give the type of results you need and perform its function correctly?

In this chapter we examine the art of finding information on the Web. We cover search engines and searching, where to find scientific articles and software, and how to use the classic online information sources such as PubMed. And once you've located your information, we help you figure out how to use it. Among the largest sources of information for biologists are the public biological databases. We discuss the history of the public databases, data annotation, the various forms the data can take, and how to get data in and out. Finally, we give you some pointers on how to judge the quality of the information you find out there.

The Internet is a tremendously useful information source for biological research. In addition to allowing researchers to exchange software and data easily, it can be a source of the kind of practical advice about computer software and hardware, experimental methods and protocols, and laboratory equipment that you once could get only by buying a beer for a seasoned lab worker or computer hacker. Use the Internet, but use it wisely.

Using Search Engines

AltaVista, Lycos, Google, HotBot, Northern Light, Dogpile, and dozens of other search engines exist to help you find your way around the billion or more pages that make up the Web. As a scientist, however, you're not looking for common web commodities such as places to order books on the Web or online news or porn sites. You're looking for perhaps a couple of needles in a large haystack.

Knowing how to structure a query to weed out the majority of the junk that will come up in a search is very useful, both in web searching and in keyword-based database searching. Understanding how to formulate boolean queries that limit your search space is a critical research skill.

Boolean Searching

Most web surfers approach searching haphazardly at best. Enter a few keywords into the little box, and look at whatever results come up. But each search engine makes different default assumptions, so if you enter *protein structure* into Excite's query field, you are asking for an entirely different search than if you enter *protein structure* into Google's query field. In order to search effectively, you need to use boolean logic, which is an extremely simple way of stating how a group of things should be divided or combined into sets.

Search engines all use some form of boolean logic, as do the query forms for most of the public biological databases. Boolean queries restrict the results that are returned from a database by joining a series of search terms with the operators AND, OR, and NOT. The meaning of these operators is straightforward: joining two keywords with AND finds documents that contain only *keyword1* and *keyword2*; using OR finds documents that contain either *keyword1* or *keyword2* (or both); and using NOT finds documents that contain *keyword1* but not *keyword2*.

However, search engines differ in how they interpret a space or an implied operator. Some search engines consider a space an OR, so when you type *protein structure*, you're really asking for protein or structure. If you search for protein *structure* on Excite, which defaults to OR, you come up with a lot of advertisements for fad diets and protein supplements before you ever get to the scientific sites you're interested in. On the other hand, Google defaults to AND, so you'll find only references that contain protein and structure, which is probably what you intended to look for in the first place. Find out how the search engine you're using works before you formulate your query.

Boolean queries are read from left to right, just like text. Parentheses can structure more complex boolean queries. For instance, if you look for documents that contain *keyword1* and one of either *keyword2* or *keyword3*, but not *keyword4*, your query would look like this: (*keyword1* AND (*keyword2* OR *keyword3*)) NOT *keyword4*.

Many search engines allow you to use quotation marks to specify a phrase. If you want to find only documents in which the words *protein structure* appear together in sequence, searching for "protein structure" is one way to narrow your results.

Let's say you want to search a literature database for references about computing electrostatic potentials for protein molecules, and you only want to look for references by two authors, Barry Honig and Andrew McCammon. You might structure a boolean query statement as follows:

```
((protein AND "electrostatic potential") AND (Honig OR McCammon))
```

This statement tells the search engine you want references that contain both the word protein and the phrase electrostatic potential, and that you require either one or the other of the names Honig and McCammon.

There are many excellent web tutorials available on boolean searching. Try a search with the phrase *boolean searching* in Google, and see what comes up.

Search Engine Algorithms

While the purpose of this book isn't to describe exhaustively how search engines work, there are significant differences in how search engines build their databases and rank sites. These differences make some search engines far more useful than others for searching science and technology web sites.

Key features to look at in a web search engine's database building and indexing strategies are free URL submission, full-text indexing, automated, comprehensive web crawling, a fast "refresh rate," and a sensible ranking strategy for results.

Our current favorite search engine is Google. Google is extremely comprehensive, indexing over 1 billion URLs. Pages are ranked based on how many times they are linked from other pages. Links from well-connected pages are considered more significant than links from isolated pages. The claim is that a Google search will bring you to the most well-traveled pages that match your search topic, and we've found that it works rather well. Google caches copies of web pages, so pages can be accessible even if the server is offline. It returns only pages that contain all the relevant query terms. Google uses a shorthand version of the standard boolean search formula, and it allows such specialized services as locating all the pages that link back to a page of interest.

For the neophyte user, however, HotBot is probably the best search engine. HotBot is relatively comprehensive and regularly updated, and it offers form-based query tools that eliminate the need for you to formulate even simple query statements.

Finding Scientific Articles

Scientists have traditionally been able to trust the quality of papers in print journals because these journals are refereed. An editor sends each paper to a group of experts who are qualified to judge the quality of the research described. These reviewers comment on the manuscript, often requiring additions, corrections, and even further experiments before the paper is accepted for publication. Print journals in the sciences are, increasingly frequently, publishing their content in an electronic format in addition to hardcopy. Almost every major journal has a web site, most of which are accessible only to subscribers, although access to abstracts usually is free. Scientific articles in these web journals go through the same process of review as their print counterparts.

Another trend is e-journals, which have no print counterpart. These journals are usually refereed, and it shouldn't be too hard to find out by whom. For instance, the *Journal of Molecular Modeling*, an electronic journal published by Springer-Verlag, has links to information about the journal's editorial policy prominently displayed on its home page.

An excellent resource for searching the scientific literature in the biological sciences is the free server sponsored by the National Center for Biotechnology Information (NCBI) at the National Library of Medicine. This server makes it possible for anyone with a web browser to search the Medline database. There are other literature databases of comparable quality available, but most of these are not free. Your institution may offer access to such sources as Lexis-Nexis or Cambridge Scientific Abstracts.

Outside of refereed resources, however, anyone can publish information on the Web. Often research groups make papers available as technical reports on their web sites. These technical reports may never be peer reviewed or published outside the research group's home organization, and your only clue to their quality is the reputation and expertise of the authors. This isn't to say that you shouldn't trust or seek out these sources. Many government organizations and academic research groups have reference material of near-textbook quality on their web sites. For example, the University of Washington Genome Center has an excellent tutorial on genome sequencing, and NCBI has a good practical tutorial on use of the BLAST sequence alignment program and its variants.

Using PubMed Effectively

PubMed (*http://www.ncbi.nlm.nih.gov/entrez/query.fcgi*) is one of the most valuable web resources available to biologists. Over 4,000 journals are indexed in PubMed, including most of the well-regarded journals in cell and molecular biology, biochemistry, genetics, and related fields, as well as many clinical publications of interest to medical professionals.

PubMed uses a keyword-based search strategy and allows the boolean operators AND, OR, and NOT in query statements. Users can specify which database fields to check for each search term by following the search term with a field name enclosed in square brackets.

Additionally, users can search PubMed using Medical Subject Heading (MeSH) terms. MeSH is a library of standardized terms that may help locate manuscripts that use alternate terms to refer to the same concept. The MeSH browser (*http:// www.nlm.nih.gov/mesh/meshhome.html*) allows users to enter a word or word fragment and find related keywords in the MeSH library. PubMed automatically finds MeSH terms related to query terms and uses them to enhance queries.

For example, we searched for "protein electrostatics" in PubMed. The terms protein and electrostatics are automatically joined with an AND unless otherwise specified. The resulting boolean query statement submitted to PubMed is actually:

```
((("proteins"[MeSH Terms] OR protein[Text Word]) AND ("electrostatics"[MeSH Terms]
   OR electrostatics[Text Word])) AND notpubref[sb])
```

The results of the search are shown in Figure 6-1.

As you can see in Figure 6-2, PubMed also allows you to use a web interface to narrow your search. The Limits link immediately below the query box on the main PubMed page takes you to this web form.

The Limits form allows you to add specificity to your query. You can limit your search to particular fields in the PubMed database record, such as the Author Name or Substance Name field. Searches can also be limited by language, content (e.g., searching for review articles or clinical trials only), and date. For clinical research publications, the search can be limited based on the species, age, and gender of the research subjects.

The Preview/Index menu allows you to build a detailed query interactively. You can select a specific data field (for instance, the Author Name field) and then enter a term you want to search for within the specified field only. Clicking the AND, OR, or NOT buttons joins the new term to your previous query terms using the specified boolean operator.

For instance, you might start with a general search for "protein AND electrostatics," then go to the Preview/Index page (Figure 6-3) and specify that you want to search for "Gilson OR McCammon" in the Author Name field only.

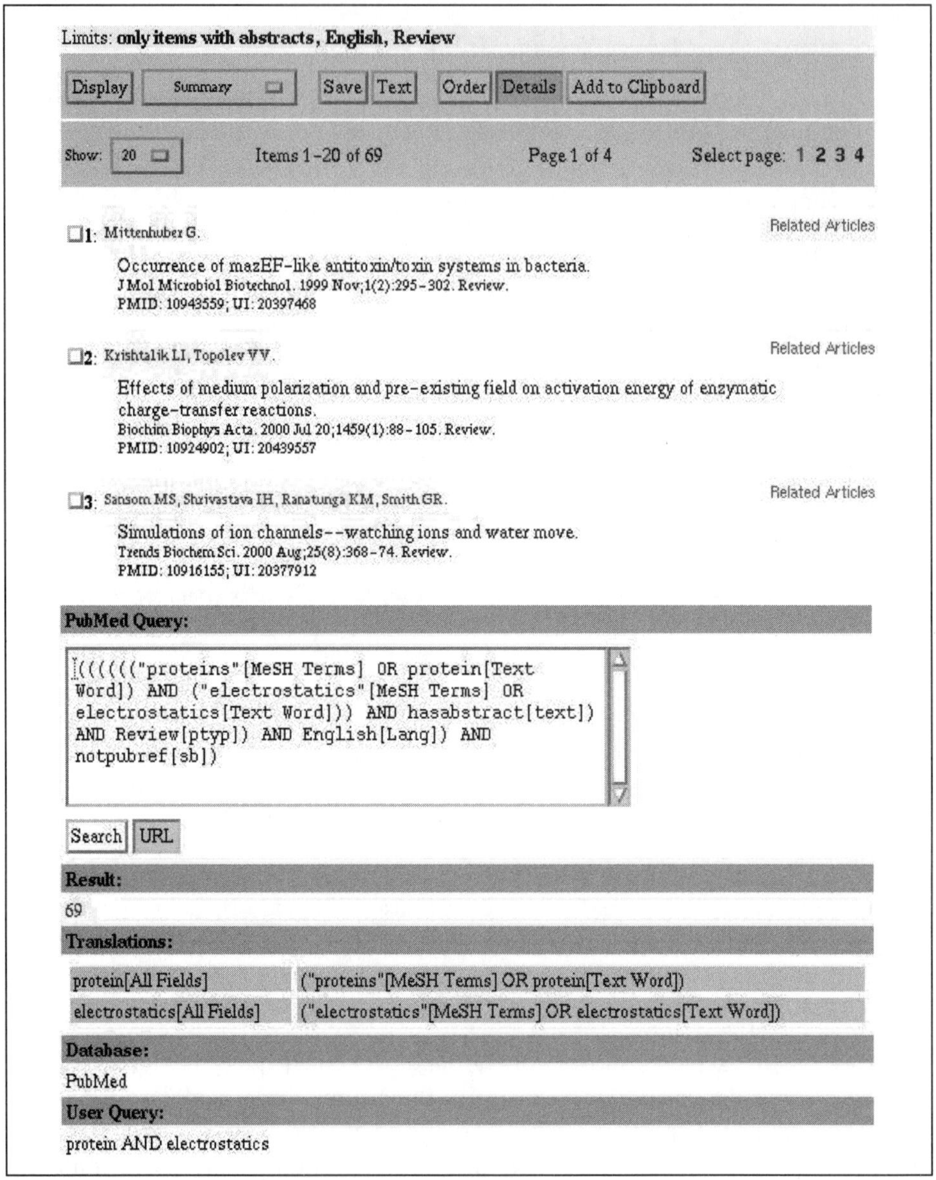

Limits: **only items with abstracts, English, Review**

| Display | Summary ⬜ | Save | Text | Order | Details | Add to Clipboard |

Show: 20 ⬜   Items 1–20 of 69   Page 1 of 4   Select page: 1 **2 3 4**

☐**1**: Mittenhuber G.   Related Articles

   Occurrence of mazEF–like antitoxin/toxin systems in bacteria.
   J Mol Microbiol Biotechnol. 1999 Nov;1(2):295–302. Review.
   PMID: 10943559; UI: 20397468

☐**2**: Krishtalik LI, Topolev VV.   Related Articles

   Effects of medium polarization and pre–existing field on activation energy of enzymatic
   charge–transfer reactions.
   Biochim Biophys Acta. 2000 Jul 20;1459(1):88–105. Review.
   PMID: 10924902; UI: 20439557

☐**3**: Sansom MS, Shrivastava IH, Ranatunga KM, Smith GR.   Related Articles

   Simulations of ion channels--watching ions and water move.
   Trends Biochem Sci. 2000 Aug;25(8):368–74. Review.
   PMID: 10916155; UI: 20377912

PubMed Query:

```
((((((("proteins"[MeSH Terms] OR protein[Text
Word]) AND ("electrostatics"[MeSH Terms] OR
electrostatics[Text Word])) AND hasabstract[text])
AND Review[ptyp]) AND English[Lang]) AND
notpubref[sb])
```

| Search | URL |

Result:

69

Translations:

| protein[All Fields] | ("proteins"[MeSH Terms] OR protein[Text Word]) |
| electrostatics[All Fields] | ("electrostatics"[MeSH Terms] OR electrostatics[Text Word]) |

Database:

PubMed

User Query:

protein AND electrostatics

Figure 6-1. Results from a PubMed search

You can also use the options in the History form to access results from earlier searches, and to narrow a search by adding new terms to the query.

If you want to collect results from multiple queries and save them into one big file, the Clipboard will allow you to do that. To save individual results to the

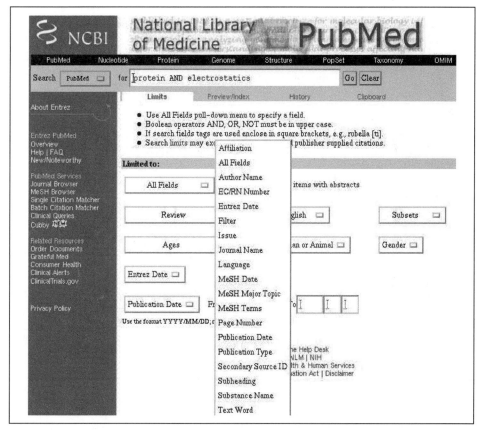

Figure 6-2. Narrowing a search strategy using the Limits menu in PubMed

Clipboard, simply click the checkbox next to the result you want to save, then click the Add to Clipboard button in the menu at the top of your results page.*

If you find a search strategy that works for you in PubMed, you can save that strategy in the form of a URL, and repeat the same search at any time in the future by visiting that URL. To save a PubMed URL, click the Details link on your results page, then click the URL link on the Details page. The URL of your search will appear in the Location field at the top of the web browser, so that you can bookmark it.

---

* You'll notice that all the checkbox-clicking to select and save individual results can get time-consuming if you're working with a lot of pages of results. It would be easier if you could come up with a search strategy that was absolutely certain to bring up only the results you want. There's no solution for this within the NCBI tools, and writing your own scripts to process batches of results may not help you either. The limitation is in the ability of computer programs to parse human language.

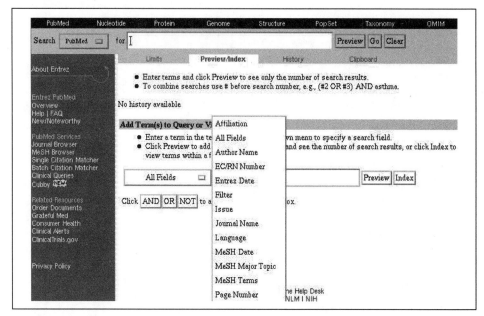

Figure 6-3. Building a PubMed query using the Preview/Index form

The "bookmarkable" URL for a PubMed search should look something like this:

```
http://www.ncbi.nlm.nih.gov:80/entrez/query.fcgi?cmd=PureSearch&db=
PubMed&details_term=%28%28%28%28%28%28%22proteins%22%5BMeSH%20Terms
%5D%20OR%20protein%5BText%20Word%5D%29%20AND%20%28%22electrostatics
%22%5BMeSH%20Terms%5D%20OR%20electrostatics%5BText%20Word%5D%29%29
%20AND%20hasabstract%5Btext%5D%29%20AND%20Review%5Bptyp%5D%29%20AND
%20English%5BLang%5D%29%20AND%20notpubref%5Bsb%5D%29
```

Spending a few hours developing some detailed PubMed search strategies that work for you, and saving them, can save you a lot of work in the future.

The Public Biological Databases

The nomenclature problem in biology at the molecular level is immense. Genes are commonly known by unsystematic names. These may come from developmental biology studies in model systems, so that some genes have names like *flightless*, *shaker*, and *antennapedia* due to the developmental effects they cause in a particular animal. Other names are chosen by cellular biologists and represent the function of genes at a cellular level, like *homeobox*. Still other names are chosen by biochemists and structural biologists and refer to a protein that was probably isolated and studied before the gene was ever found. Though proteins are direct products of genes, they are not always referred to by the same names or codes as the genes that encode them. This kind of confusing nomenclature generally means that only a scientist who works with a particular gene, gene product, or the biochemical process that it's a part of can immediately recognize what the common name of the gene refers to.

The biochemistry of a single organism is a more complex set of information than the taxonomy of living species was at the time of Linnaeus, so it isn't to be expected that a clear and comprehensive system of nomenclature will be arrived at easily. There are many things to be known about a given gene: its source organism, its chromosomal location, and the location of the activator sequences and identities of the regulatory proteins that turn it on and off. Genes also can be categorized by when during the organism's development they are turned on, and in which tissues expression occurs. They can be categorized by the function of their product, whether it's a structural protein, an enzyme, or a functional RNA. They can be categorized by the identity of the metabolic pathway that their product is part of, and by the substrate it modifies or the product it produces. They can be categorized by the structural architecture of their protein products. Clearly this is a wealth of information to be condensed into a reasonable nomenclature. Figure 6-4 shows a portion of the information that may be associated with a single gene.

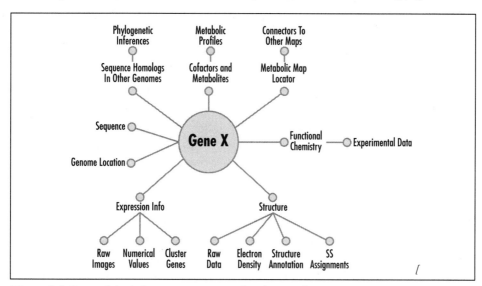

Figure 6-4. Some of the information associated with a single gene

The problem for maintainers of biological databases becomes mainly one of annotation; that is, putting sufficient information into the database that there is no question of what the gene is, even if it does have a cryptic common name, and creating the proper links between that information and the gene sequence and serial number. Correct annotation of genomic data is an active research area in itself, as researchers attempt to find ways to transfer information across genomes without propagating error.

Storage of macromolecular data in electronic databases has given rise to a way of working around the problem of nomenclature. The solution has been to give each new entry into the database a serial number and then to store it in a relational database that knows the proper linkages between that serial number, any number of names for the gene or gene product it represents, and all manner of other information about the gene. This strategy is the one currently in use in the major biological databases. The questions databases resolve are essentially the same questions that arise in developing a nomenclature. However, by using relational databases and complex querying strategies, they (perhaps somewhat unfortunately) avoid the issue of finding a concise way for scientists to communicate the identities of genes on a nondigital level.

Data Annotation and Data Formats

The representation and distribution of biological data is still an open problem in bioinformatics. The nucleotide sequences of DNA and RNA and the amino acid sequences of proteins reduce neatly to character strings in which a single letter represents a single nucleotide or amino acid. The remaining challenges in representing sequence data are verification of the correctness of the data, thorough annotation of data, and handling of data that comes in ever-larger chunks, such as the sequences of chromosomes and whole genomes.

The standard reduced representation of the 3D structure of biomolecule consists of the Cartesian coordinates of the atoms in the molecule. This aspect of representing the molecule is straightforward. On the other hand, there are a host of complex issues for structure databases that are not completely resolved. Annotation is still an issue for structural data, although the biology community has attempted to form a consensus as to what annotation of a structure is currently required.

In the last 15 years, different researchers have developed their own styles and formats for reporting biological data. Biological sequence and structure databases have developed in parallel in the United States and in Europe. The use of proprietary software for data analysis has contributed a number of proprietary data formats to the mix. While there are many specialized databases, we focus here on the fields in which an effort is being made to maintain a comprehensive database of an entire class of data.

3D Molecular Structure Data

Though DNA sequence, protein sequence, and protein structure are in some sense just different ways of representing the same gene product, these datatypes currently are maintained as separate database projects and in unconnected data formats. This is mainly because sequence and structure determination methods have separate histories of development.

The first public molecular biology database, established nearly 10 years before the public DNA sequence databases, was the Protein Data Bank (PDB), the central repository for x-ray crystal structures of protein molecules.

While the first complete protein structure was published in the 1950s, there were not a significant number of protein structures available until the late 1970s. Computers had not developed to the point where graphical representation of protein structure coordinate data was possible, at least at useful speeds. However, in 1971, the PDB was established at the Brookhaven National Laboratory, to store protein structure data in a computer-based archive. A data format developed, which owed much of its style to the requirements of early computer technology. Throughout the 1970s and 1980s, the PDB grew. From 15 sets of coordinates in 1973, it grew to 69 entries in 1976. The number of coordinate sets deposited each year remained under 100 until 1988, at which time there were still fewer than 400 PDB entries.

Between 1988 and 1992, the PDB hit the turning point in its exponential growth curve. By January 1994, there were 2,143 entries in the PDB; at the time of this writing, the PDB has nearly reached the 14,000-entry mark. Management of the PDB has been transferred to a consortium of university and public-agency researchers, called the Research Collaboratory for Structural Bioinformatics, and a new format for recording of crystallographic data, the Macromolecular Crystallographic Information File (mmCIF), is being phased in to replace the antiquated PDB format. Journals that publish crystallographic results now require submission to the PDB as a condition of publication, which means that nearly all protein structure data obtained by academic researchers becomes available in the PDB in a fairly timely fashion.

A common issue for data-driven studies of protein structure is the redundancy and lack of comprehensiveness of the PDB. There are many proteins for which numerous crystal structures have been submitted to the database. Selecting subsets of the PDB data with which to work is therefore an important step in any statistical study of protein structure. As of December 1998, only about 2,800 of the protein chains in the PDB were sufficiently different from each other (having less than 95% of their sequence in common) to be considered unique. Many statistical studies of protein structure are based on sets of protein chains that have no more than 25% of their sequence in common; if this criterion is used, there are still only around 1,000 unique protein folds represented in the PDB. As the amount of biological sequence data available has grown, the PDB now lags far behind the gene-sequence databases.

DNA, RNA, and Protein Sequence Data

Sequence databases generally specialize in one type of sequence data: DNA, RNA, or protein. There are major sequence data collections and deposition sites in Europe, Japan, and the United States, and there are independent groups that mirror all the data collected in the major public databases, often offering some software that adds value to the data.

In 1970, Ray Wu sequenced the first segment of DNA; twelve bases that occurred as a single strand at the end of a circular DNA that was opened using an enzyme. However, DNA sequencing proved much more difficult than protein sequencing, because there is no chemical process that selectively cleaves the first nucleotide from a nucleic acid chain. When Robert Holley reported the sequencing of a 76-nucleotide RNA molecule from yeast, it was after seven years of labor. After Holley's sequence was published, other groups refined the protocols for sequencing, even successfully sequencing an 3,200-base bacteriophage genome. Real progress with DNA sequencing came after 1975, with the chemical cleavage method designed by Allan Maxam and Walter Gilbert, and with Frederick Sanger's chain-terminator procedure.

The first DNA sequence database, established in 1979, was the Gene Sequence Database (GSDB) at Los Alamos National Lab. While GSDB has since been supplanted by the worldwide collaboration that is the modern GenBank, up-to-date gene sequence information is still available from GSDB through the National Center for Genome Resources.

The European Molecular Biology Laboratory, the DNA Database of Japan, and the National Institutes of Health cooperate to make all publicly available sequence data available through GenBank. NCBI has developed a standard relational database format for sequence data, known as the ASN.1 format. While this format promises to make locating the right sequences of the right kind in GenBank easier, there are still a number of services providing access to nonredundant versions of the database.

The DNA sequence database grew slowly through its first decade. In 1992, GenBank contained only 78,000 DNA sequences—a little over 100 million base pairs of DNA. In 1995, the Human Genome Project, and advances in sequencing technology, kicked GenBank's growth into high gear. GenBank currently doubles in size every 6 to 8 months, and its rate of increase is constantly growing.

Genomic Data

In addition to the Human Genome Project, there are now separate genome project databases for a large number of model organisms. The sequence content of the genome project databases is represented in GenBank, but the genome project sites also provide everything from genome maps to supplementary resources for researchers working on that organism. As of October 2000, NCBI's Entrez Genome database contained the partial or complete genomes of over 900 species. Many of these are viruses. The remainder include bacteria; archaea; yeast; commonly studied plant model systems such as *A. thaliana*, rice, and maize; animal model systems such as *C. elegans*, fruit flies, mice, rats, and puffer fish; as well as organelle genomes. NCBI's web-based software tools for accessing these databases are constantly evolving and becoming more sophisticated.

Biochemical Pathway Data

The most important biological activities don't happen by the action of single molecules, but as the orchestrated activities of multiple molecules. Since the early 20th century, biochemists have studied these functional ensembles of enzymes and their substrates. A few research groups have begun work on intelligently organizing and storing these pathways in databases. Two examples of pathway databases are WIT and KEGG. WIT, short for "What Is There?", was developed at Argonne National Labs. It's a database containing reconstructed metabolic pathways for organisms whose genomes have been entirely sequenced. The Kyoto Encyclopedia of Genes and Genomes (KEGG) stores similar data but links in information from sequence, structure, and genetic linkage databases. Both databases are queryable through web interfaces and are curated by a combination of automation and human expertise.

In addition to these whole genome "parts catalogs," other, more specialized databases that focus on specific pathways (such as intercellular signaling or degradation of chemical compounds by microbes) have been developed.

Gene Expression Data

DNA microarrays (or *gene chips*) are miniaturized laboratories for the study of gene expression. Each chip contains a deliberately designed array of probe molecules that can bind specific pieces of DNA or mRNA. Labeling the DNA or RNA with fluorescent molecules allows the level of expression of any gene in a cellular preparation to be measured quantitatively. Microarrays also have other applications in molecular biology, but their use in studying gene expression has opened up a new way of measuring genome functions.

Since the development of DNA microarray technology in the late 1990s, it has become apparent that the increase in available gene expression data will eventually parallel the growth of the sequence and structure databases, and that this is another datatype for which public access to raw data will be desirable. Raw microarray data has just begun to be made available to the public in selective databases, and talk of establishing a central data repository for such data is underway. However, formats for delivering this kind of data are still not standardized; often, it's made available in large spreadsheets or tab-delimited text. Two of the most comprehensive resources for microarray data are the National Human Genome Research Initiative's Microarray Project site and the Stanford Genome Resources site. Since many of the early microarray expression experiments were performed at Stanford, their genome resources site has links to both raw data and, in some cases, databases that can be queried using gene names or functional descriptions. Recently, the European Bioinformatics Institute has been instrumental in developing a set of standards for deposition of microarray data in databases. Several databases also exist for the deposition of 2D gel electrophoresis results, including SWISS-2DPAGE and HSC-2DPAGE. 2D-PAGE is a technology that allows quantitative study of protein concentrations in the cell, for many proteins simultaneously. The combination of these two techniques is a powerful tool for understanding how genomes work.

Table 6-1 summarizes sources on the Web for some of the most important databases we've discussed in this section.

Table 6-1. Major Biological Data and Information Sources

Subject	Source	Link
Biomedical literature	PubMed	*http://www.ncbi.nlm.nih.gov/entrez/query.fcgi*
Nucleic acid sequence	GenBank	*http://www.ncbi.nlm.nih.gov:80/entrez/query.fcgi?db=Nucleotide*
	SRS at EMBL/EBI	*http://srs.ebi.ac.uk*
Genome sequence	Entrez Genome	*http://www.ncbi.nlm.nih.gov:80/entrez/query.fcgi?db=Genome*
	TIGR databases	*http://www.tigr.org/tdb/*
Protein sequence	GenBank	*http://www.ncbi.nlm.nih.gov:80/entrez/query.fcgi?db=Protein*
	SWISS-PROT at ExPASy	*http://www.expasy.ch/spro/*
	PIR	*http://www-nbrf.georgetown.edu*
Protein structure	Protein Data Bank	*http://www.rcsb.org/pdb/*
Entrez Structure DB		
Protein and peptide mass spectroscopy	PROWL	*http://prowl.rockefeller.edu*
Post-translational modifications	RESID	*http://www-nbrf.georgetown.edu/pirwww/search/textresid.html*

Table 6-1. Major Biological Data and Information Sources (continued)

Subject	Source	Link
Biochemical and bio-physical information	ENZYME	*http://www.expasy.ch/enzyme/*
	BIND	*http://www.ncbi.nlm.nih.gov:80/entrez/ query.fcgi?db=Structure*
Biochemical pathways	PathDB	*http://www.ncgr.org/software/pathdb/*
	KEGG	*http://www.genome.ad.jp/kegg/*
	WIT	*http://wit.mcs.anl.gov/WIT2/*
Microarray	Gene Expression Links	*http://industry.ebi.ac.uk/~alan/ MicroArray/*
2D-PAGE	SWISS-2DPAGE	*http://www.expasy.ch/ch2d/ch2d-top.html*
Web resources	The EBI Biocatalog	*http://www.ebi.ac.uk/biocat/*
	IUBio Archive	*http://iubio.bio.indiana.edu*

Searching Biological Databases

There are dozens of biological databases on the Web, and many alternate web interfaces that provide access to the same sets of data. Which ones you use depends on your needs, but it's necessary for you to be aware of what the central data repositories are for various datatypes, and how often the more peripheral databases you might be using synchronize themselves with these central data sources.

Although data repositories for new types of biological data are multiplying, we focus here on two established databases: NCBI's GenBank, for DNA sequence data; and the Protein Data Bank, for molecular structure data. Every database has its own deposition procedures, and for the newer datatypes these are not yet well established or are still changing rapidly. However, both NCBI and RCSB have mature, automated, web-based deposition systems that are not likely to change drastically in the near future.

GenBank

NCBI, in cooperation with EMBL and other international organizations, provides the most complete collection of DNA sequence data in the world, as well as PubMed, a taxonomy database, and an alternate access point for protein sequence and structure data. This database, known as GenBank, may be accessed at *http:// www.ncbi.nlm.nih.gov:80/entrez/query.fcgi?db=Protein*.

NCBI maintains sequence data from every organism, every source, every type of DNA—from mRNA to cDNA clones to expressed sequence tags (ESTs) to high-throughput genome sequencing data and information about sequence polymorphisms. Users of the NCBI database need to be aware of the differences between these datatypes so that they can search the data set that's most appropriate for the work they're doing. The main sequence types that you'll encounter in a full GenBank search include:

mRNA

> Messenger RNA, the product of transcription of genomic DNA. mRNA may be edited by the cell to remove introns (in eukaryotes) or in other ways that result in differences from the transcribed genomic DNA. May be "partial" or "complete"; an mRNA may not cover the complete coding sequence of a gene.

cDNA

> A DNA sequence artificially generated by reverse transcription of mRNA. cDNA roughly represents the coding components of the genomic DNA region that produced the mRNA. May also be "partial" or "complete."

Genomic DNA

> A DNA sequence from genome sequencing that contains both coding and noncoding DNA sequences. May contain introns, repeat regions, and other features. Genomic DNA (as opposed to genome survey sequence) is generally "complete"; it's a result of multiple sequencing passes over a single stretch of a genome, and can generally be relied upon as a fairly good representation of the real DNA sequence of that region.

EST

> Short cDNA sequences prepared from mRNA extracted from a cell under particular conditions or in specific developmental phases (e.g., arabidopsis thaliana 2-week old shoots or valencia orange seeds). ESTs are used for quick identification of genes and don't cover the entire coding sequence of a gene.

GSS

> Genome survey sequence. Single-pass sequence direct from the genome projects. Covers each region of sequence only once and is likely to contain a relatively large proportion of sequencing errors. You'd include genome survey sequence in a search only if you were looking for very new hypothetical gene annotations in a genome project that's still in progress.

There are two ways to search GenBank. The first is to use a text-based query to search the annotations associated with each DNA sequence entry in the database. The second, which we'll discuss in Chapter 7, *Sequence Analysis, Pairwise Alignment, and Database Searching*, is to use a method called BLAST to compare a query DNA (or protein) sequence to a sequence database.

Here's a sample GenBank record. Each GenBank entry contains annotation—information about the gene's identity, the conditions under which it was characterized, etc.—in addition to sequence.

```
LOCUS         AB009351 1412 bp   mRNA   PLN        22-JUN-1999
DEFINITION    Citrus sinensis mRNA for chalcone synthase, complete cds, clone
              CitCHS2.
ACCESSION     AB009351 VERSION AB009351.1 GI:5106368
KEYWORDS      chalcone synthase.
SOURCE        Citrus sinensis young seed cDNA to mRNA, clone:CitCHS2.
  ORGANISM    Citrus sinensis
              Eukaryota; Viridiplantae; Streptophyta; Embryophyta; Tracheophyta;
              euphyllophytes; Spermatophyta; Magnoliophyta; eudicotyledons; core
              eudicots; Rosidae; eurosids II; Sapindales; Rutaceae; Citrus.
REFERENCE     1 (sites)
  AUTHORS     Moriguchi,T., Kita,M., Tomono,Y., EndoInagaki,T. and Omura,M.
  TITLE       One type of chalcone synthase gene expressed during embryogenesis
              regulates the flavonoid accumulation in citrus cell cultures
  JOURNAL     Plant Cell Physiol. 40 (6), 651-655 (1999)
  MEDLINE     99412624
  [...]
FEATURES      Location/Qualifiers
  Source      1..1412
              /organism="Citrus sinensis"
              /db_xref="taxon:2711"
              /clone="CitCHS2"
              /dev_stage="young seed"
              /note="Valencia orange"
  CDS         30..1205
              /codon_start=1
              /product="chalcone synthase"
              /protein_id="BAA81664.1"
              /db_xref="GI:5106369"
              /translation="MATVQEIRNAQRADGPATVLAIGTATPAHSVNQADYPDYYFRIT
              KSEHMTELKEKFKRMCDKSMIKKRYMYLTEEILKENPNMCAYMAPSLDARQDIVVVEV
              PKLGKEAATKAIKEWGQPKSKITHLIFCTTSGVDMPGADYQLTKLIGLRPSVKRFMMY
              QQGCFAGGTVLRLAKDLAENNKGARVLVVCSEITAVTFRGPADTHLDSLVGQALFGDG
              AAAVIVGADPDTSVERPLYQLVSTSQTILPDSDGAIDGHLREVGLTFHLLKDVPGLIS
              KNIEKSLSEAFAPLGISDWNSIFWIAHPGGPAILDQVESKLGLKGEKLKATRQVLSEY
              GNMSSACVLFILDEMRKKSVEEAKATTGEGLDWGVLFGFGPGLTVETVVLHSVPIKA"
  polyA_site  1412
              /note="18 a nucleotides"
BASE COUNT    331 a    358 c    372 g    351 t
ORIGIN
    1 aaacatattc attaagggtt caacttgaaa tggcaaccgt tcaagagatc agaaacgctc
   61 agcgtgccga cggcccggcc accgtcctcg ccatcggtac ggccacgcct gcccacagtg
  121 tcaaccaggc tgattatccc gactattact tcaggatcac aaagagcgag catatgacgg
  [...]
 1261 cacagttgag ttattggttg atcgtgtgaa ggtttagttt tgtcaattga gtttaaggca
 1321 tcgtgccttt tctcttatga cgtcaccaaa cctgggcaac gctttgtgtt tatgcataaa
 1381 ttcttgggaa tttgagaaag tagtaaattt gt
//
```

This sample GenBank record shows the types of fields that can be found in a record from the GenBank Nucleotide database. Everything from the identity of the protein product (in this example, chalcone synthase), the sequence of the protein product, and its starting and ending point within the gene, to the authors who submitted the record and the journal references in which the experiment was described, can be found in the record, and therefore can be used to search the database.

The GenBank search interface is nearly identical to the PubMed search interface. The Limits, Preview/Index, History, and Clipboard features for searching work the same way in the Protein, Nucleic Acid, and Genome databases as they do for PubMed, although the specific fields that can be searched and limits that can be set are somewhat different.

Saving search results

Sequences can be downloaded from NCBI in any of three file formats: the simple FASTA format, which is readable by many sequence analysis programs but contains little information other than sequence; the GenBank flat file format, which is a legacy flat file format that was used at GenBank earlier in its history; and the modern ASN.1 (Abstract Syntax Notation One) format. ASN.1 is a generic data specification, designed to promote database interoperability, that is now used for storage and retrieval of all datatypes—sequences, genomes, structure, and literature—at NCBI. The NCBI Toolkit, a code library for developing molecular biology software, relies on the ASN.1 specification. NCBI, and increasingly, other organizations, rely on the NCBI Toolkit for software development. Learning to use the NCBI Toolkit is a programming challenge well beyond the scope of this book, but there is an excellent tutorial on the Web, developed by Christopher Hogue and his research group at the Samuel Lunenfeld Research Institute.

The casual database user or depositor doesn't have to think too much about file formats, except if database files are to be exported and read by another piece of software. NCBI's forms-based interfaces convert user-entered data into the appropriate format for deposition, and the availability of GenBank files in FASTA format means that most sequence analysis software can handle sequence files you download from NCBI without complicated conversions.

When you save results of a GenBank search, you can choose the format in which to save them. Earlier, you saw what the GenBank sequence record looks like. Many of the computer programs we discuss in the following chapters can read GenBank format sequence files, but some can't. A particularly foolproof format in which to save your sequence files if you're going to process them with other software is the FASTA format. FASTA files have a simple format, a single comment line that begins with a > character, followed by single-character DNA sequence on as many lines as needed to hold the sequence, with no breaks. Of course, some information associated with the gene is lost when you save the data in FASTA format, but if the program you want to use can't read that extra data, it won't be useful to you anyway.

Here's a sample of data in FASTA format:

```
> gene identifier and comments here
MATVQEIRNAQRADGPATVLAIGTATPAHSVNQADYPDYYFRITKSEHMTELKEKFKRMCDKSMIKKRYM
YLTEEILKENPNMCAYMAPSLDARQDIVVVEVPKLGKEAATKAIKEWGQPKSKITHLIFCTTSGVDMPGA
DYQLTKLIGLRPSVKRFMMYQQGCFAGGTVLRLAKDLAENNKGARVLVVCSEITAVTFRGPADTHLDSLV
GQALFGDGAAAVIVGADPDTSVERPLYQLVSTSQTILPDSDGAIDGHLREVGLTFHLLKDVPGLISKNIE
KSLSEAFAPLGISDWNSIFWIAHPGGPAILDQVESKLGLKGEKLKATRQVLSEYGNMSSACVLFILDEMR
KKSVEEAKATTGEGLDWGVLFGFGPGLTVETVVLHSVPIKA
```

To save your files in FASTA format, simply use the pulldown menu at the top of the results page. When you first see it, it will say "Summary," but you can change it to FASTA, ASN.1, and other formats. Once you've chosen your format, you can click the Save button to save all your sequences into one big FASTA-format file. Figure 6-5 shows you how to change the file formats when doing a GenBank search.

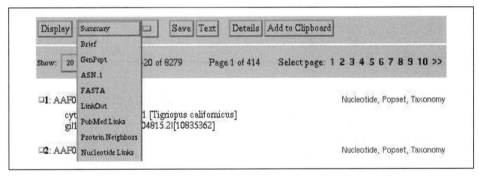

Figure 6-5. Changing the file format to write out your GenBank search results

Saving large result sets

So far, our discussion of information retrieval from databases has assumed that you need access to only a few sequences at a time. However, modern bioinformatics studies increasingly deal with large amounts of sequence data. For example, gene-finding programs (covered in Chapter 7) are trained and tested on hundreds or thousands of DNA sequences; comprehensive studies of protein families can involve analysis of up to thousands of protein sequences as well. While it's possible to select thousands of checkboxes on a web page by hand, it would be better to use an automated tool that can return a large number of sequences based on criteria you specify.

NCBI provides just such a tool in the form of Batch Entrez (*http://www.ncbi.nlm. nih.gov/Entrez/batch.html*). Batch Entrez is one of the tools accessible from the Entrez web site. It's accessed using a web form that allows the user to select sequences by source organism, by an Entrez query (using the query structure described in the section on PubMed), or by a list of accession numbers (provided by the user in the form of a text file). The results of a Batch Entrez search are then packaged in a file that is downloaded to the user's computer, where the complete result set can be edited manually or (even better) using a script.

At this time, not all the biological databases are so kind about providing such services, but all the public databases have FTP sites that allow you to download the entire database in one form or another. That can take up a lot of space on your hard disk, but disk space is cheaper these days than the time it would take you to handle a large set of results on an interactive web site. If you've got a local copy of the big databases that interest you, you can write (or perhaps even download) a script that processes the database, looking for your keyword of choice, and writes out the information you want to a file.

PDB

Unlike NCBI, the Protein Data Bank (*http://www.rcsb.org/pdb/*) is responsible for only one type of molecular data: molecular structures of molecules and, to a growing extent, the underlying raw data sets from which the molecular structures were modeled.

The PDB web site offers three options for searching the database. You can enter a four-letter PDB identifier directly, or search using the SearchLite or SearchFields interfaces. The SearchLite interface is similar to the other query tools we've discussed. You can enter a term or terms into the query box, joined by the operators AND, OR, and BUTNOT.

The SearchFields interface is an innovative design-it-yourself web form system. As you see in Figure 6-6, when you first go to SearchFields, you can scroll down to the bottom of the web form and select which parts of the form you need. If you're only going to be doing a FASTA search to find similar sequences, you don't need a search form that prompts you for keywords to use in searching the Citation Author field. You might want to add a field that lets you search for proteins with a particular ligand or prosthetic group. With the SearchFields interface, you select the form elements you want for your custom PDB search, and click the "New Form" button to generate the new query form.

Whether you use SearchLite or SearchFields, you'll come to the Query Result browser (Figure 6-7), where you can select options for refining your query, downloading your results as structure or sequence files, and even preparing a tabular

Customize the search fields on this query form
Select one or more additional search categories and hit the "New Form" button below (any data entered above will be lost).

General Information

☐ PDB Identifier   ☐ Citation | New Form |

☐ Citation Author   ☐ Compound Information

☐ Contains Chain Type (protein, DNA etc.)   ☐ EC Number and Classification

☐ PDB HEADER   ☐ Ligands and Prosthetic Groups

☐ Experimental Technique   ☐ Source

☐ Text Search   ☐ Experimental Data Availability

☐ Deposition/Release Date

Sequence and Secondary Structure

☐ Number of Chains and Chain Length   ☐ Short Sequence Pattern

☐ FASTA search   ☐ Secondary Structure Content

Crystallographic Experimental Information

☐ Resolution   ☐ Unit Cell Dimensions

☐ Space Group   ☐ Refinement Parameters

☐ Revert to default settings

Figure 6-6. Customizing the PDB's SearchFields form

report of your search results. These options are straightforward to use and well documented on the PDB web site.

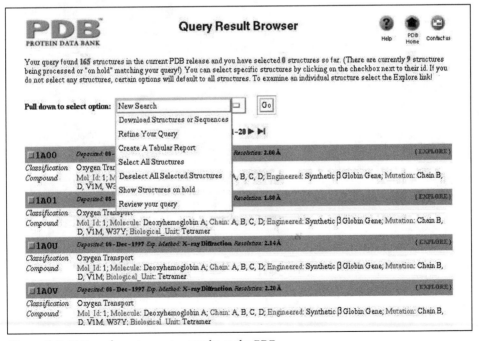

Figure 6-7. Options for using query results at the PDB

The Protein Data Bank makes data available in two formats: the legacy PDB flat-file format, and the newer mmCIF data format. We'll discuss the differences between these two file formats in more detail in Chapter 12, *Automating Data Analysis with Perl*. At this point, little of the available structure-analysis and protein-modeling software handles the mmCIF format, so you are not likely to need to download protein structure data in mmCIF format unless you are developing new software.* You can choose to download the complete set of results from your search as a *tar* archive or a zipped file in either PDB or mmCIF format, as well as in sequence-only FASTA format.

Another convenient way to view protein structure data from the PDB web site is to install a browser plug-in such as RasMol or Chime on your computer. We discuss how to do this in Chapter 9, *Visualizing Protein Structures and Computing Structural Properties*. Once the plug-in is installed and properly configured, you can simply click on a link on the protein's View Structure page and the protein structure is automatically displayed using the plug-in, as shown in Figure 6-8.

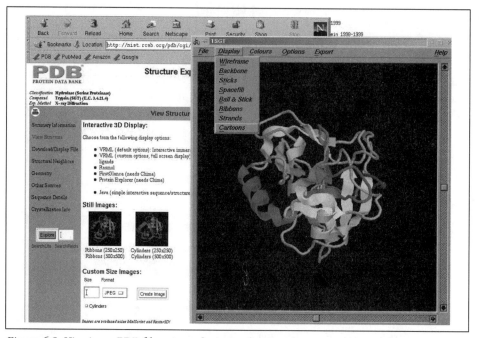

Figure 6-8. Viewing a PDB file using a browser plug-in

---

* The PDB offers a suite of mmCIF and PDB format conversion tools, as well as code libraries for working with mmCIF files.

Depositing Data into the Public Databases

In addition to downloading information from the public databases, you may also submit your own results.

GenBank Deposition

Deposition of sequences to GenBank has been made extremely simple by NCBI. Users depositing only a few sequences can use the web-based BankIt tool, which is a self-explanatory form-based interface accessible from the GenBank main page at NCBI. Users submitting multiple sequences or other complicated submissions can use NCBI's Sequin software, which is available for all major operating systems. Sequin is well documented on the NCBI site. NCBI has recently established two special submission paths: EST sequences should be submitted through dbEST, rather than to GenBank, and genome survey sequences through dbGSS.

PDB Deposition

Deposition of structures to the PDB are done using the AutoDep input tool (ADIT). AutoDep is a tool that integrates data validation software with the deposition process so that the user can receive feedback on data quality during the deposition process. AutoDep is tied in with the curation tools the PDB uses to prepare structure data for inclusion in the data bank.

Finding Software

Bioinformatics is a diffuse field, attracting researchers from many disciplines, and articles about new research developments in bioinformatics are widely distributed in the literature. If you're looking for cutting-edge developments, journals such as *Bioinformatics, Nucleic Acids Research, Journal of Molecular Biology,* and *Protein Science* often publish papers describing innovations in computational biology methods.

If you're looking for proven software for a particular application, there are a number of reliable web resource lists that link to computational biology software sites. Most of the major biological databases have software resource listings and the necessary motivation to keep their listings up-to-date. The PDB links to the best free software packages for macromolecular structure refinement, visualization, and dynamics. TIGR and NCBI provide links to many tools for protein and DNA sequence analysis.

Many organizations and groups provide web implementations of their software. These can be a great time-saver, especially if you are new to the use of noncommercial software packages in research. Many of the bioinformatics programs that we describe in this book are also available as web servers. You can use the web-server versions to get you started and understand the inputs, outputs, and options for the program. However, web servers have their drawbacks. They typically implement only the most popular options in any software package: it's difficult to design a web form that allows you to select every option in a complicated program. They often allow you to run only one calculation at a time. This is fine if you're only interested in analyzing a few sequences or structures, and not so fine if you suddenly find yourself with 500 sequences to analyze.

With a little clever programming, you can develop scripts that allow you to hit a web server with multiple requests without entering them manually into a form, but if you're capable of doing that, you're probably able to download a local copy of the software and run it on your own machine. Using your own processor in such cases avoids slow data transfer to and from remote sites and is also considered more polite than running huge jobs on someone else's web server.

In the next four chapters, we'll discuss the software packages you are most likely to want to use. We'll show you how to set them up on your own computer and use them independent of web interfaces.

We can't cover every available software package and web server in this book; there are just too many. You will eventually want to go out on your own and find new tools to use. Keep a few things in mind when searching for software, and you'll soon be able to judge for yourself if a new computer program is something you want to use.

Judging the Quality of Information

Your ability to judge the quality of information and software you find on the Web will improve as you continue to learn the field. At a more obvious level, however, some simple guidelines can help you screen the information you find. Approach software, information, and services offered on the Web with a healthy skepticism, and you're not likely to be led astray.

Authority

One of the first things to consider when evaluating software, data, or information found on the Internet is the source. Who are the authors? If you don't know the authors presenting the information by reputation, is information about their affiliation and credentials available on the web site? Is their expertise related to the topic or purpose of the web site? Do they make it possible for you to contact them and ask questions?

What is the purpose of the organization sponsoring the information? Is it an academic organization? A government agency? A company? For-profit corporations often have different motivations for offering access to their software and data than nonprofits and academic research groups; usually they are offering a stripped-down version of their software or services to get you to buy a more complete package. An individual academic researcher's site doesn't always have the same need to be all-inclusive as a publicly funded database does. There is nothing inherently wrong with these offerings, but you should be aware of whether or not they are comprehensive, whether all their features are available to the casual user, and why.

Even data and software from national or international public sites are not necessarily entirely correct. It has been estimated that any given sequence in GenBank is likely to contain at least one error. While these errors generally don't render the data meaningless, it's always best to be aware of such issues even when using top-of-the-line public resources. Like any other software you find on the Web, software offered by public agencies such as NCBI and the PDB may still be under development. You can use this software, and much of it is of good quality. If you're basing your research on a beta version (a version still under development) of a software package, just read the documentation carefully so that you know what problems still remain to be worked out.

Transparency

When you send data off to a web server for processing, do you ever wonder exactly what happens to it? You should. It's OK to use your word processor as a black box, but if you're publishing scientific conclusions based on output that you get from a web server or software package, you should definitely know at least the basics of what's under the hood. Anyone can create a web server, based on any software, whether it's good or just goofy. Creating a web server creates an illusion of authority; after all, the authors know how to build a web server that works, so their other software must work too. But that appearance of authority isn't always well founded.

Ideally, you have access to the source code (the human-readable version of a computer program) for whatever the web server is doing, and you can read the source code and know it's doing what you expect. But you might not know how to read source code, and even if you do, you might not be able to get hold of it. Unfortunately, some bioinformatics software authors don't make their source code publicly available, preferring to set up web servers that are easier to use and maintain. This can incidentally have the effect of hiding the underlying method from close scrutiny by users.

If you can't read the source code, what can you read? Most software or web servers made available by academic researchers or government institutions have online help pages and other documentation, including bibliographic information for publications in refereed journals that describe the methods encoded in the software. Read this documentation and understand the method and its results before you use it, just as you would for an experimental method that is new to you.

If the program or server you want to use has no documentation and doesn't allow you to check the source code, you should seriously consider not using that program, unless you have some way to verify its output (for instance, by comparison with the output of a well-documented program). After all, you're drawing conclusions based on your results; do you want to stake your scientific credibility on an unknown quantity?

Timeliness

One of the most frequently linked biology resource sites on the Web is Pedro's Biomolecular Research Tools (*http://www.beri.co.jp/Pedro/research_tools.html*). Sites all over the world still have pointers to this collection of links. And yet, if you click to Pedro's site, you'll find that the collection was last updated in 1996. A funny thing about the Web is that out-of-date sites don't just go away. They remain on the server, looking authoritative. Check web sites for dates. If there's no sign of activity in or reference to the current year, be skeptical.

Timeliness isn't always an issue with software. Software written in 1980 can be as useful and functional now as it was then. What you may encounter are problems compiling software that incorporates proprietary technologies that are no longer supported, or code libraries that have since ceased to be developed.

7

Sequence Analysis, Pairwise Alignment, and Database Searching

We now begin our tour of bioinformatics tools in earnest. In the next five chapters, we describe some of the software tools and applications you can expect to see in current research in computational biology. From gene sequences to the proteins they encode to the complicated biological networks they are involved in, computational methods are available to help you analyze data and formulate hypotheses. We have focused on commonly used software packages and packages we have used; to attempt to encompass every detail of every program out there, however, we'd need to turn every chapter in this book into a book of its own.

The first tools we describe are those that analyze protein and DNA sequence data. Sequence data is the most abundant type of biological data available electronically. While other databases may eventually rival them in size, the importance of sequence databases to biology remains central. Pairwise sequence comparison, which we discuss in this chapter, is the most essential technique in computational biology. It allows you to do everything from sequence-based database searching, to building evolutionary trees and identifying characteristic features of protein families, to creating homology models. But it's also the key to larger projects, limited only by your imagination—comparing genomes, exploring the sequence determinants of protein structure, connecting expression data to genomic information, and much more.

The types of analysis that you can do with sequence data are:

- Knowledge-based single sequence analysis for sequence characteristics
- Pairwise sequence comparison and sequence-based searching
- Multiple sequence alignment

- Sequence motif discovery in multiple alignments

- Phylogenetic inference

We divide our coverage of sequence analysis tools into two chapters. This chapter focuses on programs that operate on single sequences, or compare gene or protein sequences against each other. Chapter 8, *Multiple Sequence Alignments, Trees, and Profiles*, is devoted to multiple sequence alignment methods.

Pairwise sequence comparison is the primary means of linking biological function to the genome and of propagating known information from one genome to another. In this chapter, we discuss the techniques of biological sequence analysis and, most importantly, how to assess the significance of results from sequence comparison. There are also a number of software tools available for doing pairwise sequence comparison. Table 7-1 provides a summary.

Table 7-1. Sequence Analysis Tools and Techniques

What you do	Why you do it	What you use to do it
Gene finding	Identify possible coding regions in genomic DNA sequences	GENSCAN, GeneWise, PROCRUSTES, GRAIL
DNA feature detection	Locate splice sites, promoters, and sequences involved in regulation of gene expression	CBS Prediction Server
DNA translation and reverse translation	Convert a DNA sequence into protein sequence or vice versa	"Protein machine" server at EBI
Pairwise sequence alignment (local)	Locate short regions of homology in a pair of longer sequences	BLAST, FASTA
Pairwise sequence alignment (global)	Find the best full-length alignment between two sequences	ALIGN
Sequence database search by pairwise comparison	Find sequence matches that aren't recognized by a keyword search; find only matches that actually have some sequence homology	BLAST, FASTA, SSEARCH

Chemical Composition of Biomolecules

Sequence analysis techniques can be applied to DNA and RNA (nucleotide) sequences or to protein (amino-acid) sequences. To understand why DNA and protein sequences are informative, you need to know a bit about the chemistry of DNA and proteins. In the context of the sequence analysis applications we discuss in this chapter, it's perfectly fine to think of a DNA sequence as pure information. If you really want to, you can skip over the chemical structures and think of DNA as a string of letters. But keep this fact in mind: the single-letter sequence code that describes DNA and is a simplified representation of a 3D chemical entity, and in some cases the 3D structure of the DNA is really significant.

Proteins, at least at first glance, are more chemically complicated than DNA, and it's impossible to separate the information content of their sequences from the chemical properties of the amino acids they're built from. You can't safely forget about the chemistry of proteins when you're analyzing their sequences, so we'll discuss protein chemistry thoroughly at the beginning of Chapter 9, *Visualizing Protein Structures and Computing Structural Properties*, before we introduce techniques for protein structure analysis. As discussed in Chapter 2, *Computational Approaches to Biological Questions*, DNA is the medium for storing information in cells, and it stores and transmits that information through the sequence of nucleotides that make up the DNA chain. DNA occurs as a "double helix"—two long sequences of nucleotides that are chemical mirror images of each other. This double-helical structure and the chemistry that forces a specific pattern of pairing between nucleotides in the two halves of the helix is what gives DNA the ability to replicate itself and faithfully pass its information from cell to cell and generation to generation. The chemistry of pairing between nucleotide chains also allows the DNA sequence to be transcribed into RNA and translated into proteins.

Composition of DNA and RNA

DNA and RNA are polymer chains composed of a small alphabet of chemically similar compounds. The individual units are called nucleotides. As you can see in Figure 7-1, nucleotides are made up of three distinct parts: a cyclic base, a cyclic sugar (deoxyribose or ribose, respectively), and a phosphate group. Base utilization is different in DNA than in RNA. The DNA code consists of patterns built up from the A (adenine), T (thymine), G (guanine), and C (cytosine) nucleotides, while the RNA code substitutes U (uracil) for T.

Figure 7-2 shows the five nucleotides, which are also referred to as bases. In hydrolyzed double-stranded DNA, there are always equal amounts of A and T nucleotides (A = T). The amounts of G and C in the solution are also always equal (G = C). This is called Chargaff's rule after the researcher who discovered the relationships between A and T, G and C. (Note that there can different amounts of A and T, G, and C; the ratio of A-T to G-C base pairs can vary widely from species to species.)

Watson and Crick Solve the Structure of DNA

The quantitative relationships between adenine and thymine, and cytosine and guanine led Watson and Crick to propose a structural model for DNA in 1953, and

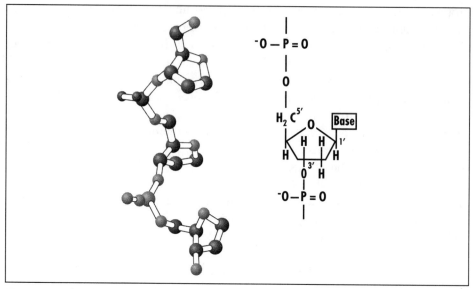

Figure 7-1. The "backbone" bits of DNA and RNA—ribose and deoxyribose phosphates

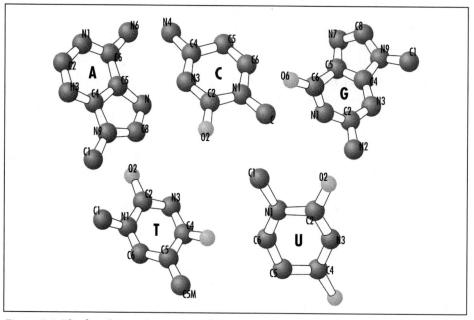

Figure 7-2. The five "bases" that commonly appear in DNA or RNA

later Crick's central dogma of biology. Watson and Crick's model of DNA was based on several observations:

- The x-ray crystallography experiments of their colleague Rosalind Franklin who observed a diffraction pattern from DNA that suggested a helical molecule with a regular repeating structure at a spacing of 3.4 angstroms

- Chargaff's rules

- Experimental evidence that the bases were connected by hydrogen bonds in the DNA molecule

- The knowledge of the correct structural conformations of the bases from x-ray crystallography

What Watson and Crick did was to combine this disparate information to propose the double helix. The double helix of DNA, which has now been determined in atomic detail using x-ray crystallography, is a structure in which adenine pairs with thymine, and guanine with cytosine by hydrogen bonding (Figure 7-3). The hydrogen bonded base pairs form the core of the molecule.

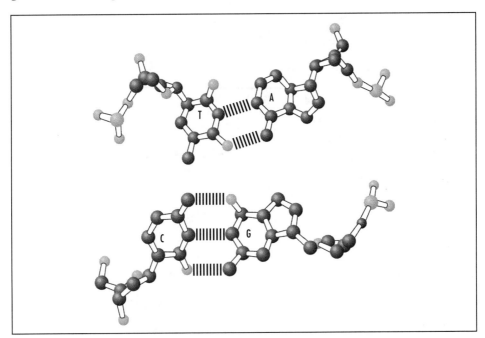

Figure 7-3. Two common base pairs, A–T and G–C

As shown in Figure 7-4, the base pairs stack on top of and parallel to each other with a spacing of 3.4 angstroms. They are held together in sequence by covalent chemical bonds between the sugar group of one nucleotide and the phosphate group of the next. This chain has a directionality: the end left with an exposed phosphate group is called the 5' end, while the end with the exposed ribose group is the 3' end.

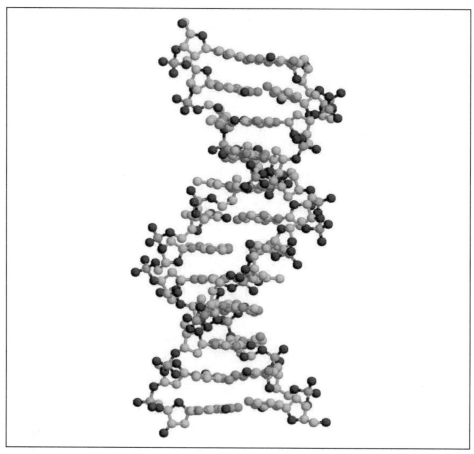

Figure 7-4. Schematic of the DNA chain

The specific chemical pairing of nucleotides in DNA and RNA sequences suggests a mechanism by which each strand of DNA can serve as the template for the synthesis of a complementary strand. The use of a similar nucleotide code in RNA suggests that DNA can also be used as a template for synthesis of RNA. From these two pieces of evidence, Crick proposed his central dogma: that DNA directs its own replication and its transcription into RNA and that RNA is translated into protein.

Development of DNA Sequencing Methods

If you just digest DNA into its four component bases and measure the quantity of each, it tells you nothing about the DNA sequence. Modern methods for DNA sequencing rely on controlled biochemical reactions that allow the base content at each position in the DNA sequence to be quantitated independently. The chemical cleavage method for sequencing DNA relies on the specificity of chemical reagents (reactive substances) to break DNA chains at four specific types of sites. There are reagents that break or cleave the chain specifically after G nucleotides and reagents that cleave specifically after C nucleotides. There are also reagents that cleave less specifically: one to cleave after A and G nucleotides and one to cleave after C and T nucleotides. The method Maxam and Gilbert designed was conceptually simple. Four samples of DNA are required for this method. One type of reagent is mixed with each sample in a quantity that causes each DNA chain in the sample to be broken only one time, on average, at a random location. One end of the DNA is radioactively labeled, and the other is not, so only one piece of each broken chain is radioactive after the chain is cleaved. DNA fragments of different sizes can be separated using an electric current to drive them through a viscous medium called a gel. The larger the fragment, the more it's slowed by the gel, so at the end of some period of time, different-sized radioactive pieces of DNA are spread out at regular intervals down the gel. Figure 7-5 shows a partial autoradiogram of a DNA sequencing gel. Each set of four closely spaced lanes represents an individual sequencing experiment. The gel is read from bottom to top. Each band on the gel identifies the nucleotide present at the position in the sequence, depending on which of the four lanes it appears in. (Image courtesy of Dr. Dennis Dean, Virginia Tech.) If each DNA chain is broken once after a random A, C, G, or T, a uniform distribution of fragments that map the entire sequence of the DNA is created. Depending on which sample the radioactive piece is from, the last base in its sequence is known, and the sequence can be read off the gel from end to end.

Sanger's chain-terminator procedure is the most commonly used sequencing chemistry in modern laboratories. This procedure takes advantage of an enzyme called DNA polymerase, which builds a complementary strand of DNA for an existing single strand. In Sanger's method, the DNA polymerase reaction is carried out in the presence of specific analogues of nucleotides that, when they are incorporated, cause the synthesis of the complementary strand to stop. Four samples are prepared, each containing a small amount of one type of chain terminator. Analogously to the Maxam and Gilbert method, a uniform distribution of DNA fragments is generated, each with a known end residue. The fragments are analyzed based on the strength of this fluorescence signal, giving the sequence of the complementary strand to the original DNA.

The chain termination method is easily automated, and computer-compatible sequencing systems that use this method are readily available. Most genome sequence data is currently generated using this method, though new sequencing methods that don't involve chain cleavage or chain termination are in

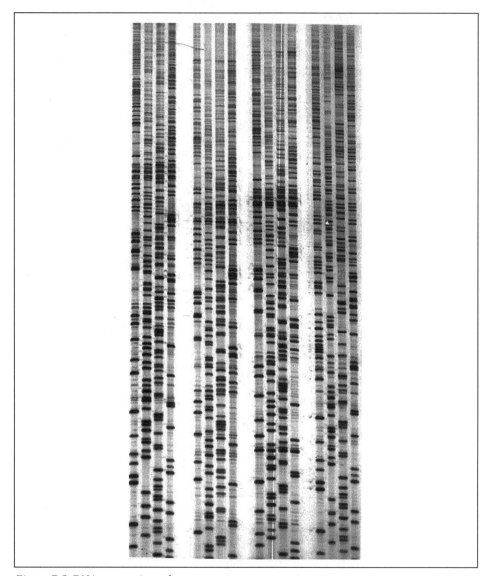

Figure 7-5. DNA sequencing gel

development. We discuss the process of sequencing data analysis and genome assembly further in Chapter 11, *Tools for Genomics and Proteomics.*

The Chemical Composition of Proteins

Unlike DNA, protein polymers consist of a common set of building blocks called amino acids. There are 20 amino acids that make up the standard chemical alphabet used to build proteins. Amino acids are small molecules that share a common motif, of three substituent chemical groups arranged around a central carbon atom. One of the substituent groups is always an amino group; another is always carboxylic acid group. To form the protein polymer, the amino and carboxyl groups react with each other and form a bond called the peptide bond. The third substituent on the central carbon of an amino acid is variable, and it's this property that makes the amino acids into a code for storing information. The sequence of amino acids in a protein is referred to as the protein's primary structure. Protein sequence can be subjected to the same analyses (described later) for DNA sequence. As we describe sequence analysis methods, we will point out ways in which these methods differ for proteins and DNA.

Mechanisms of Molecular Evolution

The discovery of DNA as the molecular basis of heredity and evolution made it possible to understand the process of evolution in a whole new way. Darwin's theory of evolution by natural selection describes the observable process of evolution and speciation. However, it doesn't explain how information is passed from generation to generation, nor does it explain the mechanisms that give rise to, or that limit, variation within each generation.

The two halves of the double-helical DNA molecule serve as a template for replication of the DNA molecule. Even though the molecular rules governing replication of DNA are specific, replication doesn't always occur with perfect fidelity. When a piece of DNA is replicated incorrectly and the error is not corrected by the cell's repair machinery, it's called a mutation.

Mutations can occur in any part of an organism's DNA: in the middle of genes that code for proteins or functional RNA molecules, in the middle of regulatory sequences that govern when a gene is turned on, or out in the "middle of nowhere", in the regions between gene sequences. Mutations can have dramatic effects on the organism's phenotype (its visible or measurable characteristics) or they can have no apparent effect. Over time—thousands or millions of years— mutations that are beneficial or at least not harmful to a species can become fixed in the population, meaning that the mutated form of the gene occurs with a certain frequency among all individuals of a particular species. Over longer time scales, enough mutations may accumulate that new species develop.

There are two classes of mutations: point mutations, in which a change affects a single nucleotide in the DNA sequence; and segmental mutations, which can affect anywhere from a few to many hundreds of adjacent nucleotides.

Point mutations usually result from a single mismatch, in which one nucleotide is mispaired with the template DNA as a new complementary DNA strand is being built. Point mutations become significant only if they occur in the middle of a coding region or signal sequence, and then only if they cause a change in functionality. In coding regions, point mutations can either be synonymous, meaning that the mutated strand codes for the same amino acid as it did before the mutation occurred, or nonsynonymous. The genetic code (which was shown back in Figure 2-3) is degenerate; that is, several different three-letter combinations code for each amino acid. The groups of codons which code for each amino acid are by no means random; instead, nature has arranged a fail-safe mechanism in which several codons that differ by only one nucleotide represent a single amino acid, thereby allowing a little room for synonymous replication errors in DNA.

Segmental mutations, which can result in insertion or deletion of long stretches of DNA, can occur by many different mechanisms, all of which involve mismatching of a strand of DNA either with the wrong partner or with a part of itself. Segmental mutations can result in duplications of whole genes or even large regions of chromosomes; some genetic events can even result in the duplication of entire genomes. Generated by gene and chromosome duplication, redundant copies of genes can be repurposed (through a slow process of mutational trial and error) to perform new functions in the cell. A detailed discussion of these mechanisms is given in the excellent book *Fundamentals of Molecular Evolution*; see the *Bibliography*.

Both types of mutation leave traces in the evolutionary record, that is, in the DNA sequences of living things. Since mutations tend to be preserved only if they are functionally useful (or at least, not harmful), there is a tendency for functionally important parts of sequences to be conserved (to remain constant throughout the evolutionary process) while noncoding or nonfunctional sequences diverge wildly. This tendency to conserve functionally important sequences is the basis for the whole field of sequence analysis; it lets us draw evolutionary connections between genes that are related in sequence.

By comparative study of DNA sequences, and on a larger scale, of whole genomes, it's possible to develop quantitative methods for understanding when and how mutational events occurred, as well as how and why they were preserved to survive in existing species and populations. Genomics and bioinformatics—the production of genome data and the development of tools for analyzing it—have made it possible to examine the evolutionary record and make increasingly quantitative statements about the evolutionary relationship of one species to another. Taxonomies can begin to be based not merely on anatomy but on quantitative measurements of differences in the genetic code. Both point mutations and segmental mutations are explicitly modeled in the scoring schemes for comparison of protein and DNA sequences discussed later in this chapter. Changes in the identity of the residue (nucleotide or amino acid) at a given position in the sequence are scored using standard substitution scores (for example, a positive score for a match and a negative score for a mismatch) or substitution matrices. Insertions and deletions are scored with penalties for gap opening and gap extension.

Genefinders and Feature Detection in DNA

Once a large chunk of DNA has been mapped and sequenced, the task of understanding its function begins. In this section, we describe some programs that search the sequence for genes and other biologically important features. A *feature* is a sequence pattern with some functional significance, such as start and stop codons, splice sites (in the case of eukaryotes), and sequences that are bound by proteins in order to regulate gene expression. Some features can be found by searching for a specific sequence, such as the restriction site cleaved by a given restriction enzyme. Others, such as promoters and genes, aren't so easy to pick out. Analysis of single DNA sequences in search of sequence features is a rapidly growing research area in bioinformatics.

There are two reasons that genefinding and feature detection are such notoriously difficult problems. First, there are a huge number of protein-DNA interactions, many of which have not yet been experimentally characterized, and some of which differ from organism to organism. More importantly, we don't always know what constitutes a binding sequence. Current promoter detection algorithms yield about 20–40 false positives for each real promoter identified. Some proteins bind to specific sequences; others are more flexible in their preference for attachment sites. To complicate matters further, a protein can bind in one part of a chromosome but affect a completely different region hundreds or thousands of base pairs away.

Predicting Gene Locations

Genefinders are programs that identify (or try to, anyway) all the open reading frames in unannotated DNA. They use a variety of approaches to locate genes, but the most successful combine content-based and pattern-recognition approaches. Content-based methods for gene prediction take advantage of the fact that the distribution of nucleotides in genes is different than in non-genes. The GRAIL family of programs developed at Oak Ridge National Laboratories uses a neural network to combine evidence from seven different statistical measures of DNA content (frame bias, periodicities, fractal dimension, coding 6-tuples, in-frame 6-tuples, k-tuple commonality, and repetitive 6-tuple words); subsequent versions measure additional features to better exploit these different types of data. At each position in the DNA sequence, the program weighs each type of information, integrates them, and comes up with a score that represents the likelihood that the region in question is in an ORF or an intergenic region. Pattern-recognition methods look for characteristic sequences associated with genes (start and stop codons, promoters, splice sites) to infer the presence and structure of a gene.

In isolation, each method goes only so far. You have a similar rate of success if you try to identify human faces by looking for either a characteristic skin texture (content) or the presence of a moustache (pattern), but not both. Not surprisingly, the current generation of genefinders combine both methods with additional knowledge, such as gene structure or sequences of other, known genes.

Some genefinders are accessible only though web interfaces, making the interaction very straightforward: the sequence that needs to be examined for genes is submitted to the program, it is processed, and the output is returned. On one hand, this eliminates the need for installation and maintenance of the genefinder on your system, and it provides a relatively uniform interface for the different programs. On the other, if you plan to rely on the results of a genefinder, you should take the time to understand underlying algorithm, find out if the model is specific for a given species or family, and, in the case of content-based models, know which sequences they are. The accuracy of a genefinder can be misleadingly high if it is trained on the same sequence with which you test it.

Some commonly used programs in gene finding include Oak Ridge National Labs' GRAIL, GENSCAN (developed by Chris Burge, now at MIT, and Samuel Karlin at Stanford), PROCRUSTES (developed by Pavel Pevzner and coworkers), and Gene-Wise (developed by Ewan Birney and Richard Durbin). GRAIL combines evidence from a variety of signal and content information using a neural network. GEN-SCAN combines information about content statistics with a probabilistic model of gene structure. PROCRUSTES and GeneWise find open reading frames by translating the DNA sequence and comparing the resulting protein sequence with known protein sequences. PROCRUSTES compares potential ORFs with close homologs, while GeneWise compares the gene against a single sequence or a model of an entire protein family.

Feature Detection

In addition to their role in genefinder systems, feature-detection algorithms can be used on their own to find patterns in DNA sequences. Frequently, these tools help interpret freshly sequenced DNA or choose targets for designing PCR primers or microarray oligomers. Some starting places for tools like these include the Center for Biological Sequence Analysis at the Technical University of Denmark (which has several web-based applications for finding intron-exon splice sites and transcription start sites in eukaryotic DNA), the CodeHop server at the Fred Hutchinson Cancer Research Center (which predicts PCR primers based on conserved protein sequences), and the Tools collection at the European Bioinformatics Institute.

In addition to these special-purpose tools, another popular approach is to use motif discovery programs that automatically find common patterns in sequences. We will examine these programs in greater detail when we look at multiple sequence analysis methods.

DNA Translation

Before a protein can be synthesized, its sequence must be translated from the DNA. Translation of DNA sequence into protein sequence isn't conceptually or computationally difficult. All that is required is the DNA sequence, a genetic code, and a program that reads in one type of sequence and outputs the other.

Any DNA sequence can be translated in six possible ways. The sequence can be translated backward and forward. Because each amino acid in a protein is specified by three bases in the DNA sequence, there are three possible translations of any DNA sequence in each direction: one beginning with the very first character in the sequence, one beginning with the second character, and one beginning with the third character.

Figure 7-6 shows "back-translation" of a protein sequence (shown on the top line) into DNA, using the bacterial and plant plastid genetic code. As you can see, back-translation of a protein sequence into DNA isn't unique. Each amino acid in the short sequence shown can be represented by as many as six codons, and the possible codons can be combined in many ways to produce not one, but hundreds of possible coding sequences, even for a short peptide. However, note that nature has grouped the codons "sensibly": alanine (A) is always specified by a "G-C-X" codon, arginine (R) is specified either by a "C-G-X" codon or an "A-G-pyrimidine" codon, etc. This reduces the number of potential sequences that have to be checked if you (for example) try to write a program to compare a protein sequence to a DNA sequence database.*

A	L	Q	E	R	T	A	S	P	G	S	G	protein sequence
GCC	CTT	CAC	GAA	CGT	ACT	GCC	TCT	CCT	GGT	TCT	GGT	possible codons
GCT	CTC	CAA	GAG	CGC	ACC	GCT	TCA	CCC	GGC	TCA	GGC	
GCA	CTA			CGA	ACA	GCA	TCC	CCA	GGA	TCC	GGA	
GCG	CTG			CGG	ACG	GCG	TCG	CCG	GGG	TCG	GGG	
	TTA			AGA			AGT			AGT		
	TTG			AGG			AGC			AGC		

Figure 7-6. Back-translation from a protein sequence

---

* The more computationally efficient solution to this problem is simply to translate the DNA sequence database in all six reading frames.

There are no markers in the DNA sequence to indicate where one codon ends and the next one begins. Consequently, unless the location of the start codon is known ahead of time, a double-stranded DNA sequence can be interpreted in any of six ways: an open reading frame can start at nucleotide *i*, at *i*+1, or at *i*+2 on either the observed or complementary strand. To account for this uncertainty, when a protein is compared with a set of DNA sequences, the DNA sequences are translated into all six possible amino acid sequences, and the protein query sequence is compared with these resulting conceptual translations. This exhaustive translation is called a "six-frame translation" and is illustrated in Figure 7-7.

```
>gi | 9858881 | gb | AF 291052 Zea mays subsp. parviglumis hemoglobin gene
DNA :  ATGGCACTCGCGGAGGCCGACGACGGCGCGGTGGTCTTCGGCGAGGAGCAG
 +3 :    G  T  R  G  G  R  R  R  R  G  G  L  R  R  G  A  G
 +2 :   W  H  S  R  R  P  T  T  A  R  W  S  S  A  R  S  R
 +1 :  M  A  L  A  E  A  D  D  G  A  V  V  F  G  E  E  Q

DNA :  GAGGCGCTGGTGCTCAAGTCGTGGGCCGTCATGAAGAAGGACGCCGCCAAC
 +3 :    G  A  G  A  Q  V  V  G  R  H  E  E  G  R  R  Q  P
 +2 :   R  R  W  C  S  S  R  G  P  S  *  R  R  T  P  P  T
 +1 :  E  A  L  V  L  K  S  W  A  V  M  K  K  D  A  A  N

DNA :  CTGGGCCTCCGCTTCTTCCTCAAGTAAGTACGTTTCCGTGCTACACACTGC
 +3 :    G  P  P  L  L  P  Q  V  S  T  F  P  C  Y  T  L  P
 +2 :   W  A  S  A  S  S  S  S  K  Y  V  S  V  L  H  T  A
 +1 :  L  G  L  R  F  F  L  K  *  V  R  F  R  A  T  H  C

DNA :  CTGCGCACGTGCGCTTGGGTTGCACCTGCACCGGCGGCCATCGAGCCTGCT
 +3 :    A  H  V  R  L  G  C  T  C  T  G  G  H  R  A  C  S
 +2 :   C  A  R  A  L  G  L  H  L  H  R  R  P  S  S  L  L
 +1 :  L  R  T  C  A  W  V  A  P  A  P  A  A  I  E  P  A
```

Figure 7-7. A DNA sequence and its translation in three of six possible reading frames

Because of the large number of codon possibilities for some amino acids, back-translation of a protein into DNA sequence can result in an extremely large number of possible sequences. However, codon usage statistics for different species are available and can be used to suggest the most likely back-translation out of the range of possibilities.

BLAST and FASTA dynamically translate query and database sequences so you don't need to worry about translating a database before you do a sequence comparison. However, in the event that you need to produce a six-frame translation of a single DNA sequence or translate a protein back into a set of possible DNA sequences, and you don't want to script it yourself, the Protein Machine server (*http://www.ebi.ac.uk/translate/*) at the European Bioinformatics Institute (EBI) will do it for you.

Pairwise Sequence Comparison

Comparison of protein and DNA sequences is one of the foundations of bioinformatics. Our ability to perform rapid automated comparisons of sequences facilitates everything from assignment of function to a new sequence, to prediction and construction of model protein structures, to design and analysis of gene expression experiments. As biological sequence data has accumulated, it has become apparent that nature is conservative. A new biochemistry isn't created for each new species, and new functionality isn't created by the sudden appearance of whole new genes. Instead, incremental modifications give rise to genetic diversity and novel function. With this premise in mind, detection of similarity between sequences allows you to transfer information about one sequence to other similar sequences with reasonable, though not always total, confidence.

Before you can make comparative statements about nucleic acid or protein sequences, a sequence alignment is needed. The basic concept of selecting an optimal sequence alignment is simple. The two sequences are matched up in an arbitrary way. The quality of the match is scored. Then one sequence is moved with respect to the other and the match is scored again, until the best-scoring alignment is found.

What sounds simple in principle isn't at all simple in practice. Choosing a good alignment by eye is possible, but life is too short to do it more than once or twice. An automated method for finding the optimal alignment out of the thousands of alternatives is clearly the right approach, but in order for the method to be consistent and biologically meaningful, several questions must be answered. How should alignments be scored? A scoring scheme can be as simple as +1 for a match and –1 for a mismatch, but what is the best scoring scheme for the data? Should gaps be allowed to open in the sequences to facilitate better matches elsewhere? If gaps are allowed, how should they be scored? Given the correct scoring parameters, what is the best algorithm for finding the optimal alignment of two sequences? And when an alignment is produced, is it necessarily significant? Can an alignment of similar quality be produced for two random sequences? Through the rest of this section, we consider each of these questions in greater detail.

Figure 7-8 shows examples of three kinds of alignment. These are three pairwise sequence alignments generated using a program called ALIGN. In each alignment, the sequences being compared are displayed, one above the other, such that matching residues are aligned. Identical matches are indicated with a colon (:) between the matching residues, while similarities are indicated with a single dot (.). Information about the alignment is presented at the top, including percent identity (the number of identical matches divided by the length of the alignment) and score. Finally, gaps in one sequence relative to another are represented by dashes (–) for each position in that sequence occupied by a gap.

The first alignment is a high-scoring one: it shows a comparison of two closely related proteins (two hemoglobin molecules, one from a sea lamprey and one from a hagfish). Compare that alignment with the second, a comparison of two

```
ALIGN calculates a global alignment of two sequences
  version 2.0uPlease cite: Myers and Miller, CABIOS (1989) 4:11-17
GENPEPT:AF248645_1                                150 aa vs.
GENPEPT:AF156936_1                                149 aa
scoring matrix: BLOSUM50, gap penalties: -12/-2
44.1% identity;        Global alignment score: 428


                   10        20        30        40        50        60
GENPEPT:AF24  MPIVDTGSVAPLSAAEKTKIRSAWAPVYSNYETSGVDILVKFFTSTPAAQEFFPKFKGLT
              :::..: :  .  :: ..: :: .: .:.:.: .: .:.:. ..:.::. ::::..
GENPEPT:AF15  MPITDQGPLPTLSEGDKKAIRESWPQIYQNFEQTGLVVLLEFLQKNPGAQQSFPKFSA--
                   10        20        30        40        50


                   70        80        90       100       110       120
GENPEPT:AF24  TADQLKKSADVRWHAERIINAVNDAVVSMDDTEKMSMKLRDLSGKHAKSFQVDPQYFKVL
              :  .:..:..:.:.: :::::: ..  ::   :.. :..:::..  ::::: .:: :
GENPEPT:AF15  TKCNLEQDNEVKWQASRIINAVNHTIGLMDKEAAMKQYLKELSAKHSSEFQVDPKLFKEL
                   60        70        80        90       100       110


                  130       140       150
GENPEPT:AF24  AAVIADTVAAGDAGFEKLMSMICILLRSAY--
              .:....: : :..::.:.:: :::::.:
GENPEPT:AF15  SAIFVSTIR-GKAAYEKLFSIICTLLRSSYDE
                  120       130       140
```

```
ALIGN calculates a global alignment of two sequences
  version 2.0uPlease cite: Myers and Miller, CABIOS (1989) 4:11-17
GENPEPT:U76030_1                                 166 aa vs.
GENPEPT:AF248645_1                               150 aa
scoring matrix: BLOSUM50, gap penalties: -12/-2
20.6% identity;        Global alignment score: 94


                   10        20        30        40        50
GENPEPT:U760  MALVEDNNAVAVSFSEEQEALVLKSWAILKKDSANIALRFFLKIFEVAPSASQMF-SF--
              : .: :...:: .:. ... .. .:: .. ..... ..:.:  .:..:.: .:
GENPEPT:AF24  MPIV-DTGSVA-PLSAAEKTKIRSAWAPVYSNYETSGVDILVKFFTSTPAAQEFFPKFKG
                   10        20        30        40        50


                   60        70        80        90       100       110
GENPEPT:U760  LRNSDVPLEKNPKLKTHAMSVFVMTCEAAAQLRKAGKVTVRDTTLKRLGATHLK-YGVGD
              : .: :::. .. :: ..  ..... .... :...  :. :   :. : : :.:
GENPEPT:AF24  LTTAD-QLKKSADVRWHAERIINAVNDAVVSMDDTEKMSMK---LRDLSGKHAKSFQVDP
                   60        70        80        90       100       110


                  120       130       140       150       160
GENPEPT:U760  AHFEVVKFALLDTIKEEVPADMWSPAMKSAWSEAYDHLVAAIKQEMKPAE
              .:.:. .. ::.           .: ...:.: . .. :
GENPEPT:AF24  QYFKVLAAVIADTV--------------AAGDAGFEKLMSMICILLRSAY
                  120                         130       140       150
```

```
ALIGN calculates a global alignment of two sequences
  version 2.0uPlease cite: Myers and Miller, CABIOS (1989) 4:11-17
GENPEPT:AF248645_1                                150 aa vs.
GENPEPT:U13831_1                                  134 aa
scoring matrix: BLOSUM50, gap penalties: -12/-2
15.2% identity;        Global alignment score: -47


                   10        20        30        40        50        60
GENPEPT:AF24  MPIVDTGSVAPLSAAEKTKIRSAWAPVYSNYETSGVDILVKFFTSTPAAQEFFPKFKGLT
              : : ...  .. .. ... ..:.. .:  ...  .:: ...: .:
GENPEPT:U138  MT-RDQNGTWEMESNE---NFEGYMKALDIDFATPKIAV---RLTQTKVIDQDGDNFKTKT
                   10        20        30        40        50


                   70        80        90       100
GENPEPT:AF24  TA---------------DQLKKSADVRWHAERIINAVNDAVVSMDDTEKMSMKLRDLSGK
              .   .. :: : : : :.. .:...   :.   .. ::  ...
GENPEPT:U138  TSTFRNYDVDFTVGVEFDEYTKSLDNR-HVKALVTWEGDVLVCVQKGEKENRGWKQW---
                   60        70        80        90       100       110


                  110       120       130       140       150
GENPEPT:AF24  HAKSFQVDPQYFKVLAAVIADTVAAGDAGFEKLMSMICILLRSAY
               .. :.:  .   .:: ...        ..: ..
GENPEPT:U138  ----IEGDKLYLEL---------TCGD--------QVCRQVFKKK
                  120                        130
```

Figure 7-8. Three alignments: high scoring, low scoring but meaningful, and random

distantly related proteins (again, two hemoglobin molecules, in this case taken from lamprey and rice). Cursory inspection shows fewer identical residues are shared by the sequences in the low-scoring alignment than in the high-scoring one. Still, there are several similarities or conservative changes—changes in which one amino acid has been replaced by another, chemically similar residue. The third alignment is a random alignment, a comparison between two unrelated sequences (the lamprey hemoglobin and a human retinol binding protein). Notice that, in addition to the few identities and conservative mutations between the two, large gaps have been opened in both sequences to achieve this alignment. Gene families aren't likely to evolve in this way, and given the lack of similarity between the sequences, you can conclude that these proteins are unrelated.

In describing sequence comparisons, several different terms are commonly used. Sequence identity, sequence similarity, and sequence homology are the most important of these terms. Each means something slightly different, though they are often casually used interchangeably.

Sequence identity refers to the occurrence of exactly the same nucleic acid or amino acid in the same position in two aligned sequences. *Sequence similarity* is meaningful only when possible substitutions are scored according to the probability with which they occur. In protein sequences, amino acids of similar chemical properties are found to substitute for each other much more readily than dissimilar amino acids. These propensities are represented in scoring matrices that score sequence alignments. Two amino acids are considered similar if one can be substituted for another with a positive log odds score from a scoring matrix (described in the next section).

Sequence homology is a more general term that indicates evolutionary relatedness among sequences. It is common to speak of a percentage of sequence homology when comparing two sequences, although that percentage may indicate a mixture of identical and similar sites. Finally, sequence homology refers to the evolutionary relatedness between sequences. Two sequences are said to be homologous if they are both derived from a common ancestral sequence. The terms similarity and homology are often used interchangeably to describe sequences, but, strictly speaking, they mean different things. Similarity refers to the presence of identical and similar sites in the two sequences, while homology reflects a stronger claim that the two sequences share a common ancestor.

Scoring Matrices

What you really want to learn when evaluating a sequence alignment is whether a given alignment is random, or meaningful. If the alignment is meaningful, you want to gauge just how meaningful it is. You attempt to do this by constructing a scoring matrix.

A scoring matrix is a table of values that describe the probability of a residue (amino acid or base) pair occurring in an alignment. The values in a scoring matrix are logarithms of ratios of two probabilities. One is the probability of random occurrence of an amino acid in a sequence alignment. This value is simply the product of the independent frequencies of occurrence of each of the amino acids. The other is the probability of meaningful occurrence of a pair of residues in a sequence alignment. These probabilities are derived from samples of actual sequence alignments that are known to be valid.

In order to score an alignment, the alignment program needs to know if it is more likely that a given amino acid pair has occurred randomly, or that it has occurred as a result of an evolutionary event. The logarithm of the ratio of the probability of meaningful occurrence to the probability of random occurrence is positive if the probability of meaningful occurrence is greater, and negative if the probability of random occurrence is greater. Because the scores are logarithms of probability ratios, they can be meaningfully added to give a score for the entire sequence. The more positive the score, the more likely the alignment is to be significant.

Figure 7-9 shows an example of a BLOSUM45 matrix, a popular substitution matrix for amino acids.

	A	R	N	D	C	Q	E	G	H	I	L	K	M	F	P	S	T	W	Y	V
A	5	-2	-1	-2	-1	-1	-1	0	-2	-1	-1	-1	-1	-2	-1	1	0	-2	-2	0
R	-2	7	0	-1	-3	1	0	-2	0	-3	-2	3	-1	-2	-2	-1	-1	-2	-1	-2
N	-1	0	6	2	-2	0	0	0	1	-2	-3	0	-2	-2	-2	1	0	-4	-2	-3
D	-2	-1	2	7	-3	0	2	-1	0	-4	-3	0	-3	-4	-1	0	-1	-4	-2	-3
C	-1	-3	-2	-3	12	-3	-3	-3	-3	-3	-2	-3	-2	-2	-4	-1	-1	-5	-3	-1
Q	-1	1	0	0	-3	6	2	-2	1	-2	-2	1	0	-4	-1	0	-1	-2	-1	-3
E	-1	0	0	2	-3	2	6	-2	0	-3	-2	1	-2	-3	0	0	-1	-3	-2	-3
G	0	-2	0	-1	-3	-2	-2	7	-2	-4	-3	-2	-2	-3	-2	0	-2	-2	-3	-3
H	-2	0	1	0	-3	1	0	-2	10	-3	-2	-1	0	-2	-2	-1	-2	-3	2	-3
I	-1	-3	-2	-4	-3	-2	-3	-4	-3	5	2	-3	2	0	-2	-2	-1	-2	0	3
L	-1	-2	-3	-3	-2	-2	-2	-3	-2	2	5	-3	2	1	-3	-3	-1	-2	0	1
K	-1	3	0	0	-3	1	1	-2	-1	-3	-3	5	-1	-3	-1	-1	-1	-2	-1	-2
M	-1	-1	-2	-3	-2	0	-2	-2	0	2	2	-1	6	0	-2	-2	-1	-2	0	1
F	-2	-2	-2	-4	-2	-4	-3	-3	-2	0	1	-3	0	8	-3	-2	-1	1	3	0
P	-1	-2	-2	-1	-4	-1	0	-2	-2	-2	-3	-1	-2	-3	9	-1	-1	-3	-3	-3
S	1	-1	1	0	-1	0	0	0	-1	-2	-3	-1	-2	-2	-1	4	2	-4	-2	-1
T	0	-1	0	-1	-1	-1	-1	-2	-2	-1	-1	-1	-1	-1	-1	2	5	-3	-1	0
W	-2	-2	-4	-4	-5	-2	-3	-2	-3	-2	-2	-2	-2	1	-3	-4	-3	15	3	-3
Y	-2	-1	-2	-2	-3	-1	-2	-3	2	0	0	-1	0	3	-3	-2	-1	3	8	-1
V	0	-2	-3	-3	-1	-3	-3	-3	-3	3	1	-2	1	0	-3	-1	0	-3	-1	5

Figure 7-9. The BLOSUM45 matrix, a popular substitution matrix for amino acids

Substitution matrices for amino acids are complicated because they reflect the chemical nature and frequency of occurrence of the amino acids. For example, in the BLOSUM matrix, glutamic acid (E) has a positive score for substitution with aspartic acid (D) and also with glutamine (Q). Both these substitutions are chemically conservative. Aspartic acid has a sidechain that is chemically similar to glutamic acid, though one methyl group shorter. On the other hand, glutamine is similar in size and chemistry to glutamic acid, but it is neutral while glutamic acid is negatively charged. Substitution scores for glutamic acid with residues such as isoleucine (I) and leucine (L) are negative. These residues have neutral, nonpolar sidechains and are chemically different from glutamic acid. The scores on the diagonal of the matrix reflect the frequency of occurrence of each amino acid. For example, with a positive score of 15, it is extremely unlikely that the alignment of a rare tryptophan (W) with another tryptophan is coincidence, while the more common serine (S) has a positive score of only 4 for a match with another serine. It's important to remember that these scores are logarithms, which means that a match of two serines is far from being mere coincidence.

Substitution matrices for bases in DNA or RNA sequence are very simple. By default, the sequence alignment program BLAST uses the scheme of assigning a standard reward for a match and a standard penalty for a mismatch, with no regard to overall frequencies of bases. In most cases, it is reasonable to assume that A:T and G:C occur in roughly equal proportions.

Commonly used substitution matrices include the BLOSUM and PAM matrices. When using BLAST, you need to select a scoring matrix. Most automated servers select a default matrix for you (usually something like BLOSUM62), and if you're just doing a quick sequence search, it's fine to accept the default.

BLOSUM matrices are derived from the Blocks database, a set of ungapped alignments of sequence regions from families of related proteins. A clustering approach sorts the sequences in each block into closely related groups, and the frequencies of substitutions between these within a family derives the probability of a meaningful substitution. The numerical value (e.g., 62) associated with a BLOSUM matrix represents the cutoff value for the clustering step. A value of 62 indicates that sequences were put into the same cluster if they were more than 62% identical. By allowing more diverse sequences to be included in each cluster, lower cutoff values represent longer evolutionary time scales, so matrices with low cutoff values are appropriate for seeking more distant relationships. BLOSUM62 is the standard matrix for ungapped alignments, while BLOSUM50 is more commonly used when generating alignments with gaps.

Point accepted mutation (PAM) matrices are scaled according to a model of evolutionary distance from alignments of closely related sequences. One PAM "unit" is equivalent to an average change in 1% of all amino acid positions. The most commonly used PAM matrix is PAM250. However, comparison of results using PAM and BLOSUM matrices suggest that BLOSUM matrices are better at detecting biologically significant similarities.

Gap Penalties

DNA sequences change not only by point mutation, but by insertion and deletion of residues as well. Consequently, it is often necessary to introduce gaps into one or both of the sequences being aligned to produce a meaningful alignment between them. Most algorithms use a gap penalty to represent the validity of adding a gap in an alignment.

The addition of a gap has to be costly enough, in terms of the overall alignment score, that gaps will open only where they are really needed and not all over the sequence. Most sequence alignment models use affine gap penalties, in which the cost of opening a gap in a sequence is different from the cost of extending a gap that has already been started. Of these two penalties—the gap opening penalty and the gap extension penalty—the gap opening penalties tend to be much higher than the associated extension penalty. This tendency reflects the tendency for insertions and deletions to occur over several residues at a time.

Gap penalties are intimately tied to the scoring matrix that aligns the sequences: the best pair of gap opening and extension penalties for one scoring matrix doesn't necessarily work with another. Scores of –11 for gap opening and –1 for gap extension are commonly used in conjunction with the BLOSUM 62 matrix for gapped-BLAST, while BLOSUM50 uses a –12/–1 penalty.

Dynamic Programming

Dynamic programming methods are a general class of algorithms that are often seen both in sequence alignment and other computational problems. They were first described in the 1950s by Richard Bellman of Princeton University as a general optimization technique. Dynamic programming seems to have been introduced[*] to biological sequence comparison by Saul Needleman and Christian Wunsch, who apparently were unaware of the similarity between their method and Bellman's.

As we mentioned, dynamic programming algorithms solve optimization problems, problems in which there are a large number of possible solutions, but only one (or a small number of) best solutions. A dynamic programming algorithm finds the best solution by first breaking the original problem into smaller subproblems and then solving. These pieces of the larger problem have a sequential dependency; that is, the fourth piece can be solved only with the answer to the third piece, the third can be solved only with the answer to the second, and so on. Dynamic programming works by first solving all these subproblems, storing each intermediate solution in a table along with a score, and finally choosing the sequence of solutions that yields the highest score. The goal of the dynamic programming algorithm is to maximize the total score for the alignment. In order to do this, the number of high-scoring residue pairs must be maximized and the number of gaps and low-scoring pairs must be minimized.

---

[*] Or, as mathematicians might say, "rediscovered." Because computational biology combines research from so many different areas, this independent discovery happens often and is only noticed later.

In sequence comparison, the overall problem is finding the best alignment between two sequences. This problem is broken down into subproblems of aligning each residue from one sequence with each residue from the other. The solution is a decision as to whether the residues should be aligned with each other, a gap should be introduced in the first sequence, or a gap should be introduced in the second sequence. Each high-scoring choice rules out the other two low-scoring possibilities, so that if information about the accumulated scores is stored at each step, every possible alignment need not be evaluated.

The algorithm uses an ($m \times n$) matrix of scores (illustrated in Figure 7-10) in which m and n are the lengths of the sequences being aligned. Starting with the alignment of a gap against itself (which is given the initial score zero), the algorithm fills in the matrix one row at a time. At each position in the matrix, the algorithm computes the scores that result for each of its three choices, selects the one that yields the highest score, then stores a pointer at the current position to the preceding position that was used to arrive at the high score. When every position in the matrix has been filled in, a traceback step is performed, and the highest-scoring path along the pointers is followed back to the beginning of the alignment.

	-	g	c	t	g	g	a	a	g	g	c	a	t
-	0	0	0	0	0	0	0	0	0	0	0	0	0
g	0	5	0	0	5	5	0	0	5	5	0	0	0
c	0	0	10	3	0	1	1	0	0	1	10	3	0
a	0	0	3	6	0	0	6	6	-g	0	3	15	8
g	0	5	0	0	11	5	0	2	11	5	0	8	11
a	0	0	1	0	4	7	10	5	4	7	1	5	4
g	0	5	0	0	5	9	3	6	10	9	3	0	1
c	0	0	10	3	0	2	5	0	3	6	14	7	0
a	0	0	3	6	0	0	7	10	3	0	7	19	12
c	0	0	5	0	2	0	0	3	6	0	5	12	15
t	0	0	0	10	3	0	0	0	0	2	0	5	17
					g	a	a	g	-	g	c	a	
					g	c	a	g	a	g	c	a	

Figure 7-10. A matrix of scores comparing two sequences; continuous high-scoring matches are highlighted

Global Alignment

One alignment scenario you may encounter is the alignment of two sequences along their whole length. The algorithm for alignment of whole sequences is called the Needleman-Wunsch algorithm. In this scenario, an optimal alignment is built up from high-scoring alignments of subsequences, stepping through the matrix from top left to bottom right. Only the best-scoring path can be traced through the matrix, resulting in an optimal alignment.

Using ALIGN to produce a global sequence alignment

Now that we have seen the theory behind the global alignment of two sequences, let's examine a program that implements this algorithm. ALIGN is a simple utility for computing global alignments. It is part of the FASTA software distribution, described later in this chapter. The programs in the FASTA distribution are easily run from the Unix command line, although many of them have been incorporated into the SDSC Biology Workbench web-based sequence analysis software, if you prefer to access them through a point-and-click interface. The FASTA programs compile easily under Linux; however, once they are compiled, you need to link them into your */usr/local/bin* directory or some other sensible location by hand.

To run ALIGN and any of the other FASTA programs, you need sequence data in FASTA format. This is one of the most frequently used sequence formats and probably the simplest. To use ALIGN, each of the sequences you are aligning should be in a separate file.

A sequence in FASTA format* looks like this:

```
>2HHB:A HEMOGLOBIN (DEOXY) - CHAIN A
VLSPADKTNVKAAWGKVGAHAGEYGAEALERMFLSFPTTKTYFPHFDLSHGSAQVKGHGK
KVADALTNAVAHVDDMPNALSALSDLHAHKLRVDPVNFKLLSHCLLVTLAAHLPAEFTPA
VHASLDKFLASVSTVLTSKYR
```

The FASTA format is very flexible, and it is one of the most commonly used formats for sequence analysis programs. A FASTA file contains one or more records in FASTA format, separated by empty lines. Each record consists of a human-readable comment followed by a nucleotide or protein sequence. The comment appears in the first line of the record; it must begin with a greater-than (>) symbol followed by one or more identifiers for the sequence. The comment may contain information about the molecule represented by the sequence, such as the protein or gene name and source organism. In the previous example, the identifier is a PDB code (2HHB), followed by a description of the sequence (the A chain of a deoxyhemoglobin protein). The remainder of the record contains the sequence itself, divided into separate lines by line breaks. Lines are usually 60 characters long, but the format doesn't specify a line length. Programs that take FASTA data as input (such as ALIGN) usually make allowances for FASTA's free-form nature.

---

* Also known as Pearson format, after the author of the FASTA software, William Pearson.

Still, it's a good practice to check the program's documentation to make sure that your data is appropriately formatted.

To use ALIGN, simply enter *align* at the command prompt. You are then prompted for sequence filenames. Results are sent to standard output. The ASCII format for pairwise alignments that is produced by FASTA is still commonly used, although there is a trend toward use of more easily parsed alignment formats:

```
Output scoring matrix: BLOSUM50, gap penalties: -12/-2 43.2% identity;
Global alignment score: 374

                  10        20        30        40                50
2HHB_A  V-LSPADKTNVKAAWGKVGAHAGEYGAEALERMFLSFPTTKTYFPHF-DLS---HGSA
        : :.: .:. : : :::: .. : :.::: :.... .: :. .: : ::: :.
2HHB:B  VHLTPEEKSAVTALWGKV-NVDEVGGEALGRLLVVYPWTQRFFESFGDLSTPDAVMGNP
                  10        20        30        40        50
                60        70        80        90       100       110
2HHB_A  QVKGHGKKVADALTNAVAHVDDMPNALSALSDLHAHKLRVDPVNFKLLSHCLLVTLAAHL
        .::.::::: :.....::.:.. .....::.:: ::.::: ::..::.. :. .:: :.
2HHB:B  KVKAHGKKVLGAFSDGLAHLDNLKGTFATLSELHCDKLHVDPENFRLLGNVLVCVLAHHF
                60        70        80        90       100       110
               120       130       140
2HHB_A  PAEFTPAVHASLDKFLASVSTVLTSKYR
        :::: :.:. .: .:.:....:. ::.
2HHB:B  GKEFTPPVQAAYQKVVAGVANALAHKYH
               120       130       140
```

The FASTA distribution contains a sample HTML form and CGI script for use with the program LALIGN, a pairwise local alignment program. The script can be modified to work with the ALIGN program if a web-based interface is desired.

Local Alignment

The most commonly used sequence alignment tools rely on a strategy called *local alignment*. The global alignment strategy discussed earlier assumes that the two sequences to be aligned are known and are to be aligned over their full length. In the scenarios that are encountered most often with sequence alignment, however, you are either searching with one sequence against a sequence database looking for unknown sequences, or searching a very long DNA sequence, such as part of a genome, for partial segments that match a query sequence. In protein or gene sequences that do have some evolutionary relatedness, but which have diverged significantly from each other, short homologous segments may be all the evidence of sequence homology that remains.

The version of the dynamic programming algorithm that performs local alignment of two sequences is known as the Smith-Waterman algorithm. Named for its inventors, Dr. Temple Smith and Dr. Michael Waterman, this algorithm is similar to the Needleman-Wunsch algorithm except that an additional choice is allowed when tracing through the matrix. A local alignment isn't required to extend from beginning to end of the two sequences being aligned. If the cumulative score up to some point in the sequence is negative, the alignment can be abandoned and a new alignment started. The alignment can also end anywhere in the matrix.

Tools for local alignment

One of the most frequently reported implementations of the Smith-Waterman algorithm for database searching is the program SSEARCH, which is part of the FASTA distribution described later. LALIGN, also part of the FASTA package, is an implementation of the Smith-Waterman algorithm for aligning two sequences.

Sequence Queries Against Biological Databases

A common application of sequence alignment is searching a database for sequences that are similar to a query sequence. In these searches, an alignment of a sequence hundreds or thousands of residues long is matched against a database of at least tens of thousands of comparably sized sequences. Using dynamic programming-based methods, this isn't very practical unless special-purpose hardware is available. Instead, for routine searches, special heuristic database-searching methods are used. Heuristic methods exploit knowledge about sequences and alignment statistics to make these large-scale searches efficient and practical. While they don't guarantee optimal alignments, they make sensitive searches of large sequence databases possible. In this section, we describe BLAST and FASTA, two commonly used database-searching programs.

Local Alignment-Based Searching Using BLAST

By far, the most popular tool for searching sequence databases is a program called BLAST (Basic Local Alignment Search Tool). BLAST is the algorithm at the core of most online sequence search servers.[*] It performs pairwise comparisons of sequences, seeking regions of local similarity, rather than optimal global alignments between whole sequences.

BLAST can perform hundreds or even thousands of sequence comparisons in a matter of minutes. And in less than a few hours, a query sequence can be compared to an entire database to find all similar sequences. BLAST is so popular for this purpose that it's become a verb in the computational biology community, as in "I BLASTed this sequence against GenBank and came up with three matches."

---

[*] To give you perspective on how long the common tools of bioinformatics have been available, the original BLAST paper by Altschul et al. was published in the *Journal of Molecular Biology* in October 1990.

The BLAST algorithm

Local sequence alignment searching using a standard Smith-Waterman algorithm is a fairly slow process. The BLAST algorithm, which speeds up local sequence alignment, has three basic steps. First, it creates a list of all short sequences (called *words* in BLAST terminology) that score above a threshold value when aligned with the query sequence. Next, the sequence database is searched for occurrences of these words. Because the word length is so short (3 residues for proteins, 11 residues for nucleic acids), it's possible to search a precomputed table of all words and their positions in the sequences for improved speed. These matching words are then extended into ungapped local alignments between the query sequence and the sequence from the database. Extensions are continued until the score of the alignment drops below a threshold. The top-scoring alignments in a sequence, or maximal-scoring segment pairs (MSPs), are combined where possible into local alignments. Originally, BLAST searched only for ungapped alignments. However, new additions to the BLAST software package that do search for gapped alignments have since been introduced.

NCBI BLAST and WU-BLAST

There are two implementations of the BLAST algorithm: NCBI BLAST and WU-BLAST. Both implementations can be used as web services and as downloadable software packages. NCBI BLAST is available from the National Center for Biotechnology Information (NCBI), while WU-BLAST is an alternate version that grew out of NCBI BLAST 1.4 and is developed and maintained by Dr. Warren Gish and coworkers at Washington University.

NCBI BLAST is the more commonly used of the two. The most recent versions of this program have focused on the development of methods for comparing multiple-sequence profiles (see Chapter 8). WU-BLAST, on the other hand, has developed a different system for handling gaps as well as a number of features (such as filtering for repeats) that are useful for searching genome sequences. Consequently, TIGR, Stanford's yeast genome server, Berkeley's Drosophila genome project, and others use WU-BLAST 2.0 as the sequence-comparison tool for searching their genome sequence data via the Web. As of this writing, WU-BLAST 2.0, the most recent version of the software, is copyrighted. NCBI BLAST and WU-BLAST's previous version, 1.4, are both in the public domain and freely available to all researchers. Because of its ubiquity we focus on NCBI BLAST in the following section, but WU-BLAST is an alternative. For more information on these flavors of BLAST see the NCBI web site at http://*ncbi.nlm.nih.gov*, or the WU-BLAST web site at *http://blast.wustl.edu.*

What do the various BLAST programs do?

Frequent users of BLAST can also download and install BLAST binaries on their own machines. BLAST installs easily on a Linux system. Simply create a new directory (e.g., */usr/local/blast*), move the archive into it, and extract. Here are the four main executable programs in the BLAST distribution:

[blastall]

> Performs BLAST searches using one of five BLAST programs: *blastp, blastn, blastx, tblastn,* or *tblastx*

[blastpgp]

> Performs searches in PSI-BLAST or PHI-BLAST mode

[bl2seq]

> Performs a local alignment of two sequences

[formatdb]

> Converts a FASTA-format flat file sequence database into a BLAST database

blastall encompasses all the major options for ungapped and gapped BLAST searches. A full list of its command-line arguments can be displayed with the command *blastall –*:

[–p]

> Program name. Its options include:
>
> *blastp*
>
> > Protein sequence (PS) query versus PS database
>
> *blastn*
>
> > Nucleic acid sequence (NS) query versus NS database
>
> *blastx*
>
> > NS query translated in all six reading frames versus PS database
>
> *tblastn*
>
> > PS query versus NS database dynamically translated in all six reading frames
>
> *tblastx*
>
> > Translated NS query versus translated NS database—computationally intensive

[–d]

> Database name. Each indexed database consists of several files; the name is the common portion of those filenames.

[–i]

> Query sequence filename. Defaults to standard input if not specified.

[–e]

> Expectation value cutoff. (See the later section "Evaluating BLAST results.")

[–m]

> Alignment view. Its options include:
>
> 0   Pairwise
>
> 1   Master-slave, show identities
>
> 2   Master-slave, no identities
>
> 3   Flat master-slave, show identities
>
> 4   Flat master-slave, no identities
>
> 5   Master-slave, no identities, blunt ends
>
> 6   Flat master-slave, no identities, blunt ends

[–o]

> Output file name. Defaults to standard output if not specified.

[–G]

> Gap opening penalty. Defaults to 11 (for BLOSUM63 matrix).

[–E]

> Gap extension penalty. Defaults to 1 (for BLOSUM63 matrix).

[–q]

> Nucleotide mismatch penalty. *blastn* only. Defaults to –3.

[–r]

> Reward for nucleotide match. *blastn* only. Defaults to 1.

[–b]

> Number of alignments to show.

[–g]

> Perform gapped alignment. T/F. Unavailable with *tblastx*.

[–M]

> Scoring matrix. Defaults to BLOSUM62.

[–T]

> Produce HTML output. T/F. Defaults to F.

These are the command-line options you are most likely to use, but there are a large number of other options available. As you become familiar with BLAST, you may want to learn to use them.

blastpgp allows you to use two new BLAST modes: PHI-BLAST (Pattern Hit Initiated BLAST) and PSI-BLAST (Position Specific Iterative BLAST). PHI-BLAST uses protein motifs, such as those found in PROSITE and other motif databases, to increase the likelihood of finding biologically significant matches. PSI-BLAST uses an iterative alignment procedure to develop position-specific scoring matrices, which increases its capability to detect weak pattern matches. Both methods are discussed further when we get to multiple sequence analysis in Chapter 8.

bl2seq allows the comparison of two known sequences using the *blastp* or *blastn* programs. Most of the command-line options for *bl2seq* are similar to those for *blastall*.

Building a local database with formatdb

> Usage: `formatdb -i araseed.nt -p F -o T`

Although BLAST is available on many web servers, one of the benefits of installing and using BLAST locally is the ability to create your own sequence databases. For instance, you may have a set of sequences that aren't yet published or publicly distributed. They're not in the GenBank database, so if you can't run BLAST on your own machine, how do you search them?

The program *formatdb* accepts an input sequence database either in FASTA format or in NCBI's ASN.1 format (described in Chapter 12, *Automating Data Analysis with Perl*). On the program command line it is necessary to specify the input filename, whether the input is a protein or nucleic acid sequence, and whether you want to create indexes for the database or not. There are other command-line options available, which can be viewed by trying to run *formatdb* with no command-line options specified.

The files created are:

```
araseed.nt.nhr
araseed.nt.nin
araseed.nt.nsd
araseed.nt.nsi
araseed.nt.nsq
```

Evaluating BLAST results

A BLAST search in a sequence database can produce dozens or hundreds of candidate alignments. Out of these alignments, how can you tell which are really significantly homologous, and which are merely the best matches between unrelated sequences? BLAST provides three related pieces of information that allow you to interpret its results: raw scores, bit scores, and E-values.

The *raw score* for a local sequence alignment is the sum of the scores of the maximal-scoring segment pairs (MSPs) that make up the alignment. Because of differences between scoring matrices, raw scores aren't always directly comparable. *Bit scores* are raw scores that have been converted from the log base of the scoring matrix that creates the alignment to log base 2. This rescaling allows bit scores to be compared between alignments.

E-values provide information about the likelihood that a given sequence alignment is significant. An alignment's E-value indicates the number of alignments one expects to find with a score greater than or equal to the observed alignment's score in a search against a random database. Thus, a large E-value (5 or 10) indicates that the alignment probably has occurred by chance, and that the target sequence has been aligned to an unrelated sequence in the database. E-values of 0.1 or 0.05 are typically used as cutoffs in sequence database searches. Using a larger E-value cutoff in a database search allows more distant matches to be found, but it also results in a higher rate of spurious alignments. Of the three, E-values are the values most often reported in the literature.

There is a limit beyond which sequence similarity becomes uninformative about the relatedness of the sequences being compared. This limit is encountered below approximately 25% sequence similarity for protein sequences of normal length, although research continues to push at this boundary. In the case of protein sequences with low sequence similarity that are still believed to be related, structural analysis techniques may provide evidence for such a relationship. Where structure is unknown, sequences with low similarity are categorized as unrelated, but that may mean only that the evolutionary distance between sequences is so great that a relationship can't be detected.

Local Alignment Using FASTA

Another heuristic method for local sequence alignment is the FASTA algorithm. FASTA predates BLAST, and it is still actively maintained by Dr. William Pearson at the University of Virginia. Like BLAST, it is available both as a service over the Web and as a downloadable set of programs. In this section, we describe the current version of the FASTA algorithm and some of the programs included in the FASTA distribution.

The FASTA algorithm

FASTA first searches for short sequences (called ktups)* that occur in both the query sequence and the sequence database. Then, using the BLOSUM50 matrix, the algorithm scores the 10 ungapped alignments that contain the most identical ktups. These ungapped alignments are tested for their ability to be merged into a gapped alignment without reducing the score below a threshold. For those merged alignments that score over the threshold, an optimal local alignment of that region

---

* An abbreviation for k tuples, or ordered sequences of k residues.

is then computed, and the score for that alignment (called the optimized score) is reported.

FASTA ktups are shorter than BLAST words, typically 1 or 2 for proteins, and 4 or 6 for nucleic acids. Lower ktup values result in slower but more sensitive searches, while higher ktup values yield faster searches with fewer false positives.

The FASTA programs

The FASTA distribution contains search programs that are analogous to the main BLAST modes, with the exception of PHI-BLAST and PSI-BLAST, as well as programs for global and local pairwise alignment and other useful functions. The FASTA programs listed here all compile easily on a Linux system:

[fasta]
> Compares a protein sequence against a protein database (or a DNA sequence against a DNA database) using the FASTA algorithm

[ssearch]
> Compares a protein sequence against a protein database (or DNA sequence against a DNA database) using the Smith-Waterman algorithm

[fastx/fasty]
> Compares a DNA sequence against a protein database, performing translations on the DNA sequence

[tfastx/tfasty]
> Compares a protein sequence against a DNA database, performing translations on the DNA sequence database

[align]
> Computes the global alignment between two DNA or protein sequences

[lalign]
> Computes the local alignment between two DNA or protein sequences

As of this writing, all these programs except ALIGN and LALIGN are available in the FASTA 3.3 package; for now, ALIGN and LALIGN are available only in the FASTA 2 distribution.

Multifunctional Tools for Sequence Analysis

Several research groups and companies have assembled web-based interfaces to collections of sequence tools. The best of these have fully integrated tools, public databases, and the ability to save a record of user data and activities from one use to another. If you're searching for matches to just one or a few sequences and you want to search the standard public databases, these portals can save you a lot of time while providing most of the functionality and ease of use of a commercial sequence analysis package. In some cases, you'll have to pay for a license or subscription to access the full functionality of these sites; others are freely accessible.

NCBI SEALS

The NCBI SEALS project aims to develop a Perl-based command-line environment for Systematic Analysis of Lots of Sequences. SEALS is far from a fully automated genome analysis tool, and it isn't intended to be. What SEALS does provide is an enhancement to the command-line environment on Unix systems. It is composed of a large suite of scripts with a variety of useful functions: converting file formats, manipulating BLAST results and FASTA files, database retrieval, piping files into Netscape, and a host of other features that make your data easier to look at without requiring a resource-sucking GUI. SEALS runs on Unix systems and is probably most useful for those who are already Unix aficionados. Before you write a script to process a lot of sequences, check to see if the process you want has been implemented in SEALS.

The Biology Workbench

The San Diego Supercomputing Center offers access to sequence-analysis tools through the Biology Workbench. This resource has been freely available to academic users in one form or another since 1995. Users obtain a login and password at the SDSC site, and work sessions and data can be saved securely on the server.

The Biology Workbench offers keyword and sequence-based searching of nearly 40 major sequence databases and over 25 whole genomes. Both BLAST and FASTA are implemented as search and alignment tools in the Workbench, along with several local and global alignment tools, tools for DNA sequence translation, protein sequence feature analysis, multiple sequence alignment, and phylogenetic tree drawing. The Workbench group has not yet implemented profile tools, such as MEME, HMMer, or sequence logo tools, although PSI-BLAST is available for sequence searches.

Although its interface can be somewhat cumbersome, involving a lot of window scrolling and button clicking, the Biology Workbench is still the most comprehensive, convenient, and accessible of the web-based toolkits. One of its main benefits is that many sequence file formats are accepted and translated by the software. Users of the Workbench need never worry about file type incompatibility and can move seamlessly from keyword-based database search, to sequence-based search, to multiple alignment, to phylogenetic analysis.

DoubleTwist

Another entry into the sequence analysis portal arena is DoubleTwist at *http://doubletwist.com*. This site allows you to submit a sequence for comparison to multiple databases using BLAST. It also provides "agents" that monitor databases for new additions that match a submitted sequence and automatically notifies the user. These services, as well as access to the EcoCyc pathways database and to an online biology research protocols database, are free with registration at the site at the time of this writing.

Multiple Sequence Alignments, Trees, and Profiles

In Chapter 7, *Sequence Analysis, Pairwise Alignment, and Database Searching*, we introduced the idea of using sequence alignment to find and compare pairs of related sequences. Biologically interesting problems, however, often involve comparing more than two sequences at once. For example, a BLAST or FASTA search can yield a large number of sequences that match the query. How do you compare all these resulting sequences with each other? In other words, how can you examine these sequences to understand how they are related to one another?

One approach is to perform pairwise alignments of all pairs of sequences, then study these pairwise alignments individually. It's more efficient (and easier to comprehend), however, if you compare all the sequences at once, then examine the resulting ensemble alignment. This process is known as *multiple sequence alignment*. Multiple sequence alignments can be used to study groups of related genes or proteins, to infer evolutionary relationships between genes, and to discover patterns that are shared among groups of functionally or structurally related sequences. In this chapter, we introduce some tools for creating and interpreting multiple sequence alignments and describe some of their applications, including phylogenetic inference and motif discovery. Phylogenetic inference and motif discovery are rooted in evolutionary theory, so before we dive into a discussion of that area of bioinformatics, let's take a minute to review the history and theory of evolution.

The Morphological to the Molecular

In order to ground our discussion of the details of multiple sequence alignment, let's take another brief look at evolution. One of the goals of biology has been the creation of a taxonomy for living things, a method of organizing species in terms of their relationships to one another. Early biologists classified species solely according to their morphology—the physical appearance of the organism—and later, as dissection became a more common practice, their anatomy.

Naturalists also discovered fossils of creatures that didn't resemble anything alive at the time, but were thought to have once been living things. This evidence introduced the possibility that life on Earth had changed over time. It also suggested that the interrelationship between species isn't static, but rather is the result of an evolutionary process. As understanding of the geophysical processes of the planet improved, the amount of time required for such changes to occur became clearer. It is now widely accepted by scientists that life on Earth is approximately 3.5 billion years old. Fossil records of single-celled organisms resembling bacteria, with an estimated age of 3.5 billion years, have been found and catalogued.

The evolutionary theory that was eventually accepted by most biologists was that of Charles Darwin. Darwin proposed that every generation of living creatures has some variability. The individuals whose variations predispose them to survive in their environment are the ones who reproduce most successfully and pass on their traits in greater numbers. In light of this theory, it has been hypothesized that the diversity of life forms on Earth is due to divergence, perhaps even from one common ancestral unicellular organism, to fill various biological niches.

Molecular evolution extends the concept of evolution to the level of DNA and protein sequences. Although the replication of DNA sequence is a very accurate process, small replication errors accumulate over time, along with radiation damage and other mutations or alterations of the genomic sequence. Instead of evolutionary pressure selecting organisms based on morphological traits, selection occurs at the level of mutations. Consequently, the only mutations observed in genes from healthy organisms are those that don't result in the organisms' death.

Because these changes between gene sequences are incremental, we can take homologous genes—genes with common evolutionary origin and related function—from a number of divergent organisms and compare them by aligning identical or similar residues. This comparison of multiple sequences shows which regions of a gene (or its derived protein) are sensitive to mutation and which are tolerant of having one residue replaced by another. Thus, we can develop hypotheses about the molecular events underlying the evolution of these sequences. Many bioinformatics methods, including pairwise sequence comparison and sequence database searching, are based on this observation that homologous genes have similar sequences.

In considering sequence similarity, there is one additional wrinkle to bear in mind: the difference between orthologs and paralogs. The chemical processes of molecular evolution are responsible for more than just giving rise to species differences.

Evolutionary change can occur within the genome of a single species as well. *Orthologs* are genes that are evolutionarily related, share a function, and have diverged by speciation. *Paralogs*, on the other hand, have a common ancestor but have diverged by gene duplication and no longer have a common functional role. In other words, orthologs have the same function but occur in different species, while paralogs exist in the same genome but have different functions. A sequence database search may return both orthologs and paralogs. Depending on the objectives of your study, you probably will not want to treat them all as members of the same set.

Multiple Sequence Alignment

Multiple sequence alignment techniques are most commonly applied to protein sequences; ideally they are a statement of both evolutionary and structural similarity among the proteins encoded by each sequence in the alignment. We know that proteins with closely related functions are similar in both sequence and structure from organism to organism, and that sequence tends to change more rapidly than structure in the course of evolution. In multiple alignments generated from sequence data alone, regions that are similar in sequence are usually found to be superimposable in structure as well.

With a detailed knowledge of the biochemistry of a protein, you can create a multiple alignment by hand. This is a painstaking process, however. The challenge of automatic alignment is that it is hard to define exactly what an optimal multiple alignment is, and impossible to set a standard for a single correct multiple alignment. In theory, there is one underlying evolutionary process and one evolutionarily correct alignment to be generated from any group of sequences. However, the differences between sequences can be so great in parts of an alignment that there isn't an apparent, unique solution to be found by an alignment algorithm. Those same divergent regions are often structurally unalignable as well. Most of the insight that we derive from multiple alignments comes from analyzing the regions of similarity, not from attempting to align the very diverged regions.

The dynamic programming algorithm used for pairwise sequence alignment can theoretically be extended to any number of sequences. However, the time and memory requirements of this algorithm increase exponentially with the number of sequences. Dynamic programming alignment of two sequences takes seconds. Alignment of four relatively short sequences takes a few hours. Beyond that, it becomes impractical to align sequences this way. The program MSA is an implementation of an algorithm that reduces the complexity of the dynamic programming problem for multiple sequences to some extent. It can align about seven relatively short (200–300) protein sequences in a reasonable amount of time. However, MSA is of little use when comparing large numbers of sequences.

Progressive Strategies for Multiple Alignment

A common approach to multiple sequence alignment is to progressively align pairs of sequences. The general progressive strategy can be outlined as follows: a starting pair of sequences is selected and aligned, then each subsequent sequence is aligned to the previous alignment. Like the Needleman-Wunsch and Smith-Waterman algorithms for sequence alignment, progressive alignment is an instance of a heuristic algorithm. Specifically, it is a greedy algorithm. *Greedy algorithms* decompose a problem into pieces, then choose the best solution to each piece without paying attention to the problem as a whole. In the case of progressive alignment, the overall problem (alignment of many sequences) is decomposed into a series of pairwise alignment steps.

Because it is a heuristic algorithm, progressive alignment isn't guaranteed to find the best possible alignment. In practice, however, it is efficient and produces biologically meaningful results. Progressive alignment methods differ in several respects: how they choose the initial pair of sequences to align, whether they align every subsequent sequence to a single cumulative alignment or create subfamilies, and how they score individual alignments and alignments of individual sequences to previous alignments.

Multiple Alignment with ClustalW

One commonly used program for progressive multiple sequence alignment is ClustalW. The heuristic used in ClustalW is based on phylogenetic analysis. First, a pairwise distance matrix for all the sequences to be aligned is generated, and a guide tree is created using the neighbor-joining algorithm. Then, each of the most closely related pairs of sequences—the outermost branches of the tree—are aligned to each other using dynamic programming. Next, each new alignment is analyzed to build a sequence profile. Finally, alignment profiles are aligned to each other or to other sequences (depending on the topology of the tree) until a full alignment is built.

This strategy produces reasonable alignments under a range of conditions. It's not foolproof; for distantly related sequences, it can build on the inaccuracies of pairwise alignment and phylogenetic analysis. But for sequence sets with some recognizably related pairs, it builds on the strengths of these methods. Pairwise sequence alignment by dynamic programming is very accurate for closely related sequences regardless of which scoring matrix or penalty values are used. Phylogenetic analysis is relatively unambiguous for closely related sequences. Using multiple sequences to create profiles increases the accuracy of pairwise alignment for more distantly related sequences.

There are many parameters involved in multiple sequence alignment. There are, of course, scoring matrices and gap penalties associated with the pairwise alignment steps. In addition, there are weighting parameters that alter the scoring matrix used in sequence-profile and profile-profile alignments. In ClustalW, these are set from the Multiple Alignment submenu or the Profile Structure Alignments submenu. In ClustalX, they are set from the Alignment pulldown menu.

The pairwise alignment parameters are familiar and have the same meaning in multiple alignment as they do in pairwise alignment. The multiple alignment parameters include gap opening and gap extension penalties for the multiple alignment process—to be used when fine-tuning alignments—and a maximum allowable delay, in terms of sequence length, for the start of divergent sequences at the beginning of the alignment.

One of ClustalW's heuristics is that, in protein sequence alignment, different scoring matrices are used for each alignment based on expected evolutionary distance. If two sequences are close neighbors in the tree, a scoring matrix optimized for close relationships aligns them. Distant neighbors are aligned using matrices optimized for distant relationships. Thus, when prompted to choose a series of matrices in the Multiple Alignment Parameters menu, it means just that: use BLOSUM62 for close relationships and BLOSUM45 for more distant relationships, rather than the same scoring matrix for all pairwise alignments.

Another heuristic that ClustalW uses is scalable gap penalties for protein profile alignments. A gap opening next to a conserved hydrophobic residue can be penalized more heavily than a gap opening next to a hydrophilic residue. A gap opening too close to another gap can be penalized more heavily than an isolated gap. These parameters are set in the Protein Gap Parameters menu.

Although ClustalW is run from the Unix command line, it is menu-driven and doesn't rely on command-line options. To start the program, you can simply type *clustalw*, and a menu of options is presented:

```
**************************************************************
******** CLUSTAL W (1.8) Multiple Sequence Alignments ********
**************************************************************
     1. Sequence Input From Disc
     2. Multiple Alignments
     3. Profile / Structure Alignments
     4. Phylogenetic trees

     S. Execute a system command
     H. HELP
     X. EXIT (leave program)
```

This menu, along with subsequent menus that appear after you input your sequences, guides you through the use of ClustalW in a fairly straightforward fashion. Alignments are written in a plain-text format.

While ClustalW is simple to install and use on a Linux workstation, ClustalX, the X Windows-based graphical user interface for ClustalW, isn't so easy to compile. However, ClustalX runs in its own X window, has pulldown menus, and allows viewing and plotting of multiple sequence alignments in a color-coded format. It also allows you to append sequences to an alignment one at a time, and to produce color PostScript output of specified sequence ranges in an alignment from different files, if desired, along with other convenient features. To install ClustalX on a Linux machine, you need:

- The ClustalX binaries

- The NCBI software toolkit source distribution

- The LessTif libraries

The first thing you need to do is install the LessTif libraries. This distribution is extremely easy to work with. The LessTif libraries are available from *http://www. lesstif.org* and may also be available within your Linux distribution. The NCBI Toolkit (available from *http://www.ncbi.nlm.nih.gov*) should compile completely as long as your LessTif libraries are installed in */usr/X11R6/lib*. If the NCBI Toolkit installation produces the file *libvibrant.a*, the command *clustalx* will work.

Viewing and Editing Alignments with Jalview

Usage: `Jalview alignmentfile FORMAT`

Viewing alignments is useful, but it's often necessary to edit them as well. Alignment editing is one of the few bioinformatics functions that's actually been done better for the Windows platform than for Unix, but if you've installed Java support on your workstation you can use a program called Jalview, written by Michele Clamp and available from the EBI at *http://www.ebi.ac.uk/~michele/jalview/ contents.html.*[*]

To use Jalview on a Linux workstation, download the full Unix distribution of the version you want. Unpack the distribution, then edit the file *Jalview* to reflect your local environment. *Jalview* is a script that sets up the environment for Jalview and actually starts the program. Specifically, you want to set the environment variable

---

[*] Installing Java support involves installing a Java Development Kit and a Java Runtime Environment. IBM has ported JDK and JRE 1.1.8 to Linux. They are available at the IBM site, *http://www.ibm.com/java/jdk /index.html*. You have to register to download the kits, but it's free. The kits are available as easy-to-install RPMs. You won't encounter a lot of Java applications for bioinformatics, but when you do, it's nice to be able to run them.

CLASSPATH to reflect the location of the class file in your JDK (Java Development Kit) and the location of the Jalview classes (your *jalview.jar* file). Set the environment variable JAVA_EXE to point to your Java executable:

```
setenv CLASSPATH /usr/jdk118/lib/classes.zip:/usr/local/jalview/jalview.jar
setenv JAVA_EXE /usr/jdk118/bin/java
```

Jalview can read an alignment (*.aln*) file from Clustal, as well as several other alignment formats. We focus on using Jalview as an alignment editor, but it does have other functions you can explore. It's also capable of searching databases if you specify them as a command-line option.

To run Jalview, make a link to the Jalview script in your working directory.

The common alignment formats that Jalview recognizes are MSF, CLUSTAL, and FASTA. These need to be indicated in all capital letters when the command is given.

The Jalview window is an active place: click with care. You can select individual sequences by clicking on their names at the left of the window, and you can select ranges of sequence by clicking on the numerical labels at the top of the sequence alignment. A red box appears to indicate the selected rows.

As in any other menu interface, the File menu contains file import and export options. Sequence alignments can be read from a file or even from a web URL. The Edit pulldown contains commands that allow you to delete, copy, and move selected sequences or columns. You can also manipulate the alignment by hand. Clicking on any letter in the alignment allows you to open a gap and move everything to the left of that letter over by dragging in either direction with the mouse. The Colour menu contains options for color-coding alignments, most of which are most informative for protein sequence. The Calculate menu contains options for calculating consensus sequences and phylogenetic trees.

Sequence Logos

Another way to view sequence alignments, and one which has become quite popular recently, is the sequence logo format developed by Tom Schneider of the National Cancer Institute. This format is especially good for shorter sequence regions, such as protein motifs. Consensus sequences represent each position in an alignment with the residue that is most commonly found in that position. Other information in the alignment, such as whether there are any other residues that occur at that site and with what relative frequencies they occur, is lost in a consensus sequence.

Sequence logos, as illustrated in Figure 8-1, are a graphical way to represent relative frequencies, information content, order of substitution preference, and other characteristics of each site in an alignment.

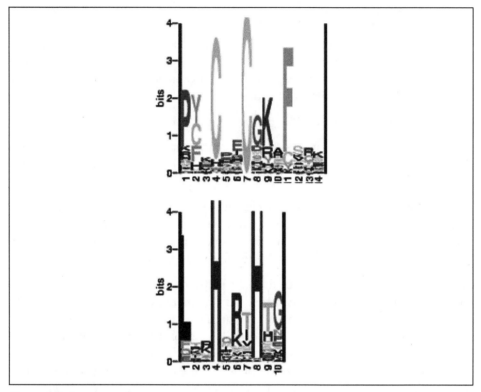

Figure 8-1. A sequence logo

In a sequence logo, the letters in the column at each sequence position represent the consensus sequence in more detail than a standard single-letter consensus sequence would. The total height of a column represents the amount of information contained in that sequence position.* The sizes of the individual letters depict their relative frequency of occurrence.

The software for creating sequence logos is part of a larger group of programs called the DELILA package, which was originally developed in the Pascal language. You actually need only two of the many DELILA programs (*alpro* and *makelogo*) to create logos from aligned sequences. Pascal compilers aren't among the compilers commonly found on Linux systems, but there is a standard GNU

---

* For a thorough discussion of sequence logos and of information content in biological sequence data, you can download some very readable papers from Dr. Tom Schneider's web site at the National Cancer Institute: *http://www-lecb.ncifcrf.gov/~toms/index.html.*

Pascal compiler you can download if you're feeling adventurous. The other way to compile the software is to use the C versions of the programs that are now available. Because these programs have been automatically translated from Pascal, they require that the p2c (Pascal-to-C) libraries are installed on your system.

An easier approach for the novice is to use the sequence logo web server at the University of Cambridge, which (as of this writing) is actually recommended by the author of the DELILA programs and hence, we assume, does exactly what it's supposed to do. Aligned sequences can be submitted to this server in FASTA alignment format, which can be generated by ClustalX.

Phylogenetic Analysis

Having covered some of the basics of multiple sequence alignment, we now introduce one of its applications: phylogenetic inference. Phylogenetic inference is the process of developing hypotheses about the evolutionary relatedness of organisms based on their observable characteristics. Traditionally, phylogenetic analyses have been based on the gross anatomy of species. When Linneaus developed the system of classification into kingdoms, phyla, genera, and species, the early biologists sorted living things into a symbolic Tree of Life, which we saw in Figure 1-3. This tree-based representation of the relationships among species is a phylogenetic tree; it has since been adopted as a convenient schematic for depicting evolutionary relatedness based on sequence similarity. The quantitative nature of sequence relationships has allowed the development of more rigorous methods and rules for tree drawing.

While hand-drawn trees of life may branch fancifully according to what is essentially an artist's conception of evolutionary relationships, modern phylogenetic trees are strictly binary; that is, at any branch point, a parent branch splits into only two daughter branches. Binary trees can approximate any other branching pattern, and the assumption that trees are binary greatly simplifies the tree-building algorithms.

The length of branches in a quantitative phylogenetic tree can be determined in more than one way. Evolutionary distance between pairs of sequences, relative to other sequences in an input data set, is one way to assign branch length.

While a phylogeny of species generally has a root, assuming that all species have a specific common ancestor, a phylogenetic tree derived from sequence data may be rooted or unrooted. It isn't too difficult to calculate the similarity between any two sequences in a group and to determine where branching points belong. It is much harder to pinpoint which sequence in such a tree is the common ancestor, or which pair of sequences can be selected as the first daughters of a common ancestor. While some phylogenetic inference programs do offer a hypothesis about the root of a tree, most simply produce unrooted trees. Figure 8-2 and Figure 8-3 illustrate rooted and unrooted phylogenetic trees.

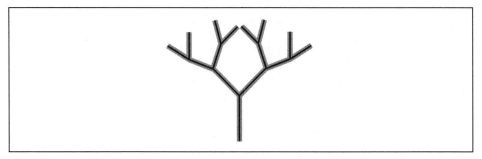

Figure 8-2. A rooted phylogenetic tree

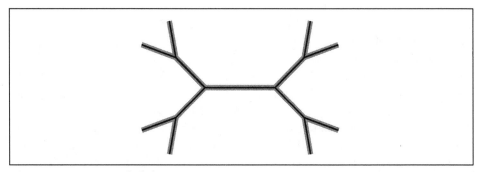

Figure 8-3. An unrooted phylogenetic tree

A phylogeny inferred from a protein or nucleic acid sequence has only a passing resemblance to a whole-organism tree of life (a true tree) that represents actual speciation events. A single phylogeny may be a tree, and it may describe a biological entity, but it takes far more than a single evolutionary analysis to draw conclusions about whole-organism phylogeny. Sequence-based phylogenies are quantitative. When they are built based on sufficient amounts of data, they can provide valuable, scientifically valid evidence to support theories of evolutionary history. However, a single sequence-based phylogenetic analysis can only quantitatively describe the input data set. It isn't valid as a quantitative tool beyond the bounds of that data set, and if you are using phylogenetic analysis tools to develop evolutionary hypotheses, it is critical to remember this point.

It has been shown, by comparative analysis of phylogenies generated for different protein and gene families, that one protein may evolve more quickly than another, and that a single protein may evolve more quickly in some organisms than in others. Thus, the phylogenetic analysis of a sequence family is most informative about the evolution of that particular gene. Only by analysis of much larger sets of data can theories of whole-organism phylogeny be suggested.

Phylogenetic Trees Based on Pairwise Distances

One of the easiest to understand algorithms for tree drawing is the pairwise distance method. This method produces a rooted tree. The algorithm is initialized by defining a matrix of distances between each pair of sequences in the input set. Sequences are then clustered according to distance, in effect building the tree from the branches down to the root.

Distances can be defined by more than one measure, but one of the more common and simple measures of dissimilarity between DNA sequences is the Jukes-Cantor distance, which is logarithmically related to the fraction of sites at which two sequences in an alignment differ. The fraction of matching positions in an ungapped alignment between two unrelated DNA sequences approaches 25%. Consequently, the Jukes-Cantor distance is scaled such that it approaches infinity as the fraction of unmatched residue pairs approaches 75%.

The pairwise clustering procedure used for tree drawing (UPGMA, unweighted pair group method using arithmetic averages) is intuitive. To begin with, each sequence is assigned to its own cluster, and a branch (or leaf) of the tree is started for that sequence at height zero in the tree. Then, the two clusters that are closest together in terms of whatever distance measure has been chosen are merged into a single cluster. A branch point (or node) is defined that connects the two branches. The node is placed at a height in the tree that reflects the distance between the two leaves that have been joined. This process is repeated iteratively, until there are only two clusters left. When they are joined, the root of the tree is defined. The branch lengths in a tree constructed using this process theoretically reflect evolutionary time.

Phylogenetic Trees Based on Neighbor Joining

Neighbor joining is another distance matrix method. It eliminates a possible error that can occur when the UPGMA method is used. UPGMA produces trees in which the branches that are closest together by absolute distance are placed as neighbors in the tree. This assumption places a restriction on the topology of the tree that can lead to incorrect tree construction under some conditions.

In order to get around this problem, the neighbor-joining algorithm searches not just for minimum pairwise distances according to the distance metric, but for sets of neighbors that minimize the total length of the tree. Neighbor joining is the most widely used of the distance-based methods and can produce reasonable trees, especially when evolutionary distances are short.

Phylogenetic Trees Based on Maximum Parsimony

A more widely used algorithm for tree drawing is called parsimony. *Parsimony* is related to Occam's Razor, a principle formulated by the medieval philosopher William of Ockham that states the simplest explanation is probably the correct one.[*] Parsimony searches among the set of possible trees to find the one requiring the least number of nucleic acid or amino acid substitutions to explain the observed differences between sequences.

The only sites considered in a parsimony analysis of aligned sequences are those that provide evolutionary information—that is, those sites that favor the choice of one tree topology over another. A site is considered to be informative if there is more than one kind of residue at the site, and if each type of residue is represented in more than one sequence in the alignment. Then, for each possible tree topology, the number of inferred evolutionary changes at each site is calculated. The topology that is maximally parsimonious is that for which the total number of inferred changes at all the informative sites is minimized. In some cases there may be multiple tree topologies that are equally parsimonious.

As the number of sequences increases, so does the number of possible tree topologies. After a certain point, it is impossible to exhaustively enumerate the scores of each topology. A shortcut algorithm that finds the maximally parsimonious tree in such cases is the branch-and-bound algorithm. This algorithm establishes an upper bound for the number of allowed evolutionary changes by computing a tree using a fast or arbitrary method. As it evaluates other trees, it throws out any exceeding this upper bound before the calculation is completed.

Phylogenetic Trees Based on Maximum Likelihood Estimation

Maximum likelihood methods also evaluate every possible tree topology given a starting set of sequences. Maximum likelihood methods are probabilistic; that is, they search for the optimal choice by assigning probabilities to every possible evolutionary change at informative sites, and by maximizing the total probability of the tree. Maximum likelihood methods use information about amino acid or nucleotide substitution rates, analogous to the substitution matrices that are used in multiple sequence alignment.

---

[*] Or, in other words, "It is futile to do with more what can be done with fewer."

Software for Phylogenetic Analysis

There is a variety of phylogenetic analysis software available for many operating systems. With such a range of choices, which package do you use? One of the most extensive listings currently available is maintained by Dr. Joe Felsenstein, the author of the PHYLIP package, and is accessible from the PHYLIP web page (*http://evolution.genetics.washington.edu/phylip.html*). If you don't want to follow our example and use PHYLIP, you can easily find information about other packages.

PHYLIP

The most widely distributed phylogenetic analysis package is PHYLIP. It contains 30 programs that implement different phylogenetic analysis algorithms. Each of the programs runs separately, from the command line. By default, most of the programs look for an input file called *infile* and write an output file called *outfile*. Rather than entering parameters via command-line flags, as with BLAST, the programs have an interactive text interface that prompts you for information.

The following are the PHYLIP programs you are most likely to use when you're just getting started analyzing protein and DNA sequence data:

PROTPARS
Infers phylogenies from protein sequence input using the parsimony method

PROTDIST
Computes an evolutionary distance matrix from protein sequence input, using maximum likelihood estimation

DNAPARS
Infers phylogenies from DNA sequence input using parsimony

DNAPENNY
Finds all maximally parsimonious phylogenies for a set of sequences using a branch-and-bound search

DNAML
Infers phylogenies from DNA sequence input using maximum likelihood estimation

DNADIST
Computes a distance matrix from DNA sequence input using the Jukes-Cantor distance or one of three other distance criteria

NEIGHBOR
Infers phylogenies from distance matrix data using either the pairwise clustering or the neighbor joining algorithm

DRAWGRAM

> Draws a rooted tree based on output from one of the phylogeny inference programs

DRAWTREE

> Draws an unrooted tree based on output from one of the phylogeny inference programs

CONSENSE

> Computes a consensus tree from a group of phylogenies

RETREE

> Allows interactive manipulation of a tree by the user—not based on data

PHYLIP is a flexible package, and the programs can be used together in many ways. To analyze a set of protein sequences with PHYLIP, you can:

1. Read a multiple protein sequence alignment using PROTDIST and create a distance matrix.

2. Input the distance matrix to NEIGHBOR and generate a phylogeny based on neighbor joining.

3. Read the phylogeny into DRAWTREE and produce an unrooted phylogenetic tree.

Or, you can:

1. Read a multiple sequence alignment using PROTPARS and produce a phylogeny based on parsimony.

2. Read the phylogeny using DRAWGRAM and produce a rooted tree.

Each of the PHYLIP programs is exhaustively documented in the *.doc* files available with the PHYLIP distribution. This documentation has been converted into HTML by several groups. Links to web-based PHYLIP documentation are available from the PHYLIP home page.

Several organizations have made PHYLIP servers available on the Web; the version of PHYLIP in the SDSC Biology Workbench produces downloadable Post-Script output.

The PHYLIP input format. PHYLIP's molecular sequence analysis programs can accept sequence data in an aligned (interleaved) format:

```
39
Archaeopt   CGATGCTTAC CGCCGATGCT
Hesperorni  CGTTACTCGT TGTCGTTACT
Baluchithe  TAATGTTAAT TGTTAATGTT
B. virgini  TAATGTTCGT TGTTAATGTT
```

```
Brontosaur CAAAACCCAT CATCAAAACC
B.subtilis GGCAGCCAAT CACGGCAGCC

TACCGCCGAT GCTTACCGC
CGTTGTCGTT ACTCGTTGT
AATTGTTAAT GTTAATTGT
CGTTGTTAAT GTTCGTTGT
CATCATCAAA ACCCATCAT
AATCACGGCA GCCAATCAC
```

where the first 10 characters are that sequence's name followed by the sequence in aligned form. Subsequent rows follow. In a sequential format, the complete first sequence is given, then the second complete sequence, etc. However, in either case, the sequences must be prealigned by another program. PHYLIP doesn't have a utility for computing multiple sequence alignments.

If you examine the phylogeny output from PHYLIP, you'll find it's represented by codes indicating each of the sequences, arranged in nested parentheses. This is called Newick notation. The pattern of the parentheses indicates the topology of the tree. The innermost parentheses surround the terminal branches of the tree, e.g., *(A,B)*, and each subsequent set of parentheses joins another pair of branches, e.g., *((A,B),(C,D))*. If the algorithm that generates the phylogeny produces branch lengths, these branch lengths are associated explicitly with each branch within the Newick notation: e.g., *((A:1.2,B:1.5):1.0,(C:2.5,D:0.5):1.2)*.

Generating input for PHYLIP with ClustalX

The multiple sequence alignment program ClustalX, which we discussed earlier in this chapter, draws phylogenetic trees with the neighbor joining method. Perhaps more importantly, it can read sequences in various input formats and then write PHYLIP-format files from multiple sequence alignments, using a simple Save As command from within the ClustalX interface.

Profiles and Motifs

In addition to studying relationships between sequences, one of the most successful applications of multiple sequence alignments is in discovering novel, related sequences. This profile- or motif-based analysis uses knowledge derived from multiple alignments to construct and search for sequence patterns. In this section, we first introduce some of the concepts behind motifs, then describe tools that use these principles to search sequence databases.

First, by way of a refresher, a multiple sequence alignment is an alignment of anywhere from three to hundreds of sequences. Multiple sequence alignments can span the full sequence of the proteins involved or a single region of similarity, depending on their purpose. Multiple sequence alignments, such as the one shown in Figure 8-4, are generally built up by iterative pairwise comparison of sequences and sequence groups, rather than by explicit multiple alignment.

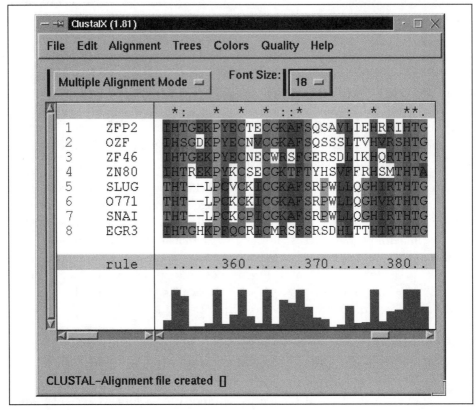

Figure 8-4. A multiple sequence alignment, shown using ClustalX

A sequence *motif* is a locally conserved region of a sequence, or a short sequence pattern shared by a set of sequences. The term "motif" most often refers to any sequence pattern that is predictive of a molecule's function, a structural feature, or family membership. Motifs can be detected in protein, DNA, and RNA sequences, but the most common use of motif-based analyses is the detection of sequence motifs that correspond to structural or functional features in proteins. Motifs are generated from multiple sequence alignments and can be displayed as patterns of amino acids (such as those in the Prosite database) or as sequence logos. For computational purposes, they can be represented as flexible patterns, position-specific scoring matrices, or profile hidden Markov models.

Motifs can be created for *protein families*, or sets of proteins whose members are evolutionarily related. Protein families can consist of many proteins that range from very similar to quite diverse. While the idea of a protein family is a fairly common concept, the method of selecting a protein family and defining its limits depends on the researcher who defines it. As in pairwise sequence comparison, there is a lower bound beyond which homology can't easily be detected. Motif-based methods can push this lower bound by detecting particularly subtle sequence patterns and distant homologs.

A sequence *profile* is a quantitative or qualitative method of describing a motif. A profile can be expressed in its most rudimentary form as a list of the amino acids occurring at each position in the motif. Early profile methods used simple profiles of this sort; however, modern profile methods usually weight amino acids according to their probability of being observed at each position.

Figure 8-5 shows a *position-specific scoring matrix* (PSSM), which is a matrix of scores representing a motif. Unlike a standard scoring matrix, the first dimension of the matrix is the length of the motif; the second dimension consists of the 20 amino acid possibilities. For each position in the matrix, there is a probability score for the occurrence of each amino acid. Most methods for developing position-specific scoring matrices normalize the raw probabilities with respect to a standard scoring matrix such as BLOSUM62.

Finally, a *profile hidden Markov model* (HMM) is the rigorous probabilistic formulation of a sequence profile. Profile HMMs contain the same probability information found in a PSSM; however, they can also account for gaps in the alignment, which tends to improve their sensitivity. Because profile analysis methods are still a subject of active research, there are many different programs and methods for motif discovery and profile building. We will focus on two of the easiest motif discovery packages to use, MEME and HMMer. We also describe the searchable databases of preconstructed protein family motifs—some with associated PSSMs or profile HMMs—offered by several organizations.

Motif Databases

We have seen that profiles and other consensus representations of sequence families can be used to search sequence databases. It shouldn't be too surprising, then, that there are motif databases that can be searched using individual sequences. Motif databases contain representations of conserved sequences shared by a sequence family. Today, their primary use is in annotation of unknown sequences: if you get a new gene sequence hot off the sequencer, scanning it against a motif database is a good first indicator of the function of the protein it encodes.

Motifs are generated by a variety of methods and with different objectives in mind. Some rely on automated analysis, but there is often a large amount of hands-on labor invested in the database by an expert curator. Because they store only those motifs that are present in reasonably large families, motif databases are small

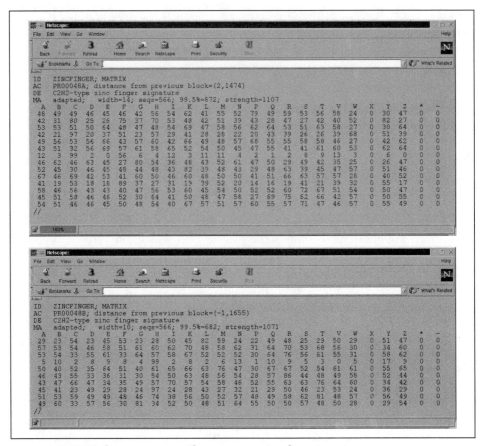

Figure 8-5. PSSMs for sequence motifs common to zinc finger proteins

relative to GenBank, and they don't reflect the breadth of the protein structure or sequence databases. Be aware that an unsuccessful search against a motif database doesn't mean your sequence contains no detectable pattern; it could be part of a family that has not yet been curated or that doesn't meet the criteria of the particular pattern database you've searched. For proteins that do match defined families, a search against the pattern databases can yield a lot of homology information very quickly.

Blocks

Blocks, a service of the Fred Hutchinson Cancer Research Center, is an automatically generated database of ungapped multiple sequence alignments that correspond to the most conserved regions of proteins. Blocks is created using a combination of motif-detection methods, beginning with a step that exhaustively searches all spaced amino acid triplets in the sequence to discover a seed alignment, followed by a step that extends the alignment to find an aligned region of maximum length. The Blocks database itself contains more than 4,000 entries; it is extended to over 10,000 entries by inclusion of blocks created from entries in several other protein family databases (see the later section "Accessing multiple databases"). The Blocks server also provides several useful search services, including IMPALA (which uses the BLAST statistical model to compare a sequence against a library of profiles) and LAMA (Local Alignment of Multiple Alignments; Shmuel Pietrokovski's program for comparing an alignment of your own sequences against a database of Blocks).

PROSITE

PROSITE is an expert-curated database of patterns hosted by the Swiss Institute of Bioinformatics. It currently contains approximately 1,200 records, and is available for download as a structured flat file from *http://ftp.expasy.ch*. PROSITE uses a single consensus pattern to characterize each family of sequences. Patterns in PROSITE aren't developed based on automated analysis. Instead, they are carefully selected based on data published in the primary literature or on reviews describing the functionality of specific groups of proteins. A humorous cartoon on the PROSITE server indicates that the optimal method for identifying patterns requires only a human, chalk, and a chalkboard. PROSITE contains pattern information as well as position-specific scoring matrices that can detect new instances of the pattern.

Pfam

Pfam is a database of alignments of protein domain families. Pfam is made up of two databases: Pfam-A and Pfam-B. Pfam-A is a curated database of over 2,700 gapped profiles, most of which cover whole protein domains; Pfam-B entries are generated automatically by applying a clustering method to the sequences left over from the creation of Pfam-A. Pfam-A entries begin with a *seed alignment*, a multiple sequence alignment that the curators are confident is biologically meaningful and that may involve some manual editing. From each seed alignment, a profile hidden Markov model is constructed and used to search a nonredundant database of available protein sequences. A full alignment of the family is produced from the seed alignments and any new matches. This process can be iterated to produce more extensive families and detect remote matches. Pfam entries are annotated with information extracted from the scientific literature, and incorporate structural data where available. As a final note, Pfam is the database of profile HMMs used by the GeneWise genefinder to search for open reading frames.

PRINTS

PRINTS is a database of protein motifs similar to PROSITE, except that it uses "fingerprints" composed of more than one pattern to characterize an entire protein sequence. Motifs are often short relative to an entire protein sequence. In PRINTS, groups of motifs found in a sequence family can define a signature for that family.

COG

NCBI's Clusters of Orthologous Groups (COG) database is a different type of pattern database. COG is constructed by comparing all the protein sequences encoded in 21 complete genomes. Each cluster must consist of protein sequences from at least three separate genomes. The premise of COG is that proteins that are conserved across these genomes from many diverse organisms represent ancient functions that have been conserved throughout evolution. COG entries can be accessed by organism or by functional category from the NCBI web site. COG currently contains more than 2,100 entries.

Accessing multiple databases

So, which motif database should you use to analyze a new sequence? Because the comparisons are performed quickly and efficiently, we recommend you use as many as possible, keeping track of the best matches from each, their scores, and (if available) the significance of the hit. While Blocks uses InterPro as one of the sources for its own patterns, as of June 2000 it contains only ungapped patterns, omitting gapped profiles such as those contained in Pfam-A and PROSITE. Fortunately, all the motif databases discussed here have search interfaces available on the Web, most of which accept input in FASTA format or FASTA alignment format.

One service that allows integrated searching of many motif databases is the European Bioinformatics Institute's Integrated Resource of Protein Domains and Functional Sites (InterPro to its friends). InterPro allows you to compare a sequence against all the motifs from Pfam, PRINTS, ProDom, and PROSITE. InterPro motifs are annotated with the name of the source protein, examples of proteins in which the motif occurs, references to the literature, and related motifs.

Constructing and Using Your Own Profiles

Motif databases are useful if you're looking for protein families that are already well documented. However, if you think you've found a new motif you want to use to search GenBank, or you want to get creative and look for patterns in unusual places, you need to build your own profiles. Several software packages and servers are available for *motif discovery*, the process of finding and constructing your own motifs from a set of sequences. The simplest way to construct a motif is to find a well-conserved section out of a multiple sequence alignment. As usual, though, we encourage you to use automated approaches instead of doing things by hand: automation makes your work faster, more reproducible, and less error-prone. In addition to Block Maker, a number of other programs are commonly used to search for and discover motifs. In this section, we discuss the use of the MEME and HMMer programs, two packages commonly used for motif analysis.

Before we begin, though, here are two observations about motif discovery. First, as InterPro and Blocks grow, it is becoming increasingly difficult to find completely novel sequence motifs undocumented by one of their member databases. Be sure to check your motif against the set of known motifs, either by searching your sequences against the databases or by using a motif-comparison tool, such as the Blocks server's LAMA program. Second, in order to find patterns reliably and search with them, you need a lot of sequences. We have used these programs in projects where very few (5–10) sequences were available, but, as a rule of thumb, more than 20 sequences are needed for reasonable motif predictions. The more sequences you have, the more reliable the resulting motifs will be.

Finding new motifs with MEME

The MEME programs are a set of tools for motif analysis developed by Charles Elkan, Tim Bailey, and William Grundy of the University of California, San Diego. MEME is short for Multiple EM for Motif Elicitation (EM, in turn, is short for Expectation Maximization, a procedure from the world of statistics for predicting the values of "missing," or unobserved, values). They can be used over the Web (*http:// meme.sdsc.edu*) or their C source code can be downloaded, compiled, and run on a local computer; here, we look at the web version. There are three programs in the MEME suite:

MEME
    Discovers shared motifs in a set of unaligned sequences

MAST
    Takes a motif discovered by MEME and uses it to search a sequence database

MetaMEME
    Constructs a model from multiple MEME motifs and uses it to search a sequence database

When you submit a set of sequences to MEME, you are testing the hypothesis that, although though you don't know the overall alignment of the sequences, they share short regions of similarity. You begin using MEME by entering on a web form your email address and a set of sequences in which you wish to search for a motif. Sequences can be in one of several formats, although FASTA is preferred. At the bottom of the sumission page are some parameters you need to set regarding the number of times per sequence you expect a motif to occur, the number of motifs you expect to find, and the approximate width of each motif.

The results will be sent back to you in three emails. The first is just a confirmation message, letting you know that the job is being processed. The second (with the subject line "MEME Job xxxxx results:", where xxxxx is the job number assigned by the MEME server) contains MEME's prediction for the motifs in both human- and machine-readable form. This message is the one you need to search the database; be sure to save the contents of this message to a text file, so you can later submit it to MAST or MetaMEME. The third message (with the subject line "MEME job... MAST analysis:") is an HTML document (making it suitable for viewing in a web browser) that shows the location of each motif in the sequences you submitted. Each message is well documented and contains detailed explanations of the contents.

Searching for motifs with MAST and MetaMEME

The next step of a motif analysis is to see whether there are new occurrences of your motif in other sequences. The MEME server provides two distinct programs, MAST and MetaMEME, that allow you to search a sequence database using your new MEME motifs. MAST simply searches for occurrences of each motif and reports matching sequences, while MetaMEME combines multiple MEME motifs into a hidden Markov model and uses that model to search the database. Both MAST and MetaMEME take the MEME motif prediction from the second email[*] as input; MetaMEME also uses the original sequence file that generates the MEME motifs in creating its HMM. Both programs return results showing the position of each match, its score, and its statistical significance.

Motif discovery with other programs

As we mentioned previously, there are a number of programs that discover motifs in groups of unaligned sequences. Besides the ones we mentioned, you may want to try these: the SAM HMM programs developed by David Haussler and coworkers at University of California, Santa Cruz; the Emotif and Ematrix servers in the Brutlag group at Stanford University; and the ASSET, gibbs, and Probe tools available for download from NCBI. Again, a good thing to do early on is to use the LAMA program to compare your motif against the motifs in the Blocks database. If it looks like you really do have a novel motif, it can be useful to compare the results of one or more of these other motif discovery tools. If all the programs predict the same motif from the same sequences, you can be more confident in your results.

---

[*] You *did* save the second email to a text file as we suggested, didn't you?

HMMer

HMMer is a software package for building profile HMMs. HMMer's central functionality is located in the *hmmbuild* program, which creates profile HMMs from sequence alignment, and the *hmmcalibrate* program, which calibrates search statistics for the HMM. The HMMer package also contains tools for generating new sequences probabilistically based on an HMM, searching sequence databases with a profile as the query, and searching profile databases with a query sequence, as well as the handy utility programs we list here:

getseq

Extracts a sequence from a large flat-file database by name. Handy to have around if you're selecting specific records out of a database from the command line.

hmmalign

Reads both a sequence file and a profile HMM and creates a multiple sequence alignment.

hmmbuild

Builds a profile HMM from a multiple sequence alignment. It can produce global results for the entire alignment or results for multiple local alignments.

hmmcalibrate

Reads an HMM and calibrates its search statistics.

hmmconvert

Converts an HMM into other profile formats, notably GCG profile format.

hmmemit

Generates sequences probabilistically based on a profile HMM. It can also generate a consensus sequence.

hmmfetch

Retrieves a profile HMM from a database if the name of the desired record is known.

hmmindex

Indexes a profile HMM database.

hmmpfam

Searches a profile HMM database (e.g., Pfam) with a query sequence. Use this if you're trying to annotate an unknown sequence.

hmmsearch

Searches a sequence database with a profile HMM. Use this if you're looking for more instances of a pattern in a sequence database.

sreformat

> Converts a sequence or alignment file from one format to another. Handy to
> have around.

HMMer reads multiple sequence alignment files from several different sequence
alignment programs, including ClustalW. The HMMer authors recommend ClustalW
as a tool to generate multiple alignments for input into *hmmbuild*.

HMMer is available for download from Dr. Sean Eddy at Washington University
(http://hmmer.wustl.edu). HMMer is a very well-behaved program, which installs
without difficulty from source on Linux systems: just follow the directions in the
INSTALL file. It even installs its own Unix manpages so you can access online help
for each of the HMMer programs using the *man* command. Specific information
about each of the HMMer programs' command-line options can also be viewed by
running the program with the *−h* option.

Incorporating Motif Information into Pairwise Alignment

Multiple sequence information can optimize pairwise alignments. The BLAST package contains two new modes that use multiple alignment information to improve
the specificity of database searches. These modes are accessed through the
blastpgp program.

Position Specific Iterative BLAST (PSI-BLAST) is an enhancement of the original
BLAST program that implements profiles to increase the specificity of database
searches. Starting with a single sequence, PSI-BLAST searches a database for local
alignments using gapped BLAST and builds a multiple alignment and a profile the
length of the original query sequence. The profile is then used to search the protein database again, seeking local alignments. This procedure can be iterated any
number of times. One caveat of using PSI-BLAST is that you need to know where
to stop. Errors in alignment can be magnified by iteration, giving rise to false positives in the ultimate sequence search. PSI-BLAST can be used as a standalone by
running the *blastpgp* program. However, the NCBI PSI-BLAST server is probably
the optimal way to run a PSI-BLAST search. The server requires you to decide after
each iteration whether to continue to another iteration, and you can hand-pick the
sequences that contribute to the profile at each step.

Pattern Hit Initiated BLAST (PHI-BLAST) takes a sequence and a preselected pattern found in that sequence as input to query a protein sequence database. The
pattern must be expressed in PROSITE syntax, which is described in detail on the
PHI-BLAST server site. PHI-BLAST can also initiate a series of PSI-BLAST itera-
tions, and can be a standalone program or a (vastly more user-friendly) web
server.

9

Visualizing Protein Structures and Computing Structural Properties

Analysis of protein 3D structures is a more mature field than biological sequence analysis. The Protein Data Bank started distributing coordinates of macromolecular crystal structures in the early 1970s, and since that time, many research groups and companies have developed software to visualize and measure the properties of protein structures.

Visualization of structure and measurement of structural properties are important tools for molecular and structural biologists. Being able to "see" the 3D structure of a protein and analyze its shape in detail can suggest the location of catalytic sites and interaction sites, and can help identify targets for the site-directed mutagenesis studies that are so often used to arrive at a detailed characterization of a protein's functional chemistry.

Here are some recent applications of this type of approach in molecular biology:

- Molecular modeling of an allergy-causing protein from mountain cedar pollen and subsequent identification of the region that causes allergic response

- Characterization of the mutagenic active site in DNA reverse transcriptase from the HIV virus; this site is thought to be responsible for the ability of the HIV virus to mutate rapidly

- Modeling of a DNA binding protein involved in Bloom syndrome, and characterization of the mutations that cause the disease

There are many specialized analysis programs in the protein structure literature, and we will not attempt to catalogue all these methods. Instead, we present an introduction to standard operations for analyzing and modeling protein structure, with examples of software for each purpose: visualization and plotting; geometric and surface property analysis; classification; analysis of intramolecular interactions and solvent interactions; and computation of some physicochemical properties.

For all-purpose molecular structure modeling, the easiest-to-use tools are still commercial packages such as MSI's Quanta and Insight, Tripos' SYBYL, and others. However, licensing for these packages, especially for multiple users, is quite expensive and they generally require specialized high-end hardware (such as SGI and IBM Unix workstations) to run. In this chapter, we again focus on software that can run on a standard desktop PC under Linux or within a web browser on any platform.

A Word About Protein Structure Data

Because protein structure analysis is a relatively old field, evolving earlier in the history of computers than sequence analysis, it has inherited some inconveniences. While many programs use the standard PDB format, others, especially molecular simulation software, expect input in slightly or significantly different forms. And because protein structure analysis software is older, many programs are written in the FORTRAN language and are very picky about data input formats. Data standardization at the PDB is excellent, but standardization at the individual software package level isn't as good. If you're going to be doing a lot of work with protein structure data it may be necessary to learn some programming to be able to convert structure files to alternate formats when necessary. We show an example of a simple structure file-format conversion in Chapter 12, *Automating Data Analysis with Perl*.

The Brookhaven PDB format is the protein structure data format that most structure-analysis programs use. This format met the needs of the protein structure field in the 1970s, and was especially human-readable, and compatible with FORTRAN programs, because of its use of rigidly structured 80-character lines. This format consists of a header section that contains miscellaneous information about the structure, including literature citations; resolution; crystallographic parameters; sequence, and sometimes secondary structure information; and a section that contains atom records. Atoms labeled *ATOM* are part of the protein chain, while atoms labeled *HETATM* (for heteroatom group) are part of cofactor molecules, substrates, ions, or other groups that aren't a covalently bound part of the protein chain. A detailed line-by-line description of the Brookhaven format is available from the RCSB PDB web site.

Protein structure files also are available from the PDB in a new format called mmCIF (the Macromolecular Crystallographic Information Format) and from NCBI in the ASN.1 file format. Both of these formats are highly parseable by computers, and if you are writing computer programs to analyze protein structures, they may be easier to use than the obsolete Brookhaven format. However, you'll need to consider that the user community is still attached to the Brookhaven format.

The Chemistry of Proteins

To work with protein sequence and structure, you need a working knowledge of protein chemistry—the kind of knowledge you'd probably have picked up in an undergraduate organic chemistry course. We'll provide you with a little of that vocabulary here, and you can find out more from the references listed in the *Bibliography*. If you already know what you need to know about protein chemistry, you can skip ahead to the section "Web-Based Protein Structure Tools."

The reason you should have a basic knowledge of organic chemistry when studying protein structures is simple. Proteins often perform their functions using standard organic reaction mechanisms, mediated by amino acids and small organic molecules (cofactors) that bind to the protein, or by metal ions. To understand how the protein structure might catalyze a reaction, you need to understand enough about organic reaction mechanisms to develop a hypothesis about how the reaction might work, given the shape of the protein and the location of various amino acids.

Even in cases in which a catalytic mechanism isn't your main concern, chemistry comes into play. Protein association is often mediated by the electrostatic properties of the protein structure; interacting molecules can be drawn together over considerable distances by strong electrostatic potentials. Within protein structures, hydrogen bonds and other interatomic interactions confer structural stability. Interatomic interactions and molecular shapes are the basis of the specificity of intermolecular interactions—the interactions of proteins with other proteins or with small molecule substrates. You are likely to be concerned about molecular specificity in practical applications of biochemistry—designing small-molecule or peptide drugs, understanding the molecular basis of disease and immunity, or delving into the specific molecules involved in sending molecular signals between cells and through the body.

The tools in this chapter enable you to look at a protein structure, see what its features are, locate different types of amino acids and visualize specific subsets of the protein, measure distances and surface areas, and compute spatially variable properties such as solvent accessibility and electrostatic potentials. However, what you can do with those tools depends on your understanding of protein chemistry.

From 1D to 3D

How does the chemistry of a protein relate to its 1D sequence? In Chapter 8, *Multiple Sequence Alignments, Trees, and Profiles*, we discussed techniques for detecting characteristic conserved patterns, called motifs, in families of protein sequences. We can find these sequence patterns in 1D data because although the 3D structure of a protein is complex, it is somehow determined by the invariant sequence of amino acids that makes up the protein. Motifs that are conserved in sequence often are related to important structural or functional features of a protein family, and those features often can be understood by their roles in the protein structure.

When amino acids come together in sequence to form a polymer, they do so by forming a peptide bond between the basic amino group and the acidic carboxyl group of each amino acid (Figure 9-1). This results in a long chain of amino acids that has a repeating backbone structure.

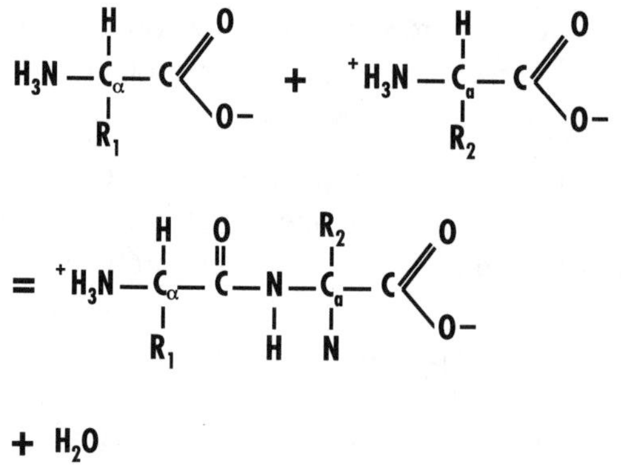

Figure 9-1. Peptide bond, peptide chain (chemical notation)

The variable group of each amino acid protrudes from the repeating backbone and is referred to in the protein structure business as a *sidechain* (Figure 9-2). Each of the 20 amino acid sidechains is chemically different from the others in some respect.

The sidechains can be classified in many ways. Some are relatively large, while others are tiny or in one case nonexistent. Some have a positive or negative charge. Some are oily, or hydrophobic (water-fearing), meaning that it's energetically unfavorable for them to be solvated in water. Others are hydrophilic (water-loving), and they solvate easily in water. Some have bulky ringlike structures, while others are straight carbon chains. Some are acids, others are bases. Amino acids are conserved through evolution at specific locations in a protein sequence

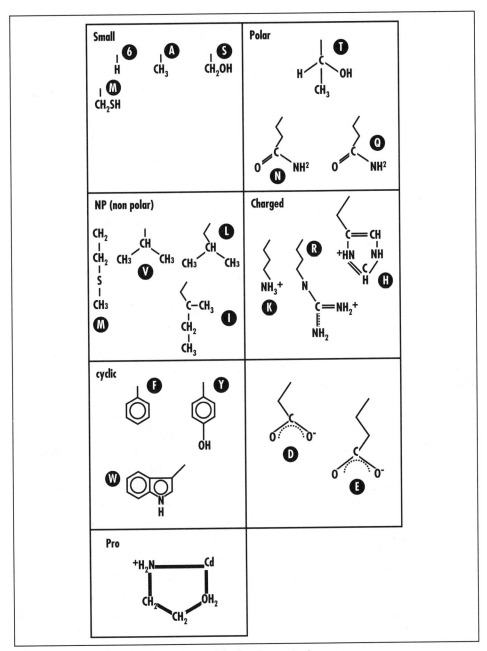

Figure 9-2. The amino acid sidechains (chemical notation)

because they are needed there, whether to stabilize the protein structure, to form a specific binding site, or to catalyze a reaction. You can detect that particular amino acids in a protein are conserved by looking at sequence data, but to develop a hypothesis about why they are conserved, it's helpful to examine the 3D protein structure. Figure 9-3 shows the 20 amino acids classified into chemically similar groups. Note that many of the amino acids fall into more than one category. An amino acid sidechain can be both "nonpolar" and "basic," for instance, like lysine, which has a long aliphatic sidechain that terminates in an amino group. Because the relationship between chemical characteristics and amino acids isn't one-to-one, but rather many-to-many, it's not always simple to predict the effects of an amino acid substitution.

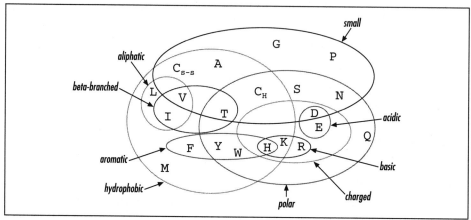

Figure 9-3. The amino acid sidechains (classification in a Venn diagram)

Interatomic forces aren't responsible only for specific interactions that form binding and interaction sites; they also are responsible for the formation of certain standard patterns that are consistently observed in protein structure. The amino acid backbone is sterically constrained—restricted from moving in certain ways because atoms will bump into each other—to follow only certain pathways. You may already be familiar with the alpha helix and beta sheet structures that commonly occur in protein structures; the reason that alpha helices and beta sheets are common is the steric restrictions on the protein backbone.

From the known structures of amino acids, Pauling and Corey first predicted the existence of alpha helices and beta sheets as a component of protein structure. Ramachandran first described exactly what range of conformations are available to amino acids in a peptide chain. Peptide chain conformation is simply described by the values of the dihedral angles in the protein backbone (i.e., the angle described by the four atoms surrounding the N-Cα bond and the angle described by the four atoms surrounding the Cα-C bond). These angles are referred to as Φ and Ψ, respectively. The chain isn't free to rotate around the third kind of bond in the protein backbone, the peptide bond, because it is a partial double bond and hence chemically constrained to be planar, so the values of Φ and Ψ for each amino acid provide a complete description of the protein backbone. A Ramachandran map is simply a plot of Ψ versus Φ for an entire protein structure. One means of evaluating a protein structure model is to compare its individual Ramachandran map with the general Ramachandran map of allowed values of Φ and Ψ.

Figure 9-4 is a general Ramachandran map that shows the allowed combinations of Φ and Ψ values for amino acids in protein structures. The small shaded region in the lower left quadrant of the map is the standard conformation of an amino acid in an alpha helix. The larger shaded region in the upper left quadrant of the map is the standard conformation of an amino acid in a beta sheet, or extended structure.

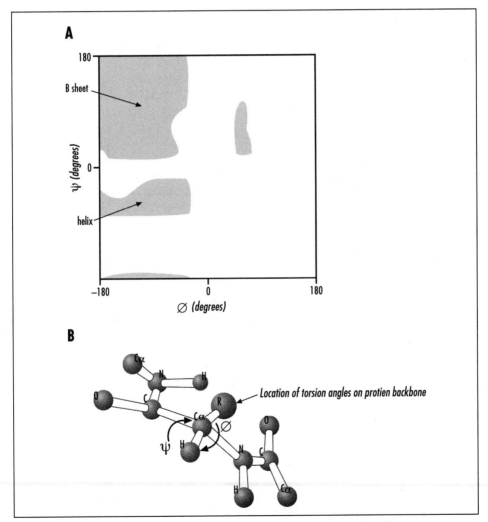

Figure 9-4. Ramachandran map of allowed conformation for protein backbones

It's apparent from the Ramachandran map that steric interactions are very important determinants of the general features of protein structure. Steric interactions instantly eliminate a large fraction of possible conformations for proteins and leave relatively few options for how a compact structure can form from a linear chain of amino acids.

The sequence of a protein is called its primary structure; the most basic level of organization in a protein is the sequence of amino acids. Alpha helix and beta sheet structures, shown in Figure 9-5, are known collectively as secondary structures and are the next level of organization. Interactions between multiple secondary structure elements give rise to supersecondary structure and tertiary structure—helices and sheets contacting each other to form larger characteristic structures, which can be described by their topology.

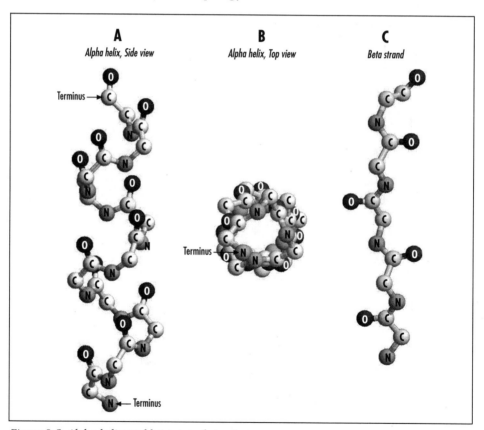

Figure 9-5. Alpha helix and beta strand structures

To create a functional protein, the sequence of amino acids in the protein chain must give rise to the proper 3D fold for the protein, and it must also place individual amino acids at appropriate points on that scaffold to carry out the protein's chemistry. Finding ways to extract those chemical instructions from the sequences of known proteins, formulating them as rules, and using those rules to predict the structure of other proteins is one of the biggest open research problems in bioinformatics.

Interatomic Forces and Protein Structure

Since the form that a protein structure can take and its chemical characteristics are governed by interatomic interactions, it is important to have at least a basic understanding of the interatomic interactions that play a role in protein structure. Interactions between atoms are physically complicated and to describe them in detail would require a whole other book, which fortunately has already been written by someone else: see the *Bibliography*. What we hope to give you is a rudimentary knowledge of these forces, to help you understand why computer methods have been developed to measure and calculate particular structural properties of proteins.

Understanding these forces gives us a basis for designing evaluative and predictive methods. Threading methods rely on the ability to discriminate between an amino acid that is in a favorable chemical environment and one that isn't. Homology modeling and structure optimization methods rely on rules for spacing between atoms, bond lengths, bond angles, and other values. These rules can be derived from chemical experiments on small molecules or from the distribution of observed values in known protein structures. However these rules are constructed, though, they reflect energetically favorable interactions between atoms.

Covalent interactions

Covalent interactions are the very short range (approximately 1 to 1.5 angstroms); they are very strong forces that bind atoms together into a molecule. In covalent bonding, the atoms involved actually share electrons. Unlike other forces encountered in protein structures, covalent bonds actually change the nature of the atoms involved to some extent. Atoms involved in covalent bonds are no longer discrete entities; instead, they combine to form a new molecule.

The protein backbone, including the peptide bond that joins one amino acid to another, is held together by covalent bonds. Amino acids retain some of their chemical individuality within the protein structure, but formally they become part of a new molecule. Atoms within individual amino acid sidechains are also covalently bonded to each other. These covalent bonds place strong constraints on the distance between atoms in a protein structure.

Because covalent interactions are strongly constrained by physicochemical rules, an important part of the verification process for structural quality is making sure that bond lengths, bond angles, and dihedral angles don't vary dramatically from their allowed values. Covalent bond lengths are determined by the size and type of the atoms involved and by the number of electrons shared between atoms. The more electrons are shared, the shorter and stronger the bond. Bond angles are constrained by the structure of atomic orbitals. *Dihedral angles*, the angles of rotation of two bonded pairs of atoms with respect to each other around a central bond, are constrained primarily by steric hindrance. These chemical constraints are also used in macromolecular simulation, where they are associated with applied forces that keep the molecule in allowed conformations.

Hydrogen bonds

Hydrogen bonds arise when two polar groups interact. The two polar groups must be of specific types. One must be a proton donor, a chemical group in which a proton (hydrogen atom) is covalently bonded to a strongly electronegative atom such as oxygen. The bond between the proton and the electronegative atom is polarized, giving the proton a partial positive charge and the electronegative atom a partial negative charge. The other group must be a proton acceptor, an electronegative atom with a partial negative charge and no attached proton. The positively polarized proton in the first group is attracted to the negatively polarized second group, and the two form a bond that isn't covalent, but is nonetheless, much shorter and stronger than a normal nonbonded interaction. Hydrogen bonds are unusual among nonbonded and electrostatic interactions because they are strongly directional; they weaken if the angle described by the three atoms involved is too large or too small.

Hydrogen bond interactions are one of the most important stabilizing forces in protein structure. The protein backbone contains a proton donor, in its N-H group, and a proton acceptor, in its carbonyl oxygen, spaced at regular intervals along the chain (Figure 9-6). The interaction of these groups stabilizes the two major types of secondary structure, the alpha helix and the beta sheet (Figure 9-7). Therefore, some structure prediction methods attempt to use the presence of potential hydrogen bond pairs to improve the accuracy of predictions.

Hydrophobic and hydrophilic interactions

A much-discussed (and frequently wrongly used) concept in protein structure analysis is that of the hydrophobic force. We've already mentioned in passing that amino acids can be classified as hydrophobic or hydrophilic. What exactly does this mean?

Proteins, except for those bound within cell membranes, always exist in aqueous solution. They constantly interact with water molecules. Water is a solution that has some interesting properties, and these properties contribute to the stability of the compact globular structures that characterize cellular proteins.

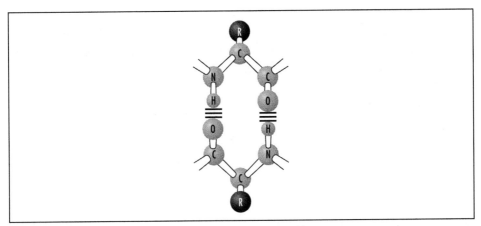

Figure 9-6. Proton donor and acceptor in the protein backbone

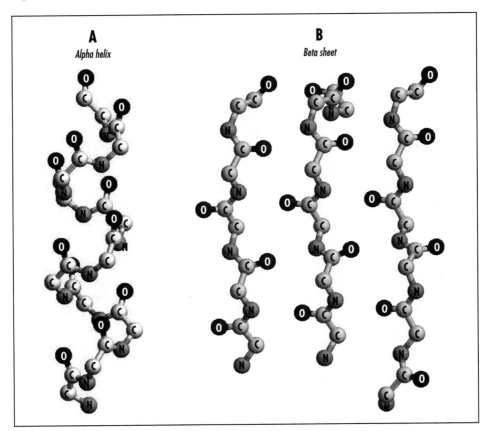

Figure 9-7. Hydrogen bonding in alpha helices and beta sheets

Water is a polar molecule. Individual water molecules in liquid water can each form four hydrogen bonds with neighboring water molecules. Liquid water is an essentially uninterrupted lattice of hydrogen bonded molecules, as seen in Figure 9-8. This unusual property contributes to the high melting and boiling points of water, as well as to such properties as low compressibility and high surface tension. It also results in interesting interactions of water with soluble proteins.

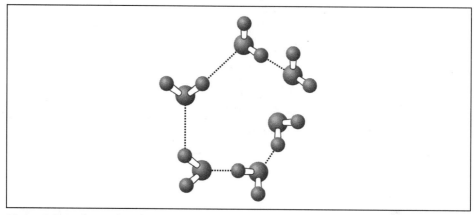

Figure 9-8. Hydrogen bonding in water

A nonpolar molecule dissolved in water interrupts the regular hydrogen bond lattice of liquid water. Individual water molecules can reorient around a small nonpolar molecule to preserve their network of hydrogen bonds, but this reorientation has a cost in terms of free energy (which is how cost is measured in chemistry). The presence of a nonpolar solute forces water molecules into a more ordered conformation than they would ordinarily assume. Instead of being able to face any which way and rotate freely, water molecules near the surface of a nonpolar solute have to work around it and form a cage. This is entropically unfavorable.

The larger a nonpolar solute gets, the more water molecules need to reorient to accommodate it, and the higher the energy cost of solvating the molecule becomes. Of course, if the nonpolar solute has some polar groups on its surface, water molecules can use those groups as hydrogen bonding partners instead of other water molecules, and the water lattice is less disturbed. Globular proteins, which exist in aqueous solution even though they are composed substantially of nonpolar groups, must present a good hydrogen-bonding surface to the world. *Hydrophilic* amino acids are those whose sidechains offer hydrogen bonding partners to the surrounding medium, while *hydrophobic* amino acids' sidechains don't. The surface of a globular protein is usually anywhere from 50%–75% polar atoms, and deviations in this pattern can suggest binding or complexation sites.

Solvent accessibility and hydrophobicity play an important role in evaluating model structures. Threading methods for protein fold recognition use amino acid environments in evaluating models. When many hydrophobic amino acids are found in solvent-exposed structural environments or hydrophilic amino acids buried in the protein interior, it is considered unlikely that the protein model is folded correctly.

Charge-charge, charge-dipole, and dipole-dipole interactions

Unlike covalent bonds, the other important interactions in protein structure are nonspecific. They don't change the discrete nature of the interacting atoms. They involve no sharing of electrons. Covalently bonded atoms are married; noncovalently bonded atoms are just shacking up.

Several kinds of important forces can arise among polar and charged atoms. An *ion* is an atom that has a net positive or negative charge due to either a surplus or a deficit of electrons. Atoms that carry a positive ionic charge are attracted to atoms that carry a negative ionic charge, with a strength that depends on the size of the charges and the inverse of the distance between the atoms. In proteins, charge-charge interactions occur between the sidechains of acidic and basic amino acids that are negatively charged or positively charged due to loss or gain of a labile proton under normal physiological conditions. The charge-charge interactions between amino acids in a protein structure are called *salt bridges*, and they can contribute a significant stabilizing force to a protein structure.

There are other, weaker interactions that occur between charges and groups that don't carry a positive or negative ionic charge. *Dipolar molecules* are molecules like those involved in hydrogen bonds, in which one end of the molecule has a partial positive charge and the other end has a partial negative charge. The dipole of a molecule is essentially a vector that describes the magnitude of the polarization along a bond. Dipolar molecules can be strongly attracted to other partial charges or to ionic charges. Many amino acid sidechains, as well as the protein backbone, have a strongly dipolar character, so charge-dipole and dipole-dipole interactions play a substantial role in stabilization of protein structure.

Van der Waals forces

The van der Waals force is a nonspecific attractive force between molecules. This force is loosely analogous to gravity, in that it exists between every pair of nonbonded atoms, and it's a fairly long-range force. However, it doesn't arise simply from the mass of the atoms involved, but from the transient attractive forces between the instantaneous dipole moments of each atom. The van der Waals force is quite strong, and because van der Waals interactions are nonspecific and numerous they play a significant role in protein folding and protein association.

Repulsive forces

Repulsive forces, or *steric* interactions, are very short range forces that increase sharply as atomic centers approach each other. The radius at which the repulsive force begins to increase sharply defines a spherical boundary around each atom center inside which another atom's spherical boundary (called the van der Waals radius) can't pass. If two nonbonded atoms in a structure get into each other's personal space, the contact is energetically unfavorable. In real molecules, atoms stay out of each other's way. However, in models of molecules, whether derived from NMR or x-ray data or built from scratch, checking for van der Waals bumps between nonbonded atoms is an important part of the structure-refinement process.

Relative strength of interatomic forces

The interaction between atoms can be described by a *pair potential*, such as the Lennard-Jones potential (Figure 9-9), which includes both an attractive and a repulsive term. The form of the potential shows that atoms tend to repel each other at very short range (positive potential energy indicating an unfavorable interaction) but to attract each other at slightly longer range. The strength of the attraction decays with distance, depending on the forces modeled.

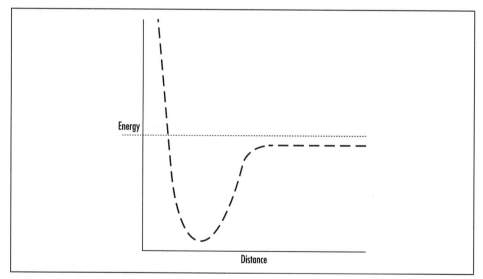

Figure 9-9. Plot of Lennard-Jones potential

When making inferences about structural stability or function based on intermolecular interactions, it is important to understand the relative strengths of these interactions, and how they scale with distance (Table 9-1).

Table 9-1. How Interatomic Forces Scale with Distance

Type of Bond	Range of Interaction
Covalent	Complicated short range
Hydrogen bond	Roughly $1/r^2$
Charge-charge	Scales with $1/r$
Charge-fixed dipole	Scales with $1/r^2$
Charge-rotating dipole	Scales with $1/r^4$
Fixed dipole-fixed dipole	Scales with $1/r^3$
Rotating dipole-rotating dipole	Scales with $1/r^6$
Charge-nonpolar	Scales with $1/r^4$
Dipole-nonpolar	Scales with $1/r^6$
Nonpolar-nonpolar	Scales with $1/r^6$

In Table 9-1, r represents the distance between two atoms in angstroms. Interactions that decrease in strength with $1/r$ are effective at a much longer range than those that decrease in strength with higher powers of r. Covalent interactions and hydrogen bonds are strong, and very energetically significant at short distances. Charge-charge interactions have some of the longest-range effects; electrostatic effects on protein activity have been experimentally shown at over 15-angstrom distance, a substantial range in molecular terms. A concentration of charges on a protein surface can create a powerful electrostatic steering effect that can attract ligand molecules or other proteins at even longer range. Hydrogen bonds and charge-dipole interactions are also relatively strong. The effects of these interactions are modeled by computing electrostatic potentials and using the computed potentials as the basis for calculating other molecular properties such as binding constants (via Brownian dynamics) or pKa values.

On the other hand, interactions between noncharged and nonpolar atoms are very weak and effective only at short range. However, the effects of these interactions can be cumulative, stabilizing structure and making intermolecular associations more favorable. The effects of these interactions are addressed when you compute the size of intermolecular contact surfaces or enumerate interactions between neighboring interactions in a protein. In the remainder of this chapter, we discuss various methods for measuring and evaluating atomic structures of proteins, all of which can be used together to add to your understanding of protein chemistry.

Web-Based Protein Structure Tools

Now that we've reviewed the basics of protein chemistry, let's turn our attention to the tools. The most important source of information about protein structure is the PDB. In addition to being an entry point to the structural data itself, the PDB web site (*http://www.rcsb.org/pdb*) contains links to many tools database you can apply to individual protein structures as you search the database. Information from the database is made available through the Protein Structure Explorer interface. For each protein, you can view the molecular structure using 3D display tools such as RasMol and the Java QuickPDB viewer. PDB files and file headers can be viewed as HTML and downloaded in a variety of formats. Links to the protein structure classification databases CATH, FSSP, and SCOP are provided, along with the tools CE and VAST, which search for structures based on structural alignment. Average geometric properties, including dihedral angles, bond angles, and bond lengths can be displayed in tabular format with extremes and deviations noted. Sequences can be viewed and labeled according to secondary structure, and sequence information downloaded in FASTA format.

You can go directly to the page for a particular protein of interest by entering that protein's four-letter PDB code in the Explore box on the PDB's main page. The PDB can also be searched using two different search tools, SearchLite and Search-Fields. SearchLite is a simple search tool that allows you to enter one or more search terms separated by boolean operators into a single search field. Search-Fields is a tool for advanced searches that provides a customizable search form that allows you to use separate keywords to search each PDB header field. You can modify the form by selecting checkboxes at the bottom of the form and regenerating the form. SearchFields supports options for searching a dozen of the most important fields in the PDB header, as well as crystallographic information. Search-Fields also allows the database to be searched using FASTA for sequence comparison, as well as secondary structure features or short sequence features.

From the individual protein page generated by the Structure Explorer, the PDB provides a menu of links through which to connect to other tools. These features are still evolving rapidly. Table 9-2 provides a brief overview of the PDB protein page. We also encourage you to explore the PDB site regularly if you are interested in tools for protein structure analysis.

Table 9-2. PDB Summary Information

Page	Description
Summary page	The Summary page shows important information from the PDB header, as well, the chain composition of the protein and chemical information about any ligands and cofactors.
View Structure	The View Structure page provides links to everything from static images to interactive protein views using VRML, RasMol, and the PDB's Protein Explorer tool.
Download/ Display File	The Download page offers several options for downloading individual protein structures and headers in both classic PDB format and the new mmCIF format.

Table 9-2. PDB Summary Information (continued)

Page	Description
Structural Neighbors	The Structural Neighbors page links to manually curated protein classification databases, such as SCOP and CATH, as well as the automated protein structure comparison tools CE and VAST.
Geometry	The Geometry page provides tabular views of bond length, bond angle, and dihedral angle data for the protein.
Other Sources	The Other Sources page is a rich catalog of links for each protein to everything from its SWISS-PROT accession code to literature references describing the structure. From this page, you can generate everything from domain analyses to structural quality reports to searches of genome catalogs and the NCBI Taxonomy database.
Sequence Details	The Sequence Details page shows the sequence of the protein and the location of its secondary structure features, as extracted from the crystallographic data. The sequences of the individual protein chains in a PDB entry are also available for download in FASTA format.

We'll discuss the specifics of some of the tools linked from the PDB web site in the upcoming sections. Again, as with any web-based tool, it's a good idea to learn as much as you can about the underlying algorithms before basing any conclusions on their results. Just because a method is endorsed by the PDB, doesn't mean that it's 100% foolproof, or that you can interpret results without understanding the method.

Structure Visualization

One of the first tools developed for structure analysis and one of the first analyses you will probably want to do is simply structure visualization. Protein structure data is stored as collections of x, y, z coordinates, but proteins can't be visualized simply by plotting those points. The connectivity between atoms in proteins has to be taken into account, and for the visualization to be effective, a virtual 3D environment, which provides the illusion of depth, needs to be created. Fortunately, all this was worked out in the 1970s and 1980s, and there are now a variety of free and commercial structure visualization tools available for every operating system.

Even with virtual 3D representation, protein structures are so complex that they are difficult to interpret visually. The human eye can interpret 3D solids, but has a difficult time with topologically complex 3D data sets. There are a number of conventional simplified representations of protein structure that allow you to see the overall topology of the protein without the confusion of atomic detail. In order to be useful, a protein structure visualization program needs to, at minimum, be able to display user-selected subsets of atoms with correct connectivity, draw standard cartoon representations of proteins such as ribbons and cylinders, and recolor subsets of a molecule according to a specified parameter.

Molecular Structure Viewers for Your Web Browser

One type of molecular structure viewers are lightweight applications that can be set up to work with your web browser. When properly configured, they will display molecular data as you access it on the Web. RasMol and CnD3 are two of the most popular viewers.

RasMol

One of the most popular molecular structure visualization program tools is RasMol. It is available for a wide range of operating systems, and it reads molecular structure files in the standard PDB format. RasMol 2.7.1, the most up-to-date version, can be downloaded from Bernstein and Sons (*http://www.bernstein-plus-sons. com*). Either source code or precompiled binary distributions can be downloaded.

RasMol comes in three display depths: 8-, 16-, and 32-bit. Eight-bit is the default, but if you have a high-resolution monitor, you may have to experiment and find out which executable is right for your system. You'll know you have a problem when you try to run RasMol and it complains that no appropriate display has been detected. Start with the 8-bit version, and work your way up.

If you plan to compile RasMol yourself, you need to get into the *src* directory and edit the *Makefile* to produce the appropriate version. To do this, open the *Makefile* with an ASCII text editor such as *vim* or Emacs and search for the variable *DEPTHDEF*. You should find something like this:

```
# DEPTHDEF = -DTHIRTYTWOBIT
DEPTHDEF = -DSIXTEENBIT
# DEPTHDEF = -DEIGHTBIT
```

In this example, *DEPTHDEF* has been defined as 16-bit.

The # character at the beginning of a line marks that line as a comment, which isn't read by the *make* program when it scans the *Makefile*. Lines of code can be skipped over by being commented out; that is, marked as a comment. Remove the # character in front of the depth definition you need to use, and add it to comment out the others. Comment characters vary from programming language to programming language, but the notion of a comment line is common to all standard languages.

You may also need to edit the *rasmol.h* file, according to the install instructions.

Once you have the proper RasMol executable, whether you download it or compile it yourself, you need to copy it into */usr/local/bin* and copy the file *rasmol.hlp* into the directory */usr/local/lib/rasmol*. Then, in your web browser's preferences, you need to add RasMol as an application. If you're using Netscape, the default browser on most Linux systems, go to the Preferences→Navigator→Applications menu, select New, and enter the following values into the dialog box:

```
Description:Brookhaven PDB
MIMEType:chemical/x-pdb
Suffixes:.pdb
Application:/usr/local/bin/rasmol
```

You may also want to create a second entry for the MIME type *chemical/x-ras.*

When run from the command line, RasMol opens a single graphics display window with a black background. The molecule can be rotated in this window either directly with the mouse, or with the sliders on the bottom and right side of the window. This window has five pulldown menus. The File menu contains commands for opening molecular structure files. The Display menu contains commands for changing the molecular display style to formats including ball and stick, cartoons, and spacefill. These display commands execute quickly, so you can try each of them out to see the different standard molecular display formats. The Colours menu allows you to change the color scheme of the entire molecule, and the Options menu changes the display style, allowing you to display the molecule in stereo, turn the display of heteroatom groups or labels on and off, etc. The Export menu allows you to write the displayed image in common electronic image formats such as GIF, PostScript, and PPM, which can be edited later using standard image manipulation programs that come with most Linux distributions, such as GIMP.

When you import or save files in RasMol, you do it from the RasMol command line. In the shell window from which you start RasMol, the command prompt changes to *RasMol>*. Enter *help commands* at this command prompt to see the full range of RasMol commands, including commands for selecting subsets of atoms. If RasMol complains that it can't find its help file, create a symbolic link to */usr/local/ lib/rasmol/rasmol.hlp* in the directory in which you installed RasMol and/or the directory in which you are running it. Help commands allow you to create your own combinations of colors and structure display formats, including some not available from the menus; create interatomic distance monitors; and display some intermolecular interactions, such as hydrogen bonds and disulfide bridges.

Cn3D

Cn3D is an application from NCBI that can view protein structure files in NCBI ASN.1 format. If you use the NCBI databases frequently, you will also want to install this tool and set it up to work as an application in your browser.

To install Cn3D on a Linux workstation and set it up as a browser application, you simply need to download the Cn3D archive from NCBI, make a *Cn3D* directory on your own machine, move the archive into that directory, and extract it.

Then, in your web browser's application preferences, make the following new entry:

```
Description:NCBI ASN.1
MIMEType:chemical/ncbi-asn1-binary
Suffixes:.prt
Application:/usr/local/cn3d/Cn3D
```

Cn3D opens two windows: a color structure viewer, in which a molecule can be rotated, colored according to different properties, and rendered in different display formats; a sequence viewer, which allows you to view sequences and alignments corresponding to the displayed protein and to add graphics to the sequence display to highlight the location of secondary structure features.

SWISS-PDBViewer

The SWISS-PDBViewer is a relatively new 3D structure display and analysis tool that complements the services offered by the Swiss Institute of Bioinformatics. It can be used to prepare input for homology modeling using the SWISS-Model web server. However, it is also useful as a standalone visualization tool. The viewer incorporates many useful functions, including superimposition of structures, calculation of molecular surfaces and electrostatic potentials, high-quality rendering, analysis of torsion angles, creation of mutations to the structure, and much more. At the time of this writing, SWISS-PDBViewer is in a phase of rapid development; if interested, you should check the Swiss Institute of Bioinformatics web site for the current version and online documentation.

Standalone Modeling Packages

Heavy-duty molecular structure viewers tend to have many more features than web applications such as RasMol and Cn3D. The most popular examples are Mol-Mol, MidasPlus, and VMD. These programs run on your desktop machine, and to use them you need copies of the PDB files you're interested in using already stored on your computer.

MolMol

If you have Cn3D and RasMol linked to your web browser, you are well-equipped to view any molecular structure on the fly. However, there are times when you need to do more extensive manipulations of a molecular structure. MolMol is a full-featured molecular structure visualization package that allows you to display molecules, edit structures, and compute molecular properties.

You run the MolMol program by issuing the command *molmol* from the command line. There are no command-line options. The program opens with one large window with a white background, and a separate smaller window, which contains sliders for *x*, *y* and *z* rotation and for changing depth and position of the clipping plane. The *clipping plane* controls the simulated depth of the display window and the point at which the display window intersects the molecular structure. Atom selection options are controlled from the menu bar to the right of the main window.

Like RasMol, MolMol has pulldown menus, but all its options are available from the pulldown menus, and there are substantially more of them. MolMol has a complete manual, which is distributed, along with the software, in HTML, and several printable formats, so we will not discuss each command here in detail. Some MolMol features you may find useful, in addition to the standard molecular display functions, are the display of Ramachandran and contact maps, calculation and display of macromolecular surfaces, and display of qualitatively accurate electrostatic potentials.

MolMol is available as a binary distribution from ETH Zurich and is simple to install on a Linux workstation. Follow the directions provided, and you can't go wrong. While the MolMol interface isn't quite as slick as that of a commercial product like MSI's Quanta, it is an amazing value for the price. A couple of general tips: be sure to close dialog boxes and windows by clicking on their OK buttons or by selecting Quit from the menus, rather than by clicking the Kill Window button at the top-right corner. If the program seems to need to take its time to do something, don't click a lot of extra buttons or try to force it to close down—just wait. This will keep the program from hanging up your machine.

MidasPlus

MidasPlus is a near commercial-quality molecular modeling package available from the University of California at San Francisco. It provides many standard molecular display functions, as well as tools for measurement, limited modeling capabilities (for instance, the ability to substitute amino acids in the structure), and computation of molecular surfaces and electrostatics. The MidasPlus source code and executables for various platforms, including some Linux systems, are available from UCSF for a licensing fee of $350—much less than comparable commercial software packages. Your Linux workstation must be equipped with a good-quality 3D graphics card in order to support MidasPlus.

VMD

Another excellent package for creating molecular graphics is VMD, the Visual Molecular Dynamics program from the Theoretical Biophysics group at the University of Illinois. VMD was designed to visualize and animate trajectories from molecular dynamics simulations, but it can also produce quite nice visualizations of single molecules. VMD is available for Linux systems and has an easy-to-use, menu-driven graphical user interface.

Creating High-Quality Graphics with MolScript

> Usage: `molscript -in` *infile* `-[`*options*`] -out` *outfile*
> Usage: `molauto -[`*options*`]` *infile* `>` *outfile*

MolScript has a completely different purpose from the other visualization packages we have discussed. It is designed to produce high-quality graphics for print publication, as you can see in Figure 9-10. It can be configured to run from the command line and to produce PostScript, Raster3D, and VRML output only; it can also be configured to run interactively in its own window, using OpenGL, and to produce output in many additional image file formats.[*]

Setting up interactive MolScript with OpenGL on a Linux workstation isn't straight-forwRasMolard; it requires the installation of Mesa (open source OpenGL) libraries and customization of the *Makefile* that comes with the distribution. However, the basic MolScript installation is quick and simple and can produce visually appealing line drawings of molecular structure cartoons in color or black and white, in a style that is uniquely elegant and appropriate for print media. To install the basic version of MolScript, simply follow the directions in the install file. Copy the resulting executables (*molscript* and *molauto*) to your */usr/local/bin* directory or to another directory in your default path. Here's what *molscript* and *molauto* do:

molscript
> The main MolScript program; generates images

molauto
> The MolScript setup program; automatically generates a rudimentary Mol-Script input file from an input PDB file

MolScript takes two input files: a MolScript command file and a PDB coordinate file. Here's the MolScript input file that produced the images in Figure 9-10:

```
! MolScript v2.1 input file
! generated by MolAuto v1.1.1
title "MYOGLOBIN  (FERRIC IRON - METMYOGLOBIN)"
plot
  read mol "1MBN.pdb";
  transform atom * by centre position atom *;
  set segments 2;
  set planecolour hsb 0.6667 1 1
coil from 1 to 3
```

---

[*] The image in Figure 9-10 was contributed by Per J. Kraulis, from "MOLSCRIPT: A Program to Produce Both Detailed and Schematic Plots of Protein Structures," *Journal of Applied Crystallography* (1991), vol. 24, pp. 946-950.

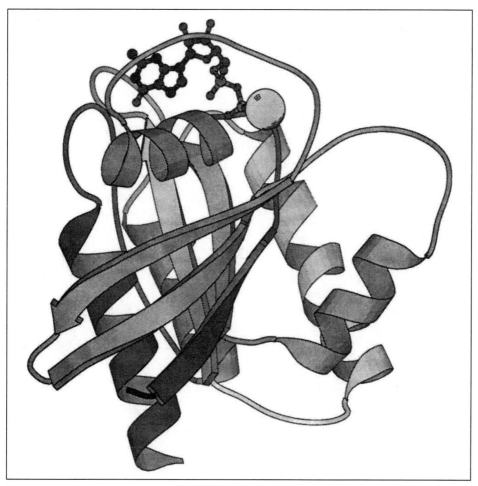

Figure 9-10. A sample image generated by molscript

```
set planecolour hsb 0.619 1 1
helix from 3 to 18
set planecolour hsb 0.5714 1 1
coil from 18 to 20
set planecolour hsb 0.5238 1 1
helix from 20 to 35
...
coil from 94 to 100
set planecolour hsb 0.1429 1 1
helix from 100 to 118
set planecolour hsb 0.09524 1 1
coil from 118 to 125
set planecolour hsb 0.04762 1 1
helix from 125 to 148
set planecolour hsb 0 1 1
coil from 148 to 153;
```

```
set colourparts on
bonds in require residue 1 and type HEM;
```

```
end_plot
```

The MolScript scripting language is unique and not really based on any standard computer language. The only way to learn it is to decide what you want to do, study the manual and examples, and learn the language. The example just shown is a simple MolScript command file; it reads in a single molecule, centers it on the molecule's center of mass, defines the locations of the various secondary structure elements and shades them through the spectrum from red to blue. MolScript can produce much more complex figures than this, however. MolScript plots can be scaled and multiple plots shown on a single page. Subsets of atoms in the molecule can be turned on, displayed in different formats, and custom colored. Labels can be added to figures.

Fortunately, the *molauto* program automatically produces simple input files for the *molscript* program, which can help you get started using the MolScript command language. *molauto* does the most tedious part of input file setup for you—assigning *helix*, *sheet*, or *coil* drawing styles, and colors, to each segment of secondary structure. *molauto* has a variety of command-line options, which you can access by entering *molauto –h. molauto* reads input in the standard PDB file format, and writes to standard output unless a redirector is used.

The following are some of the most useful command line options for *molauto*:

–ss_pdb
> Reads secondary structure assignments from the PDB file

–ss_hb
> Uses hydrogen bonding patterns to assign secondary structure

–cylinder
> Uses cylinders to indicate alpha helices

–stick
> Renders cofactor molecules using a ball-and-stick representation

–nocolour
> Leaves out the coloring commands

–nice
> Improves the quality of the rendering, using more colors and segments

The output of the *molauto* program is an input for the main *molscript* program. Command-line options for *molscript* include:

–ps
> Produces PostScript output

–v Produces VRML output

–size width height
>   Changes the size of the output image

The default input files produced by *molauto* can be hand-edited to produce various effects. One important thing you might want to do (and can't do automatically unless you have installed the MolScript package with OpenGL support) is to rotate the molecular structure until you achieve a good view.

To rotate the molecule view using the noninteractive version of *molscript*, add the following lines to your *molscript* input file, replacing the line that currently reads:

```
transform atom * by centre position atom *;
```

with:

```
transform atom * by centre position in amino-acids
               by rotation x    0.0
               by rotation y    0.0
               by rotation z    0.0
                           ;   !Be sure to include this semicolon.
```

After you generate your first version of the image, open it in a fast PostScript viewer such as *gv*. To change the view of the molecule, experiment with changing the values of *x*, *y*, and *z* rotation in your input file. Since *molscript* takes only seconds to run on any protein input file, you can make changes to the input file, save the file, and redisplay the new output several times until you like the view.

Once generated, the *molscript* image file can be viewed, converted to other file formats, and edited using standard Unix image-manipulation tools. One program you can load when you install most major Linux distributions is GIMP, the freeware package similar to Adobe Photoshop.

Active Site Visualization with LIGPLOT

>   Usage: `ligplot` *protein.pdb* `resid` *resid chain*

Another useful tool for producing graphics for publication is the program LIGPLOT (*http://www.biochem.ucl.ac.uk/bsm/ligplot/ligplot.htm*), which is available from the Structure and Modelling group at University College London (UCL). Given a molecular structure and a specific residue or heteroatom group within the structure as input, LIGPLOT automatically generates a 2D schematic drawing showing hydrogen bonds, interatomic contacts, and solvent accessibility. A sample of LIGPLOT is shown in Figure 9-11

To install LIGPLOT on a Linux workstation, simply follow the directions in the *README* file.

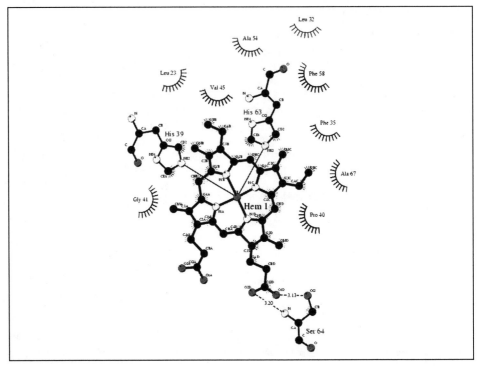

Figure 9-11. A schematic diagram of ligands to the heme cofactor in cytochrome B5, generated with LIGPLOT

In order for LIGPLOT to find its parameter files and helper programs correctly, you need to add some path information to your *.cshrc* file:

```
setenv ligdir /usr/local/ligplot
alias ligplot $ligdir'/ligplot.scr'
alias ligonly $ligdir'/ligonly.scr'
alias dimplot $ligdir'/dimplot.scr'
alias dimonly $ligdir'/dimonly.scr'
setenv hbdir /usr/local/hbplus
alias hbplus $hbdir'/hbplus'
```

The values on the command line specify a residue range in a particular protein chain. The program doesn't have to display only interactions with ligands and prosthetic groups; it can also display the network of close interactions with any residue in a protein. This works best when the residue range selected is small.

dimplot

Usage: dimplot *protein.pdb chain1 chain2*

Usage: dimplot *protein.pdb* -d *domain1 domain2*

The *dimplot* program, a variant of LIGPLOT, displays interactions across an interface between two protein chains or domains. The domain variant works only if your PDB file labels proteins at the domain level of organization.

The painful part of installing the LIGPLOT, *hbplus*, and *naccess* programs on some Linux systems is, ironically, not the installation itself, but having the capability to decrypt the encrypted archives you get from UCL. The files are encrypted using the standard Unix *crypt* command. This sounds straightforward enough, but many Linux vendors don't include *crypt* in their distributions. In order to use *crypt* on your system, you may in fact need to reinstall the latest version of *glibc-2.0*. If you don't want to deal with this, request a decrypted copy of the LIGPLOT *tar* archive from the authors when you send in your license agreement.

Structure Classification

Protein structure classification is important because it gives you an entry point into the world of protein structure that is independent of sequence similarity. Proteins are grouped not by functional families, but according to what kind of secondary structure (alpha helix, beta sheet, or both) they have. Within those larger classes, subclasses are defined based on how the secondary structures in the protein are arranged.

The focus in protein classification is on finding proteins that have similar chemical architectures; it doesn't matter if their sequences are related. Over the years, we've learned from classification that there are far fewer unique protein folds than there are protein sequence families. Protein chemists often are interested in the information that can be extracted from broader structural classes of proteins, since analyzing that information can help them better understand how proteins fold.

Classification of protein structures into families is a nontrivial task. Proteins have many levels of structure: the *primary structure*, which is the 1D sequence; the *secondary structure*, which is composed of the regular substructures that the protein polymer forms due to steric and hydrogen bond interactions; the *tertiary structure*, which is the overall 3D structure of the protein; and the *quaternary structure*, which is the most complex protein structure composed of multiple chains. The quaternary structure is required to form a functional protein. Structure classification involves developing a representation of how units of secondary structure come together to form *domains*, which are compact regions of structure within the larger protein structure. Dividing proteins into domains is another aspect of structure classification.

There isn't really a consensus as to how to classify protein structures quantitatively. Instead, structures end up in qualitatively named classes such as "greek key," "helix bundle," and "alpha-beta barrel." These fold classes are useful in that they draw attention to prominent structural features and create a frame of reference for classifying structure. However, qualitative classifications don't lend themselves to automated analysis, and such protein classification databases still require the involvement of expert curators.

If you're simply concerned with finding the close structural relatives of a published protein structure, there are a number of online classification databases in which existing structures have been annotated by a combination of automated analysis and input from protein structure experts. There are also automated tools for finding structural neighbors by structure alignment, though like any alignment method, these tools require you to understand the significance of comparison scores when analyzing results.

If you're interested in doing your own analysis of a protein structure, there are several structure classification processes and tools that might help.

Secondary Structure from Coordinates

Protein coordinate data sets don't automatically come labeled with alpha-helix and beta-sheet classifiers. Secondary structure features in the protein can be distinguished with reasonable certainty by their hydrogen bonding patterns and their backbone torsion angles.

The standard program for extracting secondary structure from sequence is the DSSP program. DSSP analyzes the geometry and backbone hydrogen bonding partners of each residue in a known protein structure, producing a tabular output that includes residue numbering, sequence, hydrogen bonding, and geometry details. The DSSP database, and DSSP executables derived from the 1995 release of the program, are available from the European Bioinformatics Institute (EBI); these executables may still cause Y2K-related errors on some older Linux systems. Updated DSSP source code is available from the Gerrit Vriend at the Center for Molecular and Biomolecular Informatics at the University of Nijmegen, Netherlands.

STRIDE

Usage: `stride -[options] infile > outfile`

An alternative to DSSP is the program STRIDE, offered in either web server or downloadable form at the European Molecular Biology Laboratory (EMBL, *http:// embl-heidelberg.de/stride/stride.html/*). STRIDE compiles easily on a Linux machine. Create a directory for the program, move the *tar* archive into the directory, and extract. Compile the program with *make*.

Command-line options for STRIDE include:

−M molscript file

> Produces a simple MolScript input

−h Reports hydrogen bond information

−o Reports secondary structure assignments only

A complete list of commands can be viewed by running STRIDE with no command-line options.

The STRIDE output format is in structured 78-character lines. The following example illustrates the hydrogen bond information output format:

```
ACC  ALA -  143  142 ->  TYR -  146  145  3.3  107.8  125.8   58.5   76.9  1MBN

ACC  ALA -  143  142 ->  LYS -  147  146  3.2  154.3  113.4    0.1   43.4  1MBN
DNR  ALA -  144  143 ->  LYS -  140  139  3.0  153.6  109.9   16.4   27.2  1MBN

ACC  ALA -  144  143 ->  GLU -  148  147  3.0  160.3  109.4   11.6    6.4  1MBN
DNR  LYS -  145  144 ->  ASP -  141  140  3.2  145.3  119.5    3.7   73.8  1MBN

ACC  LYS -  145  144 ->  LEU -  149  148  3.0  149.4  128.8    4.7   63.7  1MBN
DNR  TYR -  146  145 ->  ILE -  142  141  3.2  158.7  121.8   20.1   52.6  1MBN
DNR  TYR -  146  145 ->  ALA -  143  142  3.3  107.8  125.8   58.5   76.9  1MBN

ACC  TYR -  146  145 ->  GLY -  150  149  3.0  156.9   96.3   37.1   37.7  1MBN

ACC  TYR -  146  145 ->  TYR -  151  150  3.1  111.2  118.0    4.2   89.9  1MBN
DNR  LYS -  147  146 ->  ALA -  143  142  3.2  154.3  113.4    0.1   43.4  1MBN
```

The STRIDE source code is well constructed and documented. It's an excellent example of how molecular geometry is analyzed. Each function, e.g., surface area calculation, torsion angle calculation, etc., lives in its own separate program. If you want to understand many of the standard operations involved in analyzing geometric properties of proteins, we highly recommend the STRIDE source code.

Topology Cartoons

Topology cartoons are a 2D notation for depicting the topological arrangement of secondary structural elements in proteins. The cartoons can clarify the spatial relationships and connectivity between secondary structure elements in a protein. These relationships may not be easily seen in a 3D structure, even if only the structural backbone is displayed or a ribbon diagram is drawn. Software for generating your own cartoons may be found on the Protein topology page, *http://www.sander.embl-ebi.ac.uk/tops/.*

Topology cartoons, as illustrated in Figure 9-12, represent each secondary structural unit as a shape. Circles are helices, and triangles are beta strands. The beginning of the chain is marked with an N, the end with a C. Each element has a directionality, which can be deduced from the way the connecting segment is drawn. If the N-terminal connection is to the edge of the secondary structural element, that element is directed out of the plane of the drawing; if the N-terminal connection is to the center of the secondary structural element, it is directed back into the plane of the drawing.

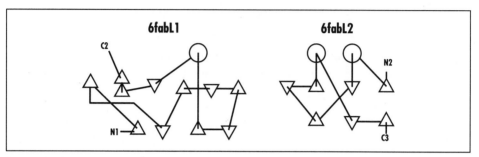

Figure 9-12. A protein topology cartoon

TOPS

Usage: `tops` *pdbcode*

The TOPS program expects a file in DSSP format, generated from your protein of interest, as its input.

In order to compile the TOPS code on your own machine, you need Java support. Linux ports of Java are available from IBM and Blackdown at *http://blackdown.org*. The Blackdown version requires that you update to *glibc2.1.2*, but the IBM version installs easily under Red Hat 6.1 using GnoRPM (if you download RPMs, of course). Once the IBM JRE and JDK are installed, TOPS installs without any difficulty. To run the EditTOPS executable, which allows you to actually view and plot topology files, be sure that these environmental variables are set correctly:

PATH
 Includes */usr/jdk118/bin* (or wherever you installed Java)

CLASSPATH
 Where you installed TOPS classes *TOPS.jar*

TOPS_HOME
 Where you installed TOPS

You can set these variables by writing a script called *topssetup*, which contains the following three lines, and placing it in your home directory. Before you try to run TOPS or EditTOPS, use *source topssetup* to set the environment variables correctly.

```
setenv PATH "/usr/sbin:/sbin:/usr/jdk118/bin:${PATH:."
setenv CLASSPATH "/usr/local/Tops/classes/TOPS.jar:${CLASSPATH"
setenv TOPS_HOME "/usr/local/Tops"
```

Topology patterns also have been implemented as data structures in web-based search tools that allow you to compare topologies of two structures or to search a protein database for structures of similar topology. These services are available from the EBI at *http://www.ebi.ac.uk*.

Classification Databases

Classification databases are taxonomies of protein structure, and they bear a strong resemblance to the morphology-based taxonomies developed by early biologists. Proteins that "look" grossly the same, in terms of shape and topology, are classified as more closely related than proteins that look substantially different. Protein structure types have whimsical names (like *Greek key beta barrel*) based on visual observation and comparison with familiar objects. The classification databases can be envisioned as trees with many branchings at each branch point—very similar to phylogenetic trees, in concept.

SCOP

The Structural Classification of Proteins (SCOP, *http://scop.mrc-1mb.cam.ac.uk/ scop/*) is a database maintained by the MRC Laboratory of Molecular Biology at Cambridge, United Kingdom. SCOP is extensively hand-curated, and tends to lag at least several months behind the PDB in terms of its content. SCOP is a simple, relatively low-tech resource composed of a hierarchy of HTML pages with links to still pictures of individual proteins and folds, as well as embedded links to structure files to be opened with RasMol or Chime plugins and links back to the PDB to download structures.

At the top level of SCOP, known proteins are generally grouped by their secondary structure characteristics into all-alpha, all-beta, coiled coil, small proteins with structural metal ions, and various types of mixed alpha-beta structures. These major types are called Classes within SCOP. The next layer of classification, the Fold level, is a mixture of topology and similarity to domains of known function: one fold can be called "globin-like" and the next "four helical up and down bundle." Beyond the Fold level, proteins are divided further into Superfamilies and Families. Superfamily and Family divisions may be purely functional, or they may also involve some structural difference.

CATH

CATH (*http://www.biochem.ac.uk/bsm/cath_new/*) is similar to SCOP in concept, but it divides up the PDB a little differently. In CATH, proteins are classified at the level of (C)lass, (A)rchitecture, (T)opology, and (H)omologous superfamily. The CATH interface is easily navigated, and it is an excellent resource for examining the variety of known protein structures. CATH can be searched by PDB code, and proteins can be displayed within the browser page. The CATH maintainers provide an excellent lexicon of protein structure description to give you a feel for the structural reality behind the somewhat whimsical protein family names. At the time of this writing, the CATH web interface is undergoing rapid revision and expansion of its capabilities, to include everything from structural assignments of uncharacterized genes that may fit into CATH classes, to new levels of classification hierarchy.

Unique protein structure data sets

The PDB is full of duplication. It's been estimated that out of the approximately 13,000 structures in the PDB at this time, only around 1,000 of them actually represent unique folds. This lack of uniqueness can bias predictive and analytical methods based on extraction of structural patterns and features from the protein database. Thus, there is a need to produce nonredundant subsets of the PDB and to select, from among groups of similar proteins, the best representative of each class. This is essentially a subset of the classification problem, and for a long time it was done based on manual examination and annotation of PDB data. But as the PDB has grown, automated methods for generating nonredundant data sets based on sequence comparison have emerged.

The process for generating such data sets is fairly standard, although the particular parameters differ. First, the PDB is culled to remove extremely short protein chains, chains of very poor resolution, and chains containing a large number of nonstandard residues. The PDB is then decomposed into individual chains, and the chains are sorted by various quality criteria. An all-against-all sequence comparison is done, and chains that don't differ sufficiently to meet a certain cutoff are removed, choosing the lowest-quality chain in a pair to be removed, until all the chains in the list meet the uniqueness criteria in a pairwise comparison. Finally, the removed chains are reintroduced and added back to the set if they don't violate the uniqueness criteria with any other chain in the final set.

At this time, nonredundant data sets can be obtained from PDB Select, at EMBL, from NCBI, and from Dr. Roland Dunbrack at the Fox Chase Cancer Center. There is no software we know of that allows you to create a unique data set based on your own choice of parameters, although the groups mentioned may be willing to generate data sets by special request. A Perl script for creation of nonredundant databases from a sequence DB, called *nrdb90.pl*, is also available from EBI; however, it's hardcoded to produce a nonredundant set at the 90% sequence identity level. If you're intrepid, you can modify this script for your own purposes.

Structural Alignment

Recently, there have been many attempts to make protein-structure classification an automatic and quantitative process, rather than an expert-curated process. Overlaying and comparing structures is a 3D problem that is much more resource-intensive than comparing 1D sequence data. The automated structure comparison tools that exist, therefore, are available primarily as online tools for searching pre-computed databases of structure comparisons.

Comparing Two Protein Structures

The most common parameter that expresses the difference between two protein structures is RMSD, or root mean squared deviation, in atomic positions between the two structures. RMSD can be computed as a function of all the atoms in a protein or as a function of some subset of the atoms, such as the protein backbone or the alpha-carbon positions only. Using a subset of the protein atoms is common, because it is likely that, when two protein structures are compared, they will not be identical to each other in sequence, and therefore the only atoms between which one-to-one comparisons in position can be made will be the backbone atoms.

This is the first context we've discussed in which the *orientation* of a molecular structure becomes important. Because protein structures are generally described in Cartesian coordinates, they essentially exist within a virtual space, and they come with a built-in orientation with respect to that space. RMSD is a function of the distance between atoms in one structure and the same atoms in another structure. Thus, if one molecule starts out in a different position with respect to the reference coordinate system, the other molecule—the RMSD between the two proteins—will be large whether they are similar or not.

In order to compute meaningful RMSDs, the two structures under consideration must first be superimposed, insofar as that is possible. Superimposition of protein structures usually starts with a sequence comparison. The sequence comparison establishes the one-to-one relationships between pairs of atoms from which the RMSD is computed. Atom-to-atom relationships, for the purpose of structure comparison, may actually occur between residues that aren't in the same relative position in the amino acid sequence. Sequence insertions and deletions can push two sequences out of register with each other, while the *core architecture* of the two structures remains similar.

Once atom-to-atom relationships between two structures are established, the task of a superposition program is to achieve an optimal superposition between the two programs—that is, the superposition with the smallest possible RMSD. Because protein scaffolds, or cores, can be similar in topology without being identical, it isn't usually possible to achieve perfect overlap in all pairs of atoms in two structures that are being compared. Overlaying one pair of atoms perfectly may push another pair of atoms further apart. Superposition algorithms optimize the orientation and spatial position of the two molecules with respect to each other.

Figure 9-13 shows an optimal alignment between atomic structures of triosephosphate isomerase and beta-mannase, shown in Compare3D. The two structures are similar enough to be classified as structural neighbors, and their chain traces are relatively similar. However, their sequence identity is only 8.5%.

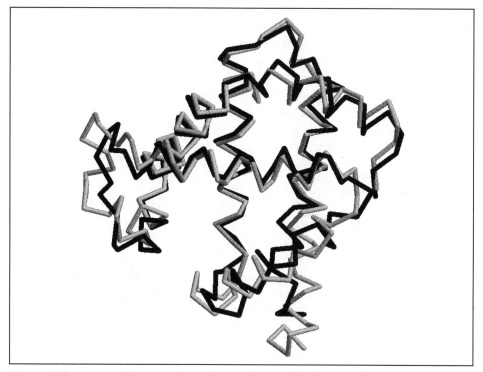

Figure 9-13. An optimal superposition of myoglobin and the 4 chain of hemoglobin, which are structural neighbors

Once optimal superpositions of all pairs of structures have been made, the RMSD values that are computed as a result can be compared with each other, because the structures have been moved to the same frame of reference before making the RMSD calculations.

ProFit

Usage: `profit` *reference.pdb mobile.pdb*

ProFit, developed by Andrew Martin at the University of Reading, United Kingdom, is an easy-to-use program for superimposing two protein structures. One protein is assigned by the user to be the reference structure, and the other protein is mobile with respect to the reference. ProFit outputs RMSD and can also write out coordinates for the superimposed proteins. ProFit allows the option of superimposing only selected regions of each protein so that domains can be examined independently. ProFit compiles and runs on any Unix workstation. ProFit may be downloaded from Andrew's web site (*http://www.bioinf.org.uk/*).

DALI Domain Dictionary

The DALI Domain Dictionary (DDD) at the EBI is based on an automatic classification of protein domains by sequence identity. Rather than using a human-designed classification scheme, DDD is constructed by clustering protein neighbors within an abstract fold space. Instead of working with whole proteins, DDD classifies structures based on compact, recurring structures (called *domains*) that may repeat themselves within, and among, different protein structures. The content of DDD may also be familiar to you as FSSP, the "Fold classification based on Structure-Structure alignment of Proteins" database.

DDD can be searched based on text keywords; it can also be viewed as a tree or a clickable graphical representation of fold space. Views of sequence data for conserved domains are available through the DDD interface, as well as connections to structural neighbors.

The superposition program (SUPPOS) that produces the structural alignments in DALI/FSSP is available within the WHAT IF software package of protein structure analysis tools, which is discussed in the later section "WHAT IF/WHAT CHECK."

CE and CL

The Combinatorial Extension of the Optimal Path (CE) is a sophisticated automatic structure alignment algorithm that uses characteristics of local geometry to "seed" structural alignments and then joins these regions of local similarity into an optimal path for the full alignment. Dynamic programming can then optimize the alignment.

CE is available either as a web server or as source code from the San Diego Supercomputer Center. The web server allows you to upload files for pairwise comparison to each other or to proteins in the PDB, to compare a structure to all structures in the PDB, to compare a structure to a list of representative chains, and review alignments for specific protein families. CE also is fully integrated with the PDB's web site, and CE searches can be initiated directly from the web page generated for any protein you identify in a sequence search. Along with the source code, you can download a current, precomputed pairwise comparison database containing all structures in the PDB. If you're doing only a few comparisons, however, you probably won't even want to do this.

When using the CE server to compute similarities, there are several parameters that you can set, including cutoffs for percent sequence identity, percent of the alignment spanned by gaps, and percent length difference between two chains. You can also set an RMSD cutoff and a Z-score cutoff. The Z-score is a measure of the significance of an alignment relative to a random alignment, analogous to a BLAST E-value. A Z-score of 3.5 or above from CE usually indicates that two proteins have a similar fold.

Along with CE, the SDSC offers the Compound Likeness (CL) server, a suite of tools for probabilistic comparison between protein structures. In CL, you select either an entire protein structure or a structure fragment to use as a probe for searching the PDB. Search features include bond length and angle parameters, surface polarity and accessibility, dihedral angles, secondary structure, shape, and predicted alpha helix and beta sheet coefficients. CL allows you to ask the question "what else is chemically similar to this protein (or fragment) that is of interest to me" and to define chemical similarity very broadly. A full tutorial on CL is available at the CL web site (*http://cl.sdsc.edu/cl1.html/*).

VAST

VAST is a pairwise structural alignment tool offered by NCBI. VAST reports slightly different parameters about structural comparison than CE does, and the underlying algorithm differs in significant respects. However, the results tend to be quite similar. VAST searches automatically allow you to view your superimposed protein structures in the Cn3D browser plug-in, with aligned sequences displayed in Cn3D as well. For practical purposes, either CE or VAST is sufficient to give you an idea of how two structures match up; if you are concerned about the algorithmic differences, both groups provide access to detailed explanations at their sites. Unlike CE, the VAST software doesn't appear to be available to download, so if you want to perform a large number of comparisons on your own server, CE may be preferable.

Structure Analysis

Geometric analysis of protein structures serves two main purposes. It is useful for verifying the chemical correctness of a protein structure, both as a means of deciding whether the structural model is ready to be submitted to the PDB and for analyzing existing structures. Geometric analysis also allows you to examine the internal contacts within a protein structure. Since protein function often depends on the interactions of amino acids that aren't adjacent in the protein sequence, contact analysis can provide insight into complex, nonsequential structural patterns in proteins.

Analyzing Structure Quality

Geometric analysis can show where a model developed from x-ray crystallography data or NMR data violates the laws of chemistry. As mentioned earlier, there are physical laws governing intermolecular interactions: nonbonded atoms can get only so close to each other because as two atoms are forced together beyond the boundary set by their van der Waals radius, the energetics of the contact become very unfavorable. These interactions limit not only the contacts between pairs of atoms in different parts of a protein chain, but also how freely atoms can rotate around the bonds that connect them. The structure of atomic orbitals and the nature of bonds between atoms place natural limits on the position of bonded atoms with respect to each other, so bond angles and dihedral angles are, in practice, restricted to a limited set of values. Tools for geometric analysis generally have been developed by crystallographers to show where their structural models violate these laws of nature; they also can be used by homology modelers or ab-initio structure modelers to evaluate the quality of a structural model.

There are a variety of tools for analyzing structure quality. Some run as standalones; others are incorporated into more comprehensive structure analysis and simulation packages. An exhaustive listing of the best of these tools can be found on the PDB web site.

PROCHECK

PROCHECK *(http://www.biochem.ucl.ac.uk/~roman/procheck/procheck.html)* is a popular software package for checking protein quality. It produces easily interpreted color PostScript plots describing a protein structure and can also compare two related protein structures. It runs on Unix systems and also been ported to Windows.

Using PROCHECK requires that you set up several aliases in your *.cshrc* file. The aliases you need are:

```
setenv prodir /usr/local/procheck
alias procheck'$prodir /procheck.scr'
alias procheck_comp'$prodir /procheck_comp.scr'
alias procheck_nmr'$prodir /procheck_nmr.scr'
alias proplot'$prodir /proplot.scr'
alias proplot_comp'$prodir /proplot_comp.scr'
```

```
alias proplot_nmr'$prodir /proplot_nmr.scr'
alias aquapro'$prodir /aquapro.scr'
alias gfac2pdb'$prodir /gfac2pdb.scr'
alias viol2pdb'$prodir /viol2pdb.scr'
```

The aliases are required by the various PROCHECK command scripts, so you can't just run PROCHECK by typing the full pathnames to each individual module. When you run PROCHECK or PROCOMP, the program you actually run is a command script that calls several other programs and scripts.

PROCHECK can be set up to produce several different kinds of output, either in color or black and white, by editing the *procheck.prm* file in the directory in which you are about to issue the *procheck* command. The parameters are edited by changing *Y* to *N* or vice versa at points in the *procheck.prm* file where those options are available. The file is self-documenting and easy to understand. The most important part of the file, for reference, is probably the portion in which you turn on or off the various types of plots that are available. The rest of the parameters in *procheck.prm* are mainly default color values for different types of plots.

```
Colour all plots?
-----------------
Y <- Produce all plots in colour (Y/N)?


Which plots to produce
----------------------
Y    <-  1. Ramachandran plot (Y/N)?
N    <-  2. Gly & Pro Ramachandran plots (Y/N)?
N    <-  3. Chi1-Chi2 plots (Y/N)?
N    <-  4. Main-chain parameters (Y/N)?
N    <-  5. Side-chain parameters (Y/N)?
N    <-  6. Residue properties (Y/N)?
N    <-  7. Main-chain bond length distributions (Y/N)?
N    <-  8. Main-chain bond angle distributions (Y/N)?
N    <-  9. RMS distances from planarity (Y/N)?
N    <- 10. Distorted geometry plots (Y/N)?
```

Once you've edited the *procheck.prm* file to your satisfaction, run PROCHECK with the command *procheck filename.pdb [chain] resolution*. The resolution parameter causes your protein to be compared to a "reference protein of X angstrom resolution" in the PROCHECK output. This parameter isn't optional. The command line for PROCOMP requires a second protein filename and chain ID instead of the resolution parameter.

WHAT IF/WHAT CHECK

WHAT IF is a multifunctional menu-driven molecular modeling package developed by Gert Vriend and now available through the University of Nijmegen. WHAT IF can calculate just about any property of proteins we discuss in this chapter, from solvent accessible surface area to pKa values to contacts to molecular dynamics using GROMOS. The full WHAT IF package is available to academic users for a small fee, and it is known to compile and run well on Linux systems.

WHAT CHECK provides access to a subset of WHAT IF structural quality checks. WHAT CHECK reports on stereochemistry, bond lengths, angles, and dihedrals, among other quantities. Complete WHAT CHECK reports for any protein in the PDB can be downloaded from the PDBREPORTS database at EMBL. WHAT CHECK also is available as part of the Biotech Validation Suite web server at EMBL, for use on models and on structures not already deposited in the PDB.

Intramolecular Interactions

Geometric analysis can also be useful in understanding a protein's fold and function. In this case, the geometry of interest isn't the chemical bonding interactions between atoms adjacent to each other in the protein chain, but the nonbonded interactions between atoms that are widely separated in the protein chain. The density of intramolecular contacts in the structural core of a domain may be quite different from the density of contacts in a region between two structural domains. Measuring this density over the whole protein may give clues as to the process by which a protein folds. The patterns of hydrogen bonds that hold a protein together may serve as an identifying signature for a protein fold. And contacts between certain chemically important residues in a protein may suggest hypotheses about the protein's catalytic mechanism or function. Protein engineers may want to examine the intramolecular contacts in a protein to determine where changes are least likely to disrupt the protein's structure.

Computing contacts with HBPLUS

Listings of intramolecular nonbonded interactions and hydrogen bonds can be computed using the standalone program HBPLUS, available from the Biomolecular Structure group at UCL. Obtaining the HBPLUS program and running it are straightforward, but because the results are produced as a single long text file, they require some scripted postprocessing to become useful. The LPC-CSU (Ligand-Protein Contacts/Contacts of Structural Units) server at the Weizmann Institute (Rehovot, Israel, *http://pdb.weizmann.ac.il:8500/oca-bin/ipcsu/*) can produce textual reports of important intra- and intermolecular contacts in any protein. Protein structures can be uploaded to the server from the user's machine or found on the server using their PDB ID codes.

Contact mapping and display functionality also can be found within the WHAT IF package. Two-dimensional contact maps are a standard feature of most molecular modeling packages. A 2D contact map is simply a plot of pairwise interactions between residues, where residue number within the protein is plotted on each axis and a dot (perhaps color-coded to indicate the contact distance) is drawn wherever residue X and residue Y come into close contact. Contact maps have distinct patterns that can help identify a protein's fold, and some efforts have even been made to predict contact maps for proteins of unknown structure based on their sequences and predicted secondary structure features.

Solvent Accessibility and Interactions

Solvent-accessible surface calculations help you figure out which chemical groups are on the surface of a protein. Amino acids on the surface of a protein usually are the ones that determine how it interacts with other molecules, such as chemical substrates, ligands, other proteins, and receptors If you know what the chemical surface of the protein looks like, you can use that information to help determine why one molecule binds to another, why an enzyme is specific for a particular substrate, or how the protein influences its environment in other ways.

Analytical shape calculations also help you describe the geometry of the protein surface. A lot of biochemistry textbooks describe intermolecular interactions in terms of locks and keys. Molecules fit together in geometrically specific ways, so the shape of the lock (e.g., the enzyme) has to complement to the shape of the key (the substrate). The shape of a receptor on the cell surface has to complement to the ligand it's supposed to respond to, or the cellular response isn't triggered. The immune system is a good example. In the immune response, the organism produces antibodies that attack antigens of a particular shape. This is why you can vaccinate an animal against a disease by injecting a sample of killed virus. The killed virus is shaped just like the live, deadly virus, but it can't harm the animal. Nonetheless, the animal develops antibodies that recognize the shape of the killed virus. Then, when the live virus comes along and tries to invade, the animal already has antibodies that are the right shape to attack the live virus.

So, for instance, if you want to design a new vaccine or engineer a protein that will carry out a particular reaction, or understand how two proteins in a metabolic pathway interact with each other, it's important to be able to measure the shape of the molecule.

The standard method for computing solvent accessibility is quite simple. Each atom in the molecular structure is represented by a sphere; there is a different sphere radius for each distinct atom type. The spheres surround the known atomic centers and are modeled by a collection of several hundred discrete points. To determine the solvent-accessible surface of the protein, solvent-accessibility calculators simulate a spherical "probe" with a radius equivalent to that of water (1.4 angstroms) rolling over the surface of the atomic spheres. The path of the center of the probe determines the solvent-accessible surface of the molecule. Because the probe (and hence, water molecules) can't fit into sharp crevices in the molecular surface, the computed solvent accessible surface is much smoother than the underlying molecular surface (Figure 9-14).

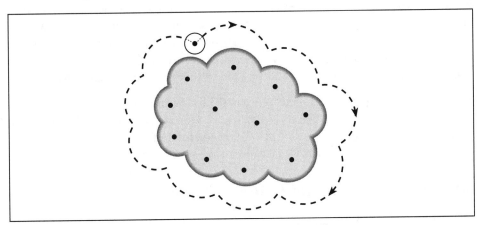

Figure 9-14. Determination of solvent accessibility by probe-rolling

Because proteins are dynamic entities rather than the rigid bodies assumed by solvent-accessibility calculations, it's likely that the interior of the molecule has more contact with solvent than can be computed using a probe-rolling algorithm. However, solvent-accessibility calculations can help develop an initial understanding of a protein molecule that will inform further experimentation. Accessibility calculations are one way of getting at the complex physicochemical properties of a protein; the nature of the protein surface affects its interaction with the surrounding media as well as with other proteins or substrates.

Computing Solvent Accessibility with naccess

Usage: naccess *pdb file* [-p *probe size*] [-r *vdw file*] [-s *stdfile*]
-[*hwyc*]

There are many programs for calculating solvent accessibility by probe-rolling. They are all straightforward and easy to use, requiring a standard PDB file as input and usually giving output in the form of a percentage of accessibility for each amino acid or atom in the protein. One popular program is *naccess*, which is available from the Biomolecular Structure and Modelling group at UCL. *naccess* can be used in combination with other programs developed by this group, such as HBPLUS (a program for computing intermolecular interactions and hydrogen bonds) and LIGPLOT, which we covered earlier. It also runs as a standalone. *naccess* is written in FORTRAN, so you'll need the *g77* compiler installed on your machine to compile it.

naccess outputs two files, an *.asa* file with accessible surface areas for each atom in the molecule and an *.rsa* file with accessible surface areas and relative accessibilities for each amino acid. It handles both protein and nucleic acid molecules and produces reports of accessibilities for individual molecular chains as well as complete structures. The *–h*, *–w*, and *–y* flags cause the program to ignore hydrogen atoms, water molecules, or heteroatoms, respectively. Run with the *–c* option, *naccess* produces intermolecular contact areas rather than accessible areas.

SURFNET is a program developed by Roman Laskowski at UCL to manipulate solvent-accessibility information and display useful representations of surface features, clefts, cavities, and binding sites. SURFNET generates surface output in formats that can be displayed in molecular visualization programs, including RasMol.

Solvent Accessibility with Alpha Shapes

The Alpha Shapes software is a mathematically exact alternative to the standard Connolly surface method of computing solvent accessibility. Developed by the research group of mathematician Herbert Edelsbrunner at NCSA (*http://www.alphashapes.org/alpha/*), the Alpha Shapes software is a general-purpose program for modeling the surfaces of objects. A set of extensions to the Alpha Shapes software, specifically for analyzing protein molecules, is also available.

The Alpha Shapes method constructs what is called a simplicial complex or alpha complex of a structure, based on a rigorous geometrical decomposition of the space surrounding the collection of points that describes the structure. Once the alpha complex is constructed for a protein structure, algorithms for inclusion and exclusion can describe exactly the surface area or volume of the structure as well as cavities, clefts, and regions of contact. The main benefit of using the Alpha Shapes algorithm to compute protein shapes is that the software comes with a sophisticated visualization program called *alvis*, which can display such geometrical features as the interior shape of an ion channel or the cavities in the interior of a protein.

Several programs make up the Alpha Shapes distribution. These programs must be run in the proper sequence to correctly analyze molecular data:

pdb2alf
>   Translates a PDB file into an alpha datafile.

delcx
>   Computes the Delaunay complex of the molecule on the output from *pdb2alf.*

mkalf
>   Computes the alpha complex from the Delaunay complex computed by *delcx.*

VOLBL

> Computes protein properties, using the alpha complex computed by *mkalf* and information from the original the PDB file. Depending on which command-line options are used, VOLBL can compute cavities in the protein interior and space-filling models of the protein, as well as volumes of molecules and cavities. Multiple VOLBL runs can produce complimentary data sets, which can be added or subtracted to determine contact areas and other molecular properties.

You can find usage details of each of these programs in a *README* file that accompanies the Alpha Shapes distribution, or by attempting to run the program with no arguments on the command line.

Using *alvis* to visualize your Alpha Shapes data can be quite interesting. To do this, you need output from *delcx* and *mkalf*, but not from VOLBL. To run *alvis* on a data set generated from *molecule.PDB*, where output files *molecule.dt* and *molecule.alf* are also present, enter *alvis molecule*. The visualizer opens with the convex hull of the molecule displayed. The standard atomic structure of the molecule can't be seen from within the current version of *alvis*, but you can compare your *alvis* view with another view of the same molecule (perhaps using RasMol or a similar molecular visualization program) side by side.

In the bottom left of the *alvis* control panel, you'll see a box containing a graph with three colored curves. This graph is called the *alpha rank* graph, and it can be used to select a desirable view of the molecule. Positioning your cursor at peaks, valleys, or intersections on these graphs gives the most interesting views of the molecular shape.

Using the Pocket Panel, available from the Gizmos pulldown in *alvis*, you can make selections that shows voids, pockets, and difference areas in a protein. The online *alvis* tutorial at *http://www.alphashapes.org* describes in full the settings needed to view these features.

Along with the main Alpha Shapes programs, a number of utility scripts are provided that can postprocess *VOLBL* output to give specific information. These include:

aacount

> Computes an itemized residue-wise contribution to area or volume from a VOLBL output file

aadiff

> Computes residue-wise differences in accessible area between two models

aanonpolar

> Outputs area or volume contributions from nonpolar atoms; *aapolar* does the same thing for polar groups

areadiff

> Computes atom-wise differences in area between two files

Analogous scripts for computing volume differences are also included.

Analytical surface potentials based on Alpha Shapes can also be accessed with the CAST-P web server at the University of Illinois at Chicago. At the time of this writing, not all protein structures in the PDB are represented on CAST-P; the site is currently under development. However, it promises to be a useful analytical tool in the future. CAST-P features an integrated Java-based visualization of cavities in protein structures and the amino acids that are in contact with cavities.

Computing Physicochemical Properties

We've already discussed forces that control the interactions between individual atoms in a protein molecule. However, to understand intermolecular interactions, it may be more interesting to learn how all the atoms in a protein act together at a distance, to influence other proteins or ligands.

The electrostatic potential of an object is a measure of the force exerted by that object on other nearby objects. The electrostatic potential of a protein molecule is a long-range force that can influence the behavior of other molecules in the environment at a range of up to 15 angstroms.

Electrostatic interactions within the macromolecule can also be important. Nearby charged groups within a protein may cause the pKa value (the pH at which an acidic or basic group loses or gains a proton) of an amino acid to shift, creating the chemistry necessary for that molecule to perform its chemical function.

Macromolecular Electrostatics

A protein molecule can be thought of as a collection of charges in a dielectric medium. In the model that computes electrostatic potentials for protein molecules, each atom is represented as a point with a partial atomic charge. The solvent accessible surface of the protein forms the boundary between the interior medium of the protein and the exterior medium surrounding the protein.

Computing the electrostatic potential of a protein structure allows you to predict quantities such as individual amino acid pKa values, solvation energies, and approximations to intermolecular binding energies. If you are interested in protein modeling, macromolecular electrostatics is a topic that you may wish to explore further. Our review of the subject in the March 2000 issue of *Methods* provides an entry point to the molecular electrostatics literature.

The University of Houston Brownian Dynamics (UHBD) package is a state-of-the-art software package for computing macromolecular electrostatics. UHBD computes electrostatic potentials and can also use those potentials as parameters in subsequent Brownian Dynamics and Molecular Dynamics simulations. The most recent release of UHBD can be compiled on Linux systems and includes several control scripts that implement UHBD to calculate pKa values for individual titrating amino acids in the protein, as well as theoretical titration curves for the protein as a whole. UHBD is accessed by a scripting language; it requires a protein structure file and a command script as input. It also requires a file containing atomic partial charges for any amino acids and other atoms in the input structure. Detailed scripting examples are provided in the UHBD distribution, along with charge datafiles that allow the program to assign correct partial atomic charges to all but unusual atom groups.

UHBD, and other similar programs such as DelPhi—which overlaps only the electrostatics functionality of UHBD—use numerical approximations to solve the Poisson-Boltzmann equation for the large number of interacting charges that make up a protein. In the finite-difference approach used by UHBD, the irregularly spaced charges in a protein molecule are mapped onto a regular 3D grid, and the Poisson-Boltzmann equation is solved iteratively for each point on the grid until the solution converges to an electrostatic potential for each point.

Visualization of Molecular Surfaces with Mapped Properties

Other than *alvis*, which doesn't truly display a molecular surface but rather a mathematically derived pseudosurface, there are several options for displaying the shapes of molecules. Most molecular modeling packages incorporate a molecular surface display feature and allow the surface to be colored according to chemical properties. However, the display schemes in programs not specifically designed for that purpose are too unsophisticated to handle data from macromolecular electrostatics calculations and other representations of physicochemical properties. An exception seems to be the SWISS-PDBViewer (discussed earlier), which can interpret data from external electrostatics calculations and analytical molecular surface calculations.

GRASP/GRASS

GRASP is a high-quality molecular surface visualization program developed by Barry Honig's group at Columbia University. GRASP can read electrostatic potential files and display them as features of a molecular surface, and has many other display options for creating really beautiful visual interpretations of electrostatic properties. Unfortunately, GRASP is available only for SGI IRIX workstations and there are no plans to make it available for other operating systems at this time.

If you're using a Mac or PC, some of GRASP's functionality can be accessed through the GRASS web interface at Columbia. However, this web interface relies heavily on an interface to either GRASP itself (on SGI workstations), the Chime browser plug-in, or a VRML viewer, all of which are still problematic or nonexistent if you're working on a Linux system. We have had some success using the *vrmlview* viewer with Netscape to visualize VRML models from the GRASS server, although the image quality is relatively low. To use *vrmlview*, download and install the program and then set your Netscape preferences to use the *vrmlview* executable to handle files with MIME type *model/vrml*. The "Handled By" entry in your Netscape applications list should read */usr/local/bin/vrmlview %s* (or wherever you installed *vrmlview*).

The GRASS interface is straightforward and clickable. You can select from several molecular display options: CPK surface, molecular surface, ribbons, or a stick model. Then, a property can be chosen to be mapped onto the molecular graphics. Available properties include electrostatic potentials computed using GRASP's built-in FDPB solver, surface curvature, hydrophobicity, and amino acid variability within the protein's sequence family. GRASS doesn't implement the full functionality of GRASP, but many of the most useful features are available.

Structure Optimization

Protein structure optimization is the process of bringing a structure into agreement with some "ideal" set of geometric parameters. As mentioned earlier when we discussed structure quality checking, protein structural models sometimes violate the laws of chemistry. Placing atoms too close together causes unfavorable intramolecular contacts, or van der Waals bumps. Bond lengths, bond angles, and dihedral angles between atoms in the protein can also be "wrong"; that is, they can fall outside some normal range of values expected for that type of bond or angle.

Structure optimization is an important issue not just to developers of theoretical models, but to researchers who experimentally determine protein structures. All protein atomic coordinates are, in an important sense, structural models. Structure optimization tools have long been part of the x-ray crystallographer's toolkit. The process of optimization can be computationally intensive. Because all atoms in a protein structure are connected by bonds with rigidly fixed lengths, moving an atom in one part of the protein structure has wide-ranging effects on its neighbors. Often moving one part of the protein into a better configuration means moving another part of the protein into an unfavorable configuration. Optimization is, essentially, an iterative series of small changes designed to converge to the best overall result. There are many methods of optimization, which is its own subdiscipline within theoretical computer science.

You won't always need to know the particulars of optimization methods, but if you begin using structure optimization and molecular simulation methods frequently, you should be aware that your choice of optimization algorithms may be an issue. It's not always certain that optimization will provide you with a better structural model; if the method is based on incorrect structural rules, or if the rules are prioritized incorrectly, optimization can actually give you a worse model than you started with.

Informatics Plays a Role in Optimization

What are the "ideal" parameters or constraints used in optimization? In some cases, they are based entirely on chemical principles: bond lengths and angles determined by steric restrictions and nonbonded interactions described as Lennard-Jones potentials. In other cases, structural constraints are based on information derived from the database of known protein structures. If a particular amino acid in a particular sequence context always has the same conformation, a higher probability can be assigned to it assuming that conformation again, rather than a different conformation. Secondary structure prediction methods use an information-based approach to predicting likely conformations for the protein backbone. Optimization methods use information to refine atomic structures at the level of individual sidechain atoms once the backbone trace has been worked out.

Rotamer Libraries

Rotamer libraries are parameter sets specifically for the optimization of sidechain positions in molecular model building. They are called *rotamer* libraries because they contain information about allowed rotations of the remote amino acid sidechain atoms around the Cα–Cβ bond, expressed as the allowed values of sidechain dihedral angles.

Because of steric constraints on bond rotation, amino acid sidechains in proteins can assume only a few conformations without unfavorable energetic consequences. Rotamer libraries can be derived using chemical bond and angle constraints, but, they are more likely to be developed by analysis of the conformations assumed by amino acid sidechains in known protein structures. Rotamer libraries can be either backbone-dependent or -independent. Backbone-independent rotamer libraries classify all instances of a particular amino acid as part of the same set, even if one occurrence is within a beta sheet and the other is within an alpha helix. Backbone-dependent rotamer libraries, on the other hand, further classify amino acids according to their occurrence in specific secondary structures.*

SCRWL, available from the Fred Cohen research group at UCSF, is a program that allows you to model sidechain conformations using a backbone-dependent rotamer library.

PDFs

The derivation of probability density functions (PDFs) is similar in concept to the development of rotamer libraries, although more mathematically rigorous. The essence of a PDF is that a mathematical function is developed to represent a distribution of discrete values. The discrete values that make up the distribution are harvested from occurrences of a situation in a representative database of samples. That mathematical function can then be used to evaluate and optimize (and in some cases even predict) the properties of future occurrences of the same situation.

In protein modeling, PDFs have been used to describe intra- and inter-residue interatomic distances, as well as bond angles, dihedral angles, and other more spatially extensive regions of protein structure. Modeller, which is discussed in Chapter 10, *Predicting Protein Structure and Function from Sequence*, uses a combination of bond angle and dihedral angle PDFs to optimize the protein structure models it builds. Modeller's internal OPTIMIZE routine can be used for PDF-based structure optimization.

The data from which PDFs are generated can be broken down into specific occurrences; for example, all contacts between Cβ in residue i and Cβ in residue $i+4$ when both residues are leucine but again, trade-offs between classification detail and class population occur. Distance PDFs for proteins have been used by several groups to evaluate and optimize protein structures. Most such work is still in its early stages, and software isn't yet available for public use.

Figure 9-15 shows a plot of a distance probability density function for tertiary interactions between sulfur atoms in cysteine residues generated from known protein structures. The function's peak near 2 angstroms corresponds to the high propensity with which the sulfur atoms form disulfide bridges between cysteine residues. These data are taken from the Biology Workbench at the San Diego Supercomputer Center *(http://workbench.sdsc.edu/)* and plotted using *xmgr*. Note

---

* When rules for structure evaluation and optimization are derived from existing occurrences of patterns in a database, there is a trade-off between highly specific classification of occurrences and the size of the data set for each type of occurrence. The more data in the data set, the better the value of the rule is likely to be; however, the less specific the classification of occurrences, the less value the rule is likely to have for prediction. This is true not only of rotamer libraries but of PDFs and any other database-derived rules.

that the Workbench PDFs make a distinction between cysteine residues participating in disulfide bridges (pictured here and referred to as CSS residues at the Workbench site) and those cysteines that don't participate in disulfide bonds (which the Workbench site calls CYS).

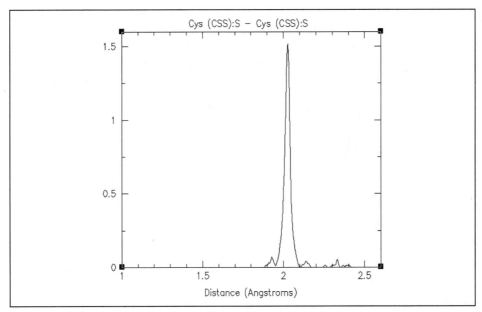

Figure 9-15. Interatomic distance probability density function

Structure evaluation based on PDFs is implemented in the Structure Tools section of the SDSC Biology Workbench (Figure 9-16). You can upload a PDB structure or a theoretical model and score the structure either on a residue-by-residue or an atom-by-atom basis. Scores can be displayed on a plot, where the Y-axis represents the relative probability of the region of structure that's being evaluated. This can be thought of in terms of the probability that a particular residue or atom is in the "correct" position, given what is known about other occurrences of that residue or atom in similar sequence environments. Regions with low probability are likely to be misfolded or poorly modeled. PDF probability scores can also be written out in a special PDB file, in place of the temperature factor values found in the original PDB file. These special PDB files can then be displayed using a visualization program such as RasMol or Chime. Coloring the molecule by temperature factor maps the PDF probability scores onto the molecular structure, highlighting regions of the structure that score poorly.

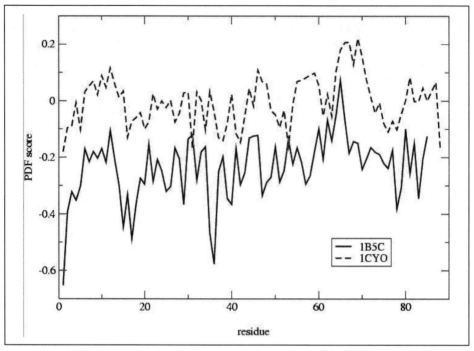

Figure 9-16. Comparing PDF scores for an obsolete PDB structure (1B5C) and (1CYO) that superseded it

Protein Resource Databases

Several new databases containing information about protein structure and function, and designed for users of genome-level information, have recently emerged on the Web. Some of the most notable are GeneCensus, PRESAGE, and BIND. These databases are still relatively lightly populated, and have not yet taken the central role in biological research that PDB and NCBI. However, certainly these or similar resources will soon become vital to molecular biology research.

GeneCensus

The GeneCensus project is a broad, sequence-based comparison of the protein content of several genomes. At the time of this writing, GeneCensus contains information from 20 genomes. GeneCensus currently can be searched with a PDB ID or an ORF ID to locate occurrences of specific protein folds in the GeneCensus genomes.

PRESAGE

PRESAGE is a database of information about experimental progress with the structures of various proteins. You can search PRESAGE with a TIGR ORF code, NCBI or SWISS-PROT accession number, and a number of other codes to find out if someone is attempting to isolate, crystallize, and solve the structure of that protein, and if so, how far along they are. PRESAGE is relatively new at press time; it currently contains only about 6,000 records and isn't guaranteed to be comprehensive. It can't be searched directly by BLAST or FASTA search with a sequence, so before checking PRESAGE for instances of an unknown sequence, you have to search for matching accession codes. However, in principle, the PRESAGE database promises to be useful, both for crystallographers and their collaborators, and for curious citizens of the molecular biology community who are wondering if the structure of their protein has been solved yet.

BIND

The Biomolecular Interaction Network Database (BIND) is another relatively new data repository offered by the Samuel Lunenfeld Research Institute. BIND was designed to be a central deposition site for known information about macromolecular interactions. BIND is a complex database, containing information about interactions between objects in the database, molecular complex information, and metabolic pathway information. The BIND format is designed to contain information about experimental conditions that observe the interactions stored in the database, as well as information about binding site location, biochemical activity, kinetics, and thermodynamics. BIND is still in its beta testing phase, containing only a few hundred interactions. However, BIND has been funded to hire indexers and it is expected to grow rapidly in the near future. One interesting aspect of the BIND data entry process is that methods for automated reading of existing journal literature are being implemented to extract known interactions from their inconvenient location in dusty library stacks and put them more effectively in the public domain.

Putting It All Together

We can't give you a single recipe for using the techniques described in this chapter to characterize a protein. There are too many variables from system to system, and too much diversity in what you as a biologist might want to know. However, some common features of a structural modeling approach include:

* Gathering useful structural and biophysical information about the system under study. Everything from site-directed mutagenesis to classic biochemical and biophysical studies may be useful.

- Using multiple sequence analysis to analyze the protein as part of a related family. This may give insight into the location of functionally important residues and active sites.

- Analyzing a crystal structure or theoretical model to identify the location of buried polar and charged residues, unusual hydrogen bonds, networks of structured solvent molecules, and other chemical features that may be involved in structural stability or function.

- Analyzing a family of related proteins by superimposing or comparing their structures to identify common features.

- Mapping identified properties—sites known to affect function if mutated, sites conserved in multiple sequences, etc.—onto the protein sequence and structure.

- Visualizing the structure and interpreting the location of potentially important amino acids and sites.

- Computing the molecular surface and characterizing possible substrate binding sites or molecular interaction regions by their shapes.

- Computing electrostatic potentials and modeling electrostatic properties such as individual amino acid pKa values or molecular interaction energies. Unusually strong electrostatic potentials or unusual pKa values may indicate regions of catalytic importance.

Obviously, this type of analysis requires a real understanding of protein chemistry. We've identified the tools of structural biology for you, but you will decide how to put them to use. To help you toward that end, Table 9-3 contains a quick reference of molecular structure tools and how they are commonly used.

Table 9-3. Structure Tools and Techniques

What you do	Why you do it	What you use to do it
View molecular structure	Computer graphics are the only way to "see" a protein structure in detail	Browser plugins: RasMol, Cn3D, SWISS-PDBViewer; standalones: MolMol, MidasPlus, VMD
Create high-quality PostScript schematic diagrams and color graphics of proteins	For publication	MolScript
Create schematic diagrams of active sites	To help identify the structural components of the functional site; for publication	LIGPLOT
Structure classification	To identify relationships among proteins	CATH, SCOP

Table 9-3. Structure Tools and Techniques (continued)

What you do	Why you do it	What you use to do it
Secondary structure analysis	To extract recognizable features at the SS level, which aids in classification	DSSP, STRIDE
Topology analysis	To extract recognizable supersecondary motifs, which aids in classification	TOPS
Domain identification	To extract recognizable domains, which aids in classification	3Dee
Unique structure database subsets	To eliminate bias in source data sets for knowledge-based modeling	PDBSelect, culled PDB databases
Structure alignment	To identify relationships among distantly related proteins that may have evolved beyond recognizable sequence similarity, while preserving structural similarity	CE, DALI, VAST
Molecular geometry analysis	To identify strained conformations or incorrectly represented regions in a structure model	PROCHECK, WHAT IF
Intramolecular contact analysis	To identify residue-residue interactions that may help identify active sites, structure-stabilizing features, etc.	CSU, HBPLUS
Solvent accessibility calculation	To identify amino acids that interact with a solvent	naccess, Alpha Shapes
Solvent modeling	To place a chemically realistic solvent shell around the molecule in preparation for some types of simulations; aids in understanding functional mechanism	HBUILD
Molecular surface visualization	To gain a visual understanding of molecular shape and chemical surface features	GRASP, GRASS server, SWISS-PDBViewer
Electrostatic potential calculation	To visualize the chemically important surface features of a protein, and as a preliminary step in pKa calculations, binding energy calculations, and Brownian dynamics simulations	UHBD, DelPhi
Protein pKa calculation	To model pH-dependent behavior of proteins, identify possible active sites, and and identify residues in unusual chemical environments	UHBD, DelPhi

10

Predicting Protein Structure and Function from Sequence

The amino acid sequence of a protein contains interesting information in and of itself. A protein sequence can be compared and contrasted with the sequences of other proteins to establish its relationship, if any, to known protein families, and to provide information about the evolution of biochemical function. However, for the purpose of understanding protein function, the 3D structure of a protein is far more useful than its sequence.

The key property of proteins that allows them to perform a variety of biochemical functions is the sequence of amino acids in the protein chain, which somehow uniquely determines the 3D structure of the protein.* Given 20 amino acid possibilities, there are a vast number of ways they can be combined to make up even a short protein sequence, which means that given time, organisms can evolve proteins that carry out practically any imaginable purpose.

Each time a particular protein chain is synthesized in the cell, it *folds* together so that each of the critical chemical groups for that particular protein's function is brought into a precise geometric arrangement. The fold assumed by a protein sequence doesn't vary. Every occurrence of that particular protein folds into exactly the same structure.

Despite this consistency on the part of proteins, no one has figured out how to accurately predict the 3D structure that a protein will fold into based on its sequence alone. Patterns are clearly present in the amino acid sequences of proteins, but those patterns are *degenerate*; that is, more than one sequence can specify a particular type of fold. While there are thousands upon thousands of ways

---

* That "somehow," incidentally, represents several decades of work by hundreds of researchers, on a fundamental question that remains open to this day.

amino acids can combine to form a sequence of a particular length, the number of unique ways that a protein structure can organize itself seems to be much smaller. Only a few hundred unique protein folds have been observed in the Protein Data Bank. Proteins with almost completely nonhomologous sequences nonetheless fold into structures that are similar. And so, prediction of structure from sequence is a difficult problem.

Determining the Structures of Proteins

If we can experimentally determine the structures of proteins, and structure prediction is so hard, why bother with predicting structure at all? The answer is that solving protein structures is difficult, and there are many bottlenecks in the experimental process. Although the first protein structure was determined decades before the first DNA sequence, the protein structure database has grown far more slowly in the interim than the sequence database. There are now on the order of 10,000 protein structures in the PDB, and on the order of 10 million gene sequences in GenBank. Only about 3,000 unique protein structures have been solved (excluding structures of proteins that are more than 95% identical in sequence). Approximately 1,000 of these are from proteins that are substantially different from each other (no more than 25% identical in sequence).

Solving Protein Structures by X-ray Crystallography

In the late 1930s, it was already known that proteins were made up of amino acids, although it had not yet been proven that these components came together in a unique sequence. Linus Pauling and Robert Corey began to use x-ray crystallography to study the atomic structures of amino acids and peptides.

Pure proteins had been crystallized by the time that Pauling and Corey began their experiments. However, x-ray crystallography requires large, unflawed protein crystals, and the technology of protein purification and crystallization had not advanced to the point of producing useful crystals. What Pauling and Corey did discover in their studies of amino acids and peptides was that the peptide bond is flat and rigid, and that the carboxylic acid oxygen is almost always on the opposite side of the peptide bond as the amino hydrogen. (See the illustration of a peptide bond in Figure 9-1). Using this information to constrain their models, along with the atomic bond lengths and angles that they observed for amino acids, Pauling and Corey built structural models of polypeptide chains. As a result, they were able to propose two types of repetitive structure that occur in proteins: the alpha helix and the beta sheet, as shown previously in Figure 9-5.

In experiments that began in the early 1950s, John Kendrew determined the structure of a protein called myoglobin, and Max Perutz determined the structure of a similar protein called hemoglobin. Both proteins are oxygen transporters, easily isolated in large quantities from blood and readily crystallized. Obtaining x-ray data of reasonably high quality and analyzing it without the aid of modern computers took several years. The structures of hemoglobin and myoglobin were found to be composed of high-density rods of the dimensions expected for Pauling's proposed alpha helix. Two years later, a much higher-quality crystallographic data set allowed the positions of 1200 of myoglobin's 1260 atoms to be determined exactly. The experiments of Kendrew and Perutz paved the way for x-ray crystallographic analysis of other proteins.

In x-ray crystallography, a crystal of a substance is placed in an x-ray beam. X-rays are reflected by the electron clouds surrounding the atoms in the crystal. In a protein crystal, individual protein molecules are arranged in a regular lattice, so x-rays are reflected by the crystal in regular patterns. The x-ray *reflections* scattered from a protein crystal can be analyzed to produce an electron density map of the protein (see Figure 10-1: images are courtesy of the Holden Group, University of Wisconsin, Madison, and Bruker Analytical X Ray Systems). Protein atomic coordinates are produced by modeling the best possible way for the atoms making up the known sequence of the protein to fit into this electron density. The fitting process isn't unambiguous; there are many incrementally different ways in which an atomic structure can be fit into an electron density map, and not all of them are chemically correct. A protein structure isn't an exact representation of the positions of atoms in the crystal; it's simply the model that best fits both the electron density map of the protein and the stereochemical constraints that govern protein structures.

In order to determine a protein structure by x-ray crystallography, an extremely pure protein sample is needed. The protein sample has to form crystals that are relatively large (about 0.5 mm) and singular, without flaws. Producing large samples of pure protein has become easier with recombinant DNA technology. However, crystallizing proteins is still somewhat of an art form. There is no generic recipe for crystallization conditions (e.g., the salt content and pH of the protein solution) that cause proteins to crystallize rapidly, and even when the right solution conditions are found, it may take months for crystals of suitable size to form.

Many protein structures aren't amenable to crystallization at all. For instance, proteins that do their work in the cell membrane usually aren't soluble in water and tend to aggregate in solution, so it's difficult to solve the structures of membrane proteins by x-ray crystallography. Integral membrane proteins account for about 30% of the protein complement (*proteome*) of living things, and yet less than a dozen proteins of this type have been crystallized in a pure enough form for their structures to be solved at atomic resolution.

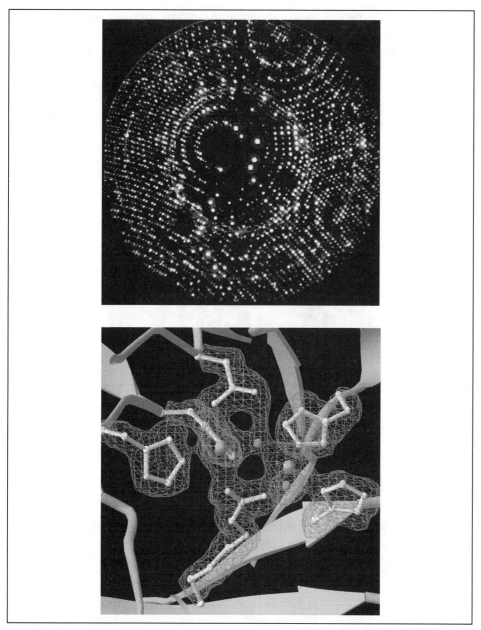

Figure 10-1. X-ray diffraction pattern and corresponding electron density map of the 3D structure of zinc-containing phosphodiesterase

Solving Structures by NMR Spectroscopy

An increasing number of protein structures are being solved by nuclear magnetic resonance (NMR) spectroscopy. Figure 10-2 shows raw data from NMR spectroscopy. NMR detects atomic nuclei with nonzero spin; the signals produced by these nuclei are *shifted* in the magnetic field depending on their electronic environment. By interpreting the chemical shifts observed in the NMR spectrum of a molecule, distances between particular atoms in the molecule can be estimated. (The image in Figure 10-2 is courtesy of Clemens Anklin, Bruker Analytical X Ray Systems.)

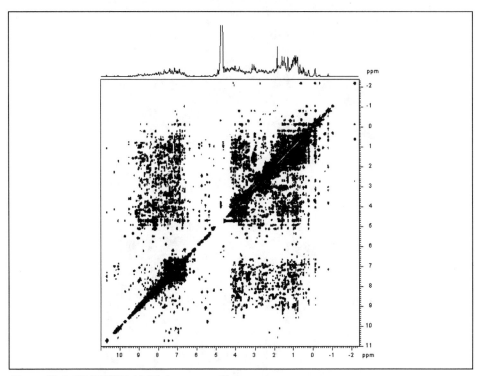

Figure 10-2. NOESY (2D NMR) spectrum of lysozyme

To be studied using NMR, a protein needs to be small enough to rotate rapidly in solution (on the order of 30 kilodaltons in molecular weight), soluble at high concentrations, and stable at room temperature for time periods as long as several days.

Analysis of the chemical shift data from an NMR experiment produces a set of distance constraints between labeled atoms in a protein. Solving an NMR structure means producing a model or set of models that manage to satisfy all the known distance constraints determined by the NMR experiment, as well as the general stereochemical constraints that govern protein structures. NMR models are often released in groups of 20–40 models, because the solution to a structure determined by NMR is more ambiguous than the solution to a structure determined by crystallography. An NMR average structure is created by averaging such a group of models (Figure 10-3). Depending on how this averaging is done, stereochemical errors may be introduced into the resulting structure, so it's generally wise to check the quality of average structures before using them in modeling.

Figure 10-3. Structural diversity in a set of NMR models

Predicting the Structures of Proteins

Ideally, what we'd like to do in analyzing proteins is take the sequence of a protein, which is cheap to obtain experimentally, and predict the structure of the protein, which is expensive and sometimes impossible to determine experimentally. It would also be interesting to be able to accurately predict function from sequence, identify functional sites in uncharacterized 3D structures, and eventually, build designed proteins—molecular machines that do whatever we need them to do. But without an understanding of how sequence determines structure, these other goals can't reliably be achieved.

There are two approaches in computational modeling of protein structure. The first is knowledge-based modeling. Knowledge-based methods employ parameters extracted from the database of existing structures to evaluate and optimize structures or predict structure from sequence (the *protein structure prediction problem*). The second approach is based on simulation of physical forces and molecular dynamics. Physicochemical simulations are often used to attempt to model how a protein folds into its compact, functional, *native* form from a nonfunctional, not-as-compact, *denatured* form (the *protein folding problem*). In this chapter we focus on knowledge-based protein structure prediction and analysis methods in which bioinformatics plays an important role.

Ab-initio protein structure prediction from protein sequence remains an unsolved problem in computational biology. Although many researchers have worked to develop methods for structure prediction, the only methods that produce a large number of successful 3D structure predictions are those based on sequence homology. If you have a protein sequence and you want to know its structure, you either need a homologous structure to use as a template for model-building, or you need to find a crystallographer who will collaborate with you to solve the structure experimentally.

The protein-structure community is addressing the database gap between sequence and structure in a couple of ways. Pilot projects in structural genomics—the effort to experimentally solve all, or some large fraction of, the protein structures encoded by an entire genome—are underway at several institutions. However, these projects stand little chance of catching up to the sheer volume of sequence data that's being produced, at least in the near future.

CASP: The Search for the Holy Grail

In light of the database gap, computational structure prediction is a hot target. It's often been referred to as the "holy grail" of computational biology; it's both an important goal and an elusive, perhaps impossible, goal. However, it's possible to track progress in the area of protein structure prediction in the literature and try out approaches that have shown partial success.

Every two years, structure prediction research groups compete in the Community Wide Experiment on the Critical Assessment of Techniques for Protein Structure Prediction (CASP, *http://predictioncenter.llnl.gov/*). The results of the CASP competition showcase the latest methods for protein-structure prediction. CASP has three areas of competition: homology modeling, threading, and ab initio prediction. In addition, CASP is a testing ground for new methods of evaluating the correctness of structure predictions.

Homology modeling focuses on the use of a structural template derived from known structures to build an all-atom model of a protein. The quality of CASP predictions in 1998 showed that structure prediction based on homology is very successful in producing reasonable models in any case in which a significantly homologous structure was available. The challenge for homology-based prediction, as for sequence alignment, is detecting meaningful sequence homology in the Twilight Zone—below 25% sequence homology.

Threading methods take the amino acid sequence of an uncharacterized protein structure, rapidly compute models based on existing 3D structures, and then evaluate these models to determine how well the unknown amino acid "fits" each template structure. All the threading methods reported in the most recent CASP competition produce accurate structural models in less than half of the cases in which they are applied. They are more successfully used to detect remote homologies that can't be detected by standard sequence alignment; if parts of a sequence fit a fold well, an alignment can generally be inferred, although there may not be enough information to build a complete model.

Ab-initio prediction methods focus on building structure with no prior information. While none of the ab-initio methods evaluated in CASP 3 produce accurate models with any reliability, a variety of methods are showing some promise in this area. One informatics-based strategy for structure prediction has been to develop representative libraries of short structural segments out of which structures can be built. Since structural "words" that aren't in the library of segments are out of bounds, the structural space to be searched in model building is somewhat constrained. Another common ab-initio method is to use a reduced representation of the protein structure to simulate folding. In these methods, proteins can be represented as beads on a string. Each amino acid, or each fixed secondary structure unit in some approaches, becomes a bead with assigned properties that attract and repel other types of beads, and statistical mechanical simulation methods are used to search the conformational space available to the simplified model. These methods can be successful in identifying protein folds, even when the details of the structure can't be predicted.

From 3D to 1D

Proteins and DNA are, in reality, complicated chemical structures made up of thousands or even millions of atoms. Simulating such complicated structures explicitly isn't possible even with modern computers, so computational biologists use *abstractions* of proteins and DNA when developing analytical methods. The most commonly used abstraction of biological macromolecules is the single-letter sequence. However, reducing the information content of a complicated structure to a simple sequence code leaves behind valuable information.

The sequence analysis methods discussed in Chapters 7 and 8, treat proteins as strings of characters. For the purpose of sequence comparison, the character sequence of a protein is almost a sufficient representation of a protein structure. However, even the need for substitution matrices in scoring protein sequence alignments points to the more complicated chemical nature of proteins. Some amino acids are chemically similar to each other and likely to substitute for each other. Some are different. Some are large, and some are small. Some are polar; some are nonpolar. Substitution matrices are a simple, quantitative way to map amino acid property information onto a linear sequence. Asking no questions about the nature of the similarities, substitution matrices reflect the tendencies of one amino acid to substitute for another, but that is all.

However, each amino acid residue in a protein structure (or each base in a DNA or RNA structure, as we are beginning to learn) doesn't exist just within its sequence context. 1D information has not proven sufficient to show unambiguously how protein structure and function are determined from sequence. The 3D structural and chemical context of a residue contains many types of information.

Until quite recently, 3D information about protein structure was usually condensed into a more easily analyzable form via 3D-to-1D mapping. A property extracted from a database can be mapped, usually in the form of a numerical or alphabetic character score, to each residue in a sequence. Knowledge-based methods for secondary structure prediction were one of the first uses of 3D-to-1D mapping. By mapping secondary structure context onto sequence information as a property—attaching a code representing "helix," "sheet," or "coil" to each amino acid—a set of *secondary structure propensities* can be derived from the structure database and then used to predict the secondary structure content of new sequences.

What important properties does each amino acid in a protein sequence have, besides occurrence in a secondary structure? Some commonly used properties are solvent accessibility, acid/base properties, polarizability, nearest sequence neighbors, and nearest spatial neighbors. All these properties have something to do with intermolecular interactions, as discussed in Chapter 9.

Feature Detection in Protein Sequences

Protein sequence analysis is based to some extent on understanding the physico-chemical properties of the chemical components of the protein chain, and to some extent on knowing the frequency of occurrence of particular amino acids in specific positions in protein structures and substructures. Although protein sequence–analysis tools operate on 1D sequence data, they contain implicit assumptions about how structural features map to sequence data. Before using these tools, it's best to know some protein biochemistry.

Features in protein sequences represent the details of the protein's function. These usually include sites of post-translational modifications and localization signals. *Post-translational modifications* are chemical changes made to the protein after it's transcribed from a messenger RNA. They include truncations of the protein (cleavages) and the addition of a chemical group to regulate the behavior of the protein (phosphorylation, glycosylation, and acetylation are common examples). *Localization* or *targeting signals* are used by the cell to ensure that proteins are in the right place at the right time. They include nuclear localization signals, ER targeting peptides, and transmembrane helices (which we saw in Chapter 9).

Protein sequence feature detection is often the first problem in computational biology tackled by molecular biologists. Unfortunately, the software tools used for feature detection aren't centrally located. They are scattered across the Web on personal or laboratory sites, and to find them you'll need to do some digging using your favorite search engine.

One collection of web-based resources for protein sequence feature detection is maintained at the Technical University of Denmark's Center for Biological Sequence Analysis Prediction Servers (*http://www.cbs.dtu.dk/services/*). This site provides access to server-based programs for finding (among other things) cleavage sites, glycosylation sites, and subcellular localization signals. These tools all work similarly; they search for simple sequence patterns, or profiles, that are known to be associated with various post-translational modifications. The programs have standardized interfaces and are straightforward to use: each has a submission form into which you paste your sequence of interest, and each returns an HTML page containing the results.

Secondary Structure Prediction

Secondary structure prediction is often regarded as a first step in predicting the structure of a protein. As with any prediction method, a healthy amount of skepticism should be employed in interpreting the output of these programs as actual predictions of secondary structure. By the same token, secondary structure predictions can help you analyze and compare protein sequences. In this section, we briefly survey secondary structure prediction methods, the ways in which they are measured, and some applications.

Protein secondary structure prediction is the classification of amino acids in a protein sequence according to their predicted local structure. Secondary structure is usually divided into one of three types (alpha helix, beta sheet, or coil), although the number of states depends on the model being used.

Secondary structure prediction methods can be divided into alignment-based and single sequence-based methods. *Alignment-based* secondary structure prediction is quite intuitive and related to the concept of sequence profiles. In an alignment-based secondary structure prediction, the investigator finds a family of sequences that are similar to the unknown. The homologous regions in the family of sequences are then assumed to share the same secondary structure and the prediction is made not based on one sequence but on the consensus of all the sequences in the set. *Single sequence-based* approaches, on the other hand, predict local structure for only one unknown.

Alignment-Based and Hybrid Methods

Modern methods for secondary structure prediction exploit information from multiple sequence alignments, or combinations of predictions from multiple methods, or both. These methods claim accuracy in the 70–77% range. Many of these programs are available for use over the Web. They take a sequence (usually in FASTA format) as input, execute some procedure on them, then return a prediction, usually by email, since the prediction algorithms are compute-intensive and tend to be run in a queue. The following is a list of six of the most commonly used methods:

PHD

> PHD combines results from a number of neural networks, each of which predicts the secondary structure of a residue based on the local sequence context and on global sequence characteristics (protein length, amino acid frequencies, etc.) The final prediction, then, is an arithmetic average of the output of each of these neural networks. Such combination schemes are known as *jury decision* or (more colloquially) *winner-take-all* methods. PHD is regarded as a standard for secondary structure prediction.

PSIPRED

> PSIPRED combines neural network predictions with a multiple sequence alignment derived from a PSI-BLAST database search. PSIPRED was one of the top performers on secondary structure prediction at CASP 3.

JPred

> JPred secondary structure predictions are taken from a consensus of several other complementary prediction methods, supplemented by multiple sequence alignment information. JPred is another one of the top-performing secondary structure predictors. The JPred server returns output that can in turn be displayed, edited, and saved for use by other programs using the Jalview alignment editor.

PREDATOR

> PREDATOR combines multiple sequence alignment information with the hydrogen bonding characteristics of the amino acids to predict secondary structure.

PSA

> PSA is another Markov model-based approach to secondary structure prediction. It's notable for its detailed graphical output, which represents predicted probabilities of helix, sheet, and coil states for each position in the protein sequence.

Single Sequence Prediction Methods

The first structure prediction methods in the 1970s were single sequence approaches. The Chou-Fasman method uses rules derived from physicochemical data about amino acids to predict secondary structure. The GOR algorithm (named for its authors, Garnier, Osguthorpe, and Robson) and its successors use information about the frequency with which residues occur in helices, sheets, and coils in proteins of known structure to predict structures. Both methods are still in use, often on multiple-tool servers such as the SDSC Biology Workbench. Modern methods based on structural rules and frequencies can achieve prediction accuracies in the 70–75% range, especially when families of related sequences are analyzed, rather than single sequences.

The surge in popularity of artificial intelligence methods in the 1980s gave rise to AI-based approaches to secondary structure prediction, most notably the pattern-recognition approaches developed in the laboratories of Fred Cohen (University of California, San Francisco) and Michael Sternberg (Imperial Cancer Research Fund), and the neural network applications of Terrence Sejnowski and N. Qian (then at Johns Hopkins). These methods exploited similar information as the earlier single-sequence methods did, using the AI techniques to automate knowledge acquisition and application.

Measuring Prediction Accuracy

Authors who present papers on secondary structure prediction methods often use a measure of prediction accuracy called Q_3. The Q_3 score is defined as:

Q = true_positives + true_negatives / total_residues

A second measure of prediction accuracy is the *segment overlap score* (Sov) proposed by Burkhard Rost and coworkers. The Sov metric tends to be more stringent than Q_3, since it gives high scores to non-overlapping segments of a single kind of secondary structure, and penalizes sparse predictions (Figure 10-4).

```
a) Good prediction
HHHHHHHHHHHEEE          EEEHHHHHHHHHHHHHHHHHHHHHHH    EEEE
TEAMRNDIIARICGEDGQVDPNCFVLAQSIVFSAMEQEHFSEFLRSHHFCKYQIE


a) Sparse prediction
H H   H H HHE E   E       E EH H HH H    H H  H HH    E E
TEAMRNDIIARICGEDGQVDPNCFVLAQSIVFSAMEQEHFSEFLRSHHFCKYQIE
```

Figure 10-4. Good and bad (sparse) secondary structure predictions

When comparing methods, it pays to be conservative; look at both the average scores and their standard deviations instead of the best reported score. As you can see, Q_3 and Sov are fairly simple statistics. Unlike E-values reported in sequence comparison, neither is a test statistic; both measure the percent of residues predicted correctly instead of measuring the significance of prediction accuracy. And, as with genefinders, make sure you know what kind of data is used to train the prediction method.

Putting Predictions to Use

Originally, the goal of predicting secondary structure was to come up with the most accurate prediction possible. Many researchers took this as their goal, resulting in many gnawed fingernails and pulled-out hairs. As mentioned earlier, the hard-won lesson of secondary structure prediction is that it isn't very accurate. However, secondary structure prediction methods have practical applications in bioinformatics, particularly in detecting remote homologs. Drug companies compare secondary structure predictions to locate potential remote homologs in searches for drug targets. Patterns of predicted secondary structure can predict fold classes of proteins and select targets in structural genomics.

Secondary structure prediction tools such as PredictProtein and JPred combine the results of several approaches, including secondary structure prediction and threading methods. Using secondary structure predictions from several complementary methods (both single-sequence and homology-based approaches) can result in a better answer than using just one method. If all the methods agree on the predicted structure of a region, you can be more confident of the prediction than if it had been arrived at by only one or two programs. This is known as a *voting* procedure in machine learning.

As with any other prediction, secondary structure predictions are most useful if some information about the secondary structure is known. For example, if the structure of even a short segment of the protein has been determined, that data can be used as a sanity check for the prediction.

Predicting Transmembrane Helices

Transmembrane helix prediction is related to secondary structure prediction. It involves the recognition of regions in protein sequences that can be inserted into cell membranes. Methods for predicting transmembrane helices in protein sequences identify regions in the sequence that can fold into a helix and exist in the hydrophobic environment of the membrane. Transmembrane helix prediction grew out of research into hydrophobicity in the early 1980s, pioneered by Russell Doolittle (University of California, San Diego). Again, there are a number of transmembrane helix prediction servers available over the Web. Programs that have emerged as standards for transmembrane helix prediction include TMHMM (*http://www.cbs.dtu.dk/services/TMHMM-1.0/*), MEMSAT (*http://insulin.brunel.ac. uk/~jones/memsat.html*), and TopPred (*http://www.sbc.su.se/~erikw/toppred2/*).

Although structure determination for soluble proteins can be difficult, a far greater challenge is structure determination for membrane-bound proteins. Some of the most interesting biological processes involve membrane proteins—for example, photosynthesis, vision, neuron excitation, respiration, immune response, and the passing of signals from one cell to another. Yet only a handful of membrane proteins have been crystallized. Because these proteins don't exist entirely in aqueous solution, their physicochemical properties are very different from those of soluble proteins and they require unusual conditions to crystallize—if they are amenable to crystallization at all.

As a result, many computer programs exist that detect transmembrane segments in protein sequence. These segments have distinct characteristics that make it possible to detect them with reasonable certainty. In order to span a cell membrane, an alpha helix must be about 17–25 amino acids in length. Because the interior of a cell membrane is composed of the long hydrocarbon chains of fatty acids, an alpha helix embedded in the membrane must present a relatively nonpolar surface to the membrane in order for its position to be energetically favorable.

Early transmembrane segment identification programs exploited these problems directly. By analyzing every 17–25 residue windows of an amino acid sequence and assigning a *hydrophobicity score* to each window, high-scoring segments can be predicted to be transmembrane helices. Recent improvements to these early methods have boosted prediction of individual transmembrane segments to an accuracy level of 90–95%.

The topology of the protein in the membrane isn't as easy to predict. The orientation of the first helix in the membrane determines the orientation of all the remaining helices. The connections of the helices can be categorized as falling on one side or the other of the membrane, but determining which side is which, physiologically, is more complicated.

Threading

The basic principle of structure analysis by threading is that an unknown amino acid sequence is fitted into (threaded through) a variety of existing 3D structures, and the fitness of the sequence to fold into that structure is evaluated. All threading methods operate on this premise, but they differ in their details.

Threading methods don't build a refined all-atom model of the protein; rather, they rapidly substitute amino acid positions in a known structure with the sidechains from the unknown sequence. Each sidechain position in a folded protein can be described in terms of its environment: to what extent the sidechain is exposed to solvent and, if it isn't exposed to solvent, what other amino acids it's in contact with. A threaded model is scored highly if hydrophobic residues are found in solvent-inaccessible environments and hydrophilic residues on the protein surface. But these high scores are possible only if buried charged and polar residues are found to have appropriate countercharges or hydrogen bonding partners, etc.

Threading is most profitably used for fold recognition, rather than for model building. For this purpose, the UCLA-DOE Structure Prediction Server (*http://www.doe-mbi.ucla.edu/people/frsur/frsur.html*) is by far the easiest tool to use. It allows you to submit a single sequence and try out multiple fold-recognition and evaluation methods, including the DOE lab's own Gon prediction method as well as EMBL's TOPITS method and NIH's 123D+ method. Other features, including BLAST and FASTA searches, PROSITE searches, and Bowie profiles, which evaluate the fitness of a sequence for its apparent structure, are also available.

Another threading server, the 3D-PSSM server offered by the Biomolecular Modelling Laboratory of the Imperial Cancer Research Fund, provides a fold prediction based on a profile of the unknown sequence family. 3D-PSSM incorporates multiple analysis steps into a simple interface. First the unknown protein sequence is compared to a nonredundant protein sequence database using PSI-BLAST, and a position-specific scoring matrix (PSSM) for the protein is generated. The query PSSM is compared to all the sequences in the library database; the query sequence is also compared to 1D-PSSMs (PSSMs based on standard multiple sequence alignments) and 3D-PSSMs (PSSMs based on structural alignments) of all the protein families in the library database. Secondary structure predictions based on these comparisons are shown, aligned to known secondary structures of possible structural matches for the query protein. The results from the 3D-PSSM search are presented in an easy-to-understand graphical format, but they can also be downloaded, along with carbon-alpha-only models of the unknown sequence built using each possible structural match as a template.

Most threading methods are considered experimental, and new methods are always under development. More than one method can be used to help identify any unknown sequence, and the results interpreted as a consensus of multiple experts. The main thing to remember about any structural model you build using a threading server is that it's likely to lack atomic detail, and it's also likely to be based on a slightly or grossly incorrect alignment. The threading approach is designed to assess sequences as likely candidates to fit into particular folds, not to build usable models. Putative structural alignments generated using threading servers can serve as a basis for homology modeling, but they should be carefully examined and edited prior to building an all-atom model.

Predicting 3D Structure

As was stated earlier in the chapter, predicting protein structure from sequence is a difficult task, and there is no method yet that satisfies all parameters. There are, however, a number of tools that can predict 3D structure. They fall into two subgroups: homology modeling and ab-initio prediction.

Homology Modeling

Let's say you align a protein sequence (a "target" sequence) against the sequence of another protein with a known structure. If the target sequence has a high level of similarity to the sequence with known structure (over the full length of the sequence), you can use that known structure as a template for the target protein with a reasonable degree of confidence.

There is a standard process that is used in homology modeling. While the programs that carry out each step may be different, the process is consistent:

1. Use the unknown sequence as a query to search for known protein structures.

2. Produce the best possible global alignment of the unknown sequence and the template sequence(s).

3. Build a model of the protein backbone, taking the backbone of the template structure as a model.

4. In regions in which there are gaps in either the target or the template, use a loop-modeling procedure to substitute segments of appropriate length.

5. Add sidechains to the model backbone.

6. Optimize positions of sidechains.

7. Optimize structure with energy minimization or knowledge-based optimization.

The key to a successful homology-modeling project isn't usually the software or server used to produce the 3D model. Your skill in designing a good alignment to a template structure is far more critical. A combination of standard sequence alignment methods, profile methods, and structural alignment techniques may be employed to produce this alignment, as we discuss in the example at the end of this chapter. Once a good alignment exists, there are several programs that can use the information in that alignment to produce a structural model.

Modeller

Modeller (*http://guitar.rockefeller.edu/modeller/modeller.html*) is a program for homology modeling. It's available free to academics as a standalone program or as part of MSI's Quanta package (*http://www.msi.com*).

Modeller has no graphical interface of its own, but once you are comfortable in the command-line environment, it's not all that difficult to use. Modeller executables can be downloaded from the web site at Rockefeller University, and installation is straightforward; follow the directions in the *README* file available with the distribution. There are several different executables available for each operating system; you should choose based on the size of the modeling problems you will use them for. The *README* file contains information on the array size limits of the various executables. There are limits on total number of atoms, total number of residues, and total number of sequences in the input alignment.

As input to Modeller, you'll need two input files, an alignment file, and a Modeller script. The alignment file format is described in detail in the Modeller manpages; the Modeller script for a simple alignment consists of just a few lines written in the TOP language (Modeller's internal language). Modeller can calculate multiple models for any input. If the *ENDING_MODEL* value in the example script shown is set to a number other than one, more models are generated. Usually, it's preferable to generate more than one model, evaluate each model independently, and choose the best result as your final model.

The example provided in the Modeller documentation shows the setup for an alignment with a pregenerated alignment file between one known protein and one unknown sequence:

```
INCLUDE                                  # Include the predefined TOP routines
SET ALNFILE = 'alignment.ali'            # alignment filename
SET KNOWNS  = '5fd1'                     # codes of the templates
SET SEQUENCE = '1fdx'                    # code of the target
SET ATOMS_FILES_DIRECTORY = './:../atom_files'# directories for input atom files
SET STARTING_MODEL= 1                    # index of the first model
SET ENDING_MODEL = 1                     # index of the last model
                                         # (determines how many models to calculate)
CALL ROUTINE = 'model'                   # do homology modeling
```

Modeller is run by giving the command *mod scriptname*. If you name your script *fdx.top*, the command is *mod fdx*.

Modeller is multifunctional and has built-in commands that will help you prepare your input:

SEQUENCE_SEARCH

Searches for similar sequences in a database of fold class representative structures

MALIGN3D

Aligns two or more structures

ALIGN

Aligns two blocks of sequences

CHECK_ ALIGNMENT

Evaluates an alignment to be used for modeling

COMPARE_SEQUENCES

Scores sequences in an alignment based on pairwise similarity

SUPERPOSE

Superimposes one model on another or on the template structure

ENERGY

Generates a report of restraint violations in a modeled structure

Each command needs to be submitted to Modeller via a script that calls that command, as shown in the previous sample script. Dozens of other Modeller commands and full details of writing scripts are described in the Modeller manual.

One caveat in automated homology modeling is that sidechain atoms may not be correctly located in the resulting model; automatic model building methods focus on building a reasonable model of the structural backbone of the protein because homology provides that information with reasonable confidence. Homology doesn't provide information about sidechain orientation, so the main task of the automatic model builder is to avoid steric conflicts and improbable conformations rather than optimize sidechain orientations. Incorrect sidechain positions may be misleading if the goal of the model building is to explore functional mechanisms.

How Modeller builds a model

Though Modeller incorporates tools for sequence alignment and even database searching, the starting point for Modeller is a multiple sequence alignment between the target sequence and the template protein sequence(s). Modeller uses the template structures to generate a set of spatial restraints, which are applied to the target sequence. The restraints limit, for example, the distance between two residues in the model that's being built, based on the distance between the two homologous residues in the template structure. Restraints can also be applied to bond angles, dihedral angles, and pairs of dihedrals. By applying enough of these spatial restraints, Modeller effectively limits the number of conformations the model can assume.

The exact form of the restraints are based on a statistical analysis of differences between pairs of homologous structures. What those statistics contribute is a quantitative description of how much various properties are likely to vary among homologous structures. The amount of allowed variation between, for instance, equivalent alpha-carbon-to-alpha-carbon distances is expressed as a PDF, or probability density function.

What the use of PDF-based restraints allows you to do, in homology modeling, is to build a structure that isn't exactly like the template structure. Instead, the structure of the model is allowed to deviate from the template but only in a way consistent with differences found between homologous proteins of known structure. For instance, if a particular dihedral angle in your template structure has a value of –60°, the PDF-based restraint you apply should allow that dihedral angle to assume a value of 60 plus or minus some value. That value is determined by what is observed in known pairs of homologous structures, and it's assigned probabilistically, according to the form of the probability density function.

Homology-based spatial restraints aren't the only restraints applied to the model. A force field controlling proper stereochemistry is also applied, so that the model structure can't violate the rules of chemistry to satisfy the spatial restraints derived from the template structures. All chemical restraints and spatial restraints applied to the model are combined in a function (called an *objective function*) that's optimized in the course of the model building process.

ModBase: a database of automatically generated models

The developers of Modeller have made available a queryable online database of annotated homology models. The models are prepared using an automated prediction pipeline. The first step in the pipeline is to compare each unknown protein sequence with a database of existing protein structures. Proteins that have significant sequence homology to domains of known structures are then modeled using those structures as templates. Unknown sequences are aligned to known structures using the *ALIGN2D* command in Modeller, and 3D structures are built using the Modeller program. The final step in the pipeline is to evaluate the models; results of the evaluation step are presented to the ModBase user as part of the search results. Since this is all standard procedure for homology-model development that's managed by a group of expert homology modelers, checking ModBase before you set off to build a homology model on your own is highly recommended.

The general procedure for building a model with Modeller is to identify homologies between the unknown sequence and proteins of known structures, build a multiple alignment of known structures for use as a template, and apply the Modeller algorithm to the unknown sequence. Models can subsequently be evaluated using standard structure-evaluation methods.

The SWISS-MODEL server

SWISS-MODEL is an automated homology modeling web server based at the Swiss Institute of Bioinformatics. SWISS-MODEL allows you to submit a sequence and get back a structure automatically. The automated procedure that's used by SWISS-MODEL mimics the standard steps in a homology modeling project:

1. Uses BLAST to search the protein structure database for sequences of known structure

2. Selects templates and looks for domains that can be modeled based on non-homologous templates

3. Uses a model-building program to generate a model

4. Uses a molecular mechanics force field to optimize the model

You must supply an unknown sequence to initiate a SWISS-MODEL run in their First Approach mode; however, you can also select the template chains that are used in the model building process. This information is entered via a simple web form. You can have the results sent to you as a plain PDB file, or as a project file that can be opened using the SWISS-PDBViewer, a companion tool for the SWISS-MODEL server you can download and install on your own machine.

Although that sounds simple, such an automatic procedure is error-prone. In a nonautomated molecular modeling project, there is plenty of room for user intervention. SWISS-MODEL actually allows you to intervene in the process using their Project Mode. In Project Mode, you can use the SWISS-PDBViewer to align your template and target sequences manually, then write out a project file, and upload it to the SWISS-MODEL server.

Tools for Ab-Initio Prediction

Since ab-initio structure prediction from sequence has not been done with any great degree of success so far, we can't recommend software for doing this routinely. If you are interested in the ab-initio structure-prediction problem and want to familiarize yourself with current research in the field, we suggest you start with any of these tools: the software package RAMP developed by Ram Samudrala, the I-Sites/ROSETTA prediction server developed by David Baker and Chris Bystroff, and the ongoing work of John Moult. Recent journal articles describing these methods can serve as adequate entry points into the ab-initio protein structure prediction literature.

Putting It All Together: A Protein Modeling Project

So how do all of these tools work to produce a protein structure model from sequence? We haven't described every single point and click in this chapter, because most of the software is web-based and quite self-explanatory in that respect. However, you may still be wondering how you'd put it all together to manage a tough modeling project.

As an example, we built a model of a target sequence from CASP 4, the most recent CASP competition. We've deliberately chosen a difficult sequence to model. There are no unambiguously homologous structures in the PDB, though there are clues that can be brought together to align the target with a possible template and build a model. We make no claims that the model is correct; its purpose is to illustrate the kind of process you might go through to build a partial 3D model of a protein based on a distant similarity.

The process for building an initial homology model when you do have an obvious, strong homology to a known structure is much more straightforward: simply align the template and target along their full length, edit the alignment if necessary, write it out in a format that Modeller can read, and submit; or submit the sequence of your unknown to SWISS-MODEL in First Approach mode.

Finding Homologous Structures

The first step in any protein modeling project is to find a template structure (if possible) to base a homology model on.

Using the target sequence T0101 from CASP 4, identified as a "400 amino acid pectate lyase L" from a bacterium called *Erwinia chrysanthemi,* we searched the PDB for homologs. We started by using the PDB SearchFields form to initiate a FASTA search.

The results returned were disheartening at first glance. As the CASP target list indicated, there were no strong sequence homologies to the target to be found in the PDB. None of the matches had E-values less than 1, though there were several in the less-than-10 range. None of the matches spanned the full length of the protein, the longest matching being a 330 amino acid overlap with a chondroitinase, with an E-value of 3.9.

Each of the top scoring proteins looked different, too, as you can see in Figure 10-5. The top match was an alpha-beta barrel type structure, while the second match (the chondroitinase) was a mainly beta structure with a few decorative alpha helices, and the third match was an entirely different, multidomain all-beta structure.

Out of curiosity, we also did a simple keyword search for pectate lyase in the PDB. There were eight pectate lyase structures listed, but none, apparently, were close enough in sequence to the T0101 target to be recognized as related by sequence information alone. None of these structures was classified as pectate lyase L; they included types A, E, and C. However, we observed that each of the pectate lyase molecules in the PDB had a common structural feature: a large, quasihelical arrangement of short beta strands known as a beta solenoid, or, less picturesquely, as a single-stranded right-handed beta helix (Figure 10-6).

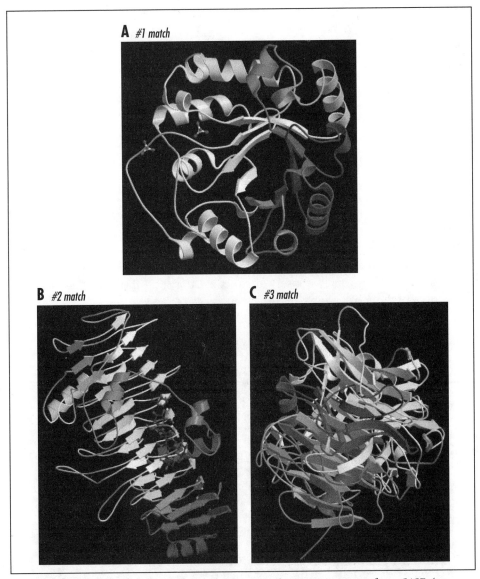

A #1 match

B #2 match

C #3 match

Figure 10-5. Pictures of top three sequence matches of a target sequence from CASP 4

Looking for Distant Homologies

We used CE to examine the structural neighbors of the known pectate lyases. Interestingly, one of the three proteins (1DBG, a chondroitinase from *Flavobacterium heparinium*) we first identified with FASTA as a sequence match for our target sequence showed up as a high-scoring structural neighbor of many of the known pectate lyases.

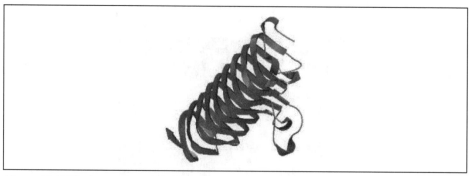

Figure 10-6. The beta-solenoid domain

Although the homology between T0101 and these other pectate lyases wasn't significant, the sequence similarity between T0101 and their close structural neighbor 1DBG seemed to suggest that the structure of our target protein *might* be distantly related to that of the other pectate lyases (Figure 10-7). Note that the alignment in the figure shows a strongly conserved structural domain—the ladderlike structure at the right of the molecule where the chain traces coincide.

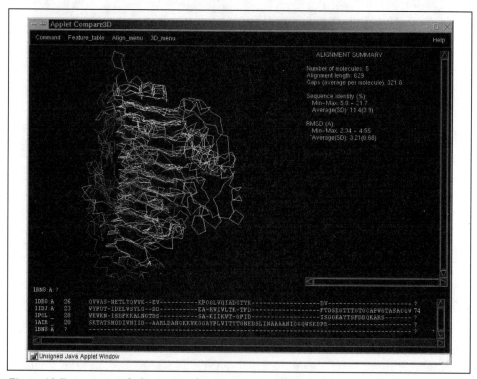

Figure 10-7. A structural alignment of known pectate lyase structures; the beta solenoid domain is visible as a ladderlike structure in the center of the molecule

However, in order to do any actual homology modeling, we need to somehow align the T0101 sequence to potential template structures. And since none of the pectate lyase sequences were similar enough to the unknown sequence to be aligned to it using standard pairwise alignment, we would need to get a little bit crafty with our alignment strategy.

Predicting Secondary Structure from Sequence

We applied several secondary structure prediction algorithms to the T0101 target sequence using the JPred structure prediction server. While the predictions from each method aren't exactly the same, we can see from Figure 10-8 that the consensus from JPred is clear: the T0101 sequence is predicted to form many short stretches of beta structure, exactly the pattern that is required to form the beta-solenoid domain.

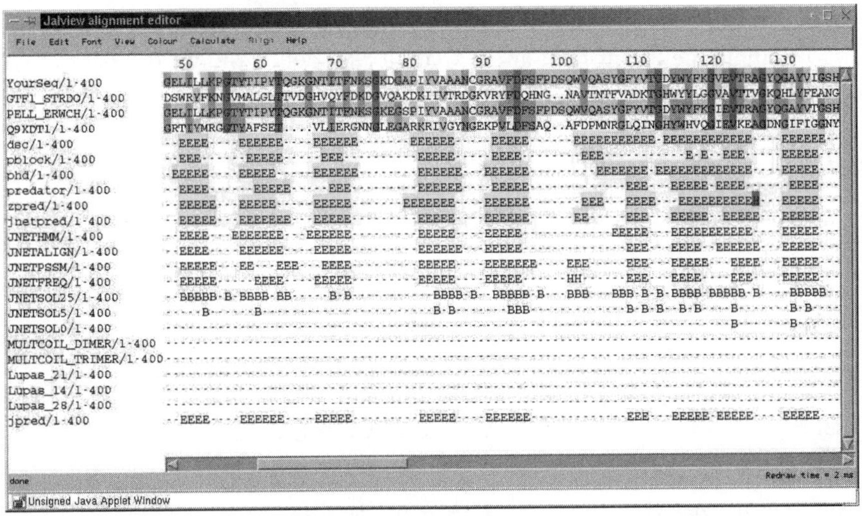

Figure 10-8. Partial secondary structure predictions for T0101, from JPred

Using Threading Methods to Find Potential Folds

We also sent the sequence to the 3D-PSSM and 123D+ threading servers to analyze its fitness for various protein folds. The top-scoring results from the 3D-PSSM threading server, with E-values in the 95% certainty range, included the proteins 1AIR (a pectate lyase), 1DBG (the chondroitinase that was identified as a homolog of our unknown by sequence-based searching), 1IDK, and 1PCL, all pectate lyases identified by CE as structural neighbors of 1DBG. These proteins were also found in the top results from 123D+.

Using Profile Methods to Align Distantly Related Sequences

We now had evidence from multiple sources that suggested the structures 1AIR, 1DBG, and 1IDK would be reasonable candidates to use as templates to construct a model of the T0101 unknown sequence. However, the remaining challenge was to align the unknown sequence to the template structures. We had many different alignments to work with: the initial FASTA alignment of the unknown with 1DBG; the CE structural alignment of 1DBG and its structural neighbors 1AIR, 1DBG, and 1IDK; and the individual alignments of predicted secondary structure in the unknown to known secondary structure for each of the database hits from 3D-PSSM. Each alignment was different, of course, because they were generated by different methods. We chose to combine the information in the individual 3D-PSSM sequence-to-structure alignments of the unknown sequence with 1AIR and 1IDK into a single alignment file. We did this by aligning those two alignments to each other using Clustal's Profile Alignment mode. Finally, we wrote out the alignment to a single file in a format appropriate for Modeller and used this as input for our first approach.

Building a Homology Model

We created the following input for Modeller:

```
The input script, peclyase.top:

Homology modelling by the MODELLER TOP routine 'model'.

INCLUDE                         # Include the predefined TOP routines
SET ALNFILE = 'peclyase.ali'    # alignment filename
SET KNOWNS  = '1air','1idk'     # codes of the templates
SET SEQUENCE = 't0101'          # code of the target
SET ATOM_FILES_DIRECTORY = './templates' # directories for input atom files
SET STARTING_MODEL= 1           # index of the first model
SET ENDING_MODEL = 3            # index of the last model
                                # (determines how many models to calculate)
CALL ROUTINE = 'model'          # do homology modeling
```

We created a sequence alignment file, *peclyase.ali*, in PIR format, built as described in the example and modified to indicate to Modeller whether each sequence was a template or a target.

We also placed PDB files, containing structural information for the template chains of 1AIR and 1IDK, in a *templates* subdirectory of our working directory. The files were named *1air.atm* and *1idk.atm*, as Modeller requires, and we then ran Modeller to create structural models. The models looked similar to their templates, especially in the beta solenoid domain, and evaluated reasonably well by standard methods of structure verification, including 3D/1D profiles and geometric evaluation methods. However, just like the actual CASP 4 competitors, we await the publication of the actual structure of the T0101 target for validation of our structural model.

Summary

Solving protein structure is complicated at best, but as you've seen, there are a number of software tools to make it easier. Table 10-1 provides a summary of the most popular structure prediction tools and techniques available to you.

Table 10-1. Structure Prediction Tools and Techniques

What you do	Why you do it	What you use to do it
Secondary structure prediction	As a starting point for classification and structural modeling	JPred, Predict-Protein
Threading	To check the fitness of a protein sequence to assume a known fold; to identify distantly related structural homologs	3D-PSSM, PhD, 123D
Homology modeling	To build a model from a sequence, based on homologies to known structures	Modeller, SWISS-MODEL
Model verification	To check the fitness of a modeled structure for its protein sequence	VERIFY-3D, PROCHECK, WHAT IF
Ab-initio structure modeling	To predict a 3D structure from sequence in the absence of homology	ROSETTA, RAMP

11

Tools for Genomics and Proteomics

The methods we have discussed so far can be used to analyze a single sequence or structure and compare multiple sequences of single-gene length. These methods can help you understand the function of a particular gene or the mechanism of a particular protein. What you're more likely to be interested in, though, is how gene functions manifest in the observable characteristics of an organism: its *phenotype*. In this chapter we discuss some datatypes and tools that are beginning to be available for studying the integrated function of all the genes in a genome.

What sets genomic science apart from the traditional experimental biological sciences is the emphasis on automated data gathering and integration of large volumes of information. Experimental strategies for examining one gene or one protein are gradually being replaced by parallel strategies in which many genes are examined simultaneously. Bioinformatics is absolutely required to support these parallel strategies and make the resulting data useful to the biology community at large. While bioinformatics algorithms may be complicated, the ultimate goals of bioinformatics and genomics are straightforward. Information from multiple sources is being integrated to form a complete picture of genomic function and its expression as the pheotype of an organism, as well as to allow comparison between the genomes of different organisms. Figure 11-1 shows the sort of flowchart you might create when moving from genetic function to phenotypic expression.

From the molecular level to the cellular level and beyond, biologists have been collecting information about pieces of this picture for decades. As in the story of the blind men and the elephant, focusing on specific pieces of the biological picture has made it difficult to step back and see the functions of the genome as a whole. The process of automating and scaling up biochemical experimentation, and treating biochemical data as a public resource, is just beginning.

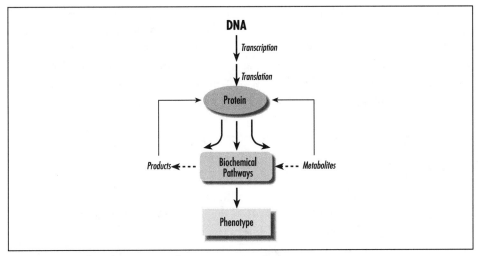

Figure 11-1. A flowchart moving from genome to phenotype

The Human Genome Project has not only made gigabytes of biological sequence information available; it has begun to change the entire landscape of biological research by its example. Protein structure determination has not yet been automated at the same level as sequence determination, but several pilot projects in structural genomics are underway, with the goal of creating a high-speed structure determination pipeline. The concept behind the DNA microarray experiment— thousands of microscopic experiments arrayed on a chip and running in parallel— doesn't translate trivially to other types of biochemical and molecular biology experiments. Nonetheless, the trend is toward efficiency, miniaturization, and automation in all fields of biological experimentation.

A long string of genomic sequence data is inherently about as useful as a reference book with no subject headings, page numbers, or index. One of the major tasks of bioinformatics is creating software systems for information management that can effectively annotate each part of a genome sequence with information about everything from its function, to the structure of its protein product (if it has one), to the rate at which the gene is expressed at different life stages of an organism. Currently, the only way to get the functional information that is needed to fully annotate and understand the workings of the genome is traditional biochemical experimentation, one gene or protein at a time. The growing genome databases are the motivation for further parallelization and automation of biological research.

Another task of genome information management systems is to allow users to make intuitive, visual comparisons between large data sets. Many new data integration projects, from visual comparison of multiple genomes to visual integration of expression data with genome map data, are under development.

Bioinformatics methods for genome-level analysis are obviously not as advanced in their development as sequence and structure analysis methods. Sequence and structure data have been publicly available since the 1970s; a significant number of whole genomes have become available only very recently. In this chapter, we focus on some data presentation and search strategies the research community has identified as particularly useful in genomic science.

From Sequencing Genes to Sequencing Genomes

In Chapter 7, *Sequence Analysis, Pairwise Alignment, and Database Searching*, we discussed the chemistry that allows us to sequence DNA by somehow producing a ladder of sequence fragments, each differing in size by one base, which can then be separated by electrophoresis. One of the first computational challenges in the process of sequencing a gene (or a genome) is the interpretation of the pattern of fragments on a sequencing gel.

Analysis of Raw Sequence Data: Basecalling

The process of assigning a sequence to raw data from DNA sequencing is called *basecalling*. As an end user of genome sequence data, you don't have access to the raw data directly from the sequencer; you have to rely on a sequence that has been assigned to this data by some kind of processing software. While it's not likely you will actually need basecalling software, it is helpful to remember what the software does and that it can give rise to errors.

If this step doesn't produce a correct DNA sequence, any subsequent analysis of the sequence is affected. All sequences deposited in public databases are affected by basecalling errors due to ambiguities in sequencer output or to equipment malfunctions. EST and genome survey sequences have the highest error rates ($1/10$–$1/100$ errors per base), followed by finished sequences from small laboratories ($1/100$–$1/1,000$ per base) and finished sequences from large genome sequencing centers ($1/10,000$–$1/100,000$ per base).[*] Any sequence in GenBank is likely to have at least one error. Improving sequencing technology, and especially the signal detection and processing involved in DNA sequencing, is still the subject of active research.

There are two popular high-throughput protocols for DNA sequencing. As discussed earlier, DNA sequencing as it is done today relies on the ability to create a ladder of fragments of DNA at single-base resolution and separate the DNA fragments by gel electrophoresis. The popular Applied Biosystems sequencers label

---

[*] These values were provided by Dr. Sean Eddy of Washington University.

the fragmented DNA with four different fluorescent labels, one for each base-specific fragmentation, and run a mixture of the four samples in one gel lane. Another commonly used automated sequencer, the Pharmacia ALF instrument, runs each sample in a separate, closely spaced lane. In both cases, the gel is scanned with a laser, which excites each fluorescent band on the gel in sequence. In the four-color protocol, the fluorescence signal is elicited by a laser perpendicular to the gel, one lane at a time, and is then filtered using four colored filters to obtain differential signals from each fluorescent label. In the single-color protocol, a laser parallel to the gel excites all four lanes from a single sequencing experiment at once, and the fluorescent emissions are recorded by an array of detectors. Each of these protocols has its advantages in different types of experiments, so both are in common use. Obviously, the differences in hardware result in differences in the format of the data collected, and the use of proprietary file formats for data storage doesn't resolve this problem.

There are a variety of commercial and noncommercial tools for automated basecalling. Some of them are fully integrated with particular sequencing hardware and input datatypes. Most of them allow, and in fact require, curation by an expert user as sequence is determined.

The raw result of sequencing is a record of fluorescence intensities at each position in a sequencing gel. Figure 11-2 shows detector ouput from a modern sequencing experiment. The challenge for automated basecalling software is to resolve the sequence of apparent fluorescence peaks into four-letter DNA sequence code. While this seems straightforward, there are fairly hard limits on how much sequence can be read in a single experiment. Because separation of bands on a sequencing gel isn't perfect, the quality of the separation and the shape of the bands deteriorates over the length of the gel. Peaks broaden and intermingle, and at some point in the sequencing run (usually 400–500 bases), the peaks become impossible to resolve. Various properties of DNA result in nonuniform reactions with the sequencing gel, so that fragment mobility is slightly dependent on the identity of the last base in a fragment; overall signal intensities can depend on local sequence and on the reagents used in the experiment. Unreadable regions can occur when DNA fragments fold back upon themselves or when a sequencing primer reacts with more than one site in a DNA sequence, leading to sample heterogeneity. Because these are fairly well-understood, systematic errors, computer algorithms can be developed to compensate for them. The ultimate goal of basecalling software development is to improve the accuracy of each sequence read, as well as to extend the range of sequencing runs, by providing means to deconvolute the more ambiguous fluorescence peaks at the end of the run.

Most sequencing projects deal with the inherent errors in the sequencing process by simply sequencing each region of a genome multiple times and by sequencing

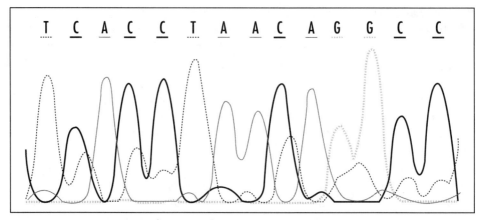

Figure 11-2. Detector output from a modern sequencing experiment

both DNA strands (which results in high-quality reads of both ends of a sequence). If you read that a genome has been sequenced with 4X coverage or 10X coverage, that means that portion of the genome has been sequenced multiple times, and the results merged to produce the final sequence.

Modern sequencing technologies replace gels with microscopic capillary systems, but the core concepts of the process are the same as in gel-based sequencing: fragmentation of the DNA and separation of individual fragments by electrophoresis.

At this point, the major genome databases don't provide raw sequence data to users, and for most applications, access to raw sequence data isn't really necessary. However, it is likely that, with the constant growth of computing power, this will change in the future, and that you may want to know how to reanalyze the raw sequence data underlying the sequences available in the public databases.

One noncommercial software package for basecalling is Phred, which is available from the University of Washington Genome Center. Phred runs on either Unix or Windows NT workstations. It uses Fourier analysis to resolve fluorescence traces to predict an evenly spaced set of peak locations, then uses dynamic programming to match the actual peak locations with the predicted results. It then annotates output from basecalling with the probability that the call is an error. Phred scores represent scaled negative log probability that a base call is in error; hence, the higher the Phred score, the lower the probability that an error has been made. These values can be helpful in determining whether a region of the genome may need to be resequenced. Phred can also feed data to a sequence-assembly program called Phrap, which then uses both the sequence information and quality scores to aid in sequence assembly.

Sequencing an Entire Genome

Genome sequencing isn't simply a scaled-up version of a gene-sequencing run. As noted earlier, the sequence length limit of a sequencing run is something like 500 base pairs. And the length of a genome can range from tens of thousands to billions of base pairs. So in order to sequence an entire genome, the genome has to be broken into fragments, and then the sequenced fragments need to be reassembled into a continuous sequence.

There are two popular strategies for sequencing genomes: the shotgun approach and the clone contig approach. Combinations of these strategies are often used to sequence larger genomes.

The shotgun approach

Shotgun DNA sequencing is the ultimate automated approach to DNA sequencing. In shotgun sequencing, a length of DNA, either a whole genome or a defined subset of the genome, is broken into random fragments. Fragments of manageable length (around 2,000 KB) are cloned into plasmids (together, all the clones are called a *clone library*). *Plasmids* are simple biological vectors that can incorporate any random piece of DNA and reproduce it quickly to provide sufficient material for sequencing.

If a sufficiently large amount of genomic DNA is fragmented, the set of clones spans every base pair of the genome many times. The end of each cloned DNA fragment is then sequenced, or in some cases, both ends are sequenced, which puts extra constraints on the way the sequences can be assembled. Although only 400–500 bases at the end or ends of the fragment are sequenced, if enough clones are randomly selected from the library and sequenced, the amount of sequenced DNA still spans every base pair of the genome several times. In a shotgun sequencing experiment, enough DNA sequencing to span the entire genome 6–10 times is usually required.

The final step in shotgun sequencing is sequence assembly, which we discuss in more detail in the next section. Assembly of all the short sequences from the shotgun sequencing experiment usually doesn't result in one single complete sequence. Rather, it results in multiple *contigs*—unambiguously assembled lengths of sequence that don't overlap each other. In the assembly process, contigs start and end because a region of the genome is encountered from which there isn't enough information (i.e., not enough clones representing that region) to continue assembling fragments. The final steps in sequencing a complete genome by shotgun sequencing are either to find clones that can fill in these missing regions, or, if there are no clones in the original library that can fill in the gaps, to use PCR or other techniques to amplify DNA sequence that spans the gaps.

Recently, Celera Genomics has shown that shotgun DNA sequencing—sequencing without a map—can work at the whole genome level even in organisms with very large genomes. The largely completed *Drosophila* genome sequence is evidence of their success.

The clone contig approach

The *clone contig* approach relies on shotgun sequencing as well, but on a smaller scale. Instead of starting by breaking down the entire genome into random fragments, the clone contig approach starts by breaking it down into restriction fragments, which can then be cloned into artificial chromosome vectors and amplified. Restriction enzymes are enzymes that cut DNA. These enzymes are sequence-specific; that is, they recognize only one specific sequence of DNA, anywhere from 6–10 base pairs in length. By pure statistics, any base has a 1 in 4 chance of occurring randomly in a DNA sequence; an N-residue sequence has a 1 in 4^N chance of occurring. Enzymes that cut at a specific 6–10 base pair sequence of DNA end up cutting genomic DNA relatively rarely, but because DNA sequence isn't random, the restriction enzyme cuts result in a specific pattern of fragment lengths that is characteristic of a genome.

Each of the cloned restriction fragments can be sequenced and assembled by a standard shotgun approach. But assembly of the restriction fragments into a whole genome is a different sort of problem. When the genome is digested into restriction fragments, it is only partially digested. The amount of restriction enzyme applied to the DNA sample is sufficient to cut at only approximately 50% of the available restriction sites in the sample. This means that some fragments will span a particular restriction site, while other fragments will be cut at that particular site and will span other restriction sites. So the clone library that is made up of these restriction fragments will contain overlapping fragments.

Chromosome walking is the process of starting with a specific clone, then finding the next clone that overlaps it, and then the next, etc. Methods such as probe hybridization or PCR are used to help identify the restriction fragment that has been inserted into each clone, and there are a number of experimental strategies that can make building up the genome map this way less time-consuming. A genome map is a record of the location of known features in the genome, which makes it relatively simple to associate particular clone sequences with a specific location in the genome by probe hybridization or other methods.

Genomes can be mapped at various levels of detail. Geneticists are used to thinking in terms of genetic linkage maps, which roughly assign the genes that give rise to particular traits to specific loci on the chromosome. However, genetic linkage maps don't provide enough detail to support the assembly of a full genome worth of sequence, nor do they point to the actual DNA sequence that corresponds to a particular trait. What genetic linkage maps do provide, though, is a set of ordered markers, sometimes very detailed depending on the organism, which can help researchers understand genome function (and provide a framework for assembling a full genome map).

Physical maps can be created in several ways: by digesting the DNA with restriction enzymes that cut at particular sites, by developing ordered clone libraries, and recently, by fluorescence microscopy of single, restriction enzyme-cleaved DNA molecules fixed to a glass substrate. The key to each method is that, using a combination of labeled probes and known genetic markers (in restriction mapping) or by identifying overlapping regions (in library creation), the fragments of a genome can be ordered correctly into a highly specific map (see Figure 11-2).

LIMS: Tracking all those minisequences

In carrying out a sequencing project, tracking the millions of unique DNA samples that may be isolated from the genome is one of the biggest information technology challenges. It's also probably one of the least scientifically exciting, because it involves keeping track of where in the genome each sample came from, which sample goes into each container, where each container goes in what may be a huge sample storage system, and finally, which data came from which sample. The systems that manage output from high-throughput sequencing are called Laboratory Information Management Systems (LIMS), and while we will not discuss them in the context of this book, LIMS development and maintenance makes up the lion's share of bioinformatics work in industrial settings. Other high-throughput technologies, such as microarrays and cheminformatics, also require complicated LIMS support.

Sequence Assembly

Basecalling is only the first step in putting together a complete genome sequence. Once the short fragments of sequence are obtained, they must be assembled into a complete sequence that may be many thousands of times their length. The next step is sequence assembly.

Sequence assembly isn't something you're likely to be doing on your own on a large scale, unless you happen to be working for a genome project. However, even small labs may need to solve sequence-assembly problems that require some computer assistance.

DNA sequencing using a shotgun approach provides thousands or millions of minisequences, each 400–500 fragments in length. The fragments are random and can partially or completely overlap each other. Because of these overlaps, every fragment in the set can be identified by sequence identity as adjacent to some number of other fragments. Each of those fragments overlaps yet another set of fragments, and so on. It's standard procedure for the sequences of both ends of some fragments to be known, and the sequences of only one end of other fragments to be known. Figure 11-3 illustrates the shotgun sequencing approach.

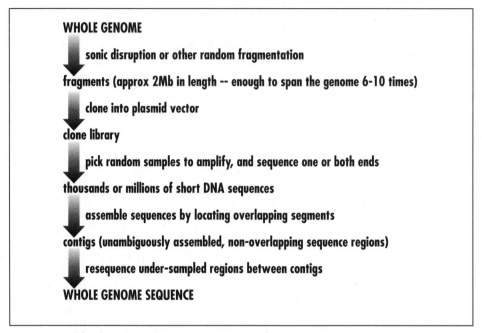

Figure 11-3. The shotgun DNA sequencing approach

Ultimately, all the fragments need to be optimally tiled together into one continuous sequence. Identifying sequence overlaps between fragments puts some constraints on how the sequences can be assembled. For some fragments, the length of the sequence and the sequences of both its ends are known, which puts even more constraints on how the sequences can be assembled. The assembly algorithm attempts to satisfy all the constraints and produce an optimal ordering of all the fragments that make up the genome.

Repetitive sequence features can complicate the assembly process. Some fragments will be uncloneable, and the sequencing process will fail in other cases, leaving gaps in the DNA sequence that must be resolved by resequencing. These gaps complicate automated assembly. If there isn't sufficient information at some point in the sequence for assembly to continue, the sequence contig that is being created comes to an end, and a new contig starts when there is sufficient sequence information for assembly to resume.

The Phrap program, available from the University of Washington Genome Center, does an effective job assembling sequence fragments, although a large amount of computer time is required. The accompanying program Consed is a Unix-based editor for Phrap sequence assembly output. TIGR Assembler is another genome assembly package that works well for small genomes, BACs, or ESTs.

Accessing Genome Information on the Web

Partial or complete DNA sequences from hundreds of genomes are available in GenBank. Putting those sequence records together into an intelligible representation of genome structure isn't so easy. There are several efforts underway to integrate DNA sequence with higher-level maps of genomes in a user-friendly format. So far, these efforts are focused on the human genome and genomes of important plant and animal model systems. They aren't collected into one uniform resource at present, although NCBI does aim to be comprehensive in its coverage of available genome data eventually.

Looking at genome data is analogous to looking at a map of the world. You may want to look at the map from a distance, to see the overall layout of continents and countries, or you may want to find a shortcut from point A to point B. Each choice requires a different sort of map. However, the maps need to be linked, because you may want to know the general directions from San Diego to Blacksburg, VA, but may also want to know exactly how to get to a specific building on the Virginia Tech campus when you get there. The approach that web-based genome analysis tools are taking is similar to the approach taken by online map databases such as MapQuest. Place names and zip codes are analogous to gene names and GenBank IDs. You can search as specifically as you wish, or you can begin with a top view of the genome and zoom in.

The genome map resources have the same limitations as online map resources, as well. You can search MapQuest and see every street in Blacksburg, but ask MapQuest for a back-road shortcut between Cochin and Mangalore on the southwest coast of India, and it can't help you. Currently, NCBI and EMBL provide detailed maps and tools for looking at the human genome, but if your major interest is the cat genome, you're (at least this year) out of luck.

Genome resources are also limited by the capabilities of bioinformatics analysis methods. The available analysis tools at the genome sites are usually limited to sequence comparison tools and whatever single-sequence feature-detection tools are available for that genome, along with any information about the genome that can be seamlessly integrated from other databases. If you are hoping to do something with tools at a genome site you can't do with existing sequence or structure analysis tools, you will still be disappointed. What genome sites do provide is a highly automated user experience and expertly curated links between related concepts and entities. This is a valuable contribution, but there are still questions that can't be answered.

NCBI Genome Resources

NCBI offers access to a wide selection of web-based genome analysis tools from the Genomic Biology section of its main web site. These tools are designed for the biologist seeking answers to specific questions. Nothing beyond basic web skills and biological knowledge is required to apply these tools to a question of interest. Their interfaces are entirely point-and-click, and NCBI supplies ample documentation to help you learn how to use their tools and databases.

Here's a list of the available tools:

Genome Information

Genome project information is available from the Entrez Genomes page at NCBI. Database listings are available for the full database or for related groups of organisms such as microorganisms, archaea, bacteria, eukaryotes, and viruses. Each entry in the database is linked to a taxonomy browser entry or a home page with further links to available information about the organism. If a genome map of the organism is available, a "See the Genome" link shows up on the organism's home page. From the home page, you can also download genome sequences and references.

Map Viewer

If a genome map is available for the organism, you can click on parts of the cartoon map that is first displayed and access several different viewing options. Depending on the genome, you can access links to overview maps, maps showing known protein-coding regions, listings of coding regions for protein and RNA, and other information. Information is generally downloadable in text format. Map Viewer distinguishes between four levels of information: the organism's home page, the graphical view of the genome, the detailed map for each chromosome (aligned to a master map from which the user can select where to zoom in), and the sequence view, which graphically displays annotations for regions of the genome sequence. Full Map Viewer functionality is available only for human and drosophila genomes at the time of this writing; however, for any complete genome, clickable genome maps and views of the annotated genome at the sequence level are available.

ORF Finder

The Open Reading Frame (ORF) Finder is a tool for locating open reading frames in a DNA sequence. ORF finders translate the sequence using standard or user-specified genetic code. In noncoding DNA, stop codons are frequently found. Only long uninterrupted stretches without stop codons are taken to be coding regions. Information from the ORF finder can provide clues about the correct reading frame for a DNA sequence and about where coding regions start and stop. For many genomes found in the Entrez Genomes database, ORF Finder is available as an integrated tool from the map view of the genome.

LocusLink

LocusLink is a curated database of genetic loci in several eukaryotic organisms that give rise to known phenotypes. LocusLink provides an alphabetical listing of traits as well as links to HomoloGene and Map Viewer.

HomoloGene

HomoloGene is a database of pairwise orthologs (homologous genes from different organisms that have diverged by speciation, as opposed to paralogs that have diverged by gene duplication) across four major eukaryotic genomes: human, mouse, rat, and zebrafish. The ortholog pairs are identified either by curation of literature reports or calculation of similarity. The HomoloGene database can be searched using gene symbols, gene names, GenBank accession numbers, and other features.

Clusters of Orthologous Groups (COG)

COG is a database of orthologous protein groups. The database was developed by comparing protein sequences across 21 complete genomes. The entries in COG represent genome functions that are conserved throughout much of evolutionary history—functions that were developed early and retained in all of the known complete genomes. The authors' assumption is that these ancient conserved sequences comprise the minimal core of functionality that a modern species (i.e., one that has survived into the era of genome sequencing) requires. The COG database can be searched by functional category, phylogenetic pattern, and a number of other properties.

NCBI also provides detailed genome-specific resources for several important eukaryotic genomes, including human, fruit fly, mouse, rat, and zebrafish.

TIGR Genome Resources

The Institute for Genome Research (TIGR, *http://www.tigr.org*) is one of the main producers of new genome sequence data, along with the other major human genome sequencing centers and commercial enterprises such as Celera. TIGR's main sequencing projects have been in microbial and crop genomes, and human chromosome 16. TIGR recently announced the Comprehensive Microbial Resource, a complete microbial genome resource for all of the genomes they have sequenced. At the present time, each microbial genome has its own web page from which various views of the genome are available. There are also tools within the resource that allow you to search the *omniome*, as TIGR designates the combined genomic information in its database. The TIGR tools aren't as visual as the NCBI genome analysis tools. Selection of regions to examine requires you to enter specific information into a form rather than just pointing and clicking on a genome map. However, the TIGR resources are a useful supplement to the NCBI tools, providing a different view on the same genetic information.

TIGR maintains many genome-specific databases focused on expressed sequence tags (ESTs) rather than complete genomic data. ESTs are partial sequences from either end of a cDNA clone. Despite their incompleteness, ESTs are useful for experimental molecular biologists. Since cDNA libraries are prepared by producing the DNA complement to cellular mRNA (messenger RNA), a cDNA library gives clues as to what genes are actually expressed in a particular cell or tissue. Therefore, a sequence match with an EST can be an initial step in helping to identify the function of a new gene. TIGR's EST databases can be searched by sequence, EST identifier, cDNA library name, tissue, or gene product name, using a simple forms-based web interface.

EnsEMBL

EnsEMBL is a collaborative project of EMBL, EBI, and the Sanger Centre (*http:// www.sanger.ac.uk*) to automatically track sequenced fragments of the human genome and assemble them into longer stretches. Automated analysis methods, such as genefinding and feature-finding tools and sequence-comparison tools, are then applied to the assembled sequence and made available to users through a web interface.

In June 2000, the Human Genome consortium announced the completion of the first map of the human genome. It's important to stress that such maps, and indeed much of the genomic information now available, are only drafts of a final picture that may take years to assemble. To remain useful, the draft maps must be constantly updated to stay in sync with the constantly updated sequence databases. The EnsEMBL project expects to apply its automated data analysis pipeline to many different genomes, beginning with human and mouse.

There are three ways to search EnsEMBL: a BLAST search of a query sequence against the database; a search using a known gene, transcript, or map marker ID; or a chromosome map browser that allows you to pick a chromosome and zoom in to ever-more specific regions. All these tools are relatively self-explanatory and available from the EnsEMBL web site. In order to use them, however, you should know something of what you are looking for or on which chromosome to look.

Other Sequencing Centers

TIGR isn't the only genome center to provide software and online tools for analyzing genomic data. Genome sequencing programs generally incorporate a bioinformatics component and attract researchers with interests in developing bioinformatics methods; their web sites are good points of entry to the bioinformatics world. The University of Washington Genome Center is known for the development of sequence assembly tools—its Phred and Phrap software are widely used. Other genome centers include, but aren't limited to, the Sanger Centre, the DOE Joint Genome Institute, Washington University in St. Louis, and many corporate centers.

A complete list of genome sequencing projects in progress and active genome centers can be found online in the Genomes OnLine Database (GOLD), a public site maintained by Integrated Genomics, Inc. (*http://wit.integratedgenomics.com/ GOLD/*).

Organism-Specific Resources

The Arabidopsis Information Resource (TAIR) is an excellent example of an organism-specific genome resource, this one focusing on the widely used plant model system *Arabidopsis thaliana*. In addition to the standard features offered at EnsEMBL and NCBI, such as clickable and zoomable chromosome maps and sequence analysis tools, TAIR offers a variety of expert-curated links to other information for users of the resource. TAIR is limited in its scope to *Arabidopsis*, but it is a much deeper resource than the general public databases. Similar resources are available for many organisms, from maize to zebrafish. Listings of online genome resources can be located at several sites, such as GOLD, NCBI, and EMBL.

Annotating and Analyzing Whole Genome Sequences

Genome data presents completely new issues in data storage and analysis:

- Genome sequences are extremely large.
- Users need to access genome data both as a whole and as meaningful pieces.
- The majority of the sequence in a genome doesn't correspond to known functionality.

Annotation of the genome with functional information can be accomplished by several means: comparison with existing information for the organism in the sequence databases, comparison with published information in the primary literature, computational methods such as ORF detection and genefinding, or propagation of information from one genome to another by evolutionary inference based on sequence comparison. Due to the sheer amount of data available, automatic annotation is desirable, but it must be automatic without propagating errors. The use of computational methods is fallible; sequence similarity searches can result in hits that aren't biologically meaningful, and genefinders often have difficulty detecting the exact start and end of a gene. Sometimes experimental information is incorrect or is recorded incorrectly in the database. Using this information to annotate genomes leaves a residue of error in the database, which can then be propagated further by use of comparative methods.

Genome Annotation

Genome annotation is a difficult business. This is in part because there are a huge number of different pieces of information attached to every gene in a genome. Not every piece of information is interesting to every user, and not every piece of this information can (or should) be crammed in a single file of information about the gene. Genome annotation relies on relational databases to integrate genome sequence information with other data.*

The primary sources of information about what genes do are laboratory experiments. It may take many experiments to figure out what a gene does. Ideally, all that diverse experimental data should somehow be associated with the gene annotation. What this means in practice is hyperlinking of content between multiple databases—sequence, structure, and functional genomics fully linked together in a queryable system. This strategy is beginning to be implemented in most of the major public databases, although the goal of "one world database" (in the user's perception) has not yet been reached and perhaps never will.

MAGPIE

MAGPIE is an environment for annotation of genomes based on sequence similarity. It can maintain status information for a genome project and make information about the genome available on the Web, as well as provide an interface for automated sequence similarity-based and manual annotation. Even if you're not maintaining a genome database for public use, a look at the features of MAGPIE may help clarify some of the information technology issues in genome annotation. The *Sulfolobus solfataricus* P2 Genome Project and many other smaller genome projects have implemented MAGPIE; the *S. solfataricus* project provides information on its web site about the role MAGPIE plays in the genome annotation process.

---

* The term *relational database* should give you a clue that the function of the database is to maintain relationships or connections among entries. We discuss this in more detail in Chapter 13, *Building Biological Databases.*

Genome Comparison

Pairwise or multiple comparison of genomes is an idea that will be useful for many studies, ranging from basic questions of evolutionary biology to very specific clinical questions, such as the identification of genetic polymorphisms, which give rise to disease states or significant variations in phenotype.

Why compare whole genomes rather than just comparing genes one at a time? As the Human Genome Project reaches completion, researchers are just beginning to explore in detail how genome structure affects genome function. Is junk DNA really junk? Are there structural features in DNA that control expression? Are there promoters and regulatory regions we haven't yet figured out? Genome comparison can help answer such questions by pointing to regions of similarity within uncharacterized or even supposedly redundant DNA. Genome comparison will also aid in genomic annotation. Prototype genome comparisons have helped to justify the sequencing of additional genomes; the comparison of mouse and human genomes is one such example. Genome comparison is useful both at the map level and directly at the sequence level.

PipMaker

PipMaker is a tool that compares two DNA sequences of up to 2 MB each (longer sequences will be handled by the new Version 2.0, to be released soon) and produces a percent identity plot as output. This is useful in identifying large-scale patterns of similarity in longer sequences, although obviously not entire larger genomes. The process of using PipMaker is relatively simple. Starting with two FASTA-format sequence files, you first generate a set of instructions for masking sequence repeats (generated using the RepeatMasker server). This reduces the number of uninformative hits in the sequence comparison. The resulting information, plus a simple file containing a numerical list of known gene positions, is submitted to the PipMaker web server at Penn State University and the results are emailed to you. A detailed PipMaker tutorial is available at the web site *(http://bio. cse.psu.edu/pipmaker/)*. PipMaker relies on BLASTZ to align sequences. BLASTZ is an experimental version of BLAST designed for extremely long sequences and developed at NCBI.

MUMmer

Another program for pairwise genome comparison is TIGR's MUMmer. MUMmer was designed to meet the needs of the sequencing projects at TIGR and is optimized for comparing microbial genome sequences that are assumed to be relatively similar. Its first application was a detailed comparison of genomes of two strains of *M. tuberculosis*. MUMmer can compare sequences millions of base pairs in length and produce colorful visualizations of regions of similarity. MUMmer is based on a computer algorithm called a *suffix tree*, which essentially makes it easy for the system to rapidly handle a large number of pairwise comparisons. The dynamic programming algorithm used in standard BLAST comparison doesn't scale well with sequence length. For genome-length sequences, dynamic programming methods are unacceptably slow. MUMmer is an example of a novel method developed to get around the problems involved in using standard pairwise sequence comparison to compare full genome sequences. MUMmer is designed for Unix systems and is freely available for use in nonprofit institutions. A new public web interface to MUMmer has recently become available on the TIGR web site.

Functional Genomics: New Data Analysis Challenges

The advent of high-speed sequencing methods has changed the way we study the DNA sequences that code for proteins. Once, finding these bits of DNA in the genome of an organism was the goal, without much concern for the context. It is now becoming possible to view the whole DNA sequence of a chromosome as a single entity and to examine how the parts of it work together to produce the complexity of the organism as a whole.

The functions of the genome break down loosely into a few obvious categories: metabolism, regulation, signaling, and construction. Metabolic pathways convert chemical energy derived from environmental sources (i.e., food) into useful work in the cell. Regulatory pathways are biochemical mechanisms that control what genomic DNA does: when it is expressed and when it isn't. Genomic regulation involves not only expressed genes but structural and sequence signals in the DNA where regulatory proteins may bind. Signaling pathways control, among other things, the movement of chemicals from one compartment in a cell to another. Teasing out the complex networks of interactions that make up these pathways is the work of biochemists and molecular biologists. Many regulatory systems for the control of DNA transcription have been studied. Mapping these metabolic, regulatory, and signaling systems to the genome sequence is the goal of the field of functional genomics.

Sequence-Based Approaches for Analyzing Gene Expression

In addition to genome sequence, GenBank contains many other kinds of DNA sequence. Expressed sequence tag (EST) data for an organism can be an extremely useful starting point for discovery-oriented exploration of gene expression. To understand why this is, you need to recall what ESTs represent. ESTs are partial sequences of cDNA clones; cDNA clones are DNA strands built using cellular mRNA as templates.* In the cell, mRNA is RNA with a mission—to be converted into protein, and soon. mRNA levels respond to changes in the cell or its environment; mRNA levels are tissue-dependent, and they change during the life cycle of the organism as well. Quantitation of mRNA or cDNA provides a pretty good measure of what a genome is doing under particular conditions.

The sequence of a cDNA molecule built off an mRNA template should be the same as the sequence of the DNA that originally served as a template for building the mRNA. Sequencing a short stretch of bases from a cDNA sequence provides enough information to localize the source of an mRNA in a genome sequence.

NCBI offers a database called dbEST that provides access to several thousand libraries of ESTs. Quite a large number of these are human EST libraries, but there are libraries from dozens of other organisms as well. NCBI's UniGene database provides fully searchable access to specific EST libraries from human, mouse, rat, and zebrafish. EST data within UniGene has been combined with sequences of well-characterized genes and clustered, using an automated clustering procedure, to identify groups of related sequences. The Library Browser can locate libraries of interest within UniGene.

Another NCBI resource for sequence-based expression analysis is SAGEmap. Serial Analysis of Gene Expression (SAGE) is an experimental technique in which the transcription products of many genes are rapidly quantitated by sequencing short "tags" of DNA at a specific position (usually a restriction site) in the sequence. SAGEmap is a specialized online resource for the SAGE user community that identifies potential SAGE tags in human DNA sequence and maps them to the genome.

DNA Microarrays: Emerging Technologies in Functional Genomics

Recently, new technology has made it possible for researchers to rapidly explore expression patterns of entire genomes worth of DNA. A *microarray* (or gene chip) is a small glass slide—like a microscope slide—about a centimeter on a side. The surface of the slide is covered with 20,000 or more precisely placed spots each containing a different DNA oligomer (short polynucleotide chain). cDNA can also be affixed to the slide to function as probes. Other media, such as thin membranes, can be used in place of slides. The key to the experiment is that each piece of DNA is immobilized—attached at one end to the slide's surface. Any reaction that results in a change in microarray signal can be precisely assigned to a specific DNA sequence.

---

* The term *transcriptome* has been used to describe the collection of sequenced transcripts from a given organism.

Microarray experiments capitalize on an important property of DNA. One strand of DNA (or RNA) can *hybridize* with a complementary strand of DNA. If the complementarity of the two strands is perfect, the bond between the two strands is difficult to break. Each oligomer in a DNA microarray can serve as a probe to detect a unique, complementary DNA or RNA molecule. These oligomers can be bound by fluorescently labeled DNA, allowing the chip to be scanned using a confocal scanner or CCD camera. The presence or absence of a complementary sequence in the DNA sample being run over the chip determines whether the position on the array "lights up" or not. Thus, the presence or absence of an average of 20,000 sequences can be experimentally demonstrated with one gene chip.

Microarrays are conceptually no different from traditional hybridization experiments such as Southern Blots (probing DNA samples separated on a filter with labeled probe sequences) or Northern Blots (probing RNA samples separated on a filter). In traditional blotting, the protein sample is immobilized; in microarray experiments, the probe is immobilized, and the amount of information that can be collected in one experiment is vastly larger. Figure 11-4 shows just a portion of a microarray scan from Arabidopsis (Image courtesy of the Arabidopsis Functional Genomics Consortium (AFGC) and the Stanford Microarray Database, *http://genome-www.stanford.edu/microarray*). Other advantages are that microarray experiments rely on fluorescent probes rather than the radioactive probes used in blotting techniques, and gene chips can be manufactured robotically rather than laboriously generated by hand.

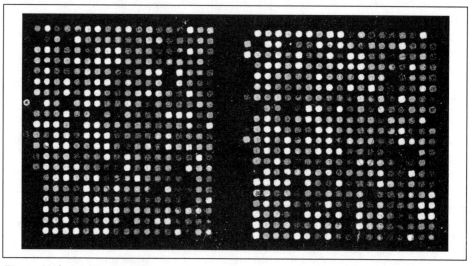

Figure 11-4. A microarray scan

Microarray technology is now routinely used for DNA sequencing experiments; for instance, in testing for the presence of polymorphisms. Another recent development is the use of microarrays for gene expression analysis. When a gene is expressed, an mRNA transcript is produced. If DNA oligomers complementary to the genes of interest are placed on the microarray, mRNA or cDNA copies can be hybridized to the chip, providing a rapid assay as to whether or not those genes are being expressed. Experiments like these have been performed in yeast to test differences in whole-genome expression patterns in response to changes in ambient sugar concentration. Microarray experiments can provide information about the behavior of every one of an organism's genes in response to environmental changes.

Bioinformatics Challenges in Microarray Design and Analysis

So why do microarrays merit a section in a book on bioinformatics? Bioinformatics plays multiple roles in microarray experiments. In fact, it is difficult to conceive of microarrays as useful without the involvement of computers and databases. From the design of chips for specific purposes, to the quantitation of signals, to the extraction of groups of genes with linked expression profiles, microarray analysis is a process that is difficult, if not impossible, to do by eye or with a pencil and a notebook.

The most popular laboratory equipment for microarray experiments, at the time of this writing, is the Affymetrix machine; however, it's been followed closely by home-built configurations. If you're working with a commercial arrayer, integrated software will probably make it relatively easy for you to analyze data. However, home-built microarray setups put out data sets of varying sizes. Arrayers may not spot quite as uniformly as commercial machines. Standardization is difficult. And running a home-built setup means you have to find software that supports all the steps of the array experiment and has the features you need for data analysis.

One of the main challenges in conducting microarray experiments with noncommercial equipment is that there are a limited number of available tools for linking expression data with associated sequences and annotations. Constructing such a database interface can be a real burden for a novice. Proprietary software, based on proprietary chip formats, is often quite well supported by a database backend specific to the chip, but it isn't always generalizable, or not easily so, to a variety of image formats and data-set sizes. In the public domain, several projects are underway to improve this situation for academic researchers, including NCGR's GeneX and EMBL-EBI's ArrayExpress. The National Human Genome Research Institute (NHGRI) is currently offering a demonstration version of an array data management system called ArrayDB (*http://genome.nhgri.nih.gov/arraydb/*) that includes both analysis tools and relational database support.* ArrayDB will also allow a community of users to add records to a central database.

The Pat Brown group at Stanford has a comprehensive listing of microarray resources on their web site, including instructions for building your own arrayer (for about 10% of the cost of a commercial setup) and the ArrayMaker software that controls the printing of arrays. This site is an excellent resource for microarray beginners.

Planning array experiments

A key element in microarray experiments is chip design. This is the aspect that's often forgotten by users of commercial devices and commercial chips, because one benefit of those systems is that chip design has been done for you, by an expert, before you ever think about doing an experiment. Chip design is a process that can take months.

Even the largest chip can't fit all the proteins in a eukaryotic genome; there may be hundreds of thousands of different targets. The chip designer has to select subsets of the genome that are likely to be informative when assayed together. EST data sets can be helpful in designing microarray primers; while they are quantitatively uninformative, ESTs do indicate which subsets of genes are likely to be active under particular conditions and hence are informative for a specific microarray experiment.

In order for microarray results to be clear and unambiguous, each DNA probe in the array must be sufficiently unique that only one specific target gene can hybridize with it. Otherwise, the amount of signal detected at each spot will be quantitatively incorrect.

What this means, in practice, is lots of sequence analysis: finding possible genes of interest, and selecting and synthesizing appropriate probes. Once the probes are selected, their sequence, plus available background information for each spot in the array, must be recorded in a database so that information is accessible when results are analyzed. Finally, the database must be robust enough to take into account changing annotations and information in the public sequence databases, so that incorrect interpretations of results can be avoided.

Some resources for probe and primer design are available on the Web. A "good" oligonucleotide—one that is useful as a probe or primer for microarrays, PCR, and other hybridization experiments shouldn't hybridize with itself to form dimers or hairpins. It should hybridize uniquely with the target sequence you are interested in. For PCR applications, primers must have an optimal melting temperature and

---

* It's in alpha release at the time of this writing.

stability. An excellent web resource for designing PCR primers is the Primer3 web site at the Whitehead Institute; CODEHOP is another primer/probe design application based on sequence motifs found in the Blocks database.

Analyzing scanned microarray images with CrazyQuant

Once the array experiment is complete, you'll find yourself in possession of a lot of very large TIFF files containing scanned images of your arrays. If you're not using an integrated analysis package, where do you go from there?

The standard for public-domain microarray analysis tools are the packages developed at Stanford. One package, ScanAlyze, available for Windows, is the image analysis tool in this group. ScanAlyze is well regarded and widely used, especially in academia and features semiautomatic grid definition and multichannel pixel analysis. It supports TIFF files as well as the Stanford SCN format. It's by far the most sophisticated of the image-analysis programs discussed here.

A relatively straightforward public-domain program for array-image analysis is CrazyQuant, a Java application available from the Hood Laboratory at the University of Washington. CrazyQuant is menu-driven and can load TIFF, JPG, or GIF format microarray images. CrazyQuant assumes a 2D matrix of regularly spaced spots, and to begin the analysis process, you need to define a 2D grid that pinpoints the spot locations. The program then computes relative intensities at each spot and stores them as integer values. CrazyQuant can quantitate both one- and two-color (differential) array data. CrazyQuant is extremely simple to install on a Linux workstation. Download the archive, move it to its own directory, unzip it, and run the program by entering *java CrazyQuant*. A sample GIF image is included in the archive so that you can see how it works.

TIGR also offers a Windows application for microarray image analysis called Spot-Finder. SpotFinder can process the TIFF-format files produced by most microarray scanners and produce output that is compatible with both TIGR's ArrayViewer and other microarray analysis software.

Visualizing high-dimensional data

Microarray results can be difficult to visualize. Array experiments generally have at least four dimensions (*x-location*, *y-location*, fluorescence intensity, and time). Straightforward plotting of array images isn't very informative. Tools that help extract features from higher-dimensional data sets and display these features in a sensible image format are needed.

TIGR offers a Java application called ArrayViewer. Currently, ArrayViewer's functions are focused on detecting differentially expressed genes and displaying differential expression results in a graphical format. ArrayViewer's parameters can be adjusted to incorporate data from arrays of any size, and it can be configured to allow straightforward access to underlying gene sequence data and annotation. Several normalization options are offered. Features for analysis of time series data and other more complicated data sets aren't yet implemented, but ArrayViewer does meet most basic array visualization needs.

Some general visualization and data-mining packages such as Xgobi, which we discuss in Chapter 14, *Visualization and Data Mining*, can also be used to examine array data.

Clustering expression profiles

At the time of this writing, the most popular strategy for analysis of microarray data is the clustering of expression profiles. An *expression profile* can be visualized as a plot that describes the change in expression at one spot on a microarray grid over the course of the experiment. The course of the experiment changes with the context, anything from changes in the concentration of nutrients in the medium in which cells are being grown prior to having their DNA hybridized to the array, to cell cycle stages.

In this context, what is clustered is essentially the shape of the plot. Different clustering methods, such as hierarchical clustering or SOMs (self-organizing maps) may work better in different situations, but the general aim of each of these methods is the same.* If two genes change expression levels in the same way in response to a change in conditions, it can be assumed that those genes are related. They may share something as simple as a promoter, or more likely, they are controlled by the same complex regulatory pathway. Automated clustering of expression profiles looks for similar symptoms (similarly shaped expression profiles) but doesn't necessarily point to causes for those changes. That's the job of the scientist analyzing the results, at least for now.

The programs Cluster and TreeView, also from Stanford, are Windows-platform tools for clustering expression profiles. Various algorithms for clustering are implemented, including SOMs and hierarchical clustering. XCluster, which implements most of the features of Cluster, is available for Unix platforms. All these programs require a specific file format (detailed in the manual, which is available online).

A note on commercial software for expression analysis

Several commercial software packages, with tools for visualizing complex microarray data sets, are available. Many of these are specific to particular hardware or

---

* We discuss clustering approaches in a little more detail in Chapter 14.

array configurations. Others, such as SpotFire and Silicon Genetics' GeneSpring, are more universal. These software packages are often rather expensive to license; however, at this stage of the development of microarray technology, their relative ease of use may make them worthwhile.

Proteomics

Proteomics refers to techniques that simultaneously study the entire protein complement of a cell. While protein purification and separation methods are constantly improving, and the time-to-completion of protein structures determined by NMR and x-ray crystallography is decreasing, there is as yet no single way to rapidly crystallize the entire protein complement of an organism and determine every structure. Techniques in biochemical characterization, on the other hand, are getting better and faster. The technological advance in biochemistry that most requires informatics support is the immobilized-gradient 2D-PAGE process and the subsequent characterization of separated protein products by mass spectrometry. Microarraying robots have begun to be used to create protein arrays, which can be used in protein interaction assays, drug discovery, and other applications. However, protein microarrays are still far from a routine approach.

Experimental Approaches in Proteomics

Knowing when and at what levels genes are being expressed is only the first step in understanding how the genome determines phenotype. While mRNA levels are correlated with protein concentration in the cell, proteins are subject to post-translational modifications that can't be detected with a hybridization experiment. Experimental tools for determining protein concentration and activity in the cell are the crucial next step in the process.

Another high-throughput technology that is emerging as a tool in functional genomics is 2D gel electrophoresis. Gels have long been used in molecular biology to separate mixtures of components. Depending on the conditions of the experiment and the type of gel used, different components will migrate through a gel matrix at different rates. (This same principle makes DNA sequencing possible).

Two-dimensional gel electrophoresis can be used to separate protein mixtures containing thousands of components. The first dimension of the experiment is separation of the components of a solution along a pH gradient (isoelectric focusing). The second dimension is separation of the components orthogonally by molecular weight. Separation in these two dimensions can resolve even a complicated mixture of components. Figure 11-5 shows a 2D-PAGE reference map from *Arabidopsis thaliana*. The 2D-PAGE experiment separates proteins from a mixed sample so that individual proteins can be identified. Each spot on the map represents a different protein. (Image © Swiss Institute of Bioinformatics, Geneva, Switzerland.)

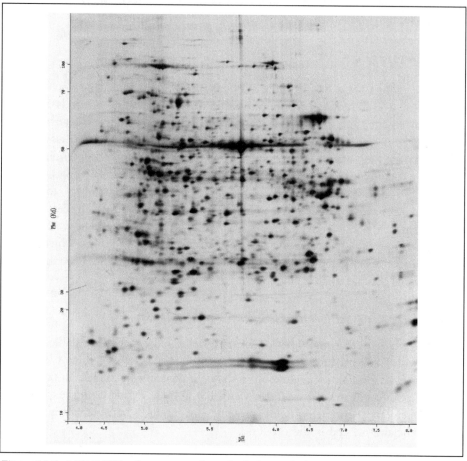

Figure 11-5. A 2D-PAGE reference map from Arabidopsis thaliana

While 2D gel electrophoresis is a useful and interesting technology in itself, the technology did not really come into its own until the development of standardized immobilized-gradient gels. These gels allow very precise protein separations, resulting in standardized high density data arrays. They can therefore be subjected to automated image analysis and quantitation and used for accurate comparative studies. The other advance that has put 2D gel technology at the forefront of modern molecular biology methods is the capacity to chemically analyze each spot on the gel using mass spectrometry. This allows the measurable biochemical phenomenon—the amount of protein found in a particular spot on the gel—to be directly connected to the sequence of the protein found at that spot.

Informatics Challenges in 2D-PAGE Analysis

The analysis pathway for 2D-PAGE gel images is essentially quite similar to that for microarrays. The first step is an image analysis, in which the positions of spots on the gel are identified and the boundaries between different spots are resolved. Molecular weight and isoelectric point (PI) for each protein in the gel can be estimated according to position.

Next, the spots are identified, and sequence information is used to make the connection between a particular spot and its gene sequence. In microarray experiments, this step is planned in advance, as the primers or cDNA fragments are laid down in the original chip design. In proteome analysis, the immobilized proteins can either be sequenced in situ or spots of protein can be physically removed from the gel, eluted, and analyzed using mass spectrometry methods such as electrospray ionization-mass spectrometry (ESI-MS) or matrix-assisted laser desorption ionization mass spectrometry (MALDI).

The essence of mass spectrometry methods is that they can determine the masses of components in a mixture, starting from a very small sample. Proteins, fragmented by various chemically specific digestion methods, have characteristic fingerprints (patterns of peptide masses) that can identify specific proteins and match them with a gene sequence.

Peptide fingerprints are sufficient to identify proteins only in cases in which the sequence of a protein is already known and can be found in a database. When full sequence information isn't available, a second mass spectrometry step can obtain partial sequence information from each individual peptide that makes up the peptide fingerprint. The initial peptide fingerprinting process separates the protein into peptides and characterizes them by mass. Within the mass spectrometer, each peptide can then be further broken down into ionized fragments. The goal of the peptide fragmentation step is to produce a ladder of fragments each differing in length by one amino acid. Because each type of amino acid has a different molecular weight, the sequence of each peptide can be deduced from the resulting mass spectrum.

Finally, staining, radiolabeling, fluorescence, or other methods are used to quantitate each protein spot on the gel. Both in the microarray experiment and the 2D-PAGE experiment, quantitation is a fairly difficult step. In this step, computer algorithms can help analyze the amount of signal at each spot and deconvolute complex patterns of spots.

Tools for Proteomics Analysis

Several public-domain programs for proteomics analysis are available on the Web. Most of these can be accessed through the excellent proteomics resource at Expert Protein Analysis System (ExPASy, *http://www.expasy.ch/tools/*), the excellent resource maintained by the Swiss Institute of Bioinformatics. ExPASy is linked with SWISS-PROT, an expert-curated database of protein sequence information, and TrEMBL, the computer-generated counterpart to SWISS-PROT. Most of its tools are web-based and tied into these and other protein databases. The Swiss Institute of Bioinformatics also maintains SWISS-2DPAGE, a database of reference gel maps that are fully searchable and integrated with other protein information. SWISS-2DPAGE, like other biological databases, is growing rapidly; however deposition of 2D-PAGE results into databases isn't, at this time, required for publication, so the database isn't comprehensive.

The Melanie3 software package, a Windows-based package for 2D-PAGE image analysis, was developed at ExPASy, although it has since been commercialized. A Melanie viewer, which allows users who don't own Melanie3 to view Melanie3 data sets generated by colleagues, is freely distributed by ExPASy.

Here are some other ExPASy proteomics tools:

AACompIdent
   Allows you to identify proteins by their amino acid composition

AACompSim
   Compares a protein's amino acid composition with other proteins in SWISS-PROT

MultiDent
   A multifunction tool that uses PI, molecular weight, mass fingerprints, and other data to help identify proteins

PeptIdent
   Compares experimentally determined mass fingerprints with theoretically calculated mass fingerprints for all proteins in SWISS-PROT

FindMod
   Predicts specific post-translational modifications to proteins based on mass differences between experimental and computed fingerprints

GlycoMod
   Predicts oligosaccharide modifications from mass differences

PeptideMass
   Computes a theoretical mass fingerprint for a SWISS-PROT or TrEMBL entry, or for a user-entered protein sequence

These tools are entirely forms-based and very approachable for the novice user. In addition, ExPASy provides links to many externally developed tools and web servers. It is an excellent starting resource for anyone interested in proteomics.

The PROWL database is a relatively new web resource for proteomics. PROWL tools can be used to search a protein database with peptide fingerprint or partial sequence information. The PROWL group also provides a suite of software for mass spectrometry data analysis.

Generalizing the Array Approach

Integration of microarray and 2D-PAGE methods—which provide information about gene transcription and translation, respectively—with genome sequence data is the best way currently available to form a picture of whole-genome function. However, these methods are still fairly new. Although the technology is moving forward by leaps and bounds, their results aren't yet fully standardized, and consensus software tools and analysis methods for these types of data are still emerging.

Array and 2D-PAGE experiments have elements in common, including the ability to separate and quantitate components in a mixture and fix particular components consistently to positions in a grid, and the ability to measure changes in signal at each position over time. Approaches for analyzing array-formatted biochemical data are likely to be similar on some level, whether the experiments involve DNA-DNA, DNA-mRNA, or even protein-protein interactions. Array strategies have recently been used to conduct a genome-wide survey of protein-protein interactions in yeast, and other applications of the strategy are, no doubt, in the works. Array methods and other parallel methods promise to continue to revolutionize biology. However, the biology community is still in the process of developing standards for reporting and archiving array data, and it is unlikely that a consensus will be reached before this book goes to press.

Biochemical Pathway Databases

Gene and protein expression are only two steps in the translation of genetic code to phenotype. Once genes are expressed and translated into proteins, their products participate in complicated biochemical interactions called *pathways*, as shown in Figure 11-6 (the image in the figure is © Kyoto Encyclopedia of Genes and Genomes). It is highly unlikely that one enzyme-catalyzed chemical reaction will produce a needed product from a material readily available to the organism. Instead, a complicated series of steps is usually required. Each pathway may supply chemical precursors to many other pathways, meaning that each protein has relationships not only to the preceding and following biochemical steps in a single pathway, but possibly to steps in several pathways. The complicated branchings of metabolic pathways are far more difficult to represent and search than the linear sequences of genes and genomes.

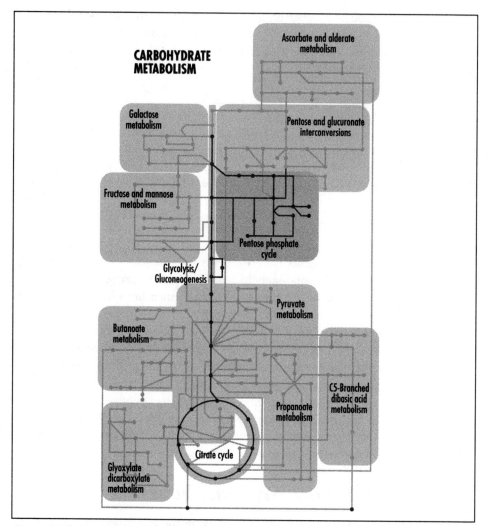

Figure 11-6. A complex metabolic pathway

Illustration of a Complex Metabolic Pathway

Several web-based services offer access to metabolic pathway information. These resources are primarily databases of information linked by search tools; at the time of this writing metabolic simulation tools, such as those we describe in the next section, have not been fully integrated with databases of known metabolic pathway information into a central web-based resource.

EC Nomenclature

Enzymes (proteins that catalyze metabolic reactions) can be described using a standard code called the *EC code*. The EC nomenclature is a hierarchical naming scheme that divides enzymes into several major classes. The first class number refers to the chemistry of the enzyme: oxidoreductase, lyase, hydrolase, transferase, isomerase, or ligase. The second class number indicates what class of substrate the enzyme acts on. The third class number, which can be omitted, indicates other chemical participants in the reaction. Finally, the fourth number narrows the search to the specific enzyme. Thus, EC number 1.1.1.1 refers to alcohol dehydrogenase, which is a (1) oxidoreductase acting on the (1) CH-OH group of donors with (1) NADH as acceptor. If you are interested in using most metabolic pathway resources, it's helpful to become familiar with EC nomenclature. The EC code and hierarchy of functional definitions can be found online at the IUBMB Biochemical Nomenclature Committee web site.

WIT and KEGG

The best known metabolic pathway resources on the Web are What is There (WIT, *http://wit.mcs.anl.gov/WIT2/*) and the Kyoto Encyclopedia of Genes and Genomes (KEGG, *http://www.genome.ad.jp/kegg/*). WIT is a metabolic pathway reconstruction resource; that is, the curators of WIT are attempting to reconstruct complete metabolic pathway models for organisms whose genomes have been completely sequenced. WIT currently contains metabolic models for 39 organisms. The WIT models include far more than just metabolism and bioenergetics; they range from transcription and translation pathways to transmembrane transport to signal transduction.

WIT can be searched and queried in a number of ways. You can browse the database beginning at the very top level, a functional overview of the WIT contents, which is found under the heading General Overview on the main page. Each heading in the metabolic outline is a clickable link that takes you to increasingly specific levels of detail about that subset of metabolism. The View Models menu takes you directly to organism-specific metabolic models.

The General Search function allows you to search all of WIT, or subsets of organisms. This type of search is based on keywords, using Unix-style regular expressions to find matches. There is also a similarity search function that allows you to search all the open reading frames (ORFs) of a selected organism for sequence pattern matches, using either BLAST or FASTA. Pathway queries require you to specify the names of metabolites and/or specific EC enzyme codes. Enzyme queries allow you to specify an enzyme name or EC code, along with location information such as tissue specificity, cellular compartment specificity, or organelle specificity. In all except the regular-expression searches, the keywords are drawn from standardized metabolic vocabularies. WIT searches require some prior knowledge of these vocabularies when you submit the query. WIT was primarily designed as a tool to aid its developers in producing metabolic reconstructions, and documentation of the vocabularies used may not always be sufficient for the novice user. WIT is relatively text-heavy, although at the highest level of detail, metabolic pathway diagrams can be displayed.

Another web-based metabolic reconstruction resource is KEGG, which provides its metabolic overviews as map illustrations, rather than text-only, and can be easier to use for the visually-oriented user. KEGG also provides listings of EC numbers and their corresponding enzymes broken down by level, and many helpful links to sites describing enzyme and ligand nomenclature in detail. The LIGAND database, associated with KEGG, is a useful resource for identifying small molecules involved in biochemical pathways. Like WIT, KEGG is searchable by sequence homology, keyword, and chemical entity; you can also input the LIGAND ID codes of two small molecules and find all of the possible metabolic pathways connecting them.

PathDB

PathDB is another type of metabolic pathway database. While it contains roughly the same information as KEGG and WIT—identities of compounds and metabolic proteins, and information about the steps that connect these entities—it handles information in a far more flexible way than the other metabolic databases. Instead of limiting searches to arbitrary metabolic pathways and describing pathways with preconceived images, PathDB allows you to find any set of connected reactions that link point A to point B, or compound A to compound B.

PathDB contains, in addition to the usual search tools, a pathway visualization interface that allows you to inspect any selected pathway and display different representations of the pathway. The PathDB developers plan to incorporate metabolic simulation into the user interface as well, although those features aren't available at the time of this writing.

The PathDB browser is a platform-independent tool you can use on any machine with a Java Runtime Environment (JRE) Version 1.1.4 or later installed. Both Sun and IBM supply a JRE for Linux systems. Once the JRE is installed, you can run the PathDB installer, making sure that the installer uses the correct version of the JRE (for this to work, you may need to add the JRE binary directory to your path). Let the installer create a link to PathDB in your home directory. To run the program, enter *PathDB*. You may be prompted to specify the correct Java virtual machine or exit; use the same Java pathway you did when you installed the software.

To sample how PathDB works, submit a simple query that will assure you get results the first time (such as "All Catalysts with EC Number like 1.1.1.1," which brings up a list of alcohol dehydrogenases). You can also follow the tutorials available from the PathDB web site.

Modeling Kinetics and Physiology

A new "omics" buzzword that has begun to crop up in the literature rather recently is "metabolomics." Researchers have begun to recognize the need to exhaustively track the availability and concentration of small molecules—everything from electrolytes to metabolic intermediates to enzyme cofactors—in biological systems. Small molecules are extremely important in biochemistry, playing roles in everything from signal transduction to bioenergetics to regulation. The populations of small molecules that interact with proteins in the cell will continue to be a key topic of research as biologists attempt to assemble the big picture of cellular function and physiology.

Mathematical modeling of biochemical kinetics and physiology is a complicated topic that is largely beyond the scope of this book. Mathematical models are generally system-specific, and to develop them requires a detailed understanding of a biological system and a facility with differential equations. However, a few groups have begun to develop context-independent software for developing biochemical and physiological models. Some of the best known of these are Gepasi, a system for biochemical modeling; XPP, a more general package for dynamical simulation; and the Virtual Cell portal.

The essential principle behind biochemical and physiological modeling is that changes in biochemical systems can be modeled in terms of chemical concentrations and associated rate equations. Each "pool" of biochemical reagent in a system has an associated rate of formation and rate of breakdown, and the model is capable of predicting how the system will behave over time under various starting conditions. A model of metabolism may consist of dozens of reagents, each being formed and consumed by multiple reactions. Models that accurately simulate the behavior of a complex biochemical pathway aren't trivially developed, but once created, they can predict the effect of perturbations to the system and help researchers develop new hypotheses.

If you're coming from a biological sciences background, you are probably familiar with the Michaelis-Menten model for describing enzyme kinetics. Biochemical modeling extends this relatively simple mathematical model of a single enzyme-catalyzed reaction to encompass multiple reactions that may feed back upon each other in complex ways. Physiological models also involve multiple compartments with barriers through which only some components can diffuse or be transported. However, the underlying principles are similar, no matter how complex the model.

Modeling Kinetics with Gepasi

Gepasi (*http://www.gepasi.org/*) is a user-friendly biochemical kinetics simulator for Windows/NT that can model systems of up to 45 metabolites and 45 rate equations. The Gepasi interface includes interactive tools for creating a new metabolic model: entering chemical reactions, adding metabolites that may be effectors or inhibitors of the reactions, defining reaction kinetics, setting metabolite concentrations, and other key steps in model development. You can apply Gepasi's predefined reaction types to your model or define your own reaction types. Gepasi automatically checks on mass conservation relations that need to be accounted for in the simulation. Gepasi has numerous options for running simulations over various time courses and testing the results of changing variable values over a user-defined range. Gepasi can also optimize metabolic models used in metabolic engineering and fit experimental data to metabolic models.

At the time of this writing, versions of Gepasi for platforms other than Windows/NT are in development.

XPP

XPP (*http://www.math.pitt.edu/~bard/xpp/xpp.html*) is a dynamical systems simulation tool that is available for both Windows/NT and Linux. While it lacks some of the user-friendly features of Gepasi, it has been used effectively to model biochemical processes ranging from biochemical reactions to cell cycles and circadian rhythms. XPP compiles easily on any Linux system with a simple *make* command; just download the archive, move it into a directory of its own, extract it, then compile the program. Documentation, as well as example files for various simulations, are included with the XPP distribution.

Using the Virtual Cell Portal

The Virtual Cell portal at the National Resource for Cell Analysis and Modeling (NRCAM, *http://www.nrcam.uchc.edu*) is the first web-based resource for modeling of cellular processes. It allows you to model cells with an arbitrary number of compartments and complex physiology. A tutorial available at the Virtual Cell site walks the first-time user through the process of developing a physiology model for a cell, choosing a cell geometry, and setting up and running a simulation. The cell physiology model includes not only a compartmentation scheme for the cell, which can be created using simple drawing tools, but the addition of specific types of ionic species and membrane transporters to the cell model.

The Virtual Cell is a Java applet, which is fully supported for Macintosh and Windows users. In order to use the Virtual Cell portal on a Linux workstation, you need to download the Java plug-in for Netscape (available from *http://www.blackdown.org*) and install it in your *~/.netscape* directory. Once the plug-in is installed, you can follow the "MacIntosh Users Run the Virtual Cell" link on the main page, even if you're running the VCell Applet on a Linux workstation, and you can try out most features of the portal. At the time of this writing, Unix users aren't explicitly supported at the Virtual Cell portal, and while correct functionality seems to be available when the Blackdown Java applet is used, it might be wise for serious users of the VCell tools to compare results for some test cases on a Linux workstation and another machine.

Summary

We've compiled a quick-reference table of genomics and proteomics tools and techniques (Table 11-1).

Table 11-1. Genomics and Proteomics Tools and Techniques

What you do	Why you do it	What you use to do it
Online genome resources	To find information about the location and function of particular genes in a genome	NCBI tools, TIGR tools, EnsEMBL, and genome-specific databases
Basecalling	To convert fluorescence intensities from the sequencing experiment into four-letter sequence code	Phred
Genome mapping and assembly	To organize the sequences of short fragments of raw DNA sequence data into a coherent whole	Phrap, Staden package
Genome annotation	To connect functional information about the genome to specific sequence locations	MAGPIE
Genome comparison	To identify components of genome structure that differentiate one organism from another	PipMaker, MUMmer
Microarray image analysis	To identify and quantitate spots in raw microarray data	CrazyQuant, SpotFinder, ArrayViewer
Clustering analysis of microarray data	To identify genes that appear to be expressed as linked groups	Cluster, TreeView
2D-PAGE analysis	To analyze, visualize, and quantitate 2D-PAGE images	Melanie3, Melanie Viewer

Table 11-1. Genomics and Proteomics Tools and Techniques (continued)

What you do	Why you do it	What you use to do it
Proteomics analysis	To analyze mass spectrometry results and identify proteins	ExPASy tools, ProteinProspector, PROWL
Metabolic pathway tools	To search metabolic pathways and discover functional relationships; to reconstruct metabolic pathways	PATH-DB, WIT, KEGG
Metabolic and cellular simulation	To model metabolic and cellular processes based on known properties and inference	Gepasi, XPP, Virtual Cell

IV

Databases and Visualization

12

Automating Data Analysis with Perl

As we've seen in previous chapters, a vast assortment of software tools exists for bioinformatics. Even though it's likely that someone has already written what you need, you will still encounter many situations in which the best solution is to do it yourself. In bioinformatics, that often means writing programs that sift through mountains of data to extract just the information you require. Perl, the Practical Extraction and Reporting Language, is ideally suited to this task.

Why Perl?

There are a lot of programming languages out there. In our survey of bioinformatics software, we have already seen programs written in Java, C, and FORTRAN. So, why use Perl? The answer is efficiency.[*] Biological data is stored in enormous databases and text files. Sorting through and analyzing this data by hand (and it can be done) would take far too long, so the smart scientist writes computer tools to automate the process. Perl, with its highly developed capacity to detect patterns in data, and especially strings of text, is the most obvious choice. The next obvious choice would probably be Python. Python, the less well known of the two, is a fully object-oriented scripting language introduced by Guido van Rossum in 1988. Python has some outstanding contributed code, including a mature library for numerical methods, tools for building graphical user interfaces quickly and easily, and even a library of functions for structural biology. At the end of the day, however, it's the wealth of existing Perl code for bioinformatics, the smooth integration of that code onto Unix-based systems, cross-platform portability, and an

---

[*] Efficiency from the programmer's point of view, that is. It takes far less programming time to extract data with Perl than with C or with Java.

incredibly enthusiastic user community that makes Perl our favorite scripting language for bioinformatics applications.

Perl has a flexible syntax, or grammar, so if you are familiar with programming in other languages such as C or BASIC, it is easy to write Perl code in a C-like or BASIC-like dialect. Perl also takes care of much of the dirty work involved in programming, such as memory allocation, so you can concentrate on solving the problem at hand. It's often the case that programming problems requiring many lines of code in C or Java may be solved in just a few lines of Perl.

Many excellent books have been written about learning and using Perl, so this single chapter obviously can't cover everything you will ever need to know about the language. Perl has a mountain of features, and it's unrealistic to assume you can master it without a serious commitment to learning the art of computer programming. Our aim in this chapter isn't to teach you how to program in Perl, but rather to show you how Perl can help you solve certain problems in bioinformatics. We will take you through some examples that are most immediately useful in real bioinformatics research, such as reading datafiles, searching for character strings, performing back-of-the-envelope calculations, and reporting findings to the user. And we'll explain how our sample programs work. The rest is up to you. The ability to program in any language—but especially in Perl, Python, or Java—is an important skill for any bioinformatician to have. We strongly suggest you take a programming class or obtain one of the books on our list of recommended reading and start from the beginning. You won't regret it.

Where Do I Get Perl?

Perl is available for a variety of operating systems, including Windows and Mac OS, as well as Linux and other flavors of Unix. It's distributed under an open source license, which means that it's essentially free. To obtain Perl from the Web, go to *http://www.perl.com/pub/language/info/software.html* and follow the instructions for downloading and installing it on your system.

Perl Basics

Once you've installed Perl, or confirmed with your system administrator that it's already installed on your system, you're ready to begin writing your first program. Writing and executing a Perl program can be broken into several steps: writing the program (or script) and saving it in a file, running the program, and reading the output.

Hello World

A Perl program is a text file that contains instructions written in the Perl language. The classic first program in Perl (and many other languages) is called "Hello, World!" It's written like this:

```
#!/usr/bin/perl -w
# Say hello
print "Hello, World!\n";
```

"Hello, World!" is a short program, but it's still complete. The first line is called the shebang line and tells the computer that this is a Perl program. All Perl programs running on Unix begin with this line.* It's a special kind of comment to the Unix shell that tells it where to find Perl, and also instructs it to look for optional arguments. In our version of "Hello World!" we've included the optional argument $-w$ at the end of the line. This argument tells Perl to give extra warning messages if you do something potentially dangerous in your program. It's a good idea to always develop your programs under $-w$.

The second line starts with a # sign. The # tells Perl that the line of text that follows is a comment, not part of the executable code. Comments are how humans tell each other what each part of the program is intended to do. Make a habit of including comments in your code. That way you and other people can add to your code, debug it successfully, and even more importantly, remember what it was supposed to do in the first place.

The third line calls the *print* function with a single argument that consists of a text string. At the end of the text string, there is a \n, which tells the computer to move to a new line after executing the *print* statement. The *print* statement ends with a semicolon, as do most statements in Perl.

To try this little program yourself, you can open a text editor such as *vi*, Emacs, or *pico*, and type the lines in. When you've finished entering the program, name the file *hello.pl* and save it in your directory of choice. While you're learning, you might consider creating a new directory (using the *mkdir* command, which we covered in Chapter 4, *Files and Directories in Unix*) called *Perl* in your home directory. That way you'll always know where to look for your Perl programs.

Now make the file executable using the command:

```
% chmod +x hello.pl
```

---

* Strictly speaking, the shebang line isn't necessary on Windows or Macintosh; neither of those systems has a *usr/bin/perl*. It's good programming form to always include the line, however, since it's the best place to indicate your optional arguments in Perl. On other platforms, you can run the program by invoking the Perl interpreter explicitly, as in *perl hello.pl*.

(If you need a refresher on *chmod*, this would be a good time to review the section on changing file permissions in Chapter 4.) To run the program, type:

```
% hello.pl
```

Because of the shebang line in our program, this command invokes the Perl interpreter, which reads the rest of the file and then translates your Perl source code into machine code the computer can execute. In this case you'll notice that *Hello, World!* appears on your computer screen, and then the cursor advances to a new line. You've now written and run your first Perl program!

A Bioinformatics Example

One of the strengths of Perl—and the reason that bioinformaticians love it—is that with a few lines of code, you can automate a tedious task such as searching for a nucleotide string contained in a block of sequence data. To do this, you need a slightly more complex Perl program that might look like this:

```perl
#!/usr/bin/perl -w
# Look for nucleotide string in sequence data

my $target = "ACCCTG";
my $search_string =
     'CCACACCACACCCACACACCCACACACCACACCACACACCACACCACACCCACACACACA'.
     'CATCCTAACACTACCCTAACACAGCCCTAATCTAACCCTGGCCAACCTGTCTCTCAACTT'.
     'ACCCTCCATTACCCTGCCTCCACTCGTTACCCTGTCCCATTCAACCATACCACTCCGAAC';

my @matches;

# Try to find a match in letters 1-6 of $search_string, then look at letters 2-7,
# and so on. Record the starting offset of each match.

foreach my $i (0..length $search_string){
    if( $target eq substr( $search_string, $i, length $target)){
       push @matches, $i;
    }
}

# Make @matches into a comma-separated list for printing
print "My matches occurred at the following offsets: @matches.\n";

print "done\n";
```

This program is also short and simple, but it's still quite powerful. It searches for the target string "ACCCTG" in a sequence of data and keeps track of the starting location of each match. The program demonstrates variables and loops, which are two basic programming constructs you need to understand to make sense of what is going on.

Variables

A *variable* is a name that is associated with a data value, such as a string or a number. It is common to say that a variable stores or contains a value. Variables allow you to store and manipulate data in your programs; they are called variables because the values they represent can change throughout the life of a program.

Our sequence matching program declares four variables: *$target*, *$search_string*, *@matches*, and *$i*. The $ and @ characters indicate the kind of variable each one is. Perl has three kinds of variables built into the language: scalars, arrays, and hashes.

Unlike other programming languages, Perl doesn't require formal declaration of variables; they simply exist upon their first use whether you explicitly declare them or not. You may declare your variables, if you'd like, by using either *my* or *our* in front of the variable name. When you declare a variable, you give it a name. A variable name must follow two main rules: it must start with a letter or an underscore (the $ and @ characters aren't considered part of the name), and it must consist of letters, digits, and underscores. The best names are ones that clearly, concisely, and accurately describe the variable's role in the program. For example, it is easier to guess the role of a variable if it is named *$target* or *$sequence*, than if it were called *$icxl*.

Scalars

A *scalar variable* contains a single piece of data that is either a number or a string. The $ character indicates that a variable is scalar. The first two variables declared in our program are scalar variables:

```
my $target = "ACCCTG";
my $search_string =
    "CCACACCACACCCACACACCCACACACCACACCACACACCACACCACACCCACACACACA".
    "CATCCTAACACTACCCTAACACAGCCCTAATCTAACCCTGGCCAACCTGTCTCTCAACTT".
    "ACCCTCCATTACCCTGCCTCCACTCGTTACCCTGTCCCATTCAACCATACCACTCCGAAC";
```

In this case, "ACCCTG" is the target string we are seeking, and "CCACACCACAC-CCACAC…" is the sequence data in which we're hoping to find it.

In a scalar variable, a number can be either an integer (0, 1, 2, 3, etc.) or a real number (a number that contains a fractional portion, such as 5.6). A string is a chunk of text that's surrounded by quotes. For example:

```
"I am a string."
'I, too, am a string'
```

One of Perl's special features is that it has a number of built-in facilities for manipulating strings, which comes in handy when working with the flat text files common to bioinformatics. We cover flat text files and their more structured relatives, relational databases, in detail in Chapter 13, *Building Biological Databases*.

Arrays

An *array* is an ordered list of data. In our sequence matching program, *@matches* is an array variable used to store the starting locations of all the matches. Each element stored in an array can be accessed by its position in the list, which is represented as a number. In Perl, array variables are given an @ prefix. For example, the following statement declares an array of numbers:

```
@a = ( 1, "4", 9 );
```

This statement declares an array of strings:

```
@names = ("T. Herman", "N. Aeschylus", "H. Ulysses", "Standish");
```

And this statement declares an array with both:

```
@mix = ("Caesar Augustus", "Tiberius", 18, "Caligula", "Claudius");
```

Note the syntax in the declarations: each element in the array is separated from its neighbors by a comma, each of the strings is quoted, and (unlike American English) the comma appears *outside* of the quotes.

Because an array is an ordered set of information, you can retrieve each element in an array according to its number. The individual elements in an array are written as *$this_array[i]*, where *i* is the index of the array element being addressed. Note that *i* can be either a bare number (such as *21*), or a numeric scalar variable (such as *$n*) that contains a bare number. Here is a Perl statement that uses the *print* operator to display the second number in *@a* and the third name in *@names* on the screen:

```
print "second number: $a[1]\n third name: $names[2]\n";
```

You may be wondering why the element numbers here are one less than what you might think they should be. The reason is that positions in Perl arrays are numbered starting from zero. That is, the first element in an array is numbered 0, the second element is numbered 1, and so on. That's why, in the previous example, the second element in *@a* is addressed as *$a[1]*. This is an important detail to remember; mistakes in addressing arrays due to missing that crucial zero element are easy to make.

Hashes

A *hash* is also known as an *associative array* because it associates a name (or key, as it's called in Perl) with each piece of data (or value) stored in it. A real-world example of a hash is a telephone book, in which you look up a person's name in order to find her telephone number. Our sequence matching program doesn't use any hashes, but they can be quite handy in bioinformatics programs, as you'll see in a later example. Perl uses the % prefix to indicate hash variables (e.g., *%sequences*). There are a number of ways to declare a hash and its contents as a list of key/value pairs. Here is the syntax for one declaration style:

```
%hash = (
    key1 => "value1",
    key2 => "value2", ...
    last_key => "last_value" );
```

A value can then be retrieved from this hash using the corresponding key, as follows:

```
$value = $hash{"key2"};
```

For example, you can declare a hash that relates each three-letter amino acid code to its one-letter symbol:

```
my %three_to_one = (
    ALA => A, CYS => C, ASP => D, GLU => E,
    PHE => F, GLY => G, HIS => H, ILE => I,
    LYS => K, LEU => L, MET => M, ASN => N,
    PRO => P, GLN => Q, ARG => R, SER => S,
    THR => T, VAL => V, TRP => W, TYR => Y
);
```

The hash entry with the one-letter code for arginine can then be displayed using the following statement:

```
print "The one-letter code for ARG is $three_to_one{ARG}\n";
```

Because there are many popular sequence databases, another place where hashes can be immediately useful is in keeping track of which sequence ID in one database corresponds to a sequence ID in the next. In the following example, we define a hash in which each of the keys is a GenBank identifier (GI) number of a particular enzyme, and each value is the corresponding SWISS-PROT identifier of the same enzyme. Using this hash, a program can take the more cryptic GI number and automatically find the associated SWISS-PROT ID:

```
#!/usr/bin/perl -w
# define the hash relating GI numbers to SWISSPROT IDs
 %sods = (
    g134606  => "SODC_DROME",
    g134611  => "SODC_HUMAN",
    g464769  => "SODC_CAEEL",
    g1711426 => "SODC_ECOLI" );

# retrieve a value from %sods
$genbank_id = "g134611";
$swissprot_id = $sods{$genbank_id};
print "$genbank_id is the same as $swissprot_id\n";
```

If you save the previous script to a file, make the file executable, and run it, you should see:

```
g134611 is the same as SODC_HUMAN
```

In the first part of this script, you are declaring the hash relating GenBank IDs to SWISS-PROT IDs. In the second part, you access the information stored in that hash. The first step is to assign one of the GenBank IDs to the variable *$genbank_ id*. Then you can retrieve the SWISS-PROT ID that *%sods* has associated with the string in *$genbank_id*, and store the SWISS-PROT ID in the variable *$swissprot_id*. Finally, print the values of the two scalar variables. This example is obviously rather contrived, but it should give you an idea of how useful hashes can be in bioinformatics programs.

Loops

Now that we've talked about scalar, array, and hash variables in Perl, let's return to our sequence matching program and talk about the other main programming construct it employs. A *loop* is a programming device that repeatedly executes a specific set of commands until a particular condition is reached. Our program uses a *foreach* loop to iterate through the search string:

```
foreach my $i (0..length $search_string){
    if( $target eq substr( $search_string, $i, length $target)){
        push @matches, $i;
    }
}
```

The first time through this loop, Perl starts at 0 and looks at the first six-letter combination in the search string, compares it to the target string, and, if there is a match, records it in *@matches*. The second cycle of the loop looks at letters 2–7, the third looks at letters 3–8, and so on. Perl stops executing this sequence when it reaches the end of the search string. At this point, the loop is done, and the program moves on to the next section, where it prints the results. Don't worry if you don't understand all the code in the loop; all that's important right now is that you have a general understanding of what the code is doing.

Subroutines

Although we don't use them in any of our example programs, the use of subroutines in programs is worth mentioning. All modern programming languages provide a way to bundle up a set of statements into a *subroutine* so that they can be invoked concisely and repeatedly. In Perl, you can create a subroutine with the *sub* declaration:

```
sub greet {
    my ($name) = shift;
```

```
      print "Hello, $name!\n";
   }
```

Once this *greet* subroutine has been declared, you can invoke it as follows:

```
   greet("world");   # Prints "Hello, world!"
   greet("Per");     # Prints "Hello, Per!"
```

Here, *"world"* and *"Per"* are *arguments*—values passed into the subroutine, where they are then stored in *$name*. Our *greet* subroutine just prints a single line and then returns. Usually, subroutines do something a bit more complicated, possibly returning a value:

```
   $length = calculate_length($sequence);
```

This sets *$length* to whatever the *calculate_length( )* subroutine returns when provided with the single argument *$sequence*. When a subroutine is used for its return value, it's often called a *function*.

Pattern Matching and Regular Expressions

A major feature of Perl is its pattern matching, and particularly its use of regular expressions. A regular expression (or *regex* in the Perl vernacular) is a pattern that can be matched against a string of data. We first encountered regular expressions in our discussion of the Unix command *grep*, back in Chapter 5, *Working on a Unix System. grep*, as you may recall, searches for occurrences of patterns in files. When you tell *grep* to search for a pattern, you describe what you're looking for in terms of a regular expression. As you know, much of bioinformatics is about searching for patterns in data.

Let's look at a Perl example. Say you have a string, such as a DNA sequence, and you want to make sure that there are no illegal characters in it. You can use a regular expression to test for illegal characters as follows:

```
#!/usr/bin/perl
# check for non-DNA characters
my $string = "CCACACCACACCCACACaCCCaCaCATCACACCACACACCACACTACACCCA*CACACACA";
if( $string =~ m/([^ATCG])/i) {
   print "Warning! Found: $1 in the string";
}
```

This program contains the regular expression *[^ATCG]*. Translated into English, the regular expression says "look for characters in *$string* that don't match A, T, C, or G." (The *i* at the end of the statement tells Perl to match case *in*sensitively; that is, to pay no attention to case. Perl's default is to treat A differently from a.) If Perl

encounters something other than the declared pattern, the program prints out the
offending character. The output of this program is:

```
Warning! Found * in the string
```

If instead you want to search for a particular combination of letters, like "CAT",
you can change the regular expression to read *CAT*:

```
#!/usr/bin/perl
# check for CATs
my $string =
   "CCACACCACACCCACACaCCCaCaCATCACACCACACACCACACTACACCCA*CACACACA";
if( $string =~ m/CAT/i ){
  print "Meow.";
}
```

The output of this modified program is:

```
Meow.
```

Parsing BLAST Output Using Perl

Now that you know enough about how Perl is written to understand these simple
programs, let's apply it to one of the most common problems in bioinformatics:
parsing BLAST output. As you already know, the result of a BLAST search is often
a multimegabyte file full of raw data. The results of several searches can quickly
become overwhelming. But by writing a fairly simple program in Perl, you can
automate the process of looking for a single string or multiple strings in your data.

Consider the following block of data:

```
. . .
gb|AC005288.1|AC005288  Homo sapiens chromosome 17, clone hC...    268  2e-68
gb|AC008812.7|AC008812  Homo sapiens chromosome 19 clone CTD...    264  3e-67
gb|AC009123.6|AC009123  Homo sapiens chromosome 16 clone RP1...    262  1e-66
emb|AL137073.13|AL137073  Human DNA sequence from clone RP11...    260  5e-66
gb|AC020904.6|AC020904  Homo sapiens chromosome 19 clone CTB...    248  2e-62
>gb|AC007421.12|AC007421 Homo sapiens chromosome 17, clone hRPC.1030_0_14,
complete sequence
Query: 3407 accgtcataaagtcaaacaattgtaacttgaaccatcttttaactcaggtactgtgtata 3466
            ||||||||||||||||||||||||||||||||||||||||||||||||||||||||||||
Sbjct: 1366 accgtcataaagtcaaacaattgtaacttgaaccatcttttaactcaggtactgtgtata 1425
Query: 3467 tacttacttctccccctcctctgttgctgcagatccgtgggcgtgagcgcttcgagatgt 3526
            ||||||||||||||||||||||||||||||||||||||||||||||||||||||||||||
Sbjct: 1426 tacttacttctccccctcctctgttgctgcagatccgtgggcgtgagcgcttcgagatgt 1485
Query: 3527 tccgagagctgaatgaggccttggaactcaaggatgcccaggctgggaaggagccagggg 3586
            ||||||||||||||||||||||||||||||||||||||||||||||||||||||||||||
Sbjct: 1486 tccgagagctgaatgaggccttggaactcaaggatgcccaggctgggaaggagccagggg 1545
Query: 3587 ggagcagggctcactccaggtgagtgacctcagcccccttcctggccctactcccctgcct 3646
            ||||||||||||||||||||||||||||||||||||||||||||||||||||||||||||
Sbjct: 1546 ggagcagggctcactccaggtgagtgacctcagcccccttcctggccctactcccctgcct 1605
Query: 3647 tcctaggttggaaagccataggattccattctcatcctgccttcatggtcaaaggcagct 3706
. . .
```

This is only a small portion of what you might find in a report from a BLAST search. (This is actual data from a BLAST report. The entire file, *blast.dat*, is too large to reproduce here.) The first six lines of this sample contain information about the BLAST search, as well as other "noise" that's of no importance to the search. The next 13 lines, and the ones that follow it in the actual report, contain the data to analyze. You want the Perl program to look at both the "Query" and "Sbjct" lines in this BLAST report and find the number of occurrences of the following substrings:

- 'gtccca'
- 'gcaatg'
- 'cagct'
- 'tcggga'
- Missing data (represented by dashes in the nucleotide sequence strings)

At the same time, you want the program to ignore irrelevant material such as information about the search and other noise. The program should then generate a report file called *report.txt* that describes the findings for these strings.

In this program you need to create two very long scalar variables to represent each sequence for searching. Let's call them $query\_src$, and $sbjct\_src$. In any BLAST output, you'll notice that sometimes the "Sbjct" and "Query" lines aren't contiguous; that is, there are gaps in the data. From a programming perspective, the fact that the gaps exist isn't important; you simply want to read the nucleotides into your scalars consecutively. Here is a sample portion of BLAST data:

```
Query: 1165   gagcccaggagttcaagaccagcctgggtaacatgatgaaacctcgtctctac 1217
              |||| ||||||||| ||||||||||||| |||| | ||||||||  ||||||||
Sbjct: 11895 gagctcaggagtttgagaccagcctggggaacacggtgaaaccctgtctctac 11843
Query: 1170   caggagttcaagaccagcctg 1190
              |||||||||||||||||||||
Sbjct: 69962 caggagttcaagaccagcctg 69942
Query: 1106   tggtggctcacacctgcaatcccagcact 1134
              |||||||||| |||| |||||||||||||
Sbjct: 77363 tggtggctcacgcctgtaatcccagcact 77335
```

In spite of the fact that the line numbers aren't contiguous, the sequence for "Query" starts with 'gagccca' and still ends with 'agcact', and will be 103 (53 + 21 + 29) characters long. As you'll see shortly, the program is designed to ignore the gaps (and the line numbers) and input the data properly. Frequent BLAST users may also notice that in a full BLAST report, each sequence is grouped by E-values. We are ignoring that (usually) important fact in the program.

The Perl program used to search for the five substrings can be broken down into three parts:

- Inputting the data and preparing it for analysis
- Searching the data and looking for the patterns
- Compiling the results and storing them in *report.txt*

Let's go through the program step by step. Here are the first few lines:

```perl
#!/usr/bin/perl
# Search through a large datafile, looking for particular sequences

use strict;

my $REPORT_FILE = "report.txt";
my $blast_file  = $ARGV[0] || 'blast.dat';

unless ( -e $blast_file ) {
  die "$0: ERROR: missing file: $blast_file";
}
```

This code makes sure that the data is in good order. Since you'll be reading large amounts of data into the variables, tell Perl to tighten up its rules with the line *use strict;*. This forces you to be more explicit about how you want Perl to do things. *use strict* is particularly useful when developing large programs or programs you want to modify and reuse. Go on to declare some variables, and in the last few lines, tell Perl to make sure that data actually exists in the input file *blast.dat*.

In the next block of code, the program reads the sequences into variables:

```perl
# First, slurp all the Query sequences into one scalar. Same for the
# Sbjct sequences.
my ($query_src, $sbjct_src);

# Open the blast datafile and end program (die) if we can't find it
open (IN, $blast_file) or die "$0: ERROR: $blast_file: $!";

# Go through the blast file line by line, concatenating all the Query and
# Sbjct sequences.
while (my $line = <IN>) {
  chomp $line;
  print "Processing line $.\n";
```

In this section you read all the "Query" sequences into one scalar variable, and the "Sbjct" sequences into another. The program then opens the file for reading with:

```perl
open (IN, $blast_file) or die "$0: ERROR: $blast_file: $!";
```

or prints an error message if for some reason it can't find the file. Next, the program goes through the file line by line, removing the line-break characters with *chomp $line;*. And finally, with a print function, you ask the program to display the current row as it reads in the data.

Now that you have the data in memory, you need to sort through it and extract the material you want. Remember that the datafile included a lot of superfluous material you want to ignore. To do that, instruct Perl to consider only those lines that begin with *Query* or *Sbjct*. Now *Query* and *Sbjct*, in addition to having the desired sequence data, also have line numbers of varying length you don't want. In order to read the sequence data correctly, you must design the program in such a way that you skip over line numbers no matter how many characters they have, and always land on the first nucleotide. You'll notice in this line of data:

```
Query: 1165 gagcccaggagttcaagaccagcctgggtaacatgatgaaacctcgtctctac 1217
```

that there is a space between *Query*, the beginning line number, the sequence data, and the ending line number. Since this happens to be true for all the query and subject lines, it becomes the key to how to read the data correctly. To be sure you get only what you want, split all the query and subject data into a four column array called *@words*. That task is accomplished by the following lines of code:

```perl
my @words = split /\s+/, $line;
if ($line =~ /^Query/) {
$query_src .= $words[2];
} elsif ($line =~ /^Sbjct/) {
$sbjct_src .= $words[2];
}
}

# We've now read the blast file, so we can close it.
close IN;
```

Once you've read the data into *@words*, you then instruct the program to take only the data from column two of *@words* (which is filled only with nucleotide sequence data) and store it in the variables *$query_src* and *$sbjct_src*. The program then closes the file and moves to a new line. You now have just the data you want, stored in a form you can use.

The next part of the program performs the analysis:

```perl
# Now, look for these given sequences...
my @patterns = ('gtccca', 'gcaatg', 'cagct', 'tcggga', '-');

# ...and when we find them, store them in these hashes
my (%query_counts, %sbjct_counts);

# Search and store the sequences
foreach my $pattern (@patterns) {
    while ( $query_src =~ /$pattern/g ) {
        $query_counts{ $pattern }++;
```

```
        }
    while ( $sbjct_src =~ /$pattern/g ) {
        $sbjct_counts{ $pattern }++;
    }
}
```

The program sets up a loop that runs five times; once for each search string or pattern. Within each iteration of the outer *foreach* loop, the program runs inner *while* loops that advance counters each time they find a pattern match. The results are stored in separate hashes called *%query_counts* and *%sbjct_counts*.

Here is the last section of the program, which produces the output:

```
# Create an empty report file
open (OUT, ">$REPORT_FILE") or die "$0: ERROR: Can't write $REPORT_FILE";

# Print the header of the report file, including
# the current date and time
print OUT "Sequence Report\n",
    "Run by O'Reilly on ", scalar localtime, "\n",
    "\nNOTE: In the following reports, a dash (-) represents\n",
    "        missing data in the chromosomal sequence\n\n",
    "Total length of 'Query' sequence: ",
    length $query_src, " characters\n", "Results for 'Query':\n";

# Print the Query matches
foreach my $key ( sort @patterns ) {
    print OUT "\t'$key' seen $query_counts{$key}\n";
}

print OUT "\nTotal length of 'Sbjct' sequence: ",
    length $sbjct_src, " characters\n", "Results for 'Sbjct':\n";

# Print the Sbjct matches
foreach my $key ( sort @patterns ) {
    print OUT "\t'$key' seen $sbjct_counts{$key}\n";
}

close OUT;

__END__
```

This code compiles and formats the results and dumps them into a file called *report.txt*. If you open *report.text* you see:

```
Sequence Report
Run by O'Reilly on Tue Jan  9 15:52:48 2001

NOTE: In the following reports, a dash (-) represents
        missing data in the chromosomal sequence

Total length of 'Query' sequence: 1115 characters
Results for 'Query':
        '-' seen 7
```

```
        'cagct' seen 11
        'gcaatg' seen 1
        'gtccca' seen 6
        'tcggga' seen 1

Total length of 'Sbjct' sequence: 5845 characters
Results for 'Sbjct':
        '-' seen 12
        'cagct' seen 2
        'gcaatg' seen 6
        'gtccca' seen 1
        'tcggga' seen 6
```

In this example the results were sent to a file. You can just as easily ask Perl to generate an HTML-coded file you can view with your web browser. Or you can make the process interactive and use Perl to create a CGI script that generates a web form to analyze the data and give you back your results.

We've only scratched the surface in terms of what this sort of program can do. You can easily modify it to look for more general patterns in the data or more specific ones. For example, you might search for 'tcggga' and 'gcaatg', but only count them if they are connected by 'cagct'. You also might search only for breaks in the data. And after all the searches are complete, you might use Perl to automatically store all the results in a database.

If you're feeling a little confused by all this, don't panic. We aren't expecting you to understand all the code we've shown you. As we said at the beginning of the chapter, the purpose of the code isn't to teach you to program in Perl, but to show you how Perl works, and also to show you that programming isn't really all that difficult. If you have what it takes to design an experiment, then you have what it takes to program in Perl or any other language.

Applying Perl to Bioinformatics

The good news is the more you practice programming, the more you learn. And the more you learn, the more you can do. Programming in Perl is all about analyzing data and building tools. As we've said before, biological data is proliferating at an astounding rate. The only chance biologists have of keeping up with the job of analyzing it is by developing libraries of reusable software tools. In Perl, there are a huge number of reusable functions available for use in your programs. Rather than being wrapped in a complete program, a group of related functions are packaged as a *module*. In your programs, you can use various modules to access the functions they support. There are Perl modules for other scientific disciplines, as well as games, graphics programming, video, artificial intelligence, statistics, and music. And they're all free.

To distinguish them from other Perl files, modules have a *.pm* suffix. To use functions from a module (say, CGI.pm) in your Perl programs, include the following line after the shebang line:

```
use CGI;
```

The primary source of all modules is the Comprehensive Perl Archive Network, or CPAN. CPAN (*http://www.cpan.org*) is a collection of sites located around the world, each of which mirrors the contents of the main CPAN site in Finland. To find the CPAN site nearest you, check the Perl web site (*http://www.perl.com*).

Because there are so many modules available, before you sit down to write a new function, it is worth your time to check the CPAN archive to see if anyone has already written it for you. In this section, we briefly describe some Perl modules that are particularly useful for solving common problems in bioinformatics. This list is by no means comprehensive; you should keep an eye on CPAN for current developments.

Bioperl

The Bioperl Project (along with its siblings, Biopython, BioJava, and Bioxml) is dedicated to the creation of an open source library of modules for bioinformatics research. The general idea is that common items in bioinformatics (such as sequences and sequence alignments) are represented as objects in Bioperl. Thus, if you use Bioperl, instead of having to constantly rewrite programs that read and write sequence files, you simply call the appropriate functions from Bio::SeqIO, and dump the resulting sequence data into a sequence object.

Bioperl isn't limited to storing sequences: it currently contains modules for generating and storing sequence alignments, managing annotation data, parsing output from the sequence-database search programs BLAST and HMMer, and has other modules on the way. In addition to the core Bioperl distribution, the ScriptCentral script repository at the Bioperl web site (*http://www.bioperl.org*) hosts a collection of biology-related scripts. To learn more about downloading, installing, and using Bioperl, see *http://www.bioperl.org*.

CGI.pm

CGI.pm is a module for programming interactive web pages. The functions it provides are geared toward formatting web pages and creating and processing forms in which users enter information. If you have used the Web, you almost certainly have used web pages written using CGI.pm. For example, let's create a page that asks the user what his favorite color is using an HTML form. When the user enters the data, the script stores it in a field named *'color'*. When the user hits "Submit," the same page is loaded, only this time, *$query->param('color')* contains the name of a color, so the *print* statement after the "else" is executed. The CGI script looks like this:

```perl
#!/usr/bin/perl

use CGI;                              # Load Perl's CGI module

my $query = new CGI;                  # Create a CGI object named $query

                                      # Send the HTML header and <HTML> tag
print $query->header, $query->start_html;

                          # If the user is visiting the site for the first time, ask him
                          # what his favorite color is

unless ($query->param('color')) {     # Page 1: Asking the user
    print $query->start_form, "What is your favorite color? ",
        $query->popup_menu( -name    => "color",
                    -values => ["red", "green", "blue"] ),
        $query->submit,
        $query->end_form;
} else {                              # Page 2: Telling the user
    print "Your favorite color is ", $query->param('color');
}

print $query->end_html;               # Send the </HTML> tag
```

The results of this script are shown in Figure 12-1.

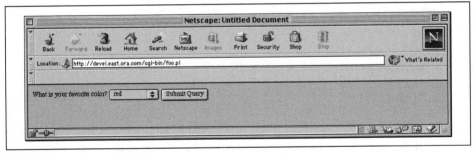

Figure 12-1. Our CGI script generates an interactive web page

LWP

If CGI.pm automates the Web from the server's perspective, the Library for Web Programming (LWP) automates web interaction from the perspective of the client. Using LWP, Perl programs can submit data to forms, retrieve web pages, and eliminate much of the tedium of manually interacting with web services through a browser. For example, let's say you want to retrieve and print out the HTML source for the main page of *http://www.oreilly.com*. You can use the LWP::Simple module as follows:

```
#!/usr/bin/perl
use LWP::Simple;
print get("http://www.oreilly.com");
```

This retrieves the HTML source code for *http://www.oreilly.com* and displays it on your screen.

PDL

The Perl Data Language (which is abbreviated PDL and pronounced "piddle") is a module for doing math with matrices. It is frequently used for scientific applications and image processing in conjunction with the GIMP (since computer representations of images are just matrices). In computational biology, PDL is invaluable for working with microarray expression data and scoring matrices, as well as data that begins as images. For example, 2D gels that measure protein-protein interaction are usually stored as images, and image processing tricks can locate and compare gel features.

Why do you need a whole library to do linear algebra with Perl? PDL allows you to work with matrices of arbitrary dimensionality as if they were scalar variables. For example, a 2D matrix constructed using standard Perl arrays looks like $a[$i][$j]. If you wanted to add two array-based matrices (let's call them @a and @b) and store the result to another matrix, @c, you have to write code that looks like this:

```
for( $i=0; $i<$row_max; $i++ ) {
    for( $j=0; $j<$col_max; $j++ ) {
        $c[$i][$j] = $a[$i][$j] + $b[$i][$j];
    }
}
```

so that you end up writing two loops, the outer one to iterate over each of the rows, and the inner to iterate over each column. With PDL, you simply write:

```
$c = $a + $b;
```

In other words, when you define your multidimensional arrays as piddles (PDL's name for its matrix data object) instead of Perl arrays, PDL makes it look like you are working with simple scalar objects, even if you are working with several-megabyte matrices. In addition, PDL comes with an interactive mode called *perldl* that is useful for trying out calculations with PDL, similar to the interactive modes provided by the numerical data analysis packages R and Octave (which we will meet in Chapter 14, *Visualization and Data Mining*).

DBI

DBI (short for database interface) is a module for writing programs that interact with relational databases. It allows you to write programs that put data into databases, query databases, and extract records from databases, without ever having to pay attention to the specific database you are using. For example, a script written with DBI can be used with a MySQL database or an Oracle database with only minor changes.

GD

The GD.pm module allows you to generate graphics using Perl programs. GD is often used to create simple, customized plots on web pages, such as web server usage statistics. PaintBlast.pm, a module that generates graphical representations of sequence alignments from BLAST output, is an example of a GD application. It 's available from Bioperl's ScriptCentral.

13

Building Biological Databases

Since the advent of the World Wide Web, biological databases have become a vital part of the biological literature. Knowing how to find information in and download information from the central biological data repositories is as important a skill for researchers now as traditional literature searching. Major online data resources, such as the Protein Data Bank and GenBank, are expertly designed to provide information to users who have no understanding of how the underlying databases function, and to allow the deposition of data to a central repository by people who wouldn't know how to, or want to, build their own private databases.

However, as web databases become more integral to sharing information within the scientific community, it is likely that more people will want to develop their own databases and allow their colleagues to access their data directly. Even something as simple as a web site for a research group can be improved greatly and made easier to maintain with databases. In this chapter, we introduce some elementary database terminology and give an example of how to set up a database for a simple data set.

If you're relatively new to the world of computers and software, you're not going to be able to read this chapter and proceed directly to setting up your own database. What we hope to give you is an idea of the steps involved in developing a database: designing a data model, choosing a database management system (DBMS), implementing your data model, and developing a user-friendly frontend to your database. What this chapter will give you is a general understanding of the issues in database development. That understanding will help you to move forward, whether on your own or with the help of a database expert.

You don't need to understand what makes a database tick in order to use it. However, providing access via the Web to data you generate is becoming more and more important in the biology community, and to do that you have to have at least a rudimentary knowledge of how databases work. Even if you've got enough money lying around the lab to spring for your own Oracle administrator, you still need to speak the language.

Types of Databases

There are two types of database management systems: flat file indexing systems and relational DBMSs. A third type, the object-oriented DBMS, is beginning to increase in popularity. Choosing to use a flat file indexing system or a relational database system is an important decision that will have long-range implications for the capacity and usefulness of your database.

Flat File Databases

Flat file databases are the easiest type of database for nonexperts to understand. A flat file database isn't truly a database, it's simply an ordered collection of similar files, usually (but not always) conforming to a standard format for their content. The emphasis in formatting data for a flat file database is at the character level; that is, at the level of how the data would appear if it were printed on a page.

A collection of flat files is analogous to having a large filing cabinet full of pieces of paper. Flat file databases are made useful by ordering and indexing. A collection of flat files on a computer filesystem can be ordered and stored in labeled folders exactly the same way as a collection of printed papers are ordered in a file cabinet drawer (Figure 13-1). When we suggested, in an earlier chapter, using the hierarchical nature of your filesystem and a sensible file-naming scheme to keep track of your files, what we were essentially encouraging you to do is to develop a rudimentary flat file database of your work. Creating a database means you can remember the rules of the database rather than the locations of individual files and so find your way around more easily.

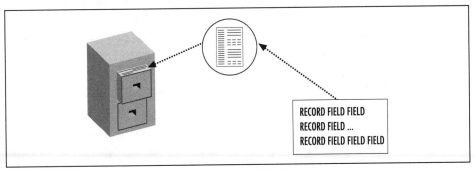

Figure 13-1. The relationship of a flat file to a flat file database

Flat file databases are often made searchable by indexing. An index pulls out a particular attribute from a file and pairs the attribute value in the index with a file-name and location. It's analogous to a book index, which for example tells you where in a book you will find the word "genome." Like book indexes, database indexes need to be carefully designed so that they point to a word only when it occurs in an informative context. Database indexes take note of context by separately indexing different fields within the file. The word "cytochrome" occurring in the Molecule Name field in a protein structure file is likely to be far more significant to the user than the same word occurring only in the file remarks. In the first context, finding the word "cytochrome" guarantees the file contains information for some kind of cytochrome molecule. In the second context, the word can appear as part of an article title or a comment about intermolecular interactions, even though the structure in the file actually belongs to a different molecule. If multiple indexes for a file are created, you can then search a particular index file based on keywords, which is less cumbersome than searching all the actual files in the database file by file.

There's nothing inherently bad about flat file databases. They do organize data in a sensible way, and with the proper indexing they can be made extensively searchable. However, as flat file collections grow larger and larger, working with them becomes inefficient. An index is one-dimensional, so it is difficult (though not impossible) to make connections between attributes within an indexed flat file database.

Flat file databases in biology

Many of the popular biological databases began as flat file databases, and it's because of their legacy that many of the programs and software packages we discussed in previous chapters have strict internal requirements for the line format of input data.

For example, the PDB began by using flat files in the well-known PDB format. The format of these flat files was designed to be read easily by FORTRAN programs, and in fact has its roots in the time when computer input data was encoded on punch cards. When there were just a few protein structure files, maintaining this database and accessing it was no problem. The PDB did not grow beyond a few hundred files until 1990, nearly 20 years after its inception.

As PDB growth increased in the 1990s, new solutions for storing data needed to be found. In practical terms, the full listing of the database was starting to be so long that, if a user entered a directory containing all the available PDB files and tried to list filenames, it could take several seconds to even produce a file list. Reading the contents of large directories slows down even simple Unix tools such as *ls*, and it is even more of a problem for computer programs that might repeatedly read a directory. At first, the PDB was split into subdirectories based on the letters of the PDB code. But as the database approached 8,000 entries, even that began to prove too cumbersome.

The PDB now uses an object-oriented database backend (the part of the operation that resides on the PDB servers and that users don't see) to support database queries and file access. However, files are still made available in the legacy PDB format, so that users can continue to work with software that was developed long before the PDB was modernized.

Beyond the PDB, flat file databases are still widely used by biologists. Many users of biological sequence data store and access sequences locally using the Sequence Retrieval System (SRS), a flat file indexing system designed with biological data in mind.

Relational Databases

Like flat file databases, relational databases are just a way of collecting all the information about something and storing it in a computer. In a flat file database, all the information about the thing is stored in one big structured text file. In a relational database, the information is stored in a collection of tables.

The flat file that describes a protein structure is like a bound book. There are chapters about the origin of the sample, how the data was collected, the sequence, the secondary structure, and the positions of the atoms.

In a relational database, the information in each chapter is put into separate tables, and instead of having its own book, each protein has its own set of tables. So, there are tables of experimental conditions, secondary structure elements, atomic positions, etc. All these tables are labeled with the identity of the protein they describe, so that connections can be made between them, but they aren't bound together like a book. The form of the tables follows rules that are uniform across the database, so you can access all the tables about atomic positions or all the chapters about experimental conditions at once, just as easily as you can access all the tables about a particular protein.

If you're interested in only one particular protein, it's not at all inconvenient to go to the library (the PDB), look the book up in the catalog, and read it straight through. The librarian can pick a few items of information out of the book (such as the name of the protein, the author who deposited it, etc.) and put them in an index (like a card catalog) that will help you find where the book is on the shelf.

But what if you're interested in getting the secondary structure chapter out of every book in the protein library? You have to go to the library, take down every book from the shelf, photocopy the secondary structure chapter, and then convert that information into a form that you can easily analyze.

A relational database management system (RDBMS) allows you to view all of the protein structure data in the database as a whole. You can "look" at the database from many different "angles," and extract only the information you need, without actually photocopying a particular chapter out of each book. Since each separate item of information about the protein is stored in its own separate table in the database, the RDBMS can assemble any kind of book about proteins you want, on the fly. If you want a book about hemoglobin, no problem. Even better, it is just as easy for the RDBMS to make you a book about the secondary structures of all proteins in the database.

All you need to do is figure out how to structure the right query to get back what you want from the database. If you want a book about hemoglobin, you can tell the RDBMS "if protein name equals hemoglobin then give me all information about this protein." If you want a book that describes only the secondary structure of each hemoglobin entry in the database, you can tell the RDBMS "if protein name equals hemoglobin then give me the secondary structure table about this protein."

How tables are organized

Data in a relational database table is organized in rows, with each row representing one record in the database. A row may contain several separate pieces of information (fields). Each field in the database must contain one distinct piece of information. It can't consist of a set or list that can be further broken into parts.

The tables in a relational database aren't just glorified flat files, though they may look that way if you print them out. Rows are synonymous with records, not with 80 characters on a line. Fields in each row aren't limited by a number of characters; they end where the value in the field ends. The job of the RDBMS is to make connections between related tables by rapidly finding the common elements that establish those relationships.

You can get an idea of the difference between data organized into tables and character-formatted flat file data by comparing the two types of protein structure datafiles available from the PDB. The standard PDB file is ordered into a series of 80 character lines. Each line is labeled, but especially in the header, the information associated with a label is quite heterogeneous. For example:

```
REMARK  1                                                         4HHB  14
REMARK  1 REFERENCE 1                                             4HHB  15
REMARK  1   AUTH   M.F.PERUTZ,S.S.HASNAIN,P.J.DUKE,J.L.SESSLER,   4HHB  16
REMARK  1   AUTH 2 J.E.HAHN                                       4HHB  17
REMARK  1   TITL   STEREOCHEMISTRY OF IRON IN DEOXYHAEMOGLOBIN    4HHB  18
```

```
REMARK  1  REF     NATURE                   V. 295    535 1982 4HHB  19 REMARK
1  REFN   ASTM NATUAS  UK ISSN 0028-0836          006  4HHB  20
REMARK  1 REFERENCE 2                                       4HHB  21
REMARK  1  AUTH    G.FERMI,M.F.PERUTZ                        4HHB  22
REMARK  1  REF     HAEMOGLOBIN AND MYOGLOBIN.   V.   2     1981 4HHB  23
REMARK  1  REF   2 ATLAS OF MOLECULAR                       4HHB  24
REMARK  1  REF   3 STRUCTURES IN BIOLOGY                    4HHB  25
REMARK  1  PUBL    OXFORD UNIVERSITY PRESS                  4HHB  26
REMARK  1  REFN              ISBN 0-19-854706-4        986 4HHB  27
```

In the PDB reference records shown here, you can see that entries in each row aren't distinct pieces of information, nor are the rows uniform. Sometimes there are four author names on one line; sometimes there are two. Sometimes there are three title lines; sometimes there is only one. This can cause difficulties in *parsing*, or reading the header with a computer program.

Compare this to an mmCIF file. mmCIF is a new data standard for results of X-ray crystallography experiments. Protein structures have been available from the PDB in mmCIF format since the management of the PDB changed in 1999.

Before you see any data in the mmCIF file, you see what looks almost like a series of commands in a computer program, lines that describe how the data in the file is to be read. Then you'll see tables of data. Here's an example:

```
loop_
_citation.id
_citation.coordinate_linkage
_citation.title
_citation.country
_citation.journal_abbrev
_citation.journal_volume
_citation.journal_issue
_citation.page_first
_citation.year
_citation.journal_id_ASTM
_citation.journal_id_ISSN
_citation.journal_id_CSD
_citation.book_title
_citation.book_publisher
_citation.book_id_ISBN
_citation.details

primary   yes
; THE CRYSTAL STRUCTURE OF HUMAN DEOXYHAEMOGLOBIN AT
    1.74 ANGSTROMS RESOLUTION
;
UK 'J.MOL.BIOL.              '  175  ?     159  1984
'JMOBAK          '  '0022-2836          '  070 ? ? ? ?

      1     no
; STEREOCHEMISTRY OF IRON IN DEOXYHAEMOGLOBIN
;
```

```
UK 'NATURE                        '  295  ?     535   1982
'NATUAS          ' '0028-0836              '  006 ? ? ? ?

2       no
?   ? ?    2 ?      ? 1981 ? ?   986
; HAEMOGLOBIN AND MYOGLOBIN.
  ATLAS OF MOLECULAR
  STRUCTURES IN BIOLOGY
;
;   OXFORD UNIVERSITY PRESS
;
'0-19-854706-4             ' ?
```

An mmCIF file contains dozens of tables that are all "about" the same protein.

The opening lines of the reference section in the mmCIF file (which is just a flat representation of the collection of tables that completely describes a protein structure) describe what the fields in each upcoming row in the table will mean. Rows don't begin arbitrarily at character 1 and end at character 80; they may stretch through several "lines" in the printout or onscreen view of the data. Rows don't end until all their fields are filled; when information is missing (as in the previous example), the fields have to be filled with null characters, such as a question mark or a space.

In the protein database, the table of literature references that describes a particular structure is associated with a particular PDB ID. However, there are other tables associated with that PDB ID as well, and they have totally different kinds of rows from the reference table. The atomic positions that describe a protein structure are contained in a separate table with a completely different format:

```
loop_
_atom_site.label_seq_id
_atom_site.group_PDB
_atom_site.type_symbol
_atom_site.label_atom_id
_atom_site.label_comp_id
_atom_site.label_asym_id
_atom_site.auth_seq_id
_atom_site.label_alt_id
_atom_site.cartn_x
_atom_site.cartn_y
_atom_site.cartn_z
_atom_site.occupancy
_atom_site.B_iso_or_equiv
_atom_site.footnote_id
_atom_site.label_entity_id
_atom_site.id
1
ATOM  N  N    VAL A   1  .   6.204  16.869   4.854  7.00 49.05   .   1  1 1
ATOM  C  CA   VAL A   1  .   6.913  17.759   4.607  6.00 43.14   .   1  2 1
ATOM  C  C    VAL A   1  .   8.504  17.378   4.797  6.00 24.80   .   1  3 1
ATOM  O  O    VAL A   1  .   8.805  17.011   5.943  8.00 37.68   .   1  4 1
```

```
ATOM  C  CB   VAL A  1  .   6.369  19.044  5.810  6.00  72.12  .  1  5  1
ATOM  C  CG1  VAL A  1  .   7.009  20.127  5.418  6.00  61.79  .  1  6  1
ATOM  C  CG2  VAL A  1  .   5.246  18.533  5.681  6.00  80.12  .  1  7  2
ATOM  N  N    LEU A  2  .   9.096  18.040  3.857  7.00  26.44  .  1  8  2
ATOM  C  CA   LEU A  2  .  10.600  17.889  4.283  6.00  26.32  .  1  9  2
ATOM  C  C    LEU A  2  .  11.265  19.184  5.297  6.00  32.96  .  1 10  2
ATOM  O  O    LEU A  2  .  10.813  20.177  4.647  8.00  31.90  .  1 11  2
ATOM  C  CB   LEU A  2  .  11.099  18.007  2.815  6.00  29.23  .  1 12  2
ATOM  C  CG   LEU A  2  .  11.322  16.956  1.934  6.00  37.71  .  1 13  2
ATOM  C  CD1  LEU A  2  .  11.468  15.596  2.337  6.00  39.10  .  1 14  2
ATOM  C  CD2  LEU A  2  .  11.423  17.268   .300  6.00  37.47  .  1 15
```

The values in the atom table are clearly *related* to the values in the reference table; they both contain information about the same PDB structure. However, the two types of data can't just be put together into one big table. It doesn't make sense to put the reference information into the same scheme of rows and columns the atom information goes into, either by tacking it on at the "bottom" of the table or by adding extra columns (although in flat files we are forced to do exactly that!). The two datatypes are related, but *orthogonal* to each other.

Anywhere in a set of information where it becomes impossible to sensibly tack rows or columns onto a table, a new table needs to be created.[*] Tables within a database may have interconnections only at the topmost level, such as the atom and reference information related to the same PDB file, or they may be more closely linked.

You may notice in the reference records two pages back that authors' names aren't listed. How can that be? Well, the answer is that they're in a separate table. Because each reference can have an arbitrary number of separate authors, that information can't just be tacked onto the reference table by adding a fixed number of extra rows or columns. So there's a separate table for authors' names:

```
loop_
_citation_author.citation_id
_citation_author.name
 primary   'Fermi, G.'
 primary   'Perutz, M.F.'
 primary   'Shaanan, B.'
 primary   'Fourme, R.'
    1      'Perutz, M.F.'
    1      'Hasnain, S.S.'
    1      'Duke, P.J.'
    1      'Sessler, J.L.'
    1      'Hahn, J.E.'
    2      'Fermi, G.'
    2      'Perutz, M.F.'
```

---

[*] The technical term for the process of separating a complex data set into a collection of mutually orthogonal, related tables is *normalization*. For a rigorous discussion of relational database theory, see the pertinent references in the *Bibliography*.

```
3        'Perutz, M.F.'
4        'TenEyck, L.F.'
4        'Arnone, A.'
5        'Fermi, G.'
6        'Muirhead, H.'
6        'Greer, J.'
```

This table is related to the previous reference table through the values in column 1, which match up with the citation IDs in the other reference table. To get from "Fermi, G." to "THE CRYSTAL STRUCTURE OF HUMAN DEOXYHAEMOGLOBIN AT 1.74 ANGSTROMS RESOLUTION" in this database, you connect through the citation ID, which specifies the relationship between the two entities.

Using an RDBMS may at first seem like an overthinking of what could be a pretty simple set of data to store. If you ever write programs that operate on the anti-quated flat-file PDB format, though, you'll realize how useful it might be to unam-biguously assign your data to tables in a relational database. Among other things, databases eliminate the need for complicated line-format statements and parsing operations that are required when using 80 character-formatted files.

The database schema

The network of tables and relationships between them that makes up a database is called the *database schema*. For a database to keep its utility over time, it's best to carefully develop the schema before you even think about beginning to populate the database. In the example later in this chapter, we develop a schema for a sim-ple database.

Getting your brain around database schemas and tables can be a challenge with-out even coming up with your own schema. However, relational databases are the standard for large database operations, and understanding RDB concepts is neces-sary for anyone who wants to build her own. Before designing your own data-base, you should definitely consult a reference that covers relational databases rigorously.

Object-Oriented Databases

You'll hear the phrase *object oriented* in connection with both programming lan-guages and databases. An object-oriented database system is a DBMS that is con-sistent with object-oriented programming principles. Some important characteristics of object-oriented databases are: they are designed to handle concurrent interac-tions by multiple clients; they can handle complex objects (beyond tables of char-acter data); and they are *persistent*—that is, they survive the execution of a process. In practice, because of the popularity of object-oriented programming strategies, most of the major relational DBMSs are compatible with an object-ori-ented approach to some extent.

The practical upshot of the object-oriented approach in the database world is the emergence of DBMSs that are flexible enough to store more than just tables and to handle functions beyond those in a rigidly defined query-language vocabulary. Since object-oriented databases handle data as objects rather than as tables, an object-oriented database can provide access to everything from simple text-format data to images and video files within the same database. Object-oriented databases don't force the use of the SQL query language, but rather provide flexible bindings to programming languages. Many DBMSs are beginning to have both object and relational characteristics, but the giants of the DBMS world are still primarily relational DBMSs.

Database Software

Databases don't just happen: they're maintained by DBMSs. There are several DBMSs, some open source and some commercial. There are flat file indexing systems, RDBMSs, object DBMSs (ODBMSs), and object-relational hybrids. Which DBMS you use depends on what you can afford, how comfortable you are with software, and what you want to do.

Sequence Retrieval System

Even if you've decided to work with a flat file indexing and retrieval system, you don't need to reinvent the wheel. The Sequence Retrieval System (SRS) is a popular system for flat file management that has been extensively used in the biology community, both in corporate and academic settings. SRS was developed at EMBL specifically for use in molecular biology database applications, and is now available as a commercial product from Lion Bioscience, *http://www.lionbioscience.com*. It is still offered for free to researchers at academic institutions, along with extensive documentation (but no tech support). A common application of the SRS database is to maintain a local mirror of the major biological sequence databases. The current release is SRS 6.

SRS can be installed on SGI, Sun, Compaq, or Intel Linux systems. To maintain your own SRS database and mirror the major biological databases requires tens of gigabytes of disk space, so it's not something to be taken on lightly. SRS has built-in parsers that know how to read EMBL nucleotide database files, SWISS-PROT files, and TrEMBL files. It's also possible to integrate other databases into SRS by using SRS's Icarus language to develop additional databank modules. For an example of the variety of databases that can be integrated under an SRS flat file management system, you only have to look at the SDSC Biology Workbench. Until its most recent release, SRS was the DBMS used within the Biology Workbench, and supported nearly the full range of databases now integrated into the Workbench.

Oracle

Oracle is the 18-wheeler of the RDBMS world. It's an industry-standard, commercial product with extremely large capacity. It's also rapidly becoming a standard for federally funded research projects. Oracle has some object capacities as well as extensive relational capacities. Potential Oracle customers can now obtain a license to try Oracle for free from *http://www.oracle.com*. If you want to provide a large-scale data resource to the biology community, you may need an Oracle developer (or a bunch of them) to help you implement it.

PostgreSQL

PostgreSQL is a full-featured object-relational DBMS that supports user-defined datatypes and functions in addition to a broad set of SQL functions and types. PostgreSQL is an open source project, and the source code can be downloaded for free from *http://www.postgresql.org*, which also provides extensive online documentation for the DBMS. PostgreSQL can also be found in most standard Linux distributions. If you plan to create a database that contains data of unusual types and you need a great degree of flexibility to design future extensions to your database, PostgreSQL may meet your needs better than MySQL. PostgreSQL is somewhat limited in its capacity to handle large numbers of operations, relative to Oracle and other commercial DBMSs, but for midrange databases it's an excellent product.

Open Source Object DBMS

Several efforts to develop open source ODBMSs are underway as of this writing. One of the most high profile of these is the Ozone project (*http://www.ozone-db.org*). Ozone is completely implemented in Java and designed for Java developers; queries are implemented in the underlying language rather than in SQL. One emphasis in Ozone development is *object persistence*, the ability of the DBMS to straightforwardly save the states of a *data object* as it is affected by transactions with the database user. Like many ODBMSs, Ozone is in a relatively early stage of development and may not be particularly easy for a new user to understand. Unless you have a compelling reason to use object-oriented principles in developing your database, it's probably wise to stick with relational database models until object technology matures.

MySQL

MySQL is an open-source relational DBMS. It's relatively easy to set up and use, and it's available for both Unix and Windows operating systems. MySQL has a rich and complex set of features, and it's somewhat different from both PostgreSQL and Oracle, two other popular RDBMSs. Each system recognizes a different subset of SQL datatypes and functions, and none of them recognizes 100% of the possible types. MySQL sets lower limits on the number of operations allowed than PostgreSQL and Oracle do, in some cases, so it's considered suitable for small and medium-sized database applications, rather than for heavy-duty database projects. However, this isn't a hard and fast rule: it depends on what you plan to do with the data in your database. MySQL is strictly a relational DBMS, so if you plan to store unusual datatypes, it may not be the right DBMS for you. For most standard database applications, however, MySQL is an excellent starting point.

MySQL's developers claim that it can manage large databases faster than other RDBMSs. While their benchmarks seem to bear out this claim, we haven't independently evaluated it. What we can say is that it's possible to learn to use MySQL and have a rudimentary database up and running within a few hours to a few days, depending on the user's level of experience with Unix and SQL.

Introduction to SQL

As a practical matter, you are most likely to work either with specialized flat file database systems for biological data, like SRS, or with some kind of RDBMS. In order to work with an RDBMS, you need to learn something about SQL.

SQL, or Structured Query Language (usually pronounced "see-kwl" by those in the know, ess-que-ell by literalists, and "squeal" by jokers) is the language RDBMSs speak. SQL commands are issued within the context of a DBMS interface; you don't give a SQL command at the Unix command line. Instead, you give the command to the DBMS program, and the program interprets the command.

SQL commands can be passed to the DBMS by another program (for instance, a script that collects data from a web form) or hand-entered. Obviously, the first option is the ideal, especially for entering large numbers of records into a database; you don't want to do that by hand. We can't teach you all of the ins and outs of programming with SQL, however; in this section we'll just focus on the basic SQL commands and what they do. Later on, we'll show an example of a web-based program that can interact with a SQL database.

SQL commands read like stilted English with a very restricted vocabulary. If you remember diagramming sentences in high-school English class, figuring out subject-verb-object relationships and conditional clauses, SQL should seem fairly intuitive. The challenge is remembering the restrictions of vocabulary and syntax, and constructing queries so that your DBMS can understand them. A SQL statement might read something like this:[*]

```
SELECT program FROM software WHERE program LIKE 'blast'
```

This says "select the names of programs from the list of software where the name of the program is like blast." This is something you might want to do if you use a searchable database of bioinformatics software.

As mentioned above, all DBMSs aren't created equal. There is a SQL standard vocabulary, called SQL 92; however, most systems implement only parts of this standard. You need to study the documentation for the particular DBMS you're using so you don't confuse it by giving unrecognized commands.

SQL Datatypes

The notion of a datatype is simple to understand. A *datatype* is an adjective that describes the data stored in a particular column of a table. In general, data stored in a table can consist of either numeric values or character strings. SQL, however, defines a multitude of subtypes within these common datatypes, mostly variants that set different upper limits on the size of a text field or numerical field, but also special numeric types such as DATE or MONEY.

When you create tables in a database, you need to define the type of each column. This means you need to know from the beginning, as you are setting up your data model, what type of data will be contained in each column. You should also have a rough idea of the likely upper and lower limits for your data, so that you can select the smallest possible type to contain them. For instance, if you know that the integer values in a column in your table will never be greater than 255, you should use the smallest possible integer type, TINYINT, for that column, rather than making space for much larger values in your database when you won't actually need that space. On the other hand, if that value will eventually grow beyond 255, then you should choose a type that allows a broader range of values for that column. Setting up a relational database requires quite a bit of intelligent forethought.

Here are some of the most popular SQL types, all of which are supported in most major RDBMS programs:

INT

> An integer number. Variations include TINYINT, SMALLINT, MEDIUMINT, and BIGINT. Each of these allows a different range of numerical values.

---

[*] SQL commands don't have to appear in all capital letters; they're case-insensitive. But we'll write them in all capital letters in our examples, so that you can distinguish them easily from the names of files, variables, and databases. File, variable, and database names are case-sensitive in SQL, so if you name a database PeOPlE, you'll have to live with that.

FLOAT

A floating-point number. Maximum value on the order of 3 E 38; minimum value on the order of 1.7 E-38.

REAL

A longer floating-point number. Maximum value on the order of 2 E 308; minimum value on the order of 2 E-308.

CHAR

A fixed-length text string. Values shorter than the fixed length are padded with spaces.

TEXT

A variable-length text string with a maximum value. Variations include TINYTEXT, MEDIUMTEXT, and LONGTEXT.

BLOB

A variable-length binary field with a maximum value. Variations include TINYBLOB, MEDIUMBLOB, and LONGBLOB. Just about anything can go in a binary field. The maximum size of a LONGBLOB is 4 GB. All sorts of interesting things, such as image data, can go into a binary field.

DECIMAL

A real number that is stored as a character string rather than as a numerical field.

DATE

A date value that stores the year, month, and day.

TIMESTAMP

A time value that updates every time the record is modified.

ENUM

A value that is one of a limited set of options and can be selected using either the option name or a numeric value that represents the name.

SET

A value that is one of a limited set of options.

SQL Commands

SQL has many commands, but it's probably most important for you to know how to create new tables, add data to them, and then search for data in your database. We'll introduce you briefly to the SQL CREATE, ALTER, INSERT, UPDATE, and SELECT commands, as they are implemented in MySQL. The references mentioned in the *Bibliography* contain full descriptions of the SQL commands available through MySQL.

Adding a new table to a database

New tables are created with the SQL CREATE statement. The syntax of the CRE-
ATE statement is simply:

```
CREATE TABLE tablename (columnname type [modifiers] columnname type
[modifiers])
```

If you want to create a table of information about software packages, for the
example database we discuss in this chapter, you can do as follows:

```
CREATE TABLE software_package
      (packid INT NOT NULL PRIMARY KEY AUTO_INCREMENT,
      packname VARCHAR(100)
      packurl VARCHAR(255)
      function TEXT
      keyword ENUM
      os SET
      format SET
      archfile VARCHAR(255)
   )
```

This command tells MySQL to set up a table in which the first column is an automatically incrementing integer; that is, the DBMS automatically assigns a unique
value to each entry you make. The second and third columns are variable-length
character strings with preset maximum lengths, in which the name and URL of the
software package will be entered. The fourth column is a text field that can contain up to 64 KB of text describing the software package. The fifth column allows
you to choose one of 64 preset keywords to describe your software package; the
sixth and seventh columns let you choose any number of values from a set of preset values to describe the operating systems the software will run under (e.g., *mac*,
windows, *linux*) and the type of archive file available (e.g., *binary*, *rpm*, *source*,
tar). The final field is another variable character string that will contain the URL of
the archive file.

Changing an existing table

If you create a table and you decide that it should look different than you originally planned, you can use the ALTER command to change it. To add another column to a table, the syntax is:

```
ALTER TABLE tablename ADD [COLUMN] (columnname type [modifiers])
```

Adding data to an existing table

The INSERT command adds a new row of data to a table. The syntax of the
INSERT command is:

```
INSERT INTO table ( colname1, colname2, colname3 ) VALUES (
'value1','value2','value3')
```

Altering existing data in a table

The UPDATE and REPLACE commands can modify an existing row in a table. Your user privileges must allow you to use UPDATE and REPLACE. These commands can take a WHERE clause, with syntax analogous to that of the SELECT command, so that you can specify under what conditions a record is updated.

Accessing Your Database with the SQL SELECT Command

The SQL SELECT command finds data in a table for you. In other words, SELECT is the command that makes the database useful once you have created it and populated it with data. It can be modified by a conditional clause that lets you determine under what conditions a record is selected from the table.

Choosing fields to select

The general syntax of the SELECT command is:

```
SELECT [fields] FROM [table] WHERE [clause]
```

To select all the fields in a particular table, the asterisk character can be used:

```
SELECT * FROM [table] WHERE [clause]
```

In this chapter's database example, if you want to select the software package name and software package URL from the software table, the SELECT command is:

```
SELECT packname, packurl FROM software
```

Using a WHERE clause to specify selection conditions

The WHERE clause allows you to specify conditions under which records are selected from a table. You can use standard operators, such as =, >=, etc., to set the conditions for your WHERE clause. MySQL also allows you to use the LIKE and NOT LIKE operators for pattern matching.

If you want to set up your SELECT statement to find only software for sequence alignment, it should look like this:

```
SELECT packname, packurl FROM software WHERE keyword = "sequence alignment";
```

If you want to find only software packages with names starting with the letter B, the SELECT statement looks like this:

```
SELECT packname, packurl FROM software WHERE packname LIKE "B%";
```

The % character is a wildcard character that represents any number of characters, so the software packages you select using this statement can have names of any length as long as the name starts with B.

Joining output from multiple tables

SELECT can also join two related tables. When we talk later about developing databases, you'll find that relationships between tables are created by replicating information called a *primary key* from one table as a *foreign key* in another table. If the foreign key in one table matches the primary key in another, the data in the two tables refers to the same record and can be *joined* to produce one set of output from SELECT. A MySQL SELECT statement for joining two tables might look like this:

```
SELECT FROM table1, table2 WHERE primarykey1=foreignkey2
```

For instance, we've already discussed creating one table that lists the names, URLs, and other details about the software packages listed in the database. In order to build the database properly, you have to have another table that lists information about the literature references that describe the functions of the software packages in the database.

What if you want to select only the names and URLs of software packages that were first described in the literature in 1998 or later? The names and URLs are found in the software table; the dates are found in the reference table. Here's the SQL:

```
SELECT packname, packurl, reference_date FROM software, reference
WHERE software.package_id = reference.package_id
AND reference_date >= "1998";
```

The variable *package_id* is the primary key from the software table, and it is replicated in the reference table to maintain a relationship between the details of software packages and the references that describe them. If the value of *package_id* is the same in both tables, the two rows being accessed are part of the same record in the database. Therefore, the first part of the WHERE clause is what joins the two tables. The second part of the WHERE clause (*AND reference_date >= "1998"*) specifies the actual selection condition.

Different database-management systems implement different levels of join functionality, so you will have to check the specific documentation for your DBMS to see how joins work.

Installing the MySQL DBMS

To set up and maintain your own database, you need to have a database server installed on the machine on which the data will be stored.

MySQL is a lightweight relational DBMS that is fairly easy to install and run. We're going to use MySQL to set up the example database, so if you're interested in trying it out, be sure the MySQL server is installed on your machine. If you're using a

Red Hat Linux distribution, this is ridiculously easy. If you didn't install MySQL when you set up your machine, simply use *kpackage* or *gnorpm* to select the MySQL components you want to install—the server, clients, and development tools. This will probably give you an older version of MySQL; to get the current version and install it easily, use the binary RPMs from the latest stable version at *http://www.mysql.com*. You'll also want to make sure the Apache web server and PHP support, available from *http://www.apache.org*, are installed. The next time you restart your machine after the install, the MySQL server daemon,* *mysqld*, is started, MySQL privilege databases are initialized, and the PHP module is made available to your Apache server.

Setting Up MySQL

When you look at RDBMS software, you usually find you have a choice of setting up a client or a server. The *server* part of the program runs on the machine on which the data is actually stored. It runs as a daemon on Unix machines; that is, as a system process that is always on, listening for and responding to requests from clients. The MySQL server program is called *mysqld*. Figure 13-2 shows an example of a client/server architecture.

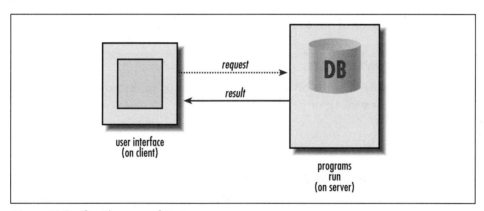

Figure 13-2. Client/server architecture

Clients are programs that connect to the server and request data. Clients can be located on the database server itself, but they also can be located on other machines on which *mysqld* isn't running and connect over the Internet to the main database.

The MySQL client programs include *mysql*, the main client that lets you do everything from designing databases to inserting records; *mysqladmin*, which performs

---

* System processes such as servers that run in the background on Unix systems are known as daemons.

selected administrative functions such as creating new databases and checking the status of the server; and *client5*. *client5* is similar to *mysql* in that it allows interactive query processing, but for security purposes, it doesn't allow you to add and modify database records.

When we talk about the MySQL DBMS as a whole, we refer to it as MySQL. When we talk about a client program that's part of MySQL, we refer to it by its specific client name.

Using the mysql client program

The *mysql* program has only a few commands of its own; the commands that are primarily directed to the *mysql* program or the *client5* program are SQL statements. When you are inside the *mysql* program, the program interprets any SQL statement you give to it as one continuous statement, until the terminating character ";" is read. Here are the *mysql* commands:

use
: Takes a database name as its argument; allows you to change which database is in active use

status
: Returns the status of the server

connect
: Reconnects with the server

go Sends a command to the MySQL server; also can be indicated by terminating a SQL statement with \g or ;

help
: Prints a complete list of *mysql* commands

Using the mysqladmin client program to set up MySQL

You can get a comprehensive listing of *mysqladmin* commands with the command:

```
mysqladmin --help
```

Here are the commands you are likely to use frequently:

create
: Takes a database name as its argument; creates a new database

drop
: Takes a database name as its argument; deletes an entire database

reload
: Reloads the grant tables

variables

Prints available variables that describe the MySQL installation

ping

Checks to see if the MySQL server is alive

shutdown

Shuts down the MySQL server on the local machine

Restarting the MySQL server

mysqladmin has an option for shutting down the server. But what about starting it up again? To start your MySQL server, use the Unix *su* command to become the MySQL administrator, whether that's user *mysql* or some other user ID. Then, start the MySQL server with the command:

```
safe_mysqld &
```

Securing Your MySQL Server

Your MySQL server isn't secure when you first install it from RPMs, although the databases are initialized. To secure your server, you should immediately set a root password for the MySQL installation. This can (and should) be different from your system root password. MySQL usernames and system usernames aren't connected, although server processes do need to run under a user ID that exists on your server. You need to use the *mysql* program directly to update the *user grant* table, the main table of permissions for MySQL users. To invoke the *mysql* program, give the command:

```
mysql -u root mysql
```

Your command prompt will change to *mysql>*, which indicates you are inside the *mysql* program until you quit using the *quit* command.

To update the grant tables, type:

```
UPDATE user SET Password=PASSWORD("your_password") WHERE User="root";
```

When you issue this command through the *mysql* program, you're giving a SQL command to update the table *user* in the database *mysql*. After you reset the root password, exit *mysql* and tell MySQL to reread the grant tables with the command:

```
mysqladmin -u root reload
```

Now you can reaccess the *mysql* program and other client programs only if you use the proper root password. To restart the *mysql* program on the *mysql* database, give the command:

```
mysql --user=root --password mysql
```

You'll be prompted for your password. If you enter the password on the command line, instead of allowing *mysql* to prompt you for the password, the password can become visible to other users (or hackers) of your system.

If you install MySQL from RPMs on a Linux system, during the installation the *mysql* user ID is added to your system. This user should own the MySQL data directory and its subdirectories. The MySQL daemon runs as a process started by system user *mysql*, and access to the database is controlled by that user. You can set the system password for user *mysql* using the Unix *passwd* command as root. To set the MySQL password for this user, you may need to use SQL commands to insert the user *mysql* into the grant tables. The SQL statement that creates the *mysql* user and grants it global access permissions for all of your databases is:

```
INSERT INTO user VALUES("localhost","mysql",PASSWORD("your_password"),
"Y","Y","Y","Y","Y","Y","Y","Y","Y","Y","Y","Y","Y","Y");}
```

For more on administration and security of MySQL databases, we suggest you consult the pertinent books listed in the *Bibliography*.

Setting Up the Data Directory

If you install MySQL from RPMs, your data directory is automatically located in */var/lib/mysql*. When you set up your workstation, you may not have left much space on the */var* partition. If you're going to be doing a lot with databases, you probably want to give the MySQL data directory some room to grow.

An easy way to do this is to relocate the data directory to a different partition and create a symbolic link from that directory to */var/lib/mysql*. If you relocate the data directory this way, you don't have to change any MySQL configuration information.

First, choose a location for your data directory. You can, for example, create a directory */home/mysql/data*. Then, shut down your MySQL daemon using:*

```
mysqladmin shutdown
```

Using the Unix *mv* command, move all the files in */var/lib/mysql* to */home/mysql/data*. Once the */var/lib/mysql* directory is empty, use *rmdir* to remove it. *cd* to the */home/mysql* directory and type:

```
chown -Rf mysql:mysql data
```

This sets the proper file ownership for all the files in that directory. Finally, use *ln −s* to create a symbolic link between the */home/mysql/data* directory and */var/lib/mysql*. Then restart your MySQL server by typing:

```
safe_mysqld &
```

---

* You also need to include *--user=mysql --password* on the *mysqladmin* command line, but from now on, we're going to assume you know that.

You'll probably need to be logged in as the superuser to do this.

Creating a New Database

Once your MySQL server is installed and running, you need to create a new database and grant yourself the correct permissions to read and write to that database. You can do this as MySQL user *mysql*, unless you want to create a separate identity for yourself right now. We're going to make a database of bioinformatics resources on the Web, so you need to create a database called *resourcedb*. To do this, simply type:

```
mysqladmin --user=mysql --password create resourcedb
```

Then run *mysql* on the *resourcedb* database with the command:

```
mysql --user=mysql --password resourcedb
```

Database Design

The example we'll walk you through is a simple example of how to use MySQL to create a searchable database of bioinformatics software web sites.* We'll also talk a little bit about a scripting language called PHP, which allows you to embed commands that let others access your database directly into an HTML file, and about other ways to access your database from the Web.

If you're looking for bioinformatics or computational biology software on the Web, there are several things you'll probably want to know about each item you find and several ways you'll want to query the database. You'll want to know the name of each item and have access to a description of what it does and the URL from which you can download it. You'll probably want to know the author of the item and what papers have been published about it. You may even want to have immediate access to a Medline link for each reference. You'll want to know what operating systems each item works under, and what format it's available in; you may even want a direct link to the archive file. You may also want to be able to search the database by keywords such as "sequence alignment" or "electrostatic potential."

That sounds pretty simple, right? You may be thinking that all that information would go nicely into one table, and a complicated RDBMS isn't needed to implement this kind of database. Figure 13-3 shows what that big table looks like.

---

* Don't run out and implement this on your machine just because we talked about how to do it. The Web is teeming with out-of-date collections of bioinformatics links (and other kinds of links), and unless you intend to be a responsible curator, no one really needs you to add to them.

Package Name	URL	Descrip	Keyword	OS	Format	Reference
package name	url	descrip	keyword	os	format	reference
package name	url	descrip	keyword	os	format	reference
package name	url	descrip	keyword	os	format	reference
package name	url	descrip	keyword	os	format	reference
package name	url	descrip	keyword	os	format	reference
package name	url	descrip	keyword	os	format	reference
package name	url	descrip	keyword	os	format	reference

Figure 13-3. The bioinformatics software DB as one big table

However, if you look more closely, you'll see it's not really possible for even a simple bioinformatics software database to fit in one table. Remember, data in tables must be *atomic*; that is, each cell must contain only one distinct item, not a list or a set.

If you think through the possibilities, you'll realize that there are several places where lists or sets might occur in a bioinformatics software database record: there might be multiple authors, and/or multiple publications describing the software; the software might be available for many different operating systems; and there might be more than one keyword used to describe each item.

On Entities and Attributes

Databases can contain two kinds of information: information that indicates an *entity* or thing that might have relationships with other things; and information that is purely descriptive of a single entity—*attributes* of that entity.

In our database example, the one thing we are sure of is that a software package is an entity. Let's begin designing the tables in this database by listing all the information associated with each software package:

```
Software package name
Software URL
Textual description of function
Descriptive keyword
Operating system
Software format
Archive filename
Reference
Author
Medline link
```

We may be able to think of more information about each software package in the database, but for the purposes of this example, we'll leave it at that.

Entities can be described by both attributes and relationships to other entities. If an entry in a database has no attributes and no relationships, it shouldn't be considered an entity. One item in our list of facts about each software package definitely has attributes; each reference has an author or authors, and each reference has a Medline link. Therefore, references should be a separate entity in the database. So we'll need at least two tables:

```
SoftwarePackage
----------------
Software package ID
Software package name
Software URL
Textual description of function
Descriptive keyword
Operating system
Software format
Archive filename

Reference
---------
Reference ID
Reference name
Reference year
Author
Medline link
```

We've included an "identifier" attribute in each table. Why? Imagine that there are two software packages named BLAST. Both do very different things. They need to be distinguished from each other in our database, but not by creating another table of "things named BLAST." The unique ID allows us to store information about two software packages named BLAST in the same table and distinguish them from each other.

Ideally, we want entities to have either one-to-one relationships or one-to-many relationships with each other. The relationship of references to software packages is a one-to-many relationship: each software package can be described by many references, but each reference describes only one software package (see Figure 13-4). Many-to-many relationships can't be sorted out by the RDBMS software, so they need to be eliminated from the data model before creating a database.

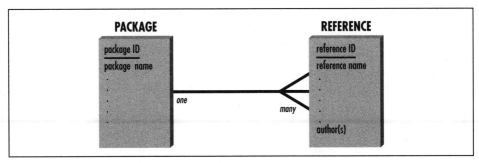

Figure 13-4. Relationship of package to reference

If you're observant, you'll notice that within the Reference table, there is a many-to-many relationship just waiting to happen. Each author can produce many references, and each reference can have many authors. The presence of that many-to-many relationship indicates that Author should probably be a separate entity, even though we haven't chosen to store any attributes about authors in our current data model. So we actually need a third table:

```
Reference
---------
Reference ID
Reference name
Medline link

Author
---------
Author ID
Author Name
```

Even after we create a new table for the Author entity, though, the relationship between authors and references is still many-to-many. This can be resolved by creating a junction entity that has no purpose other than to resolve the many-to-many relationship between the two. The junction entity could be called AuthorRef, or any other arbitrary name. Its only attributes will be its unique identifier (primary key) and the foreign keys that establish its relationship with the other tables.

Creating a Database from Your Data Model

When you actually create your database, entities become tables. Every attribute becomes a column in the table, and the ID becomes the primary key for that table. Relationships to information in other tables become foreign keys.

Before relationships are established, the four tables in our database contain the following information:

```
SoftwarePackage
----------------
Software package ID
Software package name
Software URL
Textual description of function
Descriptive keyword
Operating system
Software format
Archive filename

Reference
----------------
Reference ID
Reference name
Reference date
```

```
Medline link

AuthorRef
---------
AuthorRef ID

Author
---------
Author ID
Author Name
```

Each attribute is a column in the table, and each column must have a datatype. The primary keys can be integer values, but they can't be NULL or empty. The appropriate datatype for the primary key identifiers is thus INT_NOT_NULL; the rest of the fields can be defined as TEXT fields of one size or another.

Creating Relationships Between Tables

To store the relationships between tables in your database, you place the primary key from one table in a column in the other table; that column is called a foreign key. In our example, the primary key of the SoftwarePackage table is also entered in a column in the Reference table, because there is one software package to many references. The primary key from the Reference table and the primary key from the Author table become foreign keys in the AuthorRef table; there are many AuthorRefs for each author, and many AuthorRefs for each reference.

Once you've worked out what information your tables will contain, and what format each column will be in, you have what is called a physical model of your database and you are ready to create it using SQL CREATE statements, as we demonstrated earlier.

Developing Web-Based Software That Interacts with Databases

The purpose of public biological databases is to allow the biology community to share data in a straightforward manner. Nothing is more straightforward than the Web. Therefore, it's almost a given in developing a database (especially with federal funding involved) that you will eventually think about how to make data available on the Web. There are several technologies that allow communication between web pages and databases. The oldest of these is called Common Gateway Interface (CGI) programming, but CGI is now being augmented by other technologies such as XML and PHP.

The world of web-based software development is a rapidly changing one, and it's not our job to detail all the available technologies in this book. However, you should be aware of what these technologies are and roughly how they work, because every time you make a request that directs a web server to process some information, you are using one of them.

If you want to set up your own web server and offer data-analysis services to other users, you need to use CGI scripts or web pages that incorporate XML or PHP code. After we give brief explanations of CGI and XML, we'll show you a couple of examples of how to use PHP commands in your web pages to access the example database we've just created.

CGI

A CGI program, or *script*, is a software application that resides on a web server. When the CGI program is called by a remote user of the web server, the application executes on the server and then passes information back to the remote user in the form of a web page, as shown in Figure 13-5. CGI programs are accessed using the Hypertext Transport Protocol (HTTP) just like normal HTML web pages. Unlike normal web pages, however, CGI scripts either live in a special directory (such as */cgi* or */cgi-bin)* within the server's web documents directory, or they have a special file extension such as *.cgi*. When the server receives an HTTP request, instead of just serving the CGI code to your browser as it does for a normal web page, the server executes the CGI program. CGI is a relatively mature technology and is supported by all the major web servers.

CGI programs usually consist of multiple sections (see Figure 13-5). First, there may be a section of the program that collects user input from a web form. This is followed by the section of the program that takes the user input and does something with it. The CGI program may contain the complete code to do the input processing, but it is more likely that the program formats the input appropriately and passes it to a separate program that exists on the server, then collects the output from that program when the run is completed. The final function of the CGI program is to return the output from the process that ran on the server to the user in the form of a web page, which may contain either textual output or links to downloadable results files, or both.

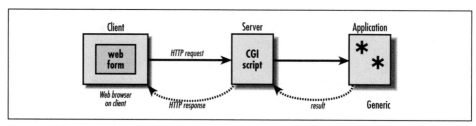

Figure 13-5. How a CGI program is executed

An example of a CGI program you might use is the BLAST server at NCBI. When you select "Basic BLAST search" from the NCBI BLAST home page, you'll notice that the URL of the new page actually points to a CGI script:

```
http://www.ncbi.nlm.nih.gov/blast/blast.cgi?Jform=0
```

The first part of the URL, up to the question mark, gives the directions to the CGI program. The second part of the URL is *state information*, which tells the CGI program what part of its functionality is needed. The state information in this particular URL is telling the BLAST CGI program to bring up an empty search form in which you can enter your sequence.

Once you click the "Submit" button, a new page appears. The new page lists your request ID and approximately how long the request will take to process. Behind the scenes, the CGI program has passed your request to the actual BLAST program, which runs on NCBI's server. When BLAST finishes running your request, the results are written out and labeled with the request ID the server assigned to you. The CGI program then looks for your results under that request ID.

After the search is run, you have the option of displaying your data. The URL still points to the BLAST CGI program, but the state information changes. The URL now looks like this:

```
http://www.ncbi.nlm.nih.gov/blast/blast.cgi?RID=965246273-2980-7926
&DESCRIPTIONS=100&ALIGNMENTS=50&ALIGNMENT_VIEW=0&&HTML=on&OVERVIEW=on
&REFRESH_DELAY=22
```

The state information that is being passed along in this URL tells the program which NCBI request ID (RID) to search for on the server and how the results should be displayed, information that you had the option of entering through the menus on the previous form. The new page that is displayed with this URL contains a listing of your BLAST results as well as links to other information at NCBI. The BLAST results and links were generated behind the scenes on the NCBI server and written to what appears to you as a normal web page (see Figure 13-6).

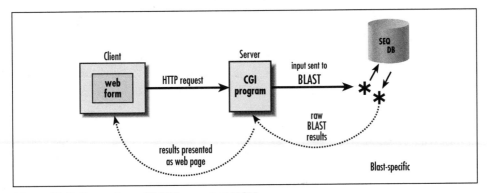

Figure 13-6. Processing a BLAST request at NCBI

CGI programs produce a lot of the dynamic content currently available on the Web, although other methods for producing dynamic content are becoming popular.

XML

The eXtensible Markup Language, better known as XML, is a data-representation scheme that has attracted a great deal of attention in the last few years. Like the HTML language that describes web pages, XML is derived from the Standard Generalized Markup Language (SGML). HTML and XML define *tags* that are used to annotate a document. Tags are surrounded by angle brackets and use the syntax *<tag>text</tag>*. HTML tags specify a web page's structure and appearance. For example, the text *<B>this is bold</B>* is rendered in boldface.

XML tags, on the other hand, define a document's content. For example, in the text:

```
homologs of the sequence <gi>g7290345</gi>
```

the GenBank ID g7290345 is unambiguously identified because it is bracketed by *<gi>* tags. If you write a program that searches a document for GenBank IDs, it's easier to find them if they're explicitly labeled than if you specify a GenBank ID regular expression. Thus, XML lends structure to flat file data such that it can be read and written in a standard way.

The tags used in a given XML document are defined in a *document type definition,* or DTD. The DTD acts as a dictionary for the data format, specifying the elements that are present in a document and the values each attribute may have. The DTD can exist in its own file, or it can be part of the XML datafile itself. Because XML allows users to define their own tags in a DTD, it provides a rich and detailed description of information that would potentially end up in a glob of free text (for example, the *REMARK* fields in a PDB file). The downside of this descriptiveness is that records can rapidly become bloated with details, especially when representing complex data such as the results of microarray experiments.

The fact that XML can mark up data in flat files in a standard and uniform way is significant for working with biological data, which is often stored in flat files. For example, if you want to use data in the ASN.1 format described earlier in this book, you need an ASN.1 parser, which reads only ASN.1 data. By the same token, if you need to read in files in PDB format, you need a different parser for PDB files. However, if your data is marked up in XML, any XML parser can read the data into your program. Here is an example of an XML representation of PDB author data:

```
<!-- Simple PDB citation DTD -->
<!ELEMENT citation (author)+>
<!ELEMENT author (first-name, last-name)>
```

```
<!ELEMENT first-name (#PCDATA)>
<!ELEMENT last-name (#PCDATA)>

<!DOCTYPE pdbcite SYSTEM "pdbcite.dtd">
<citation>
   <author>
     <name>Fermi, G.</name>
     <citation_id>primary</citation_id>
   </author>
   <author>
     <name></name>
     <citation_id></citation_id>
   </author>
   ...
</citation>
```

A number of XML parsers are available for the programming languages commonly used in bioinformatics research, including Perl, Java, Python, and C++. There are two basic types of XML parser: nonvalidating and validating. *Nonvalidating* parsers read the XML file and ensure its overall syntactic correctness. *Validating* parsers, on the other hand, can guard against missing or incorrect values. By comparing the XML document against its DTD, a validating parser ensures that the markup of the data isn't only syntactically correct but that each tag or attribute is associated with appropriate values.

XML applications

Thanks to its flexibility and success in other domains, XML has been adopted as a data description language for some bioinformatics projects. XML has caught on particularly well in genome annotation: the Genome Annotation Markup Element (GAME-XML) DTD was developed by Suzanne Lewis and coworkers at the Berkeley Drosophila Genome Project to represent sequence features in genomes. XML is also the basis for the markup scheme proposed by Lincoln Stein, Sean Eddy, and Robin Dowell for the distributed annotation system, DAS. Some other example applications of XML include the Biopolymer Markup Language (BioML) sequence description format developed at Proteometrics, the Taxonomic Markup Language developed by Ronald Gilmour of the University at Albany for representing the topology of taxonomic trees, and the Chemical Markup Language (CML) for representing small molecule structures.

Information about these and other applications of XML in bioinformatics are available at the web page of the Bioxml group, the XML-specific arm of the Bioperl Project (*http://www.bioxml.org*). Additional information about XML and its associated technologies are available from the WWW Consortium (*http://www.w3c.org*).

PHP

PHP is a hypertext preprocessor module for your web server that allows it to read and interpret PHP code embedded in web pages. PHP code resembles, but isn't identical to, familiar programming languages such as Perl and C.

PHP runs on most web servers; see *http://www.php.net* for more information. Unlike some other dynamic content technologies out there (for instance, Microsoft's ASP), PHP is an open source project that is supported on multiple operating systems. PHP also has built-in support for interacting with MySQL, PostgreSQL, and Oracle databases.

When a web page that incorporates PHP code is requested from a web server, the server processes the PHP instructions in the page before passing it to the client. The page source appears to the client as standard HTML; the PHP code remains invisible to machines beyond the web server.

PHP commands can be interspersed with HTML code in just about any order that seems useful to the page designer, and the resulting HTML will appear at that point after the PHP code is processed. PHP also has the capacity to include external files, so you can write the code that controls the appearance of the web page in the main PHP file and place subroutines in separate files to be included. PHP pages are distinguished from standard HTML files by a *.php* extension.

Accessing MySQL databases with PHP

Accessing a MySQL database with PHP doesn't take much work. You need one line of code to connect to the database, another line to select which database to use, a query statement, and a statement that sends the data as HTML to the client's web browser. A simple example might look like this:

```
<?php
$link =@mysql_pconnect ("myhost.biotech.vt.edu","cgibas","password") or
exit ();
mysql_select_db ("resourcedb") or exit ();
$result = mysql_query ("SELECT program, url, institution FROM software
WHERE program = "BLAST") or exit ();
while ($row = mysql_fetch_row ($result))
{
    print("<br>\n");
    for ($i = 0; $i < mysql_num_fields ($result); $i++)
    {
        print ($row[$i]);
    }
}
mysql_free_result ($result);
?>
```

The first line of code (*<?php*) signals the start of a chunk of PHP code. The next step is to connect to the MySQL server with the specified name and password, or terminate the script if the connection is unsuccessful:

```
$link =@mysql_pconnect ("myhost.biotech.vt.edu","cgibas","password") or
exit ();
```

Now you request the database called *resourcedb*.

```
mysql_select_db ("resourcedb") or exit ();
```

Next, issue a MySQL query that selects values from the program, URL, and institution fields in the *software* table when the program name is equal to "BLAST":

```
$result = mysql_query ("SELECT program, url, institution FROM software
WHERE program = "BLAST") or exit ();
```

Every time a row is read from the database, you break that row down into fields and assign them to the *$row* variable, then step through each of the fields in the row and print out the value of that field:*

```
while ($row = mysql_fetch_row ($result))
{
    print("<br>\n");
    for ($i = 0; $i < mysql_num_fields ($result); $i++)
    {
        print ($row[$i]);
    }
}
```

Finally, release the results from memory when the query is completed:

```
mysql_free_result ($result);
```

The last line of code (?>) terminates the PHP portion of the web page.

Collecting information from a form with PHP

Obviously, this code would be more useful if you substituted a variable name for the word "BLAST," and created a little form that would let the user input a word to be assigned to that variable name. All of a sudden, instead of a little bit of PHP code that searches the database for BLAST servers, you have a crude search engine to find a user-specified program in the *resourcedb* database.

Forms are created in PHP using PHP *print* statements to produce the HTML code for the form. For example, to produce a pair of radio buttons, the PHP code looks like this:

```
print("<INPUT TYPE=\"radio\" NAME=\"type\" VALUE=\"Yes\" CHECKED>Yes\n");
print("<INPUT TYPE=\"radio\" NAME=\"type\" VALUE=\"No\">No\n");
```

---

* The way we've done this, it will be a rather ugly plain-text printout. Adding HTML table tags at various points in the command sequence results in much prettier output.

Other form features are implemented analogously. For more information about forms, collecting data using forms, and detailed examples of how to produce a PHP form, see the MySQL references in the *Bibliography*.

Web database programming isn't something you can learn in a few pages, but we hope we've convinced you that creating a MySQL database is something that you can do if needed, and that writing the PHP code to access it won't be that much harder than working with HTML and Perl. Rather than showing the full PHP code for the MySQL database example, we'll walk you through the important things the PHP code will need to do.

To interact with our example database, you want a PHP script that does several major tasks:

1. Present a welcome page to the user. The page should allow the user the option of searching the database or adding a new entry to the database. Behind the scenes, that selection needs to be processed by the PHP script so that it subsequently presents the correct page.

2. Present a query submission form to the user. The PHP code needs to build a useful form, then grab the data the user enters in the form and use it to build SQL SELECT statements.

3. Present query results to the user. As matching records are found in the database, the program will have to format each one into a reasonably nice-looking piece of HTML code so that it displays in the user's web browser in a readable format.

4. Present a form for adding a new entry. This assumes you have granted permissions for adding entries to the database to outside users and will require you to collect username and password information.

5. Add the new entry to the database. This routine needs to take the information from the add form and actually use a SQL INSERT command to add it to the database.

14

Visualization and
Data Mining

Any result in bioinformatics, whether it is a sequence alignment, a structure prediction, or an analysis of gene expression patterns, should answer a biological question. For this reason, it is up to the investigators to interpret their results in the context of a clear question, and to make those results accessible to their colleagues. This interpretation step is the most important part of the scientific process. For your results to be useful, they must be interpretable. We'll say it again: if your results can't be interpreted, they won't help anybody, not even you.

In this chapter, we present computational tools that help you to make sense of your results. To this end, the chapter is organized so that it roughly parallels the data-analysis process. In the first part of this chapter, we introduce a number of programs that are used to visualize the sort of data arising from bioinformatics research. These programs range from general-purpose plotting and statistical packages for numerical data to programs dedicated to presenting sequence and structural information in an interpretable form. The second part of this chapter covers some tools for data mining—the process of finding, interpreting, and evaluating patterns in large sets of data—in the context of some bioinformatics applications.

The topics covered in this chapter are basically subdisciplines of the larger area of computational statistics. As you have seen in previous chapters, statistical methods are important because they provide a check on the significance of the researcher's discoveries. The human nervous system is very good at finding patterns; a little too good, in fact. If you scrutinize a protein sequence for long enough, you will begin to see patterns, whether they're biologically significant (like part of a family signature sequence, such as *P.YTVF* in chloramphenicol acetyltransferase) or not (words or names, such as *PER*) amidst the amino acids.* Thus, we use visualization to

---

* When you start to see sequence motifs in words or people's names, it's time to take a break.

exploit the abilities of the eye and brain to find patterns that may be interesting. We use statistics and data mining to keep our intuition in check and to restrict our searches to those patterns that can be quantitatively and repeatedly shown to be significant.

Preparing Your Data

Preparing your data (also known as *preprocessing* or *data cleansing*) is the most important part of data mining. It's also the least glamorous and one of the least-discussed parts. Preprocessing can be as simple as making sure your data is in the right format for the program that reads it, or it can involve extensive calculations.

As a bioinformatics researcher, you must be especially careful of your data. Your results and reputation are based on data that have been provided by other researchers. Consequently, you must be scrupulous in collecting and using that data. The following is a list of some general questions about data integrity to answer when you work on a project (this list isn't exhaustive; you will probably come up with other things to check that are specific to the project at hand):

- Is your data what you expect it to be? For example, DNA sequences should only contain As, Ts, Cs, and Gs (unless your program understands the additional IUPAC symbols). Protein sequences should contain only the 20 amino acids. You can use *grep* to quickly check if your file contains lines with bad characters.

- Are your datafiles correctly formatted for the programs you plan to use? Be wary of more flexible formats. For example, some programs apply a length limit to the comment line in FASTA files, while other programs don't.

- Be aware of sequence variants. Splice variants, mutations, deletions, sequencing errors, and inadvertent truncations of the sequence file all can result in a different sequence than you'd expect. It is up to you to track which differences in sequences or structures are biologically relevant and which are artifacts of the experimental process.

- Unless the sequences you are working with have been given to you by a collaborator who has not yet deposited them in a sequence database, make sure that you can find each of your sequences in GenBank or another database.

- When working with large tabular data, make sure that every field in the table has an appropriate value. Using a program such as XGobi is a good way to check this, since it complains if not every field has a value. A visualization tool such as XGobi is also useful if the values are out of register, since the resulting points will be outliers.

- Does the program produce meaningful results on test data? When you use a new program, you should have some data for which you know the results, so you can test the program and make sure it gives the right answer and behaves in a reasonable fashion (these tests are sometimes called *sanity checks*). For example, if a program compares two sequences or structures, does it give the same result regardless of which order you pass the data to it?

- Check for side effects produced by the programs you use. Does a program change any of its input? Changes can be as subtle as adding spaces between every 10 residues in a sequence file, normalizing numerical values, or changing the coordinate values of structural data.

- For microarray data, have the values been normalized? If the programs you are using perform any kind of normalization, it is important that you determine how the normalization was achieved.

- For protein structure data, are all the atom numbers and residue numbers sequential? Is the structure intact, or does it contain chain breaks or other anomalies? Are all residues labeled with the standard amino acid three-letter codes, and are all atoms labeled with the appropriate PDB atom codes?

Finally, make sure you understand all the programs being used, at least as far as knowing the format and meaning of their input and output.

Viewing Graphics

If you are going to be working with images, you need some basic tools for viewing graphics files under Linux and Unix. There are many graphics programs available; the three that we describe next are commonly available, easy to use, and free.

xzgv

xzgv is a program for viewing graphics files under the X Window System. It can display the more popular graphics formats (GIF, PNG, JPEG), as well as a variety of others. For a simple graphics viewer, it has some handy features. For example, it creates thumbnails (small versions of a picture that preview the file) and can step through images one at a time, as a slideshow.

Ghostview and gv

Ghostview and *gv* are viewers for PostScript and Portable Document Format (PDF) files. PostScript and PDF are page-description languages developed at Adobe

Systems, Inc.* Both programs allow you to page through a document, jump to specific pages, print whole documents or selected pages, and perform other simple document-navigation tasks. More and more journals are distributing their articles electronically as PDF files, so a document viewer such as *gv* is very useful for keeping up with literature.

Because it produces more compact files and cooperates with Windows applications, PDF seems to be overtaking PostScript as the more common format. Many documents are still distributed over the Net in PostScript, including preprints (particularly those written by people who use the LaTeX document formatting language) and the output of some web-based services (such as the BMERC secondary structure prediction server).

The GIMP

The GIMP (short for "GNU Image Manipulation Program") is an image processing package with similar functionality and features to Adobe Photoshop. While the GIMP can open and view graphics files, it is probably overkill to do so. However, when it comes to reformatting or modifying graphics to use in a presentation or paper, having image-manipulation software on hand is invaluable.

Sequence Data Visualization

Tools for viewing sequence data, particularly multiple sequence alignments, were discussed in Chapter 8, *Multiple Sequence Alignments, Trees, and Profiles*. As we mentioned in that chapter, one of the best ways to rapidly summarize information from a sequence alignment is to use a sequence logo. In this section, we discuss a geometric approach to visualizing sequence relationships and introduce TeX-shade, a program for creating publication-quality sequence alignment figures.

Making Publication-Quality Alignments with TeXshade

TeXshade (*http://homepages.uni-tuebingen.de/beitz/tse.html*) is a package for marking up sequence alignments written using LaTeX, a document markup language invented for mathematicians and computer scientists. This package is remarkably flexible, allowing you to color and label aligned residues according to conservation and chemical characteristics. In addition, TeXshade can incorporate secondary structure and accessibility information output from the DSSP program

---

* Adobe makes a PDF reader as well, named Acrobat Reader, which is available at no cost for Windows, Mac OS, Linux, and a handful of Unix systems.

(described in Chapter 6, *Biological Research on the Web*), as well as predictions of secondary structure generated by the PHD prediction server. Finally, T_EXshade can automatically create "fingerprints" that provide a bird's-eye view of an alignment, in which columns of conserved residues are represented by vertical lines. Like sequence logos, fingerprints can rapidly summarize alignment data and find clusters of neighboring conserved residues.

T_EXshade is called from within a LaT_EX document. If you have a sequence alignment stored in MSF format (the GCG multiple sequence alignment format) in the file *alignment.msf*, the following LaT_EX document produces an alignment formatted according to T_EXshade's defaults:

```
\documentclass{report}
\usepackage{texshade}
\begin{document}

\begin{texshade}{alignment.msf}
\end{texshade}

\end{document}
```

LaT_EX is a document markup language similar to HTML. In the preceding code example, the output of which is shown in Figure 14-1, you are telling the T_EX interpreter that this document has a beginning and an end, and that it contains only a T_EXshade alignment of the sequences in *alignment.msf.* You need to mark up the resulting alignment by hand. If this sounds painful, the SDSC Biology Workbench provides a graphical interface to T_EXshade and can automatically render T_EXshade-formatted sequence alignments as GIF or PostScript images.

Viewing Sequence Distances Geometrically

Multiple sequence alignments and sequence logos represent similarities at every position of a group of aligned sequences. However, even with coloring of conserved residues, it isn't always easy to tell how the sequences are related. Sometimes, it's useful to look at an even higher level of abstraction to see how the sequences cluster. Phylogenetic trees represent one way to visualize relatedness.

DGEOM, a set of programs by Mark J. Forster and coworkers, takes a set of aligned sequences (either a multiple sequence alignment in GCG's MSF format, or a set of pairwise alignments) and represents them as points in a 3D space, where the distances between the points represent the evolutionary distances between the sequences. The points are written to a PDB file and can be viewed with your choice of protein structure viewers. Some may flinch at the idea of storing a representation of a sequence alignment in a file format intended to store structural data, but the program works well, and since high-quality structure visualization packages

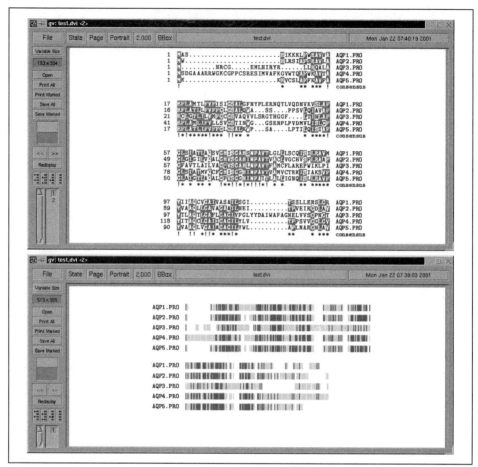

Figure 14-1. A T$_E$Xshade alignment and its corresponding fingerprint

are easy to find, this approach avoids the need for a standalone graphics system. The programs are written in Perl and C, making them fairly easy to modify.

Another implementation of the geometric approach to viewing sequence relationships is the SeqSpace package developed by Chris Dodge and Chris Sander at the EBI. This package includes C++ programs for computing the sequence distances, and it uses Java viewers to render the points in 3D.

Networks and Pathway Visualization

As of this writing, there is no standard package for visualizing interactions between molecules in a pathway or network. The most common way to represent molecular interactions schematically is in the form of a graph.* Graphs can also be useful for illustrating other data that represents interactions, including the output of cluster analyses and interacting residues in protein structures. Biological networks, such as metabolisms and signaling pathways, tend to be very densely connected, and creating readable, highly connected graphs isn't an easy task. Fortunately, AT&T Research distributes GraphViz (*http://www.research.att.com/sw/tools/graphviz/*), a freely available suite of programs that allow you to draw and edit graphs. This package has three features that make it particularly attractive: it runs quickly, it has excellent documentation, and it uses a flexible and intuitive syntax to describe graphs.

The GraphViz package consists of five programs:

dot

> Draws directed graphs

neato

> Draws undirected graphs

dotty

> A graphical interface for editing graphs

lefty

> A language for editing graphs and other diagrams; used to write *dotty*

tcldot

> A graphical interface to *dot* written in the Tcl language

To draw a directed graph of a small set of interactions, you can type the following code into a text editor and save it to a file named *morphopath.dot*:

```
digraph G {
size="3, 3";
    SHH -> "Early gene expression";
    "FGF-4" -> "Early gene expression";
    SHH -> "BMP-2";
    "BMP-2" -> "FGF-4";
    "FGF-4" -> SHH;
    "BMP-2" -> "Late gene expression";
    "FGF-4" -> "Late gene expression"; }
```

The *dot* program is invoked using the following command at the shell prompt:

```
% dot -Tps morphopath.dot -o morphopath.ps \end
```

---

* Here we are talking about the graph theory kind of graph, in which a set of dots (nodes) are connected by a set of lines (edges). *Directed* graphs are those in which the edge connecting two nodes has a direction. Edges in directed graphs are usually represented using arrows pointing in the direction of a connection. In an undirected graph, the edges have no direction.

This command tells the *dot* program in the GraphViz suite to produce a PostScript image of the graph described by *morphopath.dot* and to put the image in the file *morphopath.ps* (see Figure 14-2).

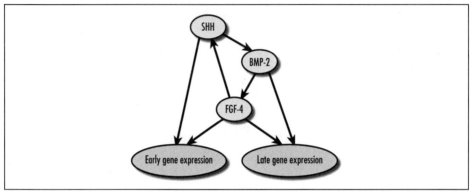

Figure 14-2. morphopath pathway output

If you have some experience with the C programming language, you might recognize the similarity of the graph description format to a struck in C. This structured approach to describing the graph's layout makes it possible to define graphs within graphs, and also makes it straightforward to generate GraphViz files from Perl scripts. In addition to specifying connectivity, graphs produced by the Graph-Viz programs can be annotated with labels, different arrow types, and highlighted boxes.

Working with Numerical Data

Numerical data can always be fed into a spreadsheet program such as Microsoft Excel or StarOffice Calc and plotted using the program's built-in graphing functions. Often, this is the best way to make plots quickly. However, you will encounter situations in which you need more control over the plotting process than the spreadsheet provides. Two common examples of this kind of situation are in formatting your plots for publication and in dealing with high-dimensional data sets. If you do have to create figures from your data, we encourage you to take a look at Edward Tufte's books on visual explanations (see the *Bibliography*). They are full of examples and tips on making clean figures that clearly say what you mean.

In this section, we describe some programs that can create plots. In addition, we introduce two special-purpose programming languages that include good facilities for visualization as well as data analysis: the statistics language R (and its commercial cousin, S-plus) and the numerical programming language Matlab (and its free counterpart, Octave).

gnuplot and xgfe

gnuplot (*http://www.gnuplot.org*) is one of the more widely used programs for producing plots of scientific data. Because of its flexibility, longevity, and open source nature, *gnuplot* is loaded with features, including scripting and facilities for including plots in documents. The dark side of this flexibility and longevity, though, is a fairly intimidating command syntax. Fortunately, a graphical interface to *gnuplot* called *xgfe* exists. *xgfe* is good for quickly plotting either data or a function, as shown in Figure 14-3. You can find out more about *xgfe* at *http://home.flash.net/~dmishee/xgfe/xgfe.html*.

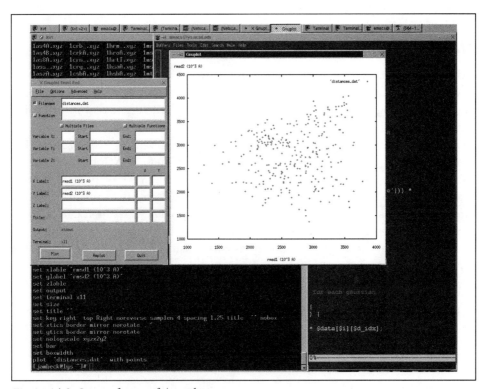

Figure 14-3. Output from xgfe/gnuplot

If you need to exert more control over the format of the output, though, it behooves you to read through the *gnuplot* documentation and see what it can do. Additionally, if you need to aumotically generate many plots from data, you may want to figure out how to control *gnuplot*'s behavior using Perl or another scripting language.

Grace: The Pocketknife of Data Visualization

Grace (*http://plasma-gate.weizmann.ac.il/Grace/*) and its predecessor, *xmgr*, are alternatives to *gnuplot* as a fairly powerful tool for plotting 2D data. Grace uses a simple graphical interface under the X Window System, which allows a fair amount of menu-driven customization of plots. Like *xgfe*, Grace provides the fairly simple 20% functionality you need 80% of the time. In addition to its current main distribution site at the Weizmann Institute of Science in Israel (which always has the latest version), there are a number of mirror sites from which Grace can be acquired. The home site also has a useful FAQ and tutorial introduction to working with Grace.

Multidimensional Analysis: XGobi and XGvis

Plotting programs such as Grace and *gnuplot* work well if your data has two or three variables that can be assigned to the plot axes. Unfortunately, most interesting data in biology has a much higher dimensionality. The science of investigating high-dimensional data is known as *multivariate* or *multidimensional* analysis. One significant problem in dealing with multidimensional data is visualization. For those who can't envision an 18-dimensional space, there is XGobi (*http://www. research.att.com/areas/stat/xgobi/*). XGobi and XGvis are a set of programs freely available from AT&T Labs. XGobi allows you to view data with many variables three dimensions at a time as a constellation of points you can rotate using a mouse. XGvis performs multidimensional scaling, the intelligent squashing of high-dimensional data into a space you can visualize (usually a 2D plot or a rotatable 3D plot). Figure 14-4 shows output from XGobi.

XGobi has a huge number of features; here is a brief explanation to get you started. XGobi takes as input a text file containing columns of data. If you have a datafile named *xgdemo.dat*, it can be viewed in XGobi by typing the following command at the shell prompt:

```
% xgobi xgdemo.dat &
```

XGobi initially presents the points in a 2D scatterplot. Selecting Rotation from the View menu at the top of the window shows a moving 3D plot of the points that you can control with the mouse by clicking within the data points and moving the mouse. Selecting Grand Tour or Correlation Tour from the View menu rotates the points in an automated tour of the data space.

The *variable widgets* (the circles along the right side of the XGobi interface) represent each of the variables in the data. The line in each widget represents the orientation of that variable's axis in the plot. If the data contains more than three variables, you can select the variables to be represented by clicking first within the widget of the variable you want to dismiss, and then within the widget of the

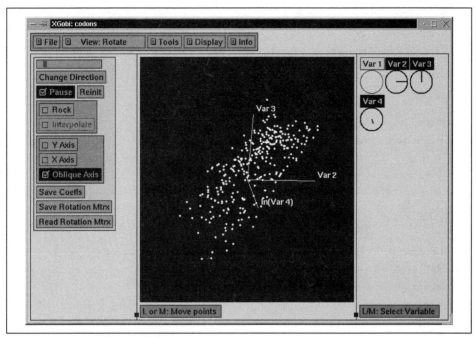

Figure 14-4. Screenshot from XGobi

variable to be displayed. Finally, clicking on the name of the corresponding variable displays a menu of transformations for that axis (e.g., natural logarithms, common logs, squares, and square roots). Like the GraphViz graph drawing programs, XGobi and XGvis are superbly documented and easy to install on Linux systems if you follow the instructions on the XGobi home page. Some Linux distributions (such as SuSE) even include XGobi.

Programming for Data Analysis

In this section, we introduce two new programming languages that are well adapted for data analysis. The proposition of learning more languages after just learning Perl may seem a little perverse. Who would want to learn a whole language just to do data analysis? If your statistics requirements can be satisfied with a spreadsheet and calculator, these packages may not be for you. Also, as we saw in the last chapter, there are facilities for creating numerically sophisticated applications using Perl, particularly the PDL.

However, many problems in bioinformatics require the use of involved numerical or statistical calculations. The time required to develop and debug such software is considerable, and it may not be worth your time to work on such code if it's used only once or twice. Fortunately, in the same way that Perl makes developing data-handling programs easy, data analysis languages (for lack of a better term) ease the prototyping and rapid development of data analysis programs. In the next sections, we introduce R (and its commercial cousin, S-plus), a language for doing statistics; and Matlab (and its free cousin, Octave), a language for doing numerical mathematics.

R and S-plus

R is a free implementation of the S statistics programming language developed at AT&T Bell Laboratories. R was developed by Ross Ihaka and Robert Gentleman at the University of Auckland. Both R and its commercial cousins (S-plus 3.x, 4.x, and 2000) are available for the Unix and Win32 platforms, and both have a syntax that has been described as "not dissimilar," so we use *R* to refer to both languages.

R is usually run within an *interpreted environment*. Instead of writing whole programs that are executed from the command line, R provides its own interactive environment in which statements can be run one at a time or as whole programs. To start the R environment, type in R at the command prompt and hit the Enter key. You should see something like this:

```
R : Copyright 2000, The R Development Core Team
Version 1.1.1  (August 15, 2000)

R is free software and comes with ABSOLUTELY NO WARRANTY.
You are welcome to redistribute it under certain conditions.
Type    "?license" or "?licence" for distribution details.

R is a collaborative project with many contributors.
Type    "?contributors" for a list.

Type    "demo()" for some demos, "help()" for on-line help, or
        "help.start()" for a HTML browser interface to help.
Type    "q()" to quit R.
```

The angle bracket (>) at the bottom of this screen is the R prompt, similar to the shell prompt in Unix. In the following examples, we write the R prompt before the things that the user (that's you) is supposed to type.

Before anything else, you should know two commands. Arguably, the most important command in any interactive environment is the one that lets you exit back out to the operating system. In R, the command to quit is:

```
> q()
```

The second most useful command is the one that provides access to R's online help system, *help()*. The default *help()* command, with no arguments, returns an explanation of how to use *help()*. If you want help on a specific R function, put the name of the function in the parentheses following *help*. So, for example, if you want to learn how the *source()* function works, you can type:

```
> help(source)
```

You can also use ? as shorthand for *help()*. So, instead of typing *help(source)* in the example, you can just enter *?source.*

As mentioned earlier, the R environment is interactive. If you type the following:

```
> 2 + 2
```

R tells you that two plus two does, in fact, equal four:

```
> 2 + 2
[1] 4
```

The R response (*4*) is preceded by a bracketed number (*[1]*), which indicates the position of the answer in the output vector. Unlike Perl, R has no scalar variables. Instead, single numbers like the previous answer are stored in a vector of length one. Also, note that the first element in the vector is numbered 1 instead of 0.*

The <- operator is used as the assignment operator. Its function is similar to the = operator in Perl. Typing:

```
> a <- 2 + 2
```

produces no output, since the result of the calculation is stored in the variable on the left side of the assignment operator. In order to see what value a variable contains, enter its name at the R prompt:

```
> a <- 2 + 2
> a
[1] 4
```

Just as Perl has basic datatypes that are useful for working with text, R has datatypes that are useful for doing statistics. We have already seen the vector; R also has matrices, arrays (which are a multidimensional generalization of matrices), and factors (lists of strings that label vectors of the same length).

Online resources for R

The place to go for more information on R is the Comprehensive R Archive Network (CRAN). You can find the CRAN site nearest to you either by using your favorite search engine or off a link from the R Project home page (*http://www.R-project.org*). CRAN has a number of packages for specific statistical applications implemented in R and available as RPM files (for information on installing RPMs, see Chapter 3, *Setting Up Your Workstation*). If your project requires sampling, clustering, regression, or

---

* Actually, R vectors do have a zero element, but it doesn't accept values assigned to it, and it returns *numeric(0)*, which is an empty vector.

factor analysis, R can be a lifesaver. R can even be made to directly access XGobi as an output system, so that the results of your computations can be plotted in two or more dimensions.

You can try R without having to install it, thanks to Rweb (*http://www.math. montana.edu/Rweb/*), a service provided by the Montana State University Mathematics Department. Rweb accepts your R code, runs it, and returns a page with the results of the calculation. If you want to use R for anything beyond simple demonstrations, though, it's faster to download the RPM files and run R on a local computer.

If you find that R is useful in your work, we vigorously recommend you supplement the R tutorial, *An Introduction to R*, and the R FAQ (*http://cran.r-project.org/*) with the third edition of *Modern Applied Statistics with S-Plus* (see the *Bibliography*). Both Venables and Ripley are now part of the R development core team, and although their text is primarily an S-plus book, supplements are available from Ripley's web site (*http://www.stats.ox.ac.uk/~ripley/*)that make the examples in book more easily used under R.

Matlab and Octave

GNU Octave (*http://www.gnu.org/software/octave/octave.html*) is a freely available programming language whose syntax and functions are similar to Matlab, a commercial programming environment from The MathWorks, Inc. (*http://www. mathworks.com/products/matlab/*). Matlab is popular among engineers for quickly writing programs that perform large numbers of numerical computations. Octave (or Matlab) is worth a look if you want to write quick prototypes of number-crunching programs, particularly for data analysis or simulation. Both Octave and Matlab are available for Unix and Windows systems. Octave source code, binaries, and documentation are all available online; they are also distributed as part of an increasing number of Linux distributions.

Octave produces graphical output using the *gnuplot* package mentioned previously. While this arrangement works well enough, it is rather spartan compared to the plotting capabilities of Matlab. In fact, if you are a student, we will take off our open source hats and strongly encourage you to take advantage of the academic pricing on Matlab; it will add years to your life. As a further incentive, a number of the data mining and machine learning tools discussed in the next section are available as Matlab packages.

Visualization: Summary

This section has described solutions to data presentation problems that arise frequently in bioinformatics. For some of the most current work on visualization in bioinformatics, see the European Bioinformatics Institute's visualization information off the Projects link on their industrial relations page (*http://industry.ebi.ac.uk*). Links to more online visualization and data mining resources are available off the web page for this book. Table 14-1 shows the tools and techniques that are used for data visualization.

Table 14-1. Data Visualization Tools and Techniques

What you do	Why you do it	What you use to do it
View graphics files	To view results and check figures	*xzgv*
View PDF or PostScript files	To read articles in electronic form	*gv*, Adobe Acrobat Reader
Manipulate graphics files	For preparation of figures	The *GIMP*
Plot data in two or three dimensions	To summarize data for presentations	Grace, *gnuplot*
Multidimensional visualization	To explore data with more than three variables	XGobi
Multidimensional scaling	To view high-dimensional data in 2D or 3D	XGvis
Plot graphical structures	To draw networks and pathways	GraphViz programs
Print sequence alignment clearly	To format sequence alignment for publication	T$_E$Xshade
Statistics-heavy programming for data analysis	For rapid prototyping of statistical data-analysis tools	R (or S-plus)
Numerically intensive programming for data analysis	For rapid prototyping of tools that make heavy use of matrices	GNU Octave (or Matlab)

Data Mining and Biological Information

One of the most exciting areas of modern biology is the application of data mining methods to biological databases. Many of these methods can equally well fall into the category of *machine learning*, the name used in the artificial intelligence community for the larger family of programs that adapt their behavior with experience. We present here a summary of some techniques that have appeared in recent work in bioinformatics. The list isn't comprehensive but will hopefully provide a starting point for learning about this growing area.

A word of caution: anthropomorphisms have a tendency to creep into discussions of data mining and machine learning, but there is nothing magical about them. Programs are said to "learn" or be "trained," but they are always just following well-defined sets of instructions. As with any of the tools we've described in this book, data mining tools are supplements, rather than substitutes, for human knowledge and intuition. No program is smart enough to take a pile of raw data and generate interesting results, much less a publication-quality article ready for submission to the journal of your choice. As we've stressed before, the creation of a meaningful question, the experimental design, and the meaningful interpretation of results are your responsibility and yours alone.

Problems in Data Mining and Machine Learning

The topics addressed by data mining are ones that statisticians and applied mathematicians have worked on for decades. Consequently, the division between statistics and data mining is blurry at best. If you do work with data mining or machine learning techniques, you will want to have more than a passing familiarity with traditional statistical techniques. If your problem can be solved by the latest data-mining algorithm or a straightforward statistical calculation, you would do well to choose the simple calculation. By the same token, please avoid the temptation to devise your own scoring method without first consulting a statistics book to see if an appropriate measure already exists. In both cases, it will be easier to debug and easier to explain your choice of a standard method over a nonstandard one to your colleagues.

Supervised and unsupervised learning

Machine learning methods can be broadly divided into supervised and unsupervised learning. Learning is said to be *supervised* when a learning algorithm is given a set of labeled examples from which to learn (the training set) and is then tested on a set of unlabeled examples (the test set). *Unsupervised* learning is performed when data is available, but the correct labels for each example aren't known. The objective of running the learning algorithm on the data is to find some patterns or trends that will aid in understanding the data. For example, the MEME program introduced in Chapter 8, *Multiple Sequence Alignments, Trees, and Profiles*, performs unsupervised learning in order to find sequence motifs in a set of unaligned sequences. It isn't known ahead of time whether each sequence contains the pattern, where the pattern is, or what the pattern looks like.

Cluster analysis is another kind of unsupervised learning that has received some attention in the analysis of microarray data. Clustering, as shown in Figure 14-5, is the procedure of classifying data such that similar items end up in the same class while dissimilar items don't, when the actual classes aren't known ahead of time. It is a standard technique for working with multidimensional data. Figure 14-5 shows two panels with unadorned dots on the left and dots surrounded by cluster boundaries on the right.

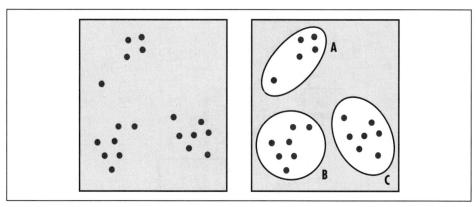

Figure 14-5. Clustering

A Collection of Data Mining Techniques

In this section, we describe some data mining methods commonly reported in the bioinformatics literature. The purpose of this section is to provide an executive summary of the complex tricks for data analysis. You aren't expected to be able to implement these algorithms in your programming language of choice. However, if you see any of these methods used to analyze data in a paper, you should be able to recognize the method and, if necessary, evaluate the way in which it was applied. Like any technique in experimental biology, it is important to have an understanding of the machine learning methods used in computational biology to know whether or not they have been used appropriately and correctly.

Decision trees

In its simplest form, a decision tree is a list of questions with yes or no answers, hierarchically arranged, that lead to a decision. For instance, to determine whether a stretch of DNA is a gene, we might have a tree like the one shown in Figure 14-6.

A tree like this one is easy to work through, since it has a finite number of possibilities at each branch, and any path through the tree leads to a decision. The structure of the tree and the rules at each of the branches are determined from the data by a learning algorithm. Techniques for learning decision trees were described by Leo Breiman and coworkers in the early 1980s, and were later popularized in the machine learning community by J. R. Quinlan, whose freely available C4.5 decision tree software and its commercial successor, C5, are standards in the field.

One major advantage of decision trees over other machine learning techniques is that they produce models that can be interpreted by humans. This is an important feature, because a human expert can look at a set of rules learned by a decision

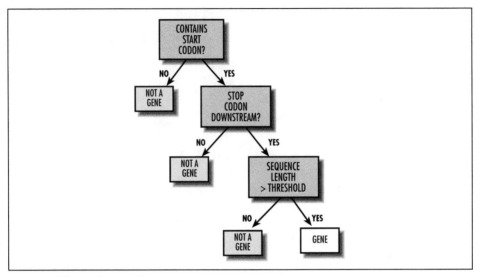

Figure 14-6. Simple gene decision tree

tree and determine whether the learned model is plausible given real-world constraints.* In biology, tree classifiers tend to be used in pattern recognition problems, such as finding gene splice sites or identifying new occurrences of a protein family member. The MORGAN genefinder developed by Steven Salzberg and coworkers is an example of a decision tree approach to genefinding.

Neural networks

Neural networks are statistical models used in pattern recognition and classification. Originally developed in the 1940s as a mathematical model of memory, neural networks are sometimes also called *connectionist models* because of their representation as nodes (which are usually variables) connected by weighted functions. Figure 14-7 shows the process by which a neural network is constructed. Please note, though, that there is nothing particularly "neural" about these models, nor are there actually physical nodes and connections involved. The idea behind neural networks is that, by working in concert, these simple processing elements can perform more complex computations.

A neural network is composed of a set of nodes that are connected in a defined topology, where each node has input and output connections to other nodes. In general, a neural network will receive an input pattern (for example, an amino acid

---

* The canonical decision-tree urban legend comes from an application of trees by a long-distance telephone company that wanted to learn about *churn*, the process of losing customers to other long-distance companies. They discovered that an abnormally large number of their customers over the age of 70 were subject to churn. A human recognized something the program did not: humans can die of old age. So, being able to interpret your results can be useful.

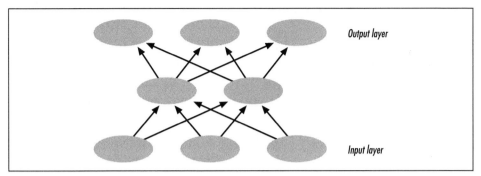

Figure 14-7. Neural network diagram

sequence whose secondary structure is to be predicted), which sets the values of the nodes on the first layer (the input layer). These values are propagated according to transfer functions (the connections) to the next layer of nodes, which propagate their values to the next layer, until the output layer is reached. The pattern of activation of the output layer is the output of the network. Neural networks are used extensively in bioinformatics problems; examples include the PHD (*http://www. embl-heidelberg.de/predictprotein/predictprotein.html*) and PSIPRED (*http://insulin. brunel.ac.uk/psipred/*) secondary structure predictors described in Chapter 9, *Visualizing Protein Structures and Computing Structural Properties*, and the GRAIL genefinder (*http://compbio.ornl.gov/grailexp/*) mentioned in Chapter 7, *Sequence Analysis, Pairwise Alignment, and Database Searching*.

Genetic algorithms

Genetic algorithms are optimization algorithms. They search a large number of possible solutions for the best one, where "best" is determined by a *cost function* or *fitness function*. Like neural networks, these models were inspired by biological ideas (in this case, population genetics), but there is nothing inherently biological about them. In a genetic algorithm, a number of candidate solutions are generated at random. These candidate solutions are encoded as chromosomes. Parts of each chromosome are then exchanged à la homologous recombination between real chromosomes. The resulting recombined strategies are then evaluated according to the fitness function, and the highest scoring chromosomes are propagated to the next generation. This recombination and propagation loop continues until a suitably good solution is found. Genetic algorithms are frequently used in molecular simulations, such as docking and folding of proteins.

Support vector machines

In late 1998, a machine learning tool called the *support vector machine* (SVM) began to attract a great deal of attention in bioinformatics. Support vector machines were developed by Vladimir Vapnik of Bell Laboratories, an early pioneer of machine learning methods. They have been applied to a wide range of problems, from optical character recognition to financial time series analysis and recognizing spam (the email variety, not the lunch meat). SVMs were first applied to biological problems by Tommi Jaakola (now at MIT), David Haussler, and coworkers at UC Santa Cruz, who used them for protein sequence classification. They have since been applied to many of the standard computational biology challenge problems (function prediction, structure prediction, and genefinding) but have gained the most attention for their use in microarray analysis.

Support vector machines are supervised classifiers that try to find a linear separation between different classes of points in a high-dimensional space. In a 2D space, this separator is a line; in 3D, it's a plane. In general, this separating surface is called a *hyperplane.* Support vector machines have two special features. First, instead of just finding any separating hyperplane, they are guaranteed to find the optimal one, or the one whose placement yields the largest separation between the two classes. The data points nearest the frontier between the two classes are called the *support vectors.** Second, although SVMs are linear classifiers, they can classify nonlinearly separable sets of points by transforming the original data points into a higher dimensional space in which they can be separated by a linear surface.

Table 14-2 shows some of the most popular data-mining tools and techniques.

Table 14-2. Data Mining Tools and Techniques

What you do	Why you do it	What you use to do it
Clustering	To find similar items when a classification scheme isn't known ahead of time	Clustering algorithms, self-organizing maps
Classification	To label each piece of data according to a classification scheme	Decision trees, neural networks, SVMs
Regression	To extrapolate a trend from a few examples	Regression algorithms, neural networks, SVMs, decision trees
Combining estimators	To improve reliability of prediction	Voting methods, mixture methods

---

* Vectors, in this case, refer to the coordinates of the data points. For example, on a 2D map, you might have pairs of *(x,y)* coordinates representing the location of the data points. These ordered pairs are the vectors.

Bibliography

Unix

Learning Red Hat Linux and *Learning Debian GNU Linux*. B. McCarty. O'Reilly & Associates. Good introductory guides to setting up systems with these releases of Linux.

Learning the Unix Operating System. J. Peek, G. Todino, and J. Strang. O'Reilly & Associates. A concise introduction to Unix for the beginner.

The Linux Desk Reference. S. Hawkins and J. Brockmeier. Prentice Hall.

Linux in a Nutshell. Siever, et al. O'Reilly & Associates. A no-nonsense quick-reference guide to Linux commands.

Running Linux. M. Welsh and L. Kaufman. O'Reilly & Associates. A relatively comprehensive how-to guide for setting up a Linux system.

Unix for the Impatient. P. Abrahams and B. Larson. Addison Wesley. A detailed yet user-friendly presentation of everything a Unix user needs to know. (My first and still favorite Unix guide. CJG)

Unix in a Nutshell. A. Robbins. O'Reilly & Associates. A no-nonsense quick-reference guide to Unix commands.

SysAdmin

Essential System Administration. A. Frisch. O'Reilly & Associates. A detailed guide to administration of Unix systems.

Using csh & tcsh. P. DuBois. O'Reilly & Associates. A detailed guide to using two of the most common shell environments.

Perl

Elements of Programming in Perl. A. L. Johnson. Manning Publications. Good introduction to Perl as a first programming language

Learning Perl. R. Schwartz and T. Christiansen. O'Reilly & Associates. Introduction to Perl but assumes prior experience with another programming language.

For a more detailed, biology-oriented Perl tutorial, we recommend the one available online at Lincoln Stein's laboratory page at Cold Spring Harbor Labs, *http://stein.cshl.org.*

Mastering Algorithms in Perl. J. Orwant, J. Hietaniemi, and J. Macdonald. O'Reilly & Associates. Both this book and the next cover interesting things that can be done with Perl.

Perl Cookbook. T. Christiansen and N. Torkington. O'Reilly & Associates.

Programming Perl. L. Wall, T. Christiansen, and J. Orwant. O'Reilly & Associates. The bible of Perl.

General Reference

Finding Out About: Search Engine Technology from a Cognitive Perspective. R. Belew. Cambridge University Press. A fascinating discussion of information retrieval and the process of web-based research from a cognitive science perspective. Both practical and philosophical aspects are covered.

All three of the following books cover general programming techniques:

Code Complete. S. McConnell. Microsoft Press.

The Practice of Programming. B. W. Kernighan and R. Pike. Addison Wesley

Programming Pearls. J. Bentley. Addison Wesley

Bioinformatics Reference

Bioinformatics: A Machine Learning Approach. P. Baldi and S. Brunak. MIT Press. The authors have firsthand experience with applying neural networks and hidden Markov models to sequence analysis, including genefinding, DNA feature detection, and protein family modeling.

Bioinformatics: A Practical Guide to the Analysis of Genes and Proteins. A. D. Baxevanis and B. F. F. Ouellette. John Wiley & Sons. A gentle introduction to biological information and bioinformatics tools on the Web, focused on NCBI tools.

Biological Sequence Analysis: Probabilistic Models of Proteins and Nucleic Acids. R. Durbin, S. Eddy, A. Krogh, and G. Mitchison. Cambridge University Press. A rigorous presentation of the statistical and algorithmic basis of sequence analysis methods, including pairwise and multiple sequence analysis, motif discovery, and phylogenetic analysis.

Molecular Systematics. D. M. Hillis, C. Moritz, and B. K. Mable, Eds. Sinauer and Associates. Although the first two-thirds of the book are devoted to experimental methods, the chapters on the methods for inferring and applying phylogenies provide a rigorous and comprehensive follow-up to the Graur and Li book.

Molecular Biology/Biology Reference

Fundamentals of Molecular Evolution. D. Graur, W-H. Li. Sinauer and Associates. A readable explanation of the mechanisms by which genomes change over time, with a discussion of phylogenetic inference based on molecular data.

Molecular Systematics. D. M. Hillis, C. Moritz, and B. K. Mable, eds. Sinauer and Associates. Although the first two-thirds of the book are devoted to experimental methods, the chapters on the methods for inferring and applying phylogenies provide a rigorous and comprehensive follow-up to the Graur and Li book.

Protein Structure and Biophysics

Intermolecular and Surface Forces. J. Israelachvili. Academic Press. A must-have book for any serious student of macromolecular structure and molecular biophysics. This book details the physical chemistry of interactions among molecules and between molecules and surfaces.

Introduction to Protein Structure. C-I. Branden and J. Tooze. Garland Publishing. An illustrated guide to the basic principles of protein structure and modeling.

Genomics

Genomes. T. A. Brown. Wiley-Liss. A thorough presentation of molecular genetics from the genomics perspective.

Genomics: The Science and Technology Behind the Human Genome Project. C. R. Cantor and C. L. Smith. John Wiley & Sons. If you want to understand, in detail, how genomic sequence data is obtained, this is the book to have. It exhaustively details experimental protocols for sequencing and mapping and explores the future of sequencing technology.

Biotechnology

DNA Microarrays: A Practical Approach. M. Schena, ed. Oxford University Press. An introduction to the basics of DNA microarray technology and its applications.

Proteome Research: New Frontiers in Functional Genomics. M. R. Wilkins, K. L. Williams, R. D. Appel, and D. F. Hochstrasser, eds. Springer. An introduction to new techniques for protein identification and analysis, from 2D-PAGE to MALDI-TOF and beyond.

Databases

CGI Programming with Perl. S. Guelich, S. Gundavaram, and G. Birznieks. O'Reilly & Associates. An introduction to the CGI protocol for generating active-content web pages. If you are interested in web software development, this book is an essential starting point.

Joe Celko's Data and Databases: Concepts in Practice. J. Celko. Morgan Kaufman. A good introduction to relational database concepts and the use of SQL.

MySQL. P. DuBois. New Riders. A detailed guide to using MySQL. Detailed coverage of administration and security issues.

MySQL & mSQL. R. J. Yarger, G. Reese, and T. King. O'Reilly & Associates. An introduction to using MySQL and mSQL; also contains an introduction to RDB concepts and database normalization. O'Reilly also publishes a collection of reference books about Oracle, if you prefer to start using Oracle from the beginning.

Visualization

Understanding Robust and Exploratory Data Analysis. D. C. Hoaglin, et al. eds. John Wiley & Sons. A classic book on visualization techniques. Don't be put off by the fact that the focus of the book is on techniques for doing analysis by hand rather than the latest computational tricks: the methods described are implemented in many visualization packages and are easily applicable to the latest bioinformatics problems.

The Visual Display of Quantitative Information, Envisioning Information, and *Visual Explanations*. E Tufte. Graphics Press. In each book, Tufte illustrates good and bad practices in visual data analysis using examples from newspapers, advertising campaigns, and train schedules (to name a few).

The Visualization Toolkit: An Object-Oriented Approach to 3-D Graphics. W. Schroeder, K. Martin, and B. Lorensen. Prentice Hall Computer Books. For those readers who want a more active role in designing visualization tools, this book combines introductions to computer graphics and visualization practices with a description of a working implementation of a complete visualization system, the Visualization Toolkit (VTK). VTK is an object-oriented, scriptable framework for building visualization tools. It is available from *http://www.kitware.com.*

Data Mining

Data Mining: Practical Machine Learning. I. Witten and E. Frank. Morgan Kaufman. A clearly written introduction to data mining methods. It comes with documentation for the authors' WEKA program suite, a set of data mining tools written in Java that can be freely downloaded from their web site.

Data Preparation for Data Mining. D. Pyle. Morgan Kaufman. For readers looking for more insight into the data-preparation process.

Machine Learning. T. Mitchell. McGraw-Hill. Provides a complementary treatment of the same methods as the previous book and is more formal but no less practical.

Modern Applied Statistics with S-Plus. Brian D. Ripley and William N. Venables. Springer Verlag.

Numerical Recipes in C. W. H. Press, S. A. Teukolsky, W. T. Vetterling, and B. P. Flannery. Cambridge University Press. A comprehensive introduction to the techniques that underlie all nontrivial methods for data analysis. Combines mathematical explanations with efficient C implementations. In addition to the hardcopy form, the entire book and all its source code are available online at no charge from *http://www.nr.com.*

Index

Symbols

Φ angle in Ramachandran map, 220
Ψ angle in Ramachandran map, 220
* (asterisk) in regular expressions, 111
\ (backslash) in regular expressions, 111
∧ (caret) in regular expressions, 111
character in Perl, 333
% character in Perl, 337
@ character in Perl, 335
$ (dollar sign)
  in Perl, 335
  in regular expressions, 111
. (dot) in regular expressions, 111
| (pipe), 93
< redirector, 91
> redirector, 91
>> redirector, 91
[] square brackets, 111

Numbers

1D protein sequences, relating to
    3D, 218–223
1D protein structures, relating to 3D, 275
1D-PSSMs, 282
2D gel electrophoresis, 317
2D structures, depicting topology
    cartoons, 243
2D-PAGE, 146
  analysis of, 319
  finding data from the Web, 147
generalizing array approaches, 321
proteomics and, 320
3D structures
  accessing through 1D
      representation, 27–29, 275
  from RNA, 24
  ModBase database, building with, 286
  modeling protein, 29
  predicting, 283–287
  public databases and, 142
  relating to 1D structures, 218–223
  web-based tools for, 230
3D-PSSM threading servers, 282, 293

A

AACompIdent/AACompSim (ExPASy
    proteomics tool), 320
aacount/aadiff utility script, 257
aanonpolar utility scripts, 258
ab-initio prediction methods, 275
  tools for, 287
absolute paths, 66
Abstract Syntax Notation One format (see
    ASN.1)
abstractions of proteins, 275
acceptor (proton), 224
adenine (A), 4
ADIT (AutoDep input tool), 155
Adobe Acrobat Reader, 397
Affymetrix machine, 313
AI-based structure prediction, 279

About the Authors

Cynthia Gibas is an assistant professor of biology at Virginia Tech, in Blacksburg, Virginia. She's been a computational biologist since before computational biology was cool, and is currently learning to drive her spankin' new home-built Linux cluster. Her research interests include the structure and evolution of genomes, the properties of protein surfaces and interfaces, and prediction of protein structure. She teaches introductory courses in bioinformatics methods for biologists and is looking forward to her next real vacation, sometime in 2006.

Per Jambeck is a Ph.D. student in the bioengineering department at the University of California, San Diego. He has worked on computational biology problems since 1994, concentrating on machine learning applications in understanding multidimensional biological data. Per smiles wistfully at the mention of free time, but he manages to host shows at community and student-run radio stations anyway.

Colophon

Our look is the result of reader comments, our own experimentation, and feedback from distribution channels. Distinctive covers complement our distinctive approach to technical topics, breathing personality and life into potentially dry subjects.

The animal on the cover of *Developing Bioinformatics Computer Skills* is *Caenorhabditis elegans*, a small nematode worm. Unlike many of its nastier parasitic cousins, *C. elegans* lives in the soil where it feeds on microbes and bacteria. It grows to about 1 mm in length.

In spite of its status as a "primitive" organism, *C. elegans* shares with *H. sapiens* many essential biological characteristics. *C. elegans* begins life as a single cell that divides and grows to form a multicellular adult. It has a nervous system and a brain (more properly known as the circumpharyngeal ring) and a muscular system that supports locomotion. It exhibits behavior and is capable of rudimentary learning. Like humans, it comes in two sexes, but in *C. elegans* those sexes consist of a male and a self-fertilizing hermaphrodite. *C. elegans* is easily grown in large numbers in the laboratory, has a short (2-3 week) lifespan, and can be manipulated in sophisticated experiments. These characteristics make it an ideal organism for scientific research.

The *C. elegans* hermaphrodite has 959 cells, 300 of which are neurons, and 81 of which are muscle cells. The entire cell lineage has been traced through development. The adult has a number of sensory organs in the head region which respond to taste, smell, touch, and temperature. Although it has no eyes, it does react slightly to light. *C. elegans* has approximately 17,800 distinct genes, and its genome has been completely sequenced. Along with the fruit fly, the mouse, and the weed *Arabidopsis, C. elegans* has become one of the most studied model organisms in biology since Sydney Brenner first focused his attention on it decades ago.

Mary Anne Weeks Mayo was the production editor and copyeditor for *Developing Bioinformatics Computer Skills.* Rachel Wheeler proofread the book. Linley Dolby and Sheryl Avruch provided quality control. Gabe Weiss, Edie Shapiro, Matt Hutchinson, and Sada Preisch provided production assistance. Joe Wizda wrote the index.

Ellie Volckhausen designed the cover of this book, based on a series design by Edie Freedman. The cover image is an original illustration created by Lorrie LeJeune, based on a photograph supplied by Leon Avery at the University of Texas Southwestern Medical Center. Emma Colby produced the cover layout with QuarkXPress 4.1 using Adobe's ITC Garamond font.

Melanie Wang designed the interior layout based on a series design by Nancy Priest. Cliff Dyer converted the files from MSWord to FrameMaker 5.5 using tools created by Mike Sierra. The text and heading fonts are ITC Garamond Light and Garamond Book; the code font is Constant Willison. The illustrations for this book were created by Robert Romano and Lucy Muellner using Macromedia Freehand 9 and Adobe Photoshop 6. This colophon was written by Lorrie LeJeune.

Whenever possible, our books use a durable and flexible lay-flat binding. If the page count exceeds this binding's limit, perfect binding is used.

How to stay in touch with O'Reilly

1. Visit Our Award-Winning Web Site

http://www.oreilly.com/

★ "Top 100 Sites on the Web" —*PC Magazine*
★ "Top 5% Web sites" —*Point Communications*
★ "3-Star site" —*The McKinley Group*

Our web site contains a library of comprehensive product information (including book excerpts and tables of contents), downloadable software, background articles, interviews with technology leaders, links to relevant sites, book cover art, and more. File us in your Bookmarks or Hotlist!

2. Join Our Email Mailing Lists

New Product Releases

To receive automatic email with brief descriptions of all new O'Reilly products as they are released, send email to:
ora-news-subscribe@lists.oreilly.com
Put the following information in the first line of your message (*not* in the Subject field):
subscribe ora-news

O'Reilly Events

If you'd also like us to send information about trade show events, special promotions, and other O'Reilly events, send email to:
ora-news-subscribe@lists.oreilly.com
Put the following information in the first line of your message (*not* in the Subject field):
subscribe ora-events

3. Get Examples from Our Books via FTP

There are two ways to access an archive of example files from our books:

Regular FTP

- ftp to:
  ftp.oreilly.com
  (login: anonymous
  password: your email address)
- Point your web browser to:
  ftp://ftp.oreilly.com/

FTPMAIL

- Send an email message to:
  ftpmail@online.oreilly.com
  (Write "help" in the message body)

4. Contact Us via Email

order@oreilly.com
To place a book or software order online. Good for North American and international customers.

subscriptions@oreilly.com
To place an order for any of our newsletters or periodicals.

books@oreilly.com
General questions about any of our books.

software@oreilly.com
For general questions and product information about our software. Check out O'Reilly Software Online at **http://software.oreilly.com/** for software and technical support information. Registered O'Reilly software users send your questions to: **website-support@oreilly.com**

cs@oreilly.com
For answers to problems regarding your order or our products.

booktech@oreilly.com
For book content technical questions or corrections.

proposals@oreilly.com
To submit new book or software proposals to our editors and product managers.

international@oreilly.com
For information about our international distributors or translation queries. For a list of our distributors outside of North America check out:
http://www.oreilly.com/distributors.html

5. Work with Us

Check out our website for current employment opportunites:
http://jobs.oreilly.com/

O'Reilly & Associates, Inc.
101 Morris Street, Sebastopol, CA 95472 USA
TEL   707-829-0515 or 800-998-9938
          (6am to 5pm PST)
FAX   707-829-0104

International Distributors

http://international.oreilly.com/distributors.html

UK, EUROPE, MIDDLE EAST AND AFRICA (EXCEPT FRANCE, GERMANY, AUSTRIA, SWITZERLAND, LUXEMBOURG, AND LIECHTENSTEIN)

INQUIRIES
O'Reilly UK Limited
4 Castle Street
Farnham
Surrey, GU9 7HS
United Kingdom
Telephone: 44-1252-711776
Fax: 44-1252-734211
Email: information@oreilly.co.uk

ORDERS
Wiley Distribution Services Ltd.
1 Oldlands Way
Bognor Regis
West Sussex PO22 9SA
United Kingdom
Telephone: 44-1243-843294
UK Freephone: 0800-243207
Fax: 44-1243-843302 (Europe/EU orders)
or 44-1243-843274 (Middle East/Africa)
Email: cs-books@wiley.co.uk

FRANCE

INQUIRIES & ORDERS
Éditions O'Reilly
18 rue Séguier
75006 Paris, France
Tel: 1-40-51-71-89
Fax: 1-40-51-72-26
Email: france@oreilly.fr

GERMANY, SWITZERLAND, AUSTRIA, LUXEMBOURG, AND LIECHTENSTEIN

INQUIRIES & ORDERS
O'Reilly Verlag
Balthasarstr. 81
D-50670 Köln, Germany
Telephone: 49-221-973160-91
Fax: 49-221-973160-8
Email: anfragen@oreilly.de (inquiries)
Email: order@oreilly.de (orders)

CANADA (FRENCH LANGUAGE BOOKS)

Les Éditions Flammarion ltée
375, Avenue Laurier Ouest
Montréal (Québec) H2V 2K3
Tel: 00-1-514-277-8807
Fax: 00-1-514-278-2085
Email: info@flammarion.qc.ca

HONG KONG

City Discount Subscription Service, Ltd.
Unit A, 6th Floor, Yan's Tower
27 Wong Chuk Hang Road
Aberdeen, Hong Kong
Tel: 852-2580-3539
Fax: 852-2580-6463
Email: citydis@ppn.com.hk

KOREA

Hanbit Media, Inc.
Chungmu Bldg. 210
Yonnam-dong 568-33
Mapo-gu
Seoul, Korea
Tel: 822-325-0397
Fax: 822-325-9697
Email: hant93@chollian.dacom.co.kr

PHILIPPINES

Global Publishing
G/F Benavides Garden
1186 Benavides Street
Manila, Philippines
Tel: 632-254-8949/632-252-2582
Fax: 632-734-5060/632-252-2733
Email: globalp@pacific.net.ph

TAIWAN

O'Reilly Taiwan
1st Floor, No. 21, Lane 295
Section 1, Fu-Shing South Road
Taipei, 106 Taiwan
Tel: 886-2-27099669
Fax: 886-2-27038802
Email: mori@oreilly.com

INDIA

Shroff Publishers & Distributors Pvt. Ltd.
12, "Roseland", 2nd Floor
180, Waterfield Road, Bandra (West)
Mumbai 400 050
Tel: 91-22-641-1800/643-9910
Fax: 91-22-643-2422
Email: spd@vsnl.com

CHINA

O'Reilly Beijing
SIGMA Building, Suite B809
No. 49 Zhichun Road
Haidian District
Beijing, China PR 100080
Tel: 86-10-8809-7475
Fax: 86-10-8809-7463
Email: beijing@oreilly.com

JAPAN

O'Reilly Japan, Inc.
Yotsuya Y's Building
7 Banch 6, Honshio-cho
Shinjuku-ku
Tokyo 160-0003 Japan
Tel: 81-3-3356-5227
Fax: 81-3-3356-5261
Email: japan@oreilly.com

SINGAPORE, INDONESIA, MALAYSIA AND THAILAND

TransQuest Publishers Pte Ltd
30 Old Toh Tuck Road #05-02
Sembawang Kimtrans Logistics Centre
Singapore 597654
Tel: 65-4623112
Fax: 65-4625761
Email: wendiw@transquest.com.sg

ALL OTHER ASIAN COUNTRIES

O'Reilly & Associates, Inc.
101 Morris Street
Sebastopol, CA 95472 USA
Tel: 707-829-0515
Fax: 707-829-0104
Email: order@oreilly.com

AUSTRALIA

Woodslane Pty., Ltd.
7/5 Vuko Place
Warriewood NSW 2102
Australia
Tel: 61-2-9970-5111
Fax: 61-2-9970-5002
Email: info@woodslane.com.au

NEW ZEALAND

Woodslane New Zealand, Ltd.
21 Cooks Street (P.O. Box 575)
Waganui, New Zealand
Tel: 64-6-347-6543
Fax: 64-6-345-4840
Email: info@woodslane.com.au

ARGENTINA

Distribuidora Cuspide
Suipacha 764
1008 Buenos Aires
Argentina
Phone: 5411-4322-8868
Fax: 5411-4322-3456
Email: libros@cuspide.com

O'REILLY®

TO ORDER: **800-998-9938** • order@oreilly.com • http://www.oreilly.com/
OUR PRODUCTS ARE AVAILABLE AT A BOOKSTORE OR SOFTWARE STORE NEAR YOU.
FOR INFORMATION: **800-998-9938** • 707-829-0515 • info@oreilly.com

O'REILLY®

O'Reilly & Associates, Inc.
101 Morris Street
Sebastopol, CA 95472-9902
1-800-998-9938

Visit us online at:
http://www.oreilly.com/
orders@oreilly.com

O'REILLY WOULD LIKE TO HEAR FROM YOU

Nineteenth century wood engraving
of a bear from the O'Reilly &
Associates Nutshell Handbook®
Using & Managing UUCP.

BUSINESS REPLY MAIL

FIRST CLASS MAIL   PERMIT NO. 80   SEBASTOPOL, CA

Postage will be paid by addressee

O'Reilly & Associates, Inc.
101 Morris Street
Sebastopol, CA 95472-9902